THE PROTECTION OF FUNDAMENTAL RIGHTS IN THE EU AFTER LISBON

The changes made by the Lisbon Treaty suggest that its entry into force in December 2009 marks a new stage in the shaping of the EU's commitment to the protection of fundamental rights, and the book's concern is to provide an examination of the several (and interlocking) challenges. This book will not only address the fresh and intriguing challenges for the EU as an entity committed to the protection and promotion of fundamental rights presented by developments 'post-Lisbon', but also a number of conundrums about the scope and method of protection of fundamental rights in the EU which existed 'pre-Lisbon' and which endure.

The book consists of three parts. The first part is concerned with the safeguarding of fundamental rights in Europe's internal market. The second part of the book is entitled 'The Scope of Fundamental Rights in EU Law' and the chapters discuss the reach of fundamental rights and the horizontal dimension of fundamental rights. The last part of this book deals with 'The Constitutional Dimension of Fundamental Rights' analysing the special relationship between the ECJ and the ECtHR and the issue of rights competition between the EU Charter on Fundamental Rights, the European Convention on Human Rights and national rights catalogues.

Volume 15: Studies of the Oxford Institute of European and Comparative Law

Studies of the Oxford Institute of European and Comparative Law

Editor
Professor Stefan Vogenauer

Board of Advisory Editors
Professor Mark Freedland, FBA
Professor Stephen Weatherill
Professor Derrick Wyatt, QC

Volume 1: The Harmonisation of European Contract Law: Implications for European Private Laws, Business and Legal Practice
Edited by Stefan Vogenauer and Stephen Weatherill

Volume 2: The Public Law/Private Law Divide
Edited by Mark Freedland and Jean-Bernard Auby

Volume 3: Constitutionalism and the Role of Parliaments
Edited by Katja Ziegler, Denis Baranger and AW Bradley

Volume 4: The Regulation of Unfair Commercial Practices under EC Directive 2005/29: New Rules and Techniques
Edited by Stephen Weatherill and Ulf Bernitz

Volume 5: Human Rights and Private Law: Privacy as Autonomy
Edited by Katja Ziegler

Volume 6: Better Regulation
Edited by Stephen Weatherill

Volume 7: Forum Shopping in the European Judicial Area
Edited by Pascal de Vareilles-Sommières

Volume 8: The Reform of Class and Representative Actions in European Legal Systems: A New Framework for Collective Redress in Europe
Christopher Hodges

Volume 9: Reforming the French Law of Obligations: Comparative Reflections on the Avant-projet de réforme du droit des obligations et de la prescription ('the Avant-projet Catala')
Edited by John Cartwright, Stefan Vogenauer and Simon Whittaker

Volume 10: Performance-Oriented Remedies in European Sale of Goods Law
Vanessa Mak

Volume 11: Current Issues in European Financial and Insolvency Law: Perspectives from France and the UK
Edited by Wolf-Georg Ringe, Louise Gullifer and Philippe Thery

Volume 12: Article 82 EC: Reflections on its Recent Evolution
Edited by Ariel Ezrachi

Volume 13: Prohibition of Abuse of Law: A New General Principle of EU Law?
Edited by Rita de la Feria and Stefan Vogenauer

Volume 14: Constitutional Pluralism in the European Union and Beyond
Edited by Matej Avbelj and Jan Komárek

The Protection of Fundamental Rights in the EU After Lisbon

Edited by

Sybe de Vries, Ulf Bernitz and Stephen Weatherill

OXFORD AND PORTLAND, OREGON
2013

Published in the United Kingdom by Hart Publishing Ltd
16C Worcester Place, Oxford, OX1 2JW
Telephone: +44 (0)1865 517530
Fax: +44 (0)1865 510710
E-mail: mail@hartpub.co.uk
Website: http://www.hartpub.co.uk

Published in North America (US and Canada) by
Hart Publishing
c/o International Specialized Book Services
920 NE 58th Avenue, Suite 300
Portland, OR 97213-3786
USA
Tel: +1 503 287 3093 or toll-free: (1) 800 944 6190
Fax: +1 503 280 8832
E-mail: orders@isbs.com
Website: http://www.isbs.com

© The editors and contributors severally 2013

The editors and contributors have asserted their right under the Copyright, Designs and Patents Act 1988, to be identified as the authors of this work.

All rights reserved. No part of this publication may be reproduced, stored in a retrieval system, or transmitted, in any form or by any means, without the prior permission of Hart Publishing, or as expressly permitted by law or under the terms agreed with the appropriate reprographic rights organisation. Enquiries concerning reproduction which may not be covered by the above should be addressed to Hart Publishing Ltd at the address above.

British Library Cataloguing in Publication Data
Data Available

ISBN: 978-1-84946-443-7

Typeset by Hope Services, Abingdon
Printed and bound in Great Britain by
MPG Books Ltd

PREFACE

This book is a development pursuant to a conference held under the title 'The Protection of Fundamental Rights in the EU After Lisbon' in Oxford on 11 March 2011. The conference was organised by Sybe de Vries, Ulf Bernitz and Stephen Weatherill under the auspices of the Institute of European and Comparative Law in the Oxford University Law Faculty. At the conference, our speakers were Sacha Prechal (European Court of Justice and Utrecht), who offered some introductory remarks, and then Stephen Weatherill (Oxford), Catherine Barnard (Cambridge), Sybe de Vries (Utrecht), Ulf Bernitz (Stockholm and Oxford), Martin Mörk (Öberg & Associés), Xavier Groussot (Lund), Sionaidh Douglas-Scott (Oxford), Iain Cameron (Uppsala), and Katja Ziegler (Oxford).

The general theme of the conference was targeted at interrogation of the development of the protection of fundamental rights in the European Union and in particular the impact of the Lisbon Treaty, which came into force in December 2009 but the full implications of which are far from clear and will not become clear for some considerable time. At least three aspects of the changes made by the Lisbon Treaty suggest that its entry into force marks a new stage in the shaping of the EU's commitment to the protection of fundamental rights, and the book's concern is to provide an examination of the several (and interlocking) challenges. The three aspects are: first, respect for human rights has been inscribed more deeply as a foundational value of the EU (in particular Articles 2, 3(5), 6 and 21 TEU); secondly, there is provision in Article 6(2) TEU for the accession of the European Union to the European Convention on Human Rights (which had previously been beyond the competence of the EU); and thirdly the EU's Charter of Fundamental Rights, 'solemnly proclaimed' at Nice in 2001 but not then granted binding effect, has now been elevated to formally-binding status.

The developments 'post-Lisbon' present a number of fresh and intriguing challenges for the EU as an entity committed to the protection and promotion of fundamental rights. It is now even clearer than before that fundamental rights are of central importance to the EU. Fundamental rights cannot and should not be seen as a mere addendum of EU law. The issues evolving around the Lisbon Treaty and its possible impact on fundamental rights protection in Europe therefore require close attention, and this book is motivated by concern to pursue such inquiries.

Without the help and support of some persons neither the conference, nor the book would have become a reality. The conference was generously supported by the Wallenberg Foundation, Stockholm, for which we would like to express our gratitude. Jenny Dix helped very much in the organisation of this conference and we would like to thank her. Wei Pao Chan undertook the task of carefully copy-editing for which we are very grateful.

As ever, Hart Publishing have offered an exemplary service.

Sybe de Vries,
Ulf Bernitz and
Stephen Weatherill

TABLE OF CONTENTS

Preface v
List of Contributors ix
Table of Cases xi

Introduction 1
Sybe deVries, Ulf Bernitz and Stephen Weatherill

Part I: Safeguarding Fundamental Rights in Europe's Internal Market

1. From Economic Rights to Fundamental Rights 11
Stephen Weatherill

2. The Protection of Fundamental Social Rights in Europe after Lisbon:
A Question of Conflicts of Interests 37
Catherine Barnard

3. The Protection of Fundamental Rights within Europe's Internal Market
after Lisbon – An Endeavour for More Harmony 59
Sybe A de Vries

Part II: The Scope of Fundamental Rights in EU Law

4. The Reach of Fundamental Rights on Member State Action after Lisbon 97
Xavier Groussot, Laurent Pech and Gunnar Thor Petursson

5. An End to the Possibilities – on Horizontal Liability in *Laval* and the
Limits of Judicial Rights Protection 119
Martin Mörk

6. Horizontal Effects of Private Rights Vested by Union Law on Damages
to be Paid by another private Party: The *Laval* Case as Model 139
Ulf Bernitz

Part III: The Constitutional Dimension of Fundamental Rights

7. The Court of Justice of the European Union and the European Court of
Human Rights after Lisbon 153
Sionaidh Douglas-Scott

8. Competing Rights? 181
Iain Cameron

Conference Report 207
Eva Suzanne Lachnit

Index 215

LIST OF CONTRIBUTORS

Catherine Barnard MA (Cantab), LLM (EUI), PhD (Cantab) is Professor in European Union and Employment Law at the University of Cambridge and a fellow of Trinity College. She specialises in EU law, employment law and discrimination law. She is co-director of the Centre for European Legal Studies at Cambridge. She is author of *EC Employment Law*, 3rd edn (Oxford, OUP, 2006), *The Substantive Law of the EU: The Four Freedoms*, 3rd edn (Oxford, OUP, 2010), editor of a collection of essays entitled *The Fundamentals of EU Law Revisited* (Oxford, OUP, 2007), editor of the *Cambridge Yearbook of European Legal Studies 2006–07* and *2007–08*, co-editor of *2008–09* and *2009–10* (with O Odudu), and co-editor of a collection of essays entitled *The Law of the Single European Market* (Oxford, Hart Publishing, 2002) (with J Scott), of another volume entitled *The Future of Labour Law*, (Oxford, Hart Publishing, 2004) (with S Deakin and Morris) and of a book aimed at prospective law students entitled *What about Law?* (with G Virgo and J O'Sullivan).

Ulf Bernitz is Professor of European Law at Stockholm University, as well as Senior Research Fellow at St Hilda's College, University of Oxford. He is also Director for the Wallenberg Foundation Oxford/Stockholm Association in European Law, based at the Institute of European and Comparative Law, University of Oxford. His research interests are in the field of European law and private law (especially competition and marketing law, intellectual property law and consumer law).

Iain Cameron is Professor in Public International Law at the University of Uppsala, where he teaches international law and constitutional law. His research interests lie in human rights/civil liberties, international criminal law and international police/security cooperation. He has written extensively (over 70 publications) in the fields of international law and constitutional law, particularly on international criminal law and human rights issues. He has served as an expert to a number of Swedish government commissions of inquiry proposing legislation, and has written major reports for the Swedish government, the Council of Europe and the European Parliament on targeted sanctions. In 2006, the Swedish government appointed him as a member of the European Commission on Democracy through Law (Venice Commission), the advisory body of the Council of Europe on constitutional law and international law.

Sionaidh Douglas-Scott is Professor of European and Human Rights Law at the University of Oxford. She is the author of 'Constitutional Law of the European Union' as well as numerous articles on European human rights law and on the legal, social and political theory of the European Union.

Xavier Groussot is professor of EU Law at Lund University and guest professor at the European College of Paris (Université Panthéon-Assas, Paris II). His fields of research are related to EU constitutional law, free movement and procedural law.

x   *List of Contributors*

Eva Lachnit is a PhD candidate in the field of Public Economic Law. Her thesis is entitled 'Alternative Enforcement of Competition Law' and concerns the enforcement practice of the European Commission and the national competition authorities. She is a researcher at the Europa Institute of Utrecht University, where she also earned her master's degrees in Corporate Law and European Law.

Martin Mörk MJur (Oxf) is Head of Litigation at the Swedish Equality Ombudsman. A former legal advisor to the Chancellor of Justice of Sweden, he has argued several *Francovich* liability cases for the Swedish state.

Laurent Pech is *Jean Monnet* Lecturer in EU Public Law in the School of Law, National University of Ireland Galway. A graduate of the Faculty of Law of Aix-en-Provence (France), he has written extensively in the fields of EU Constitutional Law and European Human Rights Law. Amongst his recent publications are: 'The Institutional Development of the EU post-Lisbon' in Ashiagbor, Countoris and Lianos, *The European Union after the Treaty of Lisbon* (Cambridge University Press, 2012); 'Between judicial minimalism and avoidance: the Court of Justice's sidestepping of fundamental constitutional issues in *Römer and Dominguez*' (2012) 49 *Common Market Law Review* 1841.

Gunnar Thor Petursson is a Senior Specialist at the School of Law, Reykjavik University. He graduated as a Cand jur from the Faculty of Law, University of Iceland in 1997, and with a LLM degree in European Law from the Faculty of Law, University of Lund, Sweden in 1998. He was a Deputy Director at the EFTA Surveillance Authority 1999–2004, admitted to practice before Iceland's District Courts in 2002, Attorney-at-law at Logos Legal Service, 2004–2005, and Head of Legal, Actavis Group in 2005–2008. Gunnar Thor has been an Adjunct Faculty Member at the School of Law, Reykjavik University since 2005 and a full time Faculty Member since 2008. Gunnar Thor is also a guest lecturer at the Faculty of Law, Panthéon-Assas (Paris II), France, and at the Faculty of Law, University of Lund, Sweden.

Sybe de Vries is Associate Professor of European Law at the Europa Institute of Utrecht University and Jean Monnet Chair in EU Single Market Law and Fundamental Rights. In 2006, he obtained his PhD at Utrecht University for his dissertation 'Tensions within the Internal Market – The Functioning of the Internal Market and the Development of Horizontal and Flanking Policies'. From 2001 until 2004, he was a legal secretary of the Advisory Appeal Committee of the Netherlands Competition Authority. In 2010 he was a visiting researcher at the Institute of European and Comparative Law of the University of Oxford. His research focused on the protection of fundamental rights within the EU internal market. He has authored and co-authored a number of articles in law journals and books in the field of European law and public economic law.

Stephen Weatherill is the Jacques Delors Professor of European Law in the University of Oxford. He is also Deputy Director for European Law in the Institute of European and Comparative Law and is a Fellow of Somerville College, Oxford

TABLE OF CASES

European Union

Court of Justice, Case Number Order

Case 7/61 Commission v Italy [1961] ECR 317 .... 11, 19
Case 26/62 Van Gend en Loos v Nederlandse Administratie der Belastingen
  [1963] ECR 1 11
Case 20/64 SARL Albatros v Société des Petroles et des Combustibles
  Liquides (SOPECO) [1965] ECR 29 11
Case 29/69 Erich Stauder v City of Ulm – Sozialamt [1969] ECR 419 .... 2, 61
Case 11/70 Internationale Handelsgesellschaft mbH v Einfuhr- und
  Vorratsstelle für Getreide und Futtermittel [1970] ECR 1125 .... 2, 61
Case 4/73 Nold v European Commission [1974] ECR 491 2
Case 8/74 Procureur du Roi v Benoit et Gustave Dassonville [1974]
  ECR 837 .... 16, 19–20, 83
Case 36/74 BNO Walrave and LJN Koch v Association Union cycliste
  internationale, Koninklijke Nederlandsche Wielren Unie and Federación
  Española Ciclismo [1974] ECR 1405 126–7
Case 36/75 Rutili v Ministre de l'Interiori [1975] ECR 1219 .... 101, 157
Case 43/75 Gabrielle Defrenne v Société Anonyme Belge de Navigation
  Aerienne (SABENA) (Defrenne II) [1976] ECR 455 .... 106–7, 113, 132–3
Case 30/77 R v Bouchereau [1977] ECR 1999 67
Case 106/77 Amministrazione delle Finanze dello Stato v Simmenthal
  SpA [1978] ECR 629 109
Case 120/78 Rewe-Zentrale AG v Bundesmonopolverwaltung für
  Branntwein (Cassis de Dijon) [1979] ECR 649 .... 14–15, 19–20, 30
Case 61/79 Amministrazione delle finanze dello Stato v Denkavit italiana
  Srl [1980] ECR 1205 133
Case 53/80 Officier van Justitie v Koninklijke Kaasfabriek Eyssen [1981]
  ECR 409 19
Case 158/80 Rewe-Handelsgesellschaft Nord mbH and Rewe-Markt Steffen v
  Hauptzollamt Kiel [1981] ECR 1805 124
Case 169/80 Administration des douanes v Société anonyme Gondrand
  Frères and Société anonyme Garancini [1981] ECR 1931 132
Case C–283/81 Srl CILFIT and Lanificio di Gavardo SpA v Ministry of
  Health [1982] ECR 3415 170

xii *Table of Cases*

Case 240/83 Procureur de la République v Association de défense des brûleurs
   d'huiles usagées [1985] ECR 531 80
Case 152/84 M Helen Marshall v Southampton and South-West Hampshire
   Area Health Authority [1986] ECR 723...134
Case 178/84 European Commission v Germany [1987] ECR 1227 82
Joined Cases 201/85 and 202/85 Klensch and Others v Secrétaire d'Etat
   [1986] ECR 3477.....113
Case 314/85 Foto-Frost v Hauptzollamt Lübeck-Ost [1987] ECR 1129.............169
Case 302/86 European Commission v Denmark [1988] ECR 4607......................80
Joined Cases 46/87 and 227/88 Hoechst AG v European Commission
   [1989] ECR 2859.. 159, 197
Case 374/87 Orkem v Commission [1989] ECR 3283..159
Case 382/87 Buet and Educational Business Services v Ministère Public
   [1989] ECR 1235..19
Case 5/88 Hubert Wachauf v Bundesamt für Ernährung und Forstwirtschaft
   [1989] ECR 2609..3, 61, 72, 98, 102, 105, 108,
                                                     110–11, 113–14, 116–17, 187
Case 145/88 Torfaen Borough Council v B & Q plc [1989] ECR 3851 15
Case C–49/89 Corsica Ferries France v Direction générale des douanes
   françaises [1989] ECR I–4441 83
Case C–260/89 Elliniki Radiophonia Tileorassi AE (ERT) v Dimotiki Etairia
   Pliroforissis and Sotirios Kouvelas [1991] ECR I–2925............. 3, 23, 61, 72, 98,
                                                     101–3, 105, 108, 113–14, 116, 186
Case C–2/90 European Commission v Belgium [1992] ECR I–4431 89
Joined Cases C–6/90 and C–9/90 Francovich and Others v Italy [1991]
   ECR I–5357 ....120, 126–31, 135, 139, 142, 145, 148–9, 211
Case C–159/90 Society for the Protection of Unborn Children Ireland v
   Grogan and others [1991] ECR I–4685 ....13–14, 78
Case C–72/91 Firma Sloman Neptun Schiffahrts AG v Seebetriebsrat Bodo
   Ziesemer der Sloman Neptun Schiffahrts AG [1993] ECR I–887 ....38, 43
Case C–169/91 Stoke on Trent and Norwich City Councils v B & Q plc
   [1992] ECR I–6635 15
Cases C–267/91 and C–268/91 Criminal proceedings against Keck and
   Mithouard [1993] ECR I–6097 .... 11, 14, 16, 62, 85
Case C–271/91 M Helen Marshall v Southampton and South-West
   Hampshire Area Health Authority [1993] ECR I–4367....................................146
Case C–91/92 Paola Faccini Dori v Recreb Srl [1994] ECR I–3325 134
Case C–128/92 HJ Banks & Co Ltd v British Coal Corporation [1994]
   ECR I–1209 147
Joined Cases C–46/93 and C–48/93 Brasserie de Pêcheur SA v Germany
   and The Queen v Secretary of State for Transport, *ex parte* Factortame
   Ltd and others [1996] ECR I–1029................................ 129, 141–2, 146, 149, 211
Case C–143/93 Gebroeders van Es Douane Agenten BV v Inspecteur der
   Invoerrechten en Accijnzen [1996] ECR I–431 132

Cases C–363/93 and C–407/93 to C–411/93 René Lancry SA v Direction
  Générale des Souanes and Société Dindar Confort and others [1994]
  ECR I–3957 85
Case C–415/93 Union Royale Belge des Sociétés de Football Association
  ASBL v Jean-Marc Bosman [1995] ECR I–4921 .... 18, 21, 113, 116–17, 126–7
Case C–470/93 Verein gegen Unwesen in Handel und Gewerbe Köln v Mars
  GmbH [1995] ECR I–1923..15
Joined Cases C–485/93 and C–486/93 Simitzi v Dimos Kos [1995]
  ECR I–2655 85
C-286/94 Garage Molenheide BVBA and Others v Belgian State[1997]
  ECR I-7281 113
Case C–13/94 P v S and Cornwall County Council [1996] ECR
  I–2143 .... 41, 125, 158
Case C–3/95 Reisebüro Broede v Gerd Sandker [1996] ECR I–6511...................20
Case C–84/95 Bosphorus Hava Yollari Turizm ve Ticaret AS v Minister
  for Transport [1996] ECR I–3953 113–14
Case C–265/95 European Commission v France [1997] ECR I–6959
  (Spanish Strawberries) 18, 64, 78–9, 83, 117, 127–8
Case C–368/95 Vereinigte Familiapress Zeitungsverlags- und vertriebs
  GmbH v Heinrich Bauer Verlag [1997] ECR I–3689 .... 3, 23, 25, 113–14, 157
Case C–67/96 Albany International BV v Stichting Bedrijfspensioenfonds
  textielindustrie [1999] ECR I–5751 42
Case C–129/96 Inter-Environnement Wallonie ASBL v Région Wallonne
  [1997] ECR I–7411 108
Case C–158/96 Raymond Kohll v Union des Caisses de Maladie [1998]
  ECR I–1931 88
Case C–184/96 European Commission v France [1998] ECR I–6197 85
Case C–249/96 Lisa Jacqueline Grant v South-West Trains Ltd [1998]
  ECR I–621 125
Case C–309/96 Annibaldi [1997] ECR I–7493, judgment of 18 December
  1997 ....72, 102
Case C–348/96 Criminal proceedings against Donatella Calfa [1999]
  ECR I–11 ....67, 88
Case T–163/96 Connolly v European Commission [1999] ECR II–463.............154
Case C–225/98 European Commission v France [2000] ECR I–7445 51
Case C–254/98 Schutzverband gegen unlauteren Wettbewerb v TK-Heimdienst
  Sass GmbH [2000] ECR I–151..85
Case C–281/98 Roman Angonese v Cassa di Risparmio di Bolzano SpA
  [2000] ECR I–4139 .... 83, 85, 106, 113, 126–7, 140, 147
Case C–352/98P Laboratoires pharmaceutiques Bergaderm SA (in
  liquidation) and Jean-Jacques Goupil v European Commission [2000]
  ECR I–5291 149
Case C–379/98 PreussenElektra AG v Schleswag AG [2001] ECR I–2099......30, 89
Case C–398/98 European Commission v Greece [2001] ECR I–7915 78

xiv *Table of Cases*

Case C–405/98 Konsumentombudsmannen v Gourmet International
Products AB [2001] ECR I–1795 15
Case C–448/98 Criminal proceedings against Jean-Pierre Guimont [2000]
ECR I–10663 85
Case C–88/99 Roquette Frères SA v Direction des Services Fiscaux du
Pas-de-Calais [2000] ECR I–10465 159
Case C-413/99 Baumbast and R v Secretary of State for the Home
Department [2002] ECR I–7091 113
Case C–453/99 Courage Ltd v Bernard Crehan [2001] ECR
I–6297 .... 32, 120, 141, 145
Cases C–515/99, C–519/99-524/99 and C–526-540/99 Hans Reisch and
others Grundverkehrslandeskommission des Landes Salzburg [2002]
ECR I–2157 85
Cases C–20/00 and C–64/00 Booker Aquaculture Ltd (trading as Marine
Harvest McConnell) and Hydro Seafood GSP Ltd v Scottish Ministers
[2003] ECR I–7411 .... 3, 113–14
Case C–60/00 Mary Carpenter v Secretary of State for the Home
Department [2002] ECR I–6279 .... 28, 113, 194
Case C–94/00 Roquette Frères SA v Directeur général de la concurrence,
de la consommation et de la répression des fraudes, and European
Commission [2002] ECR I–9011 .... 197, 212
Case C–112/00 Eugen Schmidberger, Internationale Transporte und
Planzüge v Austria [2003] ECR I–5659 .... 3, 5, 12, 24–6, 48, 60, 62–4,
78, 81, 83, 87–90, 92–4, 113–16, 127–30, 133, 194, 209
Case C–294/00 Deutsche Paracelsus Schulen für Naturheilverfahren
GmbH v Kurt Gräbner [2002] ECR I–6515 20
Case C–442/00 Ángel Rodríguez Caballero v Fondo de Garantía Salarial
(Fogasa) [2002] ECR I–11915 3
Case C–101/01 Criminal proceedings against Bodil Lindqvist [2003]
ECR I–12971 113–14
Case C–276/01 Joachim Steffenson [2003] ECR I–3735 113–14
Case C–36/02 Omega Spielhallen- und Automatenaufstellungs-
GmbH v Oberbürgermeisterin der Bundesstadt Bonn [2004]
ECR I 9609 .... 3, 12, 25, 31 2, 60, 62, 65 8, 83,
89–90, 92–4, 113, 115, 193, 209
Case C–71/02 Herbert Karner Industrie-Auktionen GmbH v Troostwijk
GmbH [2004] ECR I–3025 .... 24, 62, 113, 116
Case C–200/02 Kunqian Catherine Zhu and Man Lavette Chen v Secretary
of State for the Home Department [2004] ECR I–9925 104
Case C–201/02 The Queen (on the application of Delena Wells) v Secretary
of State for Transport, Local Government and the Regions [2004]
ECR I–723 134
Case C–309/02 Radlberger Getränkegesellschaft mbH and S Spitz KG v
Land Baden-Württemberg [2004] ECR I–11763 80

Case C–334/02 European Commission v France [2004] ECR I–2229 88
Case C–376/02 Stichting 'Goed Wonen' v Staatssecretaris van Financiën
    [2005] ECR I–3445 3
Cases C–391/02 and C–403/02 Criminal proceedings against Silvio
    Berlusconi and Others [2005] ECR I–3565 159
Case C-6/03 Deponiezweckverband Eiterköpfe v Land Rheinland-Pfalz
    [2005] ECR I-2753 113
Case C–17/03 Vereniging voor Energie, Milieu en Water (VEMW) and
    thers v Directeur van de Dienst uitvoering en toezicht energie [2005]
    ECR I–4983 132
Case C–105/03 Criminal Proceedings against Maria Pupino [2005]
    ECR I–5285 .... 3, 157–8, 164
Case C–110/03 Belgium v European Commission [2005] ECR I–2801 132
Case C–446/03 Marks & Spencer plc v David Halsey (HM Inspector of
    Taxes) [2005] ECR I–10837 .... 18, 88
Case C–470/03 AGM-Cos.MET Srl v Suomen valtio and Tarmo Lehtinen
    [2007] ECR I–2749 .... 121, 146
Case C–512/03 JEJ Blanckaert Inspecteur van de Belastingdienst/Particulieren/
    Ondernemingen buitenland te Heerlen [2005] ECR I–7685 17
Case C–144/04 Werner Mangold v Rüdiger Helm [2005] ECR
    I–9981 .... 3, 107–11, 113, 116, 133–5, 164
Case C–295/04 to C–298/04 Vincenzo Manfredi and others v Lloyd
    Adriatico Assicurazioni SpA et al [2006] ECR I–6619 .... 120, 141, 145
Case C–308/04P SGL Carbon v European Commission [2006] ECR
    I–5977 177
Case C–344/04 The Queen (on the application of International Air
    Tranport Association and European Low Fares Airline Association) v
    Department for Transport [2006] ECR I–403 .... 132, 170
Case C–372/04 *ex parte* Watts *see* Case C–372/04 The Queen (on the
    application of Yvonne Watts) v Bedford Primary Care Trust and Secretary
    of State for Health [2006]
Case C–372/04 The Queen (on the application of Yvonne Watts) v Bedford
    Primary Care Trust and Secretary of State for Health [2006]
    ECR I–4325 .... 17, 20, 34, 69, 82
Case C–81/05 Anacleto Cordero Alonso v Fondo de Garantía Salarial
    (Fogasa) [2006] ECR I–7569 3
Case C–142/05 Åklagaren v Percy Mickelsson and Joakim Roos [2009]
    ECR I–4273 15
Case C–307/05 Del Cerro Alonso v Osakidetza-Servicio Vasco de Salud
    [2007] ECR I–7109 52
Case C–341/05 Laval un Partneri Ltd v Svenska Byggnadsarbetareförbundet
    and others [2007] ECR I–11767 .... 3, 6, 26–8, 33–4, 38–9, 42, 44–6,
                49, 60, 62, 69, 78, 83, 87–94, 103, 113, 116–17, 119,
                122, 126–30, 132, 135–7, 140, 142–5, 147–50, 195, 209–11

xvi *Table of Cases*

Case C–380/05 Centro Europa 7 Srl v Ministerio delle Comunicazioni
[2008] ECR I–349 179
Joined Cases C–402/05P and C–415/05P Yassin Abdullah Kadi and Al
Barakaat International Foundation v European Council (Kadi I)
[2008] ECR I–6351 .... 26, 44, 158, 163–4, 168, 179, 201
Case C–411/05 Félix Palacios de la Villa v Cortefiel Servicios SA [2007]
ECR I–8531 .... 43, 47, 110–11, 134
Case C–432/05 Unibet (London) Ltd and Unibet (International) Ltd v
Justitiekanslern [2007] ECR I–2271 .... 121, 124–6, 131
Case C–438/05 International Transport Workers' Federation and Finnish
Seamen's Union v Viking Line ABP and OÜ Viking Line Eesti [2007]
ECR I–10779 .... 6, 12, 18, 26–8, 33–4, 38–9, 42–6,
49–50, 60, 69–70, 78, 83, 87–94, 103, 113,
116–17, 122, 136–7, 143–5, 195, 209–10
Case C–244/06 Dynamic Medien Vertriebs GmbH v Avides Media AG
[2008] ECR I–505 .... 15, 20, 30, 68, 74–5, 79, 82, 89–90
Case C–250/06 United Pan-Europe Communications Belgium SA and
others v Belgian State [2007] ECR I–11135 (ECJ) 82
Case C–267/06 Tadao Maruko v Versorgungsanstalt der deutschen Bühnen
[2008] ECR I–1757 .... 41, 52
Case C–268/06 Impact [2008] ECR I–2483 88
Case C–275/06 Productores de Música de España (Promusicae) v Telefónica
de España SAU [2008] ECR I–271 194–5
Case C–303/06 Coleman v Attridge Law and Steve Law [2008] ECR I–5603 41
Case C–346/06 Dirk Rüffert v Land Niedersachsen [2008]
ECR I–1989 .... 40, 44–5, 49
Case C–427/06 Bartsch v Bosch und Siemens Hausgeräte (BSH)
Altersfürsorge GmbH [2008] ECR I–7245 .... 97, 110–11, 116
Cases C–55/07 and C–56/07 Michaeler, Subito GmbH, and Volgger v
Amt für sozialen Arbeitsschutz, Autonome Provinz Bozen [2008]
ECR I–3135 111
Case C–73/07 Tietosuojavaltuutettu v Satakunnan Markkinapörssi Oy
and Satamedia Oy [2008] ECR I–9831 112
Case C 94/07 Andrea Raccanelli v Max Planck Gesellschaft zur Förderung
der Wissenschaften eV [2008] ECR I–5939 .... 120, 145
Case C–388/07 The Queen (on the application of The Incorporated Trustees
of the National Council on Ageing (Age Concern England)) v Secretary of
State for Business, Enterprise and Regulatory Reform [2009] ECR I–1569 47
Case C–555/07 Seda Kücükdeveci v Swedex GmbH & Co KG [2010]
ECR I–365 .... 62, 73, 106–7, 110–13, 116, 164
Case C–50/08 European Commission v France (ECJ, 24 May 2011), nyr 83
Case C–58/08 The Queen (on the application of Vodafone Ltd and others) v
Secretary of State for Business, Enterprise and regulatory reform (ECJ,
8 June 2010), nyr 84

Case C–73/08 Nicolas Bressol and others, Céline Chaverot and others v
 Gouvernment de la Communauté française [2010] ECR I–2735 18
Case C–135/08 Janko Rottman v Freistaat Bayern [2010] ECR I–1449 17
Case C–147/08 Jürgen Römer v Freie und Hansestadt Hamburg (ECJ,
 10 May 2011), nyr 111
Case C–160/08 European Commission v Germany [2010] ECR I–3713 49
Case C–271/08 European Commission v Germany [2010]
 ECR I–7091 .... 42, 48–9, 89–90, 92, 94
Case C–499/08 Ole Andersen v Region Syddanmark (CJEU, 12 October
 2010) [2011] 1 CMLR 35..47, 50
Case C–515/08 Criminal proceedings against Vitor Manuel Santos Palhota
 and others (CJEU, 7 October 2010) 46
Case C–34/09 Gerardo Ruiz Zambrano v Office national de l'emploi
 (ONEm) (ECJ, 8 March 2011), nyr 4, 62–3, 74, 85, 103–4, 113, 164, 211–12
Case C–52/09 Konkurrensverket v TeliaSonera Sverige AB (ECJ,
 17 February 2011), nyr 33
Joined Cases C–92/09 and C–93/09 Volker and Markus Schecke GbR
 and Hartmut Eifert v Land Hessen [2010] ECR I–11063 .... 3, 57, 61,
 75–6, 93, 161, 188, 198
Case C–104/09 Roca-Álvarez v Sesa Start Espana ETT SA (ECJ,
 30 September 2010), nyr..112
Case C–137/09 Marc Michel Josemans v Burgemeester van Maastricht
 (ECJ, 16 December 2010), nyr... 13–14, 67, 77–8
Case C–208/09 Ilonka Sayn-Wittgenstein v Landeshauptmann von Wien
 (ECJ, 22 December 2010), nyr............... 12, 31, 66, 68, 89–94, 113, 115, 193, 209
Case C–279/09 Deutsche Energiehandels- und Beratungsgesellschaft
 mbH (DEB) v Germany [2010] ECR I–13849 .... 74, 103, 113
Case C–434/09 Shirley McCarthy v Secretary of State for the Home
 Department (ECJ, 5 May 2011), nyr 112, 164
Case C–447/09 Reinhard Prigge and others v Deutsche Lufthansa AG
 (ECJ, 13 September 2011), nyr...62, 73, 148
Case C–70/10 Scarlet Extended SA v Société belge des auteurs, compositeurs
 et éditeurs SCRL (SABAM), (CJEU, 24 November 2011), nyr 148, 188
Case C–108/10 Ivana Scattolon v Ministerio dell'Istruzione, dell'Università e
 della Ricerca (ECJ, 6 September 2011), nyr 97
Case C–282/10 Maribel Dominguez v Centre informatique du Centre Ouest
 Atlantique and Préfet de la région Centre (ECJ, 24 January 2011), nyr 112, 141
Case C–400/10 PPU J McB v LE (ECJ, 5 October 2010), nyr 163
Joined Cases C–411/10 and C–493/10 N. S. v Secretary of State for the Home
 Department and M. E. and Others v Refugee Applications Commissioner
 and Minister for Justice, Equality and Law Reform (ECJ, Grand Chamber),
 21 December 2011 .... 106, 113, 172
Case C–491/10 PPU Aguirre Zarraga v Pelz (ECJ, 22 December 2010), nyr 172
Case C–617/10 Åklagaren v Hans Åkerberg Fransson 196

xviii *Table of Cases*

Case C–40/11 Yoshikazu Iida v City of Ulm (decision of ECJ pending) 73
Case C–256/11 Murat Dereci and others v Bundesministerium für Inneres
  (ECJ, 15 November 2011), nyr 4, 63, 103, 113, 164

Court of Justice, Name Order

Administration des Douanes v Société anonyme Gondrand Frères and Société
  anonyme Garancini, Case 169/80 [1981] ECR 1931 132
AGM-Cos.MET Srl v Suomen valtio and Tarmo Lehtinen, Case C–470/03
  [2007] ECR I–2749 .... 121, 146
Åklagaren v Hans Åkerberg Fransson, Case C–617/10 196
Åklagaren v Percy Mickelsson and Joakim Roos, Case C–142/05 [2009]
  ECR I–4273 15
Albany International BV v Stichting Bedrijfspensioenfonds textielindustrie,
  Case C–67/96 [1999] ECR I–5751 42
Amministrazione delle finanze dello Stato v Denkavit italiana Srl, Case 61/79
  [1980] ECR 1205 133
Amministrazione delle Finanze dello Stato v Simmenthal SpA, Case 106/77
  [1978] ECR 629 109
Anacleto Cordero Alonso v Fondo de Garantía Salarial (Fogasa), Case
  C–81/05 [2006] ECR I–7569 3
Annibaldi, Case C–309/96 [1997] ECR I–7493, judgment of 18 December
  1997 .... 72, 102
Bartsch v Bosch und Siemens Hausgeräte (BSH) Altersfürsorge GmbH,
  Case C–427/06 [2008] ECR I–7245 .... 97, 110–11, 116
Baumbast and R v Secretary of State for the Home Department, Case
  C-413/99 [2002] ECR I–7091 113
Belgium v European Commission, Case C–110/03 [2005] ECR I–2801 132
BNO Walrave and LJN Koch v Association Union cycliste internationale,
  Koninklijke Nederlandsche Wielren Unie and Federación Española
  Ciclismo, Case 36/74 [1974] ECR 1405 126–7
Booker Aquaculture Ltd (trading as Marine Harvest McConnell) and Hydro
  Seafood GSP Ltd v Scottish Ministers, Cases C–20/00 and C–64/00 [2003]
  ECR I–7411 .... 3, 113–14
Bosphorus Hava Yollari Turizm ve Ticaret AS v Minister for Transport, Case
  C–84/95 [1996] ECR I–3953 113–14
Brasserie de Pêcheur SA v Germany and The Queen v Secretary of State for
  Transport, *ex parte* Factortame Ltd and others, Joined Cases C–46/93 and
  C–48/93 [1996] ECR I–1029 .... 129, 141–2, 146, 149, 211
Bressol (Nicolas) and others, Céline Chaverot and others v Gouvernment
  de la Communauté française, Case C–73/08 [2010] ECR I–2735 18
Buet and Educational Business Services v Ministère Public, Case 382/87
  [1989] ECR 1235 19
Caballero (Ángel Rodríguez) v Fondo de Garantía Salarial (Fogasa), Case

Table of Cases xix

C–442/00 [2002] ECR I–11915 3
Centro Europa 7 Srl v Ministerio delle Comunicazioni, Case C–380/05
 [2008] ECR I–349 179
Coleman v Attridge Law and Steve Law, Case C–303/06 [2008] ECR I–5603 41
Commission v Italy, Case 7/61 [1961] ECR 317 .... 11, 19
Connolly v European Commission, Case T–163/96 [1999] ECR II–463 154
Corsica Ferries France v Direction générale des douanes françaises, Case
 C–49/89 [1989] ECR I–4441 83
Courage Ltd v Bernard Crehan, Case C–453/99 [2001] ECR
 I–6297 .... 32, 120, 141, 145
Criminal proceedings against Bodil Lindqvist, Case C–101/01 [2003]
 ECR I–12971 113–14
Criminal proceedings against Donatella Calfa, Case C–348/96 [1999]
 ECR I–11 .... 67, 88
Criminal proceedings against Jean-Pierre Guimont, Case C–448/98
 [2000] ECR I–10663 85
Criminal proceedings against Keck and Mithouard, Cases C–267/91
 and C–268/91 [1993] ECR I–6097 .... 11, 14, 16, 62, 85
Criminal proceedings against Maria Pupino, Case C–105/03 [2005]
 ECR I–5285 .... 3, 157–8, 164
Criminal proceedings against Silvio Berlusconi and Others, Cases C–391/02
 and C–403/02 [2005] ECR I–3565 159
Criminal proceedings against Vitor Manuel Santos Palhota and others,
 Case C–515/08 (CJEU, 7 October 2010) 46
Defrenne (Gabrielle) v Société Anonyme Belge de Navigation Aerienne
 (SABENA) (Defrenne II), Case 43/75 [1976] ECR 455 .... 106–7, 113, 132–3
Del Cerro Alonso v Osakidetza-Servicio Vasco de Salud, Case C–307/05
 [2007] ECR I–7109 52
Dereci (Murat) and others v Bundesministerium für Inneres, Case
 C–256/11 (ECJ, 15 November 2011), nyr 4, 63, 103, 113, 164
Deponiezweckverband Eiterköpfe v Land Rheinland-Pfalz, Case C-6/03
 [2005] ECR I-2753 113
Deutsche Energiehandels- und Beratungsgesellschaft mbH (DEB) v
 Germany, Case C–279/09 [2010] ECR I–13849 .... 74, 103, 113
Deutsche Paracelsus Schulen für Naturheilverfahren GmbH v Kurt Gräbner,
 Case C–294/00 [2002] ECR I–6515 20
Dynamic Medien Vertriebs GmbH v Avides Media AG, Case C–244/06
 [2008] ECR I–505 .... 15, 20, 30, 68, 74–5, 79, 82, 89–90
Elliniki Radiophonia Tileorassi AE (ERT) v Dimotiki Etairia Pliroforissis and
 Sotirios Kouvelas, Case C–260/89 [1991] ECR I–2925 .... 3, 23, 61, 72, 98,
 101–3, 105, 108, 113–14, 116, 186
Eugen Schmidberger, Internationale Transporte und Planzüge v Austria,
 Case C–112/00 [2003] ECR I–5659 .... 3, 5, 12, 24–6, 48, 60, 62–4,
 78, 81, 83, 87–90, 92–4, 113–16, 127–30, 133, 194, 209

European Commission v Belgium, Case C–2/90 [1992] ECR I–4431....................89
European Commission v Denmark, Case 302/86 [1988] ECR 4607.....................80
European Commission v France, Case C–50/08 (ECJ, 24 May 2011), nyr............83
European Commission v France, Case C–184/96 [1998] ECR I–6197 85
European Commission v France, Case C–225/98 [2000] ECR I–7445 51
European Commission v France, Case C–265/95 [1997] ECR I–6959
 (Spanish Strawberries) 18, 64, 78–9, 83, 117, 127–8
European Commission v France, Case C–334/02 [2004] ECR I–2229 88
European Commission v Germany, Case 178/84 [1987] ECR 1227......................82
European Commission v Germany, Case C–160/08 [2010] ECR I–3713 49
European Commission v Germany, Case C–271/08 [2010]
 ECR I–7091 .... 42, 48–9, 89–90, 92, 94
European Commission v Greece, Case C–398/98 [2001] ECR I–7915 78
Félix Palacios de la Villa v Cortefiel Servicios SA, Case C–411/05 [2007]
 ECR I–8531 .... 43, 47, 110–11, 134
Firma Sloman Neptun Schiffahrts AG v Seebetriebsrat Bodo Ziesemer der
 Sloman Neptun Schiffahrts AG, Case C–72/91 [1993] ECR I–887..............38, 43
Foto-Frost v Hauptzollamt Lübeck-Ost, Case 314/85 [1987] ECR 1129............169
Francovich and Others v Italy, Joined Cases C–6/90 and C–9/90 [1991]
 ECR I–5357 ....120, 126–31, 135, 139, 142, 145, 148–9, 211
Garage Molenheide BVBA and Others v Belgian State, C-286/94 Garage
 [1997] ECR I-7281...113
Gebroeders van Es Douane Agenten BV v Inspecteur der Invoerrechten en
 Accijnzen, Case C–143/93 [1996] ECR I–431 132
Grant (Lisa Jacqueline) v South-West Trains Ltd, Case C–249/96 [1998]
 ECR I–621 125
Herbert Karner Industrie-Auktionen GmbH v Troostwijk GmbH, Case
 C–71/02 [2004] ECR I–3025 .... 24, 62, 113, 116
HJ Banks & Co Ltd v British Coal Corporation, Case C–128/92 [1994]
 ECR I–1209 147
Hoechst AG v European Commission, Joined Cases 46/87 and 227/88
 [1989] ECR 2859...159, 197
Impact, Case C–268/06 [2008] ECR I–2483...88
Inter Environnement Wallonie ASBL v Région Wallonne, Case C–129/96
 [1997] ECR I–7411 108
International Transport Workers' Federation and Finnish Seamen's Union v
 Viking Line ABP and OÜ Viking Line Eesti, Case C–438/05 [2007]
 ECR I–10779 ....6, 12, 18, 26–8, 33–4, 38–9, 42–6, 49–50, 60, 69–70,
              78, 83, 87–94, 103, 113, 116–17, 122, 136–7, 143–5, 195, 209–10
Internationale Handelsgesellschaft mbH v Einfuhr- und Vorratsstelle
 für Getreide und Futtermittel, Case 11/70 [1970] ECR 1125........................2, 61
Janko Rottman v Freistaat Bayern, Case C–135/08 [2010] ECR I–1449...............17
JEJ Blanckaert Inspecteur van de Belastingdienst/Particulieren/Ondernemingen
 buitenland te Heerlen, Case C–512/03 [2005] ECR I–7685 17

Table of Cases xxi

Josemans (Marc Michel) v Burgemeester van Maastricht, Case C–137/09
  (ECJ, 16 December 2010), nyr 13–14, 67, 77–8
Klensch and Others v Secrétaire d'Etat, Joined Cases 201/85 and 202/85
  [1986] ECR 3477 113
Konkurrensverket v TeliaSonera Sverige AB, Case C–52/09 (ECJ, 17 February
  2011), nyr 33
Konsumentombudsmannen v Gourmet International Products AB, Case
  C–405/98 [2001] ECR I–1795 15
Kücükdeveci (Seda) v Swedex GmbH & Co KG, Case C–555/07 [2010]
  ECR I–365 .... 62, 73, 106–7, 110–13, 116, 164
Kunqian Catherine Zhu and Man Lavette Chen v Secretary of State for the
  Home Department, Case C–200/02 [2004] ECR I–9925 104
Laboratoires pharmaceutiques Bergaderm SA (in liquidation) and
  Jean-Jacques Goupil v European Commission, Case C–352/98P [2000]
  ECR I–5291 149
Laval un Partneri Ltd v Svenska Byggnadsarbetareförbundet and others,
  Case C–341/05 [2007] ECR I–11767 .... 3, 6, 26–8, 33–4, 38–9, 42, 44–6,
                              49, 60, 62, 69, 78, 83, 87–94, 103, 113, 116–17, 119,
                              122, 126–30, 132, 135–7, 140, 142–5, 147–50, 195, 209–11
Mangold (Werner) v Rüdiger Helm, Case C–144/04 [2005]
  ECR I–9981 .... 3, 107–11, 113, 116, 133–5, 164
Maribel Dominguez v Centre informatique du Centre Ouest Atlantique
  and Préfet de la région Centre, Case C–282/10 (ECJ, 24 January 2011),
  nyr 112, 141
Marks & Spencer plc v David Halsey (HM Inspector of Taxes), Case
  C–446/03 [2005] ECR I–10837 .... 18, 88
Marshall (M Helen) v Southampton and South-West Hampshire Area
  Health Authority, Case 152/84 [1986] ECR 723 134
Marshall (M Helen) v Southampton and South-West Hampshire Area
  Health Authority, Case C–271/91 [1993] ECR I–4367 146
Mary Carpenter v Secretary of State for the Home Department, Case
  C–60/00 [2002] ECR I–6279 .... 28, 113, 194
Michaeler, Subito GmbH, and Volgger v Amt für sozialen Arbeitsschutz,
  Autonome Provinz Bozen, Cases C–55/07 and C–56/07 [2008]
  ECR I–3135 111
Nold v European Commission, Case 4/73 [1974] ECR 491 2
NS v Secretary of State for the Home Department and M. E. and Others v
  Refugee Applications Commissioner and Minister for Justice, Equality
  and Law Reform, Joined Cases C–411/10 and C–493/10 (ECJ, Grand
  Chamber), 21 December 2011 .... 106, 113, 172
Officier van Justitie v Koninklijke Kaasfabriek Eyssen, Case 53/80 [1981]
  ECR 409 19
Ole Andersen v Region Syddanmark, Case C–499/08 (CJEU, 12 October
  2010) [2011] 1 CMLR 35 .... 47, 50

Omega Spielhallen- und Automatenaufstellungs- GmbH v Oberbürger-
meisterin der Bundesstadt Bonn, Case C–36/02 [2004]
ECR I–9609 .... 3, 12, 25, 31–2, 60, 62, 65–8,
83, 89–90, 92–4, 113, 115, 193, 209
Orkem v Commission, Case 374/87 [1989] ECR 3283 159
P v S and Cornwall County Council, Case C–13/94 [1996]
ECR I–2143 .... 41, 125, 158
Paola Faccini Dori v Recreb Srl, Case C–91/92 [1994] ECR I–3325 134
PPU Aguirre Zarraga v Pelz, Case C–491/10 (ECJ, 22 December 2010),
nyr...172
PPU J McB v LE, Case C–400/10 (ECJ, 5 October 2010), nyr 163
PreussenElektra AG v Schleswag AG, Case C–379/98 [2001]
ECR I–2099 ....30, 89
Prigge (Reinhard) and others v Deutsche Lufthansa AG, Case C–447/09
(ECJ, 13 September 2011), nyr..62, 73, 148
Procureur de la République v Association de défense des brûleurs d'huiles
usagées, Case 240/83 [1985] ECR 531 80
Procureur du Roi v Benoit et Gustave Dassonville, Case 8/74 [1974]
ECR 837.. 16, 19–20, 83
Productores de Música de España (Promusicae) v Telefónica de España
SAU, Case C–275/06 [2008] ECR I–271 194–5
Queen, The (on the application of Delena Wells) v Secretary of State for
Transport, Local Government and the Regions, Case C–201/02 [2004]
ECR I–723 134
Queen, The (on the application of International Air Tranport Association
and European Low Fares Airline Association) v Department for Transport,
Case C–344/04 [2006] ECR I–403 ....132, 170
Queen, The (on the application of The Incorporated Trustees of the
National Council on Ageing (Age Concern England)) v Secretary of State
for Business, Enterprise and Regulatory Reform, Case C–388/07 [2009]
ECR I–1569 47
Queen, The (on the application of Vodafone Ltd and others) v Secretary of
State for Business, Enterprise and regulatory reform, Case C–58/08 (ECJ,
8 June 2010), nyr..84
Queen, The (on the application of Yvonne Watts) v Bedford Primary Care
Trust and Secretary of State for Health, Case C–372/04 [2006]
ECR I–4325 .... 17, 20, 34, 69, 82
R v Bouchereau, Case 30/77 [1977] ECR 1999...67
Raccanelli (Andrea) v Max-Planck-Gesellschaft zur Förderung der Wissen-
schaften eV, Case C–94/07 [2008] ECR I–5939..120, 145
Radlberger Getränkegesellschaft mbH and S Spitz KG v Land Baden-Württem-
berg, Case C–309/02 [2004] ECR I–11763 80
Raymond Kohll v Union des Caisses de Maladie, Case C–158/96 [1998]
ECR I–1931 88

Reisch (Hans) and others Grundverkehrslandeskommission des Landes
  Salzburg, Cases C–515/99, C–519/99-524/99 and C–526-540/99 [2002]
  ECR I–2157 85
Reisebüro Broede v Gerd Sandker, Case C–3/95 [1996] ECR I–6511 20
René Lancry SA v Direction Générale des Souanes and Société Dindar Confort
  and others, Cases C–363/93 and C–407/93 to C–411/93 [1994] ECR I–3957 85
Rewe-Handelsgesellschaft Nord mbH and Rewe-Markt Steffen v
  Hauptzollamt Kiel, Case 158/80 [1981] ECR 1805 124
Rewe-Zentrale AG v Bundesmonopolverwaltung für Branntwein (Cassis
  de Dijon), Case 120/78 [1979] ECR 649 .... 14–15, 19–20, 30
Roca-Álvarez v Sesa Start Espana ETT SA, Case C–104/09 (ECJ, 30 September
  2010), nyr 112
Roman Angonese v Cassa di Risparmio di Bolzano SpA, Case C–281/98
  [2000] ECR I–4139 .... 83, 85, 106, 113, 126–7, 140, 147
Romer (Jürgen) v Freie und Hansestadt Hamburg, Case C–147/08
  (ECJ, 10 May 2011), nyr 111
Roquette Frères SA v Directeur général de la concurrence, de la consommation
  et de la répression des fraudes, and European Commission, Case C–94/00
  [2002] ECR I–9011 .... 197, 212
Roquette Frères SA v Direction des Services Fiscaux du Pas-de-Calais,
  Case C–88/99 [2000] ECR I–10465 159
Rüffert (Dirk) v Land Niedersachsen, Case C–346/06 [2008]
  ECR I–1989 ....40, 44–5, 49
Rutili v Ministre de l'Interiori, Case 36/75 [1975] ECR 1219 ....101, 157
SARL Albatros v Société des Petroles et des Combustibles Liquides
  (SOPECO), Case 20/64 [1965] ECR 29 11
Sayn-Wittgenstein (Ilonka) v Landeshauptmann von Wien, Case C–208/09
  (ECJ, 22 December 2010), nyr 12, 31, 66, 68, 89–94, 113, 115, 193, 209
Scarlet Extended SA v Société belge des auteurs, compositeurs et éditeurs
  SCRL (SABAM), Case C–70/10 (CJEU, 24 November 2011), nyr 148, 188
Scattolon (Ivana) v Ministerio dell'Istruzione, dell'Università e della Ricerca,
  Case C–108/10 (ECJ, 6 September 2011), nyr 97
Schutzverband gegen unlauteren Wettbewerb v TK-Heimdienst Sass GmbH,
  Case C–254/98 [2000] ECR I–151 85
SGL Carbon v European Commission, Case C–308/04P [2006]
  ECR I–5977 177
Shirley McCarthy v Secretary of State for the Home Department,
  Case C–434/09 (ECJ, 5 May 2011), nyr... 112, 164
Simitzi v Dimos Kos, Joined Cases C–485/93 and C–486/93 [1995]
  ECR I–2655 85
Society for the Protection of Unborn Children Ireland v Grogan and others,
  Case C–159/90 [1991] ECR I–4685 .... 13–14, 78
Spanish Strawberries case *see* European Commission v France, Case C–265/95
  [1997] ECR I–6959

Srl CILFIT and Lanificio di Gavardo SpA v Ministry of Health, Case C–283/81 [1982] ECR 3415 170
Stauder (Erich) v City of Ulm – Sozialamt, Case 29/69 [1969] ECR 419 ....2, 61
Steffenson (Joachim), Case C–276/01 [2003] ECR I–3735 113–14
Stichting 'Goed Wonen' v Staatssecretaris van Financiën, Case C–376/02 [2005] ECR I–3445 3
Stoke on Trent and Norwich City Councils v B & Q plc, Case C–169/91 [1992] ECR I–6635 15
Tadao Maruko v Versorgungsanstalt der deutschen Bühnen, Case C–267/06 [2008] ECR I–1757 ....41, 52
Tietosuojavaltuutettu v Satakunnan Markkinapörssi Oy and Satamedia Oy, Case C–73/07. [2008] ECR I–9831 112
Torfaen Borough Council v B & Q plc, Case 145/88 [1989] ECR 3851 15
Unibet (London) Ltd and Unibet (International) Ltd v Justitiekanslern, Case C–432/05 [2007] ECR I–2271 ....121, 124–6, 131
Union Royale Belge des Sociétés de Football Association ASBL v Jean-Marc Bosman, Case C–415/93 [1995] ECR I–4921 .... 18, 21, 113, 116–17, 126–7
United Pan-Europe Communications Belgium SA and others v Belgian State, Case C–250/06 [2007] ECR I–11135 (ECJ) 82
Van Gend en Loos v Nederlandse Administratie der Belastingen, Case 26/62 [1963] ECR 1 11
Verein gegen Unwesen in Handel und Gewerbe Köln v Mars GmbH, Case C–470/93 [1995] ECR I–1923 15
Vereinigte Familiapress Zeitungsverlags- und vertriebs GmbH v Heinrich Bauer Verlag, Case C–368/95 [1997] ECR I–3689 .... 3, 23, 25, 113–14, 157
Vereniging voor Energie, Milieu en Water (VEMW) and thers v Directeur van de Dienst uitvoering en toezicht energie, Case C–17/03 [2005] ECR I–4983 ... 132
Vincenzo Manfredi and others v Lloyd Adriatico Assicurazioni SpA et al, Case C–295/04 to C–298/04 [2006] ECR I–6619 ....120, 141, 145
Volker and Markus Schecke GbR and Hartmut Eifert v Land Hessen, Joined Cases C–92/09 and C–93/09 [2010] ECR I–11063 .... 3, 57, 61, 75–6, 86, 93, 161, 188, 198
Wachauf (Hubert) v Bundesamt für Ernährung und Forstwirtschaft, Case 5/88 [1989] ECR 2609 .... 3, 61, 72, 98, 102, 105, 108, 110–11, 113–14, 116–17, 187
Watts, *ex parte see* Case C–372/04 The Queen (on the application of Yvonne Watts) v Bedford Primary Care Trust and Secretary of State for Health [2006]
Yassin Abdullah Kadi and Al Barakaat International Foundation v European Council (Kadi I), Joined Cases C–402/05P and C–415/05P [2008] ECR I–10889 .... 26, 44, 158, 163–4, 168, 179, 201
Yoshikazu Iida v City of Ulm, Case C–40/11 (decision of ECJ pending)..............73
Zambrano (Gerardo Ruiz) v Office national de l'emploi (ONEm), Case C–34/09 (ECJ, 8 March 2011), nyr........ 4, 62–3, 74, 85, 103–4, 113, 164, 211–12

International

European Court of Human Rights

A, B and C v Ireland, App no 25579/05 (ECtHR, 16 December 2010) 190, 200
Association for European Integration and Human Rights and Ekimzhiev v Bulgaria, App no 62540/00 (ECtHR, 28 June 2007) 192
Axel Springer AG v Germany, App no 39954/08 (ECtHR, 7 February 2012) 191, 200
Bayatyan v Armenia, App no 23459/03 (ECtHR, 7 July 2011) 196
Bosphorus Hava Yollari Turizm ve Ticaret Anonim Sirketi v Ireland, App no 45036/98 (ECtHR, 30 June 2005); (2006) 42 EHRR 1 .... 155–6, 173–4, 177, 195–6
Broniowski v Poland, App no 31443/96 (ECHR, 22 June 2004) 200
Cantoni v France, ECHR 1996-V 52 156
CFTD v European Communities, App no 8030/77 (1978) 13 DR 213 154
Chassagou and others v France, App nos 25088/94, 28331/95 and 28443/95 (ECtHR, 24 April 1999) 77
Connolly v 15 Member States of the European Union, App no 73274/01 (ECtHR, 9 December 2008) 154
Cooperatieve Producentenorganisatie van de Nederlandse Kokkelvisserij UA v Netherlands, App no 13645/05 (ECtHR, 20 January 2009) 155
Demir and Baykara v Turkey, App no 34503/97 (ECtHR, 12 November 2008), [2008] ECHR 1345 .... 43, 106, 190
Dogru v France, App no 27058/05 (ECtHR, 16 December 2008) 190
Dudgeon v United Kingdom (1981), Series A no 45 (ECtHR, 22 October 1981) 199
Enerji Yapi-Yol Sen v Turkey, Application no 68959/01 (ECtHR, 21 April 2009) 43
Goodwin (Christine) v UK (2002) 35 EHRR 18 159
Ezelin v France (1991) Series A no 202 187
Görgülü (Kazim) v Germany, App no 74969/01 (ECtHR, 26 February 2004) 164, 191–2
Greens and MT v United Kingdom [2010] ECHR 1826 176
Heinz v Parties to European Patent Convention (1994) 76A DR 125 156
Hirst v United Kingdom (No 2) [2005] ECHR 681 176
Inze v Austria, Series A no 126 (ECtHR, 28 October 1987) 176
Johnston and others v Ireland (1986) Series A no 112 186
Kervanci v France, App no 31645/04 (ECtHR, 16 December 2008) 190
Krone Verlag GmbH & Co KG v Austria, App no 34315/96 (ECtHR, 26 February 2002) 189
Lautsi (Soile) and others v Italy, App no 30814/06 (ECtHR, 18 March 2011) 204

M & Co v Federal Republic of Germany, App no 13258/87 (1990) 64 DR
138 .... 154, 156
Martinie v France (2006) 42 EHRR 15 159
Matthews v United Kingdom (1999) 28 EHRR 361 .... 155, 173
Moustaquim v Belgium (1991) Series A no 193 (ECtHR, 18 February
1991) 157
MSS v Belgium and Greece, App no 30696/09 (ECtHR, 21 January
2011) 172, 196
Nada (Youssef) v Switzerland, App no 10593/08 (ECtHR, 23 March
2011) 158
Neulinger and Shuruk v Switzerland, App no 41615/07 (ECtHR (Grand
Chamber), 6 July 2010) 159
News Verlags GmbH & Co KG v Austria, App no 31457/96 (ECtHR,
11 January 2000) 189
Niemietz v Germany (1992), Series A no 251-B, 16 EHRR 97 197
Nilsson (Christoffer) v Sweden, App no 73661/01 (ECtHR, 13 December
2005) 202
Opuz v Turkey, App no 33401/02 (ECtHR, 9 June 2009) 192
Osman (Mulkiye and Ahmed) v UK, App no 23452/94 [1998] ECHR 101 204
Osterreichischer Rundfunk v Austria, App no 35841/02 (ECtHR, 7 December
2006) 113, 189
Rees v United Kingdom (1986) Series A no 106 (ECtHR) 158
Roche v UK, App no 32555/96 (ECtHR, 2005-X) 191
Rosenquist (Nils-Inge) v Sweden, App no 60619/00 (ECtHR, 14 September
2004) 202
S and Marper v UK, App nos 30562/04 and 30566/04 (ECtHR, 4 December
2008) 190
Sahin (Leyla) v Turkey, App no 44774/98 (ECtHR, 29 June 2004) 190
Sánchez (Palomo) and Others v Spain, App nos 28955/06, 28957/06, 28959/06
and 28964/06 (ECtHR (Grand Chamber), 12 September 2011) 191
Schalk and Kopf v Austria, App no 30141/04 (ECtHR, 24 June 2010) 196
Scoppolla v Italy, App no 1024/03 (ECtHR (Grand Chamber), 17 September
2009) 159
Társaság a Szabadságjogokért v Hungary, App no 37374/05 (ECtHR, 14 April
2009) 197
Tyrer v United Kingdom (1978) 2 EHRR 1 176
Tyrer v United Kingdom (1978) Series A no 26, (1978) 2 EHRR 1 .... 162, 176
Tysiac v Poland, App no 5410/03 (ECtHR, 20 March 2007) 200
Ullens de Schooten and Rezabek v Belgium, Application nos 3989/07 and
38353/07 (ECtHR, 20 September 2011) 170
von Hannover v Germany, App no 59320/00 (ECtHR, 24 June 2004) [2004]
ECHR 294; (2005) 40 EHRR 1 .... 176, 190, 203
von Hannover (No 2) v Germany, App nos 40660/08 and 60641/08 (ECtHR,
7 February 2012) 190, 204

Wizerkaniuk v Poland, App no 18990/05 (ECtHR, 5 July 2011) 190
Young, James and Webster v United Kingdom (1981) Series A no 44 187
Z and others v UK, App no 29392/95 (ECtHR, 10 May 2001) 204
Zolotukhin (Sergey) v Russia, App no 14939/03 (ECtHR (Grand Chamber),
    10 February 2009) 196, 202

European Committee on Social Rights

GENOP-DEI v Greece, decisions of 23 May 2012, FSC 1961 Nos 65/2011 and
    66/2011 44

Germany

Brunner (Mannfred) v European Union Treaty [1994] 1 CMLR 57 163
'Caroline II' case, BVerfG, 1 BvR 1602/07, judgment of 26 February 2008 203
Görgülü case, Decision of the German Federal Constitutional Court, 2 BvR
    1481/04 of 14 October 2004 164
Honeywell, BVerfG, 2 BvR 2661/06, judgment of 6 July 2010 134
Solange I, 29 May 1974, BVerfGe, 37, 271 165
Solange II, Case No 2 BvR 197/83 (BVerfG) BVerfGE 73, 339 (Neue Juristische
    Wochenschrift (NJW) 1987, 577) (22 October 1986) 42, 156

Sweden

Laval un Partneri Ltd v Svenska byggnadsarbetareförbundet et al, Case
    No A 268/04, Judgment of the Labour Court (Arbetsdomstolen)
    No 89/2009, 2 December 2009 ....119–20, 122, 126, 131, 133, 137, 147, 149–50
NJA 2001 s 409 185
NJA 2005 s 805 191
NJA 2010 s 168 I–II 202
RÅ 2006 ref 87 191
RÅ 2009 ref 96 202

United Kingdom

Balpa 136
R v Horncastle and others [2009] UKSC 14; [2009] WLR (D) 358 ....164, 204
R (on the application of NS) v Secretary of State for the Home Department, 12
    July 2010 [2010] CA Civ 990 105
Seldon v Clarkson Wright [2012] UKSC 16 50

United States of America

Gitlow v People of the State of New York, 268 US 652 (1925) 101, 105
Lawrence et al v Texas, 539 US 558 (2003) 199
Roe v Wade, 410 US 113 (1973) 199–200

Roper v Simmons, 543 US 551; 125 SCt 1183, 1226 (2005) 158

International Arbitral Awards

Robert E Brown Claim (United States v Great Britain) (1923) 6 RIAA 120.......189

Introduction

SYBE DE VRIES, ULF BERNITZ AND STEPHEN WEATHERILL

I. The Origin of Fundamental Rights Protection in Europe

According to the joint communication from Presidents Costa (European Court of Human Rights – (ECtHR)) and Skouris (Court of Justice of the European Union – (ECJ)) '[t]he accession of the EU to the Convention constitutes a major step in the development of the protection of fundamental rights in Europe. The Member States of the EU have enshrined the principle of that accession in the Treaty of Lisbon'.

The Treaty of Lisbon (December 2009), of which this declaration of the Presidents of the Courts forms the 'offspring', brings the remarkable expansion of the protection of fundamental rights at the level of the European Union to a climax. At least three aspects of the changes made by the Lisbon Treaty suggest that its entry into force marks a new stage in the shaping of the EU's commitment to the protection of fundamental rights, and the book's concern is to provide an examination of the several (and interlocking) challenges. The three aspects are: first, respect for human rights has been inscribed more deeply as a foundational value of the EU (in particular Articles 2, 3(5), 6 and 21 TEU); secondly, there is provision in Article 6(2) TEU for the accession of the European Union to the European Convention on Human Rights (which had previously been beyond the competence of the EU); and thirdly, the EU's Charter of Fundamental Rights, 'solemnly proclaimed' at Nice in 2001 but not then granted binding effect, has now been elevated to formally binding status.

There are, moreover, a number of conundrums about the scope and method of protection of fundamental rights in the EU which existed 'pre-Lisbon' and which endure, and these too will be the subject of examination in the book. But these developments 'post-Lisbon' present a number of fresh and intriguing challenges for the EU as an entity committed to the protection and promotion of fundamental rights. After all, in the European Economic Community originally the focus was on the safeguarding of (economic) rights of free movement and residence. Citizens in Europe first had as *market citizens* and only later as *EU citizens* acquired rights of free movement and residence in the European Union.[1] The Treaties, however, did recognise rights that were similar to fundamental rights, such as the principle of non-discrimination and the right to equal pay for men and women.[2] Nevertheless, fundamental or human rights in the first place were a matter for the Council of Europe and the ECtHR in Strasbourg.

This does not mean that no attempts were made in Europe at all by those states promoting integration in Europe, which finally resulted in the establishment of the European Communities. Already in the early 1950s several European states sought to engage themselves in human or fundamental rights protection. Although the effort to set up a European political community was ultimately unsuccessful, it was an important first step in the European integration process for the development of a European identity for human rights protection.[3]

The primarily economic orientation of the European Communities did not appear to be a handicap for the ECJ to develop a European fundamental rights dimension, partially influenced by the discussions in Germany regarding the assumed power of the German constitutional court (Bundesverfassungsgericht) to assess EU law in the light of the German Constitution.[4] Hence, long before the inclusion of a provision in the Maastricht Treaty (1992) recognising fundamental rights as part of EU law, the proclamation of the Charter of Fundamental Right in Nice (2000) and much later the Lisbon Treaty in 2009, fundamental rights had already been 'discovered' and recognised by the ECJ as general principles of Community law. In cases like *Stauder*, *Nold* and *Internationale Handelsgesellschaft* the ECJ decided that fundamental human rights are enshrined in the general principles of Community law.[5] Furthermore, the Court referred to the constitutional traditions common to the Member States as source of inspiration.

This case law, also referred to as 'triptych' of cases, had produced a new constitutional setting for fundamental rights protection in Europe, whereby fundamental or human rights became an integral part of Community law and later EU law.[6] Ever since, the ECJ has been 'forced' to pronounce itself on the application of fundamental rights. Not only has the ECJ granted protection to citizens against infringements of fundamental rights by *EU institutions*, which was the issue in cases as *Stauder*, *Internationale Handelsgesellschaft* and more recently *Volker and Schecke*, wherein the Court declared invalid certain provisions of an EU agricultural regulation as they

---

[1] See also N Nic Shuibhne, 'The Resilience of EU Market Citizenship' (2010) 47 *CML Rev* 1597–1628; H van Eijken and SA de Vries, 'A new route into the promised land? Being a European citizen after Ruiz Zambrano' (2011) 36 *EL Rev* 704.

[2] PJG Kapteyn, 'Stauder' in TWB Beukers, HJ van Harten and S Prechal (eds), *Het recht van de Europese Unie in 50 klassieke arresten* (Den Haag, Boom Juridische uitgevers, 2010) 39.

[3] G de Búrca, 'The Evolution of EU Human Rights Law' in P Craig and G de Búrca, *The Evolution of EU Law* (Oxford, Oxford University Press, 2011) 466.

[4] Kapteyn, 'Stauder', above n 2, 40.

[5] Case 29/69 *Erich Stauder v City of Ulm – Sozialamt* [1969] ECR 419; Case 4/73 *Nold v European Commission* [1974] ECR 491; Case 11/70 *Internationale Handelsgesellschaft mbH v Einfuhr- und Vorratsstelle für Getreide und Futtermittel* [1970] ECR 1125.

[6] De Búrca, 'The Evolution of EU Human Rights Law', above n 3, 478.

constituted an unjustified interference with the Charter.⁷ For that matter, this was for the first time that the ECJ struck down secondary EU law as being incompatible with the *Charter*.

The ECJ has also declared that actions by the *Member States* or private individuals (associations) may lead to an infringement of fundamental rights, against which EU citizens should be protected. This may be the case where Member States implement EU law,⁸ or amend national legislation within the discretion left by a directive, or anticipate an amending directive.⁹ Even in situations where Member States, or private associations, in the wake of the Treaty exceptions or 'rule of reason' case law deviate from the free movement rules, they will have to respect fundamental rights. This appeared from the *ERT* case, where the Greek state, in seeking to justify a restriction on the free movement of services as a result of the television monopoly, had to take into account Article 10 of the ECHR, the freedom of expression.¹⁰ In a similar vein an Austrian prohibition on prize competitions in magazines restricting the free movement of goods could only be justifiable by reasons related to press diversity when due account was given to fundamental rights.¹¹

Member States – or private associations – may also rely on fundamental rights as a *justification* per se for restrictions on free movement. In several cases, like *Schmidberger*, *Omega*, or *Laval*, the ECJ has accepted that fundamental rights may be relied upon to derogate from the Treaty freedoms.¹²

II. The Current Challenges After Lisbon and the Background of this Book

So what, now the Lisbon Treaty has entered into force, is the role of the Court, now that it is operating in an environment that is much more crowded with relevant

---

[7] Cases C-92/09 and C-93/09 *Volker und Markus Schecke GbR and Hartmut Eifert v Land Hessen* [2010] ECR I-11063.

[8] Cases C-20/00 and C-64/00 *Booker Aquaculture Ltd (trading as Marine Harvest McConnell) and Hydro Seafood GSP Ltd v Scottish Ministers* [2003] ECR I-7411; Case C-144/04 *Werner Mangold v Rüdiger Helm* [2005] ECR I-9981; Case C-442/00 *Ángel Rodríguez Caballero v Fondo de Garantía Salarial (Fogasa)* [2002] ECR I-11915; Case C-105/03 *Criminal Proceedings against Maria Pupino* [2005] ECR I-5285; Case 5/88 *Hubert Wachauf v Bundesamt für Ernährung und Forstwirtschaft* [1989] ECR 2609.

[9] Case C-376/02 *Stichting 'Goed Wonen' v Staatssecretaris van Financiën* [2005] ECR I-3445; Case C-81/05 *Anacleto Cordero Alonso v Fondo de Garantía Salarial (Fogasa)* [2006] ECR I-7569.

[10] Case C-260/89 *Elliniki Radiophonia Tiléorassi AE (ERT) v Dimotiki Etairia Pliroforissis* [1991] ECR I-2925.

[11] Case C-368/95 *Vereinigte Familiapress Zeitungs- und vertriebs GmbH v Heinrich Bauer Verlag* [1997] ECR I-3689, paras 24–26.

[12] Case C-112/00 *Schmidberger* [2003] ECR I-5659; Case C-36/02 *Omega Spielhallen- und Automatenaufstellungs- GmbH v Oberbürgermeisterin der Bundesstadt Bonn* [2004] ECR I-9609; Case C-341/05 *Laval un Partneri Ltd v Svenska Byggnadsarbetareförbundet and others* [2007] ECR I-11767.

legislative texts? Will it be more restrained in pushing the frontiers of fundamental rights protection in the EU? Should it be? Such inquiry is also influenced by appreciation that although the Member States have taken important steps to write the protection of fundamental rights more deeply into the fabric of the EU's legal order, they have also added new layers of ambiguity. A persisting anxiety among at least some Member States is that infusing the EU with deeper commitments to human rights might generate unforeseen extension in the scope of its competence. This anxiety is reflected in a second sentence added to Article 6(2) TEU: 'Such accession [to the European Convention] shall not affect the Union's competences as defined in the Treaties'. Moreover, a supplementary Protocol relating to Article 6(2) TEU states that accession is to 'make provision for preserving the specific characteristics of the Union and Union law'. And it is to be ensured that accession 'shall not affect the competences of the Union or the powers of its institutions'. But it is notorious that the EU's competences, though in principle limited, are in practice broad and hard to define and, crucially, have tended to be driven by an expansionist dynamic embraced by the EU's legislative and judicial institutions. Furthermore, a narrow interpretation of the text of the Charter may be at odds with the generally broad scope of application of EU law and the case law of the Court on fundamental rights as general principles of EU law. The cases on rights of EU citizens like *Ruiz Zambrano* or *Dereci* demonstrate how intriguing and difficult the questions are that the ECJ faces and needs to solve.[13] Since the main rule in *Ruiz Zambrano* is that whenever the substance of citizens' rights, which constitutes the 'spine' of European citizenship, is at risk, Article 20 TFEU on citizenship can be invoked, it can be argued that the enjoyment of – at least certain domestic or EU – fundamental rights could be qualified as crucial for the enjoyment of European citizenship rights.[14]

These issues require close attention, and this book is motivated by the concern to pursue such inquiries.

III. The Structure of the Book

The book consists of three parts. The first part is concerned with the safeguarding of fundamental rights in Europe's internal market. After all, the internal market has for a long time been the cornerstone of European integration. In the case law of the ECJ the Treaty provisions on free movement have been awarded a 'fun-

---

[13] Case C-34/09 *Gerardo Ruiz Zambrano v Office national de l'emploi (ONEm)* (ECJ, 8 March 2011), nyr; Case C-256/11, *Murat Dereci and others v Bundesministerium für Inneres* (ECJ, 15 November 2011), nyr. See also N Nic Shuibhne 'Case Law – (Some of) The Kids Are All Right' (2012) 49 *CML Rev* 349–80.

[14] See also L Azoulai, 'A comment on the Ruiz Zambrano judgment: a genuine European integration', *EUDOCitizenship*: eudo-citizenship.eu/citizenship-news/457-a-comment-on-the-ruiz-zambrano-judgment-a-genuine-european-integration (Accessed 4 April 2012). See also A von Bogdandy, M Kottmann, C Antpöhler, J Dickschen, S Hentrei and M Smrkolj, 'Reverse Solange – Protecting the Essence of Fundamental Rights against EU Member States' (2012) 49 *CML Rev* 489, 507.

damental status' as they constitute the 'building blocks' of the European single market. In the first chapter of this book Stephen Weatherill discusses the pivotal role the Treaty freedoms have played in the integration process so far and the particularly important role of the ECJ herein, having been 'induced to take free movement far from its roots'. The has led to criticism, that is to say that EU free movement law has too much interfered with Member States' autonomy in certain policy areas. He therefore raises the question of how the Court has addressed this criticism of the scope of EU free movement law – 'that it is disrupting the shaping of matters of cherished importance within the Member States'.

In the second chapter Catherine Barnard focuses on the protection of fundamental social rights in Europe after Lisbon. She argues that the changes brought about by the Lisbon Treaty do not only give the European Union a greater 'social face', but also create more difficulties for the European Union to further define its social dimension. Three difficulties are discussed by Barnard. The first concerns the increasing proliferation of sources of social rights at EU, national and international levels and the question as to how these levels interact. The second difficulty relates to the increasing number of individual interests that need to be balanced, for instance, the interests of the workers of the 'old Member States' vis-à-vis the interests of the workers of the new Member States. Barnard questions the use of the proportionality test as a suitable instrument to balance these conflicting interests.

The third and last difficulty arises at macro-level, where the EU is seeking to attain a social market economy while the Eurozone is in a serious crisis. Does the EU's response to this crisis meet the objective set out in Article 151 TFEU of improving living and working conditions?

The first part is concluded by the contribution of Sybe de Vries, who draws the attention to the conflict that exists between fundamental rights and fundamental freedoms and the possibilities for the ECJ to balance these conflicting rights and principles. His central question is whether the balance between protecting fundamental rights and Treaty freedoms has been rightly struck, taking into account the changed EU legal framework. After discussing the case law of the ECJ, the point of departure for De Vries' analysis is that there is not a priori a hierarchy between fundamental rights and Treaty freedoms. The Treaty freedoms, particularly in their capacity of prohibiting discriminatory practices, can be and often are qualified as fundamental rights as well.

Furthermore, the case law of the ECJ starting with *Schmidberger*, the *locus classicus* for conflicting rights in EU law, shows that there is no consistent approach as to how fundamental rights are balanced with Treaty freedoms. In balancing conflicting rights and freedoms the 'good old' principle of proportionality plays a crucial role, which is traditionally used by the ECJ to balance within the context of the Treaty exceptions or rule of reason public interests (mandatory requirements) and Treaty freedoms. But is proportionality equally suitable in cases where fundamental rights conflict with fundamental freedoms?

The second part of the book is entitled 'The scope of fundamental rights in EU law' and the chapters discuss the reach of fundamental rights and the horizontal dimension of fundamental rights. In his contribution Xavier Groussot focuses on the 'potential "federalising effect"' of the Charter as well as the possible impact of its new legally-binding status as regards the 'horizontal' application of EU fundamental rights. Regarding the scope of the Charter he argues that the ECJ should not act as a Supreme Court, developing a federal standard against which all national rules must be evaluated. With respect to the horizontal application of fundamental rights, Groussot submits that the material scope of the Charter is broader than the general principles of EU law.

Martin Mörk then discusses the question of horizontal liability arising out of the *Laval* case law and the limits of judicial rights protection. Laval was a Latvian company, which won a contract to refurbish a school near Stockholm. The Latvian workers earned 40 per cent less than the Swedish workers. The Swedish Labour Union representing them wanted Laval to apply the collective agreement, but it refused, which led to a blockade of the building site by the Swedish construction workers. According to the ECJ the collective action constituted a restriction on the free movement of services and could not be justified by the fundamental right to collective action for the benefit of the interests of the workers.

In the subsequent proceedings the Swedish Labour Court held the trade unions liable for a breach of Article 56 TFEU and awarded damages to Laval.

Mörk examines whether as a matter of effective judicial protection, or in his words 'effective rights protection', the Swedish Labour Court was legally obliged to provide Laval with a horizontal damages action. And he points to the danger of extending damages actions to horizontal situations like Laval.

Ulf Bernitz's contribution on the horizontal effects of private rights, which also focuses on the *Laval* and *Viking* cases, reveals a more positive stance on the ECJ's case law and the resulting possibilities for the national court to award damages in these situations. He is more critical about Mörk's observations that the damages actions in horizontal situations like *Laval* should be limited, however.

The last part of this book deals with 'the Constitutional Dimension of Fundamental Rights' and includes contributions by Sionaidh Douglas-Scott and by Iain Cameron respectively. The chapter written by Sionaidh Douglas-Scott analyses the special relationship between the ECJ and the ECtHR and does not only embroider on past practice and current case law but also examines the issue of accession of the European Union to the European Convention on the Protection of Human Rights and how this is likely to affect both Courts. The question is whether this will further complicate the already complex relationship between these two institutions. The negotiations for the accession of the European Union to the ECHR are 'in full swing' and so far no unanimous EU position has been reached. Douglas-Scott also argues that EU accession to the ECHR is by no means straightforward. The consequence of accession is that the ECHR will have a more direct impact on EU and national law.

Iain Cameron concludes this book by examining the issue of rights competition between the EU Charter on Fundamental Rights, the European Convention on Human Rights and national rights catalogues. He discusses the different approaches of the ECJ, the ECtHR and the national constitutional courts to rights and principles, the possible competition between the courts responsible for applying the human rights catalogues and whether and how clashes between these courts can be avoided.

IV. Fundamental Rights at the Heart of EU Law?

Not only do the authors come up with interesting ideas as to how EU law can more fully embrace fundamental rights, they also raise new and captivating questions relating to the three main themes of this book. After more than two years since the Lisbon Treaty entered into force and the EU Charter of Fundamental Rights was given binding effect it is, of course, too early to draw well-founded conclusions on their actual bearing on fundamental rights protection in the EU. But with a gradual increase in case law on the Charter, it will not take long before a more comprehensive picture can be drawn as to its scope and impact on EU and national law.

Looking at the Lisbon Treaty, fundamental rights are more than ever put at the heart of EU law. According to Article 2 TEU 'the Union is founded on the values of respect for human dignity, freedom, democracy, equality, the rule of law and respect for human rights'. Considering this Treaty provision and Article 6 TEU, as well as the binding nature of the Charter and the forthcoming accession of the EU to the ECHR – although up until this moment tough negotiations are taking place – the protection of fundamental rights has indeed become of central importance for the EU and its Member States, and cannot be considered as a mere afterthought anymore.

Nevertheless, this 'constitutional framework' clearly has its limitations. After all, the Member States deliberately sought to constrain the powers of the EU in the field of fundamental rights protection, which makes the claim of the EU as a 'human rights organisation' rather weak. According to De Búrca 'while the claim that the EU can be understood as a human rights organization remains untenable, human rights certainly feature prominently both in the constitutional self-understanding of the EU and its international self-representation'.[15] This brings us back to the role of the Court and to the question whether fundamental or human rights can really develop in a substantive way through a court-led means.[16] The role of other EU institutions, like the EU legislature, the Member States and other, for instance non-governmental, bodies is important as well.

The many uncertainties connected to the scope and application of the EU Charter on fundamental rights are treated in several contributions to this book. Hence, the story of EU fundamental rights protection does not end with this book. This book is just the beginning!

---

[15] De Búrca, 'The Evolution of EU Human Rights Law', above n 3, 495.
[16] See Douglas-Scott in her contribution to this book (ch 7).

Part I

Safeguarding Fundamental Rights in Europe's Internal Market

1

From Economic Rights to Fundamental Rights

STEPHEN WEATHERILL*

I. Introduction: The Source(s) and Shape(s) of the Challenge

The Court of Justice's first ruling concerning the free movement of goods arrived in December 1961. It concerned Italian measures suspending the importation of pigs and pig products.[1] It was a (successful) application by the Commission under what we know today as the Article 258 TFEU infringement procedure. In February 1963 the Court delivered its first preliminary ruling concerning the free movement of goods: that was the celebrated ruling in *Van Gend en Loos*, remembered today for its landmark introduction of the principle of direct effect, but forgotten for its facts, which concerned the imposition of customs duties on ureaformaldehyde imported into the Netherlands.[2] The first preliminary ruling dealing with what we know today as Article 34 TFEU on the free movement of goods was delivered in February 1965, the utterly unmemorable ruling in *SARL Albatros v SOPECO*.[3]

That was the nature of the early years. Litigation was largely targeted at border controls, administrative formalities and customs duties – obvious obstacles to inter-state trade. Things have changed: the case law today is much richer and varied. The types of practices that are subject to challenge are much more subtle barriers to inter-state trade or sometimes not barriers to inter-state trade at all. In the last decade the Court of Justice (and national courts) have been forced to address national practices forbidding the resale of certain products at a loss,[4] acquiescence in protests by those who oppose the environmental damage caused

---

* Jacques Delors Professor of European Law, Somerville College, Oxford.
[1] Case 7/61 *European Commission v Italy* [1961] ECR 317.
[2] Case 26/62 *Van Gend en Loos v Nederlandse Administratie der Belastingen* [1963] ECR 1.
[3] Case 20/64 *SARL Albatros v Société des Petroles et des Combustibles Liquides (SOPECO)* [1965] ECR 29.
[4] Cases C-267 and C268/91 *Criminal Proceedings against Keck and Mithouard* [1993] ECR I-6097.

by the movement of goods through the Brenner Pass,[5] the suppression of imported games involving simulated killing which are regarded locally as demeaning to human dignity,[6] and collective labour action aimed at deterring the 'reflagging' of ships from one Member State to another.[7] The recent litigation in which a seller of castles complained that because the name she used in Germany, Ilonka Fürstin von Sayn-Wittgenstein, was forbidden in Austria (where, in deference to Austrian rules promoting equality through the suppression of old names of the nobility), she had to style herself plain old Ilonka Sayn-Wittgenstein, provides a gloriously vivid example of just how far free movement law has travelled from its roots in pig meat and ureaformaldehyde.[8] There is a natural trajectory to this narrative in the sense that obvious – physical, discriminatory – trade barriers get tackled first, leading then in time to the excavation of and challenge to more subtle trade barriers. But the process is driven by ingenious and well-funded litigants, able to exploit the ambiguous outer reaches of EU trade law, and strengthened further by the constitutional principles of direct effect and supremacy which ensure easy access to (national) courts in pursuit of their quest to liberalise the EU market. This chapter takes as its topic this expansion: the Court has been induced to take free movement far from its roots – too far, perhaps. The anxiety: too much EU law, too little local autonomy.

This investigation centres on how the Court has addressed the obvious criticism of this spread of EU free movement law – that it is disrupting the shaping of matters of cherished importance within the Member States. That must involve separating out, on the one hand, matters that should not be addressed by free movement law at all and, on the other, matters that must fall within an understanding of the scope of free movement law but which require the taking into account by that law of their special character. In strictly legal terms two distinct questions are at stake in examining practices that are potentially antagonistic to inter-state trade: first, does EU trade law apply at all and, secondly, if it does, to what extent is its application sensitive to (in short) non-economic concerns in shaping permitted justification for such practices? The chapter will explain how the threshold for finding that EU law applies is remarkably ill-defined but that, most significant of all, it is low. This then loads the emphasis in considering whether national practices are compatible with EU law on to the second strand of the legal analysis – is there a recognised justification? Here the chapter looks in particular at protection of fundamental (social, political) rights at national level as a basis for justifying restrictions on (fundamental) economic rights guaranteed by EU law. The chapter also considers whether the entry into force of the Lisbon

---

[5] Case C-112/00 *Eugen Schmidberger, Internationale Transporte und Planzüge v Austria* [2003] ECR I-5659.

[6] Case C-36/02 *Omega Spielhallen- und Automatenaufstellungs GmbH v Oberbürgermeisterin der Bundesstadt Bonn* [2004] ECR I-9609.

[7] Case C-438/05 *International Transport Workers' Federation and Finnish Seamen's Union v Viking Line ABP and OÜ Viking Line Eesti* [2007] ECR I-10779.

[8] Case C-208/09 *Ilonka Sayn-Wittgenstein v Landeshauptmann von Wien* (ECJ, 22 December 2010), nyr.

Treaty in December 2009 has altered the law. Its conclusion is that although elements of the Lisbon Treaty may be treated as serving to 'soften' the commercially-driven cutting edge of EU economic law in favour of greater respect for social and cultural concerns expressed through (trade-restrictive) national law, nonetheless that shift may fairly be deemed more rhetorical than real, for even before the advent of the Treaty of Lisbon the Court was receptive to several devices which are apt to generate a 'softened' interpretation of EU economic law. And ultimately the ambiguity of the relevant legal material ensures that considerable power has been delegated to the Court to choose between competing interpretations: a familiar theme in the history of EU law.

II. The Internal *Market*

Not all national measures that have an impact on cross-border mobility fall within the scope of application of EU free movement law. The relevant provisions are driven by the quest to establish an internal market in the European Union, as mandated since the entry into force of the Treaty of Lisbon by Article 3(3) TEU. And Article 26(2) TFEU defines the internal market to 'comprise an area without internal frontiers in which the free movement of goods, persons, services and capital is ensured in accordance with the provisions of the Treaties'.

The pursuit of an internal market assumes there is a 'market' element to the national provision under challenge. Absent any such necessary economic dimension, the matter escapes the scope of application of EU law. And occasionally these limits to the reach of EU economic law are visible in the case law.

In *SPUC v Grogan* students' unions in Dublin were providing information about abortion services available in London.[9] Such services were regularly used by Irish migrants seeking to evade the tight restrictions placed on abortion in Ireland. Could EU free movement law assist the students' unions when they were faced with restrictions on information provision imposed by the Irish authorities? No. The students' unions were acting without economic motivation. They simply provided the information for free, not for any commercial return. Accordingly EU law was not engaged. *Marc Michel Josemans v Burgemeester van Maastricht* offers a recent example of the limits of EU economic law.[10] In Maastricht, 'coffee shops' are licensed: only 14 are allowed and they are restricted to residents. The aim is to restrict 'drug tourism', but such a rule appears to amount to a barrier to inter-state trade (in drugs and in drug tourists). The Court found that there is no lawful trade in such products, so the free movement and non-discrimination provisions of the Treaty simply did not apply.

---

[9] Case C-159/90 *Society for the Protection of the Unborn Child v Grogan* [1991] ECR I-4685.
[10] Case C-137/09 *Marc Michel Josemans v Burgemeester van Maastricht* (ECJ, 16 December 2010), nyr.

The Court possesses devices to restrain the 'marketising' effect of EU trade law on national practices which are motivated by matters remote from economic concerns. But these limits to EU law are fragile. Had one replaced the students' union with an advertising agency accepting fees in *SPUC v Grogan*, then the matter would, without any further factual alteration, plainly have fallen within the scope of EU economic law. Irish laws governing abortion would, as restrictions on the cross-border provision of services, have been subject to review in the name of EU trade law.[11] And the reasoning in *Josemans* is so absurd that it exposes the intellectual contortions that must be endured to elude the grip of EU economic law. 'Drug tourism' is big business: the Court itself tells us in its judgment that the 14 Maastricht coffee shops attract a little more than 3.9 million visitors per year, 70 per cent of whom are not resident in the Netherlands. It is comical to claim there is no lawful trade in cannabis when the litigation with which the Court is dealing exists only because there *is* such lawful trade, or at least such tolerated trade (in the Netherlands).

Very few activities truly escape the scope of application of EU economic law. Exceptions of the type mentioned in this section – unconvincing exceptions in at least one instance – aside, it is normally a low threshold to insist that EU economic law applies only where there is an internal *market* element.

III. The *Internal* Market

A similar story applies to the requirement that there must be an effect on the *internal* market before a national practice falls within the scope of application of EU economic law. The principle is clear – a cross-border element must be at stake in the challenged national practice – but the practice is rather different. The limits of EU law are ambiguous but they are easily satisfied. The threshold for the application of EU economic law is low.

The famous *Cassis de Dijon* ruling of the Court serves as a powerful illustration of this trend.[12] The Court's early cases involved physical barriers to trade (frontier controls, obligations to provide a licence, and so on) and practices which were discriminatory on the basis of nationality. The necessary identification of an impediment to cross-border trade – that is, a problem pertaining to the creation of an *internal* market – was very straightforward and uncontroversial. In *Cassis de Dijon* the Court took this reasoning a step further and for the first time offered a sophisticated and elaborate explanation of how and why national technical standards governing product composition may fall within the scope of free movement law. Such standards do not cause any blockage to the movement of goods across

---

[11] The Opinion of AG van Gerven in the case explored the possibility of justifying such rules: it was exactly this sensitive inquiry which the Court evaded by finding no sufficient economic dimension to the case.

[12] Case 120/78 *Rewe-Zentrale AG v Bundesmonopolverwaltung für Branntwein* [1979] ECR 649.

physical frontiers. Nor do they discriminate according to nationality: all goods, irrespective of origin, must comply with local standards. But there is an obstacle to inter-state trade because standards *differ*, with the result that a product made lawfully in one Member State according to the standards prevailing in that jurisdiction is excluded from another jurisdiction where a different rulebook is in force. A host of regulatory specifications were thus brought within the net of EU free movement law.

The Court mistakenly went even further when, without explaining why, it brought within that net even national rules disassociated from product standards. In the notorious 'Sunday Trading' cases shop-opening hours, varying Member State by Member State, were treated as limiting the volume of products sold and therefore potentially incompatible with EU free movement law: they required justification.[13] This was an unacknowledged step beyond *Cassis de Dijon*, for doing damage to the volume of sales of *all* products, imported and domestic alike, is a less exacting pre-condition to the application of EU economic law than finding a particular detriment felt by the subjection of *cross-border* products to national measures – which was the key feature of the fact pattern at stake in *Cassis*. And in *Keck and Mithouard* the Court then retreated and (by implication, if not explicitly) overruled the Sunday Trading cases as improper encroachments upon national regulatory autonomy in the name of EU free movement law.[14]

The precise extent of that retreat is a matter of persisting debate, fuelled by yet more waves of litigation initiated by traders ambitious to exploit EU economic law to set aside obstructive national measures of market regulation. Certainly *Keck* was *not* designed to set aside *Cassis de Dijon*.[15] But tough questions surround the identification of whether and, if so, why and when Article 34 TFEU catches in its net non-discriminatory rules that do not affect the composition of a product. A case by case inquiry seems to be required. A ban on *advertising* a product may cover all products of a similar type, irrespective of their origin, but it is capable of impeding access to the market by products from other Member States more than it impedes access by domestic products because local consumers are typically more familiar with products that have long been available on their shop shelves. The factual, if not the formal, application of the ban is uneven in its effect to the detriment of imported goods, and it amounts to a barrier to inter-state trade.[16] Similarly a rule *restricting the use* of a product may not be tainted by discrimination, yet may raise a sufficient 'internal market' problem for the Article 34 net to catch it. *Åklagaren v Mickelsson and Roos*[17] concerned Swedish rules restricting the waterways on which jet skis could be used. There was no discrimination based on

---

[13] Case 145/88 *Torfaen Borough Council v B & Q plc* [1989] ECR 3851; Case C-169/91 *Stoke on Trent and Norwich City Councils v B & Q plc* [1992] ECR I-6635.
[14] Cases C-267 and C268/91 *Keck and Mithouard*, above n 4.
[15] eg Case C-470/93 *Verein gegen Unwesen in Handel und Gewerbe Köln v Mars GmbH* [1995] ECR I-1923; Case C-244/06 *Dynamic Medien Vertriebs GmbH v Avides Media AG* [2008] ECR I-505.
[16] Case C-405/98 *Konsumentombudsmannen v Gourmet International Products AB* [2001] ECR I-1795.
[17] Case C-142/05 *Åklagaren v Percy Mickelsson and Joakim Roos* [2009] ECR I-4273.

the origin of the goods, nor did the rules require any technical adaption of imported goods in order to comply with local standards. It was simply the case that the use of the product was restricted. The Court chose to focus on the rule's impact on consumer demand, and ruled that a restriction on use which has a 'considerable influence on the behaviour of consumers' may affect the access of the product to the market of a Member State in such a way as to trigger the application of Article 34. The Court's cautious insertion of the adjective 'considerable' into its definition of the reach of Article 34 aims to capture the notion that just because national laws vary does not of itself mean there is (in short) 'an internal market problem'. The threshold at which inter-state regulatory divergence becomes a matter of concern for the EU is higher. The risk is that the effect of *Keck* may be undone altogether if the Court is *too* quick to review these types of national measures.[18] But definitional precision remains elusive: how does one measure this jurisdictionally crucial 'considerable' influence on consumer behaviour? Moreover, the debate about convergence – whether the '*Keck* solution' (such as it is) does or should apply across the sweep of free movement law or whether it is confined to the particular case of the free movement of goods – remains unsettled too.[19] But the illuminating theme is that although on occasion a matter will be found to fall beyond the scope of EU free movement law, this is not the norm. It is in general remarkably easy to find the indirect or potential effect on inter-state trade which, ever since the Court introduced its *Dassonville* formula in 1974,[20] has been sufficient to impose on the regulator an obligation to justify its practices. Even *Keck*, a restraining influence on the reach of EU free movement law, has been subsequently interpreted as a much less radical limiting device than might initially have been anticipated.

The occasional case emerges in which the Court is able to conclude that there is no adequate impact on inter-state trade patterns for EU economic law to be triggered, but, without here embarking on an exhaustive inquiry, the thematically consistent point in the case law holds that the threshold for the application of EU free movement law is low.

IV. EU Competence is not Simply *Legislative* Competence

The expansionist character of EU economic law is not simply driven by the ease with which the Court is able to find a sufficient obstacle to inter-state trade. It is

---

[18] See especially P Oliver and S Enchelmaier, 'Free Movement of Goods: Recent Developments in the Case Law' (2007) 44 *CML Rev* 649, 679–83 and 704.

[19] *cf* eg S Prechal and S de Vries, 'Seamless web of judicial protection in the internal market?' (2009) 34 *EL Rev* 5; A Tryfonidou, 'Further steps on the road to convergence among the market freedoms' (2010) 35 *EL Rev* 36.

[20] Case 8/74 *Procureur du Roi v Benoit et Gustave Dassonville* [1974] ECR 837.

also the *functional* breadth of Article 34 TFEU and the other Treaty freedoms which is highly relevant to their deep impact on national regulatory autonomy. Where a national practice acts as a barrier to inter-state trade, review is not confined to areas in which the EU has *legislative* competence. Take, for example, the case of a patient wishing to receive medical treatment in another Member State and then to have the costs incurred reimbursed by his or her home state's health system. The EU is not granted by its Treaty a legislative competence of sufficient breadth to put in place all the rules that would be necessary to create and (still less) to fund such a system. However, where national measures obstruct patients wishing to exercise such a right of free movement, EU law demands that such practices be shown to be justified. So in this way EU economic law breaks the bounds of legislative competence granted by the Treaty. So, in *ex parte Watts*, a case of this type dealing with healthcare rules that obstructed the free movement of services (now covered by Article 56 TFEU), the Court declared that although EU law

> does not detract from the power of the Member States to organise their social security systems and decide the level of resources to be allocated to their operation, the achievement of the fundamental freedoms guaranteed by the Treaty nevertheless inevitably requires Member States to make adjustments to those systems. It does not follow that this undermines their sovereign powers in the field.[21]

Naturally one may argue that the Court is thoroughly disingenuous when it declares that the achievement of the fundamental freedoms requires an adjustment by the Member States which does not undermine 'their sovereign powers in the field'. EU free movement law subjects the exercise of 'sovereign powers' to conditions in a way that makes use of the word 'sovereign' arguably unhelpful and inappropriate. Be that as it may, the inevitable consequence of this approach is that a whole range of areas in which the principal site of regulatory authority is national and which are subject to relatively little or even no *legislative* influence exercised by the EU nevertheless become incapable of being studied or understood without assessment of the actual or potential impact of EU free movement law. Nationality law, for example, is predominantly determined by the Member States' own choices but it is misleading to treat national autonomy as absolute because decisions about the grant or withdrawal of nationality may in certain circumstances exert effects on cross-border mobility, thereby triggering review rooted in the rules of free movement.[22] There is an illuminatingly large number of instances of EU free movement law influencing national practice where EU legislative activity is thin or non-existent. Social security is a common example;[23]

---

[21] Case C-372/04 *The Queen (on the application of Yvonne Watts) v Bedford Primary Care Trust and Secretary of State for Health* [2006] ECR I-4325, para 121.
[22] Case C-135/08 *Janko Rottman v Freistaat Bayern* [2010] ECR I-1449.
[23] cf eg Case C-512/03 *JEJ Blanckaert Inspecteur van de Belastingdienst/Particulieren/Ondernemingen buitenland te Heerlen* [2005] ECR I-7685.

taxation is another;[24] also education;[25] so too action taken collectively to pursue the interests of organised labour;[26] and even the maintenance of public order and the safeguarding of internal security has been revealed as a matter of national competence that is nevertheless reviewable in so far as its pursuit impedes cross-border trade.[27] Some, though not all, of the rules on free movement bind private as well as public parties, and so here too a model arises according to which the EU lacks the competence to command by legislation but nonetheless curtails private autonomy in the name of securing free movement. Sport is a good example: the famous *Bosman* ruling tested international sporting regulations against the law governing the free movement of workers (and found them wanting).[28]

Perhaps the Court could have avoided this result by using the absence of, or weak nature of, legislative competence under the Treaty as a reason to insulate such sectors from free movement law. But the Treaty offers no such direction. And such an approach would have damaged the making of an internal market which *requires* a functionally broad legal regime within which there is no logical reason to align legislative competence at EU level with competence to check national practices that obstruct cross-border trade. So, in consequence, the fundamental economic freedoms are read in a way that causes a significant curtailment of national autonomy in circumstances where the EU's sector-specific *legislative* competence could not extend so far: but this is how the Treaty is structured.

V. The (Broader, Broadening) Shape of Justification

Few areas of national regulatory activity are immune from the potential incursion of EU law. As explained, finding the necessary economic dimension is rarely difficult; practices are commonly found to have at least some impact on inter-state trade; and the scope of EU free movement law is not confined by the limited legislative competence granted to the EU by its Treaties. None of this challenges *in principle* the constitutionally fundamental statement in Article 5 TEU that the EU operates according to the *limited* competences and powers conferred on it by its Member States, but it means that *in practice* the functionally broad project of building an internal market ensures that those limits are very broadly, and at times ambiguously, drawn. And in consequence of the operationally poor record of EU law in insulating national practices from its influence the Court has found

---

[24] cf eg Case C-446/03 *Marks and Spencer plc v David Halsey (HM Inspector of Taxes)* [2005] ECR I-10837.
[25] Case C-73/08 *Nicolas Bressol and others, Céline Chaverot and others v Gouvernment de la Communauté française* [2010] ECR I-2735.
[26] Case C-438/05 *Viking Line*, above n 7.
[27] Case C-265/95 *European Commission v France* [1997] ECR I-6959.
[28] Case C-415/93 *Union royale belge des sociétés de football association ASBL v Jean-Marc Bosman* [1995] ECR I-4921.

itself under pressure to develop a much broader framework for assessing the possible justification of practices than is explicitly allowed by the Treaty. This in turn has demanded some considerable judicial flexibility and dexterity.

This was the road on which the Court set out in *Dassonville*,[29] in which it expressed the requirement that national measures be 'reasonable', but which was developed further in *Cassis de Dijon*.[30] In that landmark case the Court was asked to consider the application of what is today Article 34 TFEU to German technical standards, in casu rules requiring a minimum amount of alcohol in particular types of beverage. It concluded that the matter fell within the scope of the Treaty: a French-made blackcurrant liqueur could not be sold in Germany because the French rules, with which the product complied, were different from those prevailing in Germany, with which the product did not comply. The possibility of showing justification for trade barriers is recognised in the Treaty – in what is now Article 36 TFEU. That list of justifications covers public health (one of the grounds on which Germany wished to rely) but it does not cover protection of the consumer (another of the German grounds). The Court did not feel constrained by the textual limitations of the Treaty. It ruled that

> the requirements relating to the minimum alcohol content of alcoholic beverages do not serve a purpose which is in the general interest and such as to take precedence over the requirements of the free movement of goods, which constitutes one of the fundamental rules of the Community.[31]

Germany had no plausible justification on the facts, but the Court did not rule out *in principle* the possibility of invoking consumer protection as a justification. Instead it adopted this much wider test, involving balancing of the general interest pursued by the German rules and the interest in the free movement of goods which would be served by holding the German rules incompatible with EU law, and on the facts the latter prevailed.

Cassis de Dijon extended the reach of available justification beyond (what is now) Article 36 TFEU, creating a general public interest test. The Court has maintained this approach, regularly assessing alleged consumer protection measures and occasionally agreeing, unlike in *Cassis*, that the interest in national-level regulation is more important than the interest in integration expressed through setting aside the national rules.[32]

The test of justification is not completely open-ended. The Court has long ruled out the possibility of invoking purely economic justifications for obstructing inter-state trade – in fact, this appears in *Commission v Italy*, the first ever decision of the Court dealing with the free movement of goods.[33] But even this restriction on the scope of possible justification for trade restrictions is not all that

---

[29] Case 8/74 *Dassonville*, above n 20.
[30] Case 120/78 *Rewe-Zentrale*, above n 12.
[31] Ibid, para 14.
[32] eg Case 53/80 *Officier van Justitie v Koninklijke Kaasfabriek Eyssen* [1981] ECR 409; Case 382/87 *Buet and Educational Business Services v Ministère Public* [1989] ECR 1235.
[33] Case 7/61 *Commission v Italy*, above n 1.

it may seem, for the Court has allowed a repackaging of what appear to be at least in part economic justifications – protecting the financial balance of a social security system, or maintaining a balanced medical and hospital service open to all – as permissible means to attain a high level of health protection.[34]

The very broad approach taken by the Court to the possibility in principle to justify national measures that impede cross-border free movement is well illustrated by its ruling in *Dynamic Medien*.[35] The case concerned German rules dealing with the labelling of videos and related media products. It was factually similar to *Cassis de Dijon* in the sense that barriers to inter-state trade arose as a result of differences between German regulatory requirements and those applicable in other Member States. But were the rules, which inter alia aimed to protect children from unsuitable images, justified? The Court stated that

> [t]he protection of the child is also enshrined in instruments drawn up within the framework of the European Union, such as the Charter of fundamental rights of the European Union, proclaimed on 7 December 2000 in Nice (OJ 2000 C 364, p. 1), Article 24(1) of which provides that children have the right to such protection and care as is necessary for their well-being . . . Furthermore, the Member States' right to take the measures necessary for reasons relating to the protection of young persons is recognised by a number of Community-law instruments, such as Directive 2000/31.[36]

The most striking feature is the Court's readiness to draw on a plurality of sources remote from the key Treaty provisions dealing with the free movement of goods. The Charter was at the time not binding, and the cited Directive is a harmonisation measure dealing with e-commerce which has some peripheral association with the protection of minors but which is principally a measure designed to promote the development of information society services within the internal market. The Court proceeded to accept that conceptions of the necessary level of protection vary from one Member State to another on the basis of moral or cultural views and that accordingly Member States 'must be recognised as having a definite margin of discretion'.[37] The German rules restricted trade but were justified: free movement law does not force standards of regulatory protection down to the lowest common denominator to be found among the Member States. This is a general principle of interpretation in the law of free movement. The Court has insisted that 'the fact that one Member State imposes less strict rules than another Member State does not mean that the latter's rules are disproportionate' and hence incompatible with EU law.[38] The space allowed for justification of trade barriers ensures limits to the deregulatory impetus of EU free movement law.

---

[34] Case C-372/04 *ex parte Watts*, above n 21, paras 103–105.
[35] Case C-244/06 *Dynamic Medien*, above n 15.
[36] Ibid, para 41.
[37] Ibid, para 44.
[38] Eg, in connection with the free movement of goods Case C-294/00 *Deutsche Paracelsus Schulen für Naturheilverfahren GmbH v Kurt Gräbner* [2002] ECR I-6515 and in connection with the free movement of services Case C-3/95 *Reisebüro Broede v Gerd Sandker* [1996] ECR I-6511.

Where the Court applies free movement law in circumstances where the Treaty offers no or little guidance on the proper range and scope of justification – which is especially salient where the matter escapes the EU's *legislative* competence – the job becomes particularly sensitive. Does the Court have the expertise to piece together an understanding of what should constitute the permitted scope of justification? Sport provides a good example. The Treaty contained no explicit reference whatsoever to sport until as late as December 2009, when the Treaty of Lisbon introduced a slender legislative competence and a direction in Article 165 TFEU to take account of the specific nature of sport. But in fact far in advance of this shift the Court had been grappling with the need to shape some understanding of the function of sport in the EU given that sporting practices readily, if not explicitly, fell within the scope of application of the rules on free movement. So in *Bosman* the Court was asked to consider the application of the Treaty provisions on the free movement of workers to a footballer wishing to move from a Belgian to a French club, but thwarted by the peculiar rules that distinguish footballers who have reached the end of their contract from ordinary employees.[39] Did the 'transfer system' which hinders player mobility comply with EU law? The Court held that it did not, but did not rule out the possibility that an amended transfer system might be justified as a means to preserve special features of the sport:

> In view of the considerable social importance of sporting activities and in particular football in the Community, the aims of maintaining a balance between clubs by preserving a certain degree of equality and uncertainty as to results and of encouraging the recruitment and training of young players must be accepted as legitimate. [40]

This identification of the special character of sport could not be drawn from the Treaty because the Treaty did not at the time even mention sport. The Court, applying the functionally broad free movement rules, chose to shape its own understanding of the character of the particular industry under examination – professional sport – and to extract the shape of available justification. Football chooses how to structure its transfer system and it duly adjusted it after the *Bosman* ruling. EU free movement law does not dictate what *shall* be done, but it places limits on what *may* be done – but it is EU free movement law applied and interpreted with respect for the 'legitimate' aims of sport of which the Court was persuaded in *Bosman*.

Assessing justification demands a creative Court. The internal market as a legal concept, built on a shared competence to open up markets and to regulate them, forces the Court to develop its own notions of what is proper and tolerable when pursued at national level. The regulatory concern expressed through the national rule is absorbed by and reflected in the EU test of justification. One may certainly question whether the scope for justifying restrictive rules is sufficiently attuned to their local cultural, political and social motivation, and one may plainly complain about the wisdom of particular rulings. So, for example, the Court's intrusion

---

[39] Case C-415/93 *Bosman*, above n 28.
[40] Ibid, para 106.

into healthcare law has been savagely criticised for failing fully to grasp the consequences for Member States, in particular with regard to setting priorities for the application of finite resources.[41] Similarly some have accused the Court of a troubling inability sensibly to adjudicate on matters of sports governance for want of adequate appreciation of the breadth of implications flowing from its judgments.[42] It is not the place here to examine the merits of such criticism. For the purposes of this chapter, the key point is *structural* – the law of the internal market, rooted in the Treaty and developed over time by the Court of Justice, is not just concerned with market freedom, it also involves market regulation, and national barriers to trade may in principle be upheld as justified.

One could understand this as a search for a 'porous' trade law: that is, the rules should be interpreted to allow for a softening or a balancing, dictated by the inevitable association between their economic effects and their wider social or cultural context.[43] Another metaphor is to treat this as the quest for 'safety valves' in EU law: the economic imperative should not be allowed to oppress all other interests, but rather devices must be created which are apt to let off steam.[44] On the most benevolent reading of EU economic law, national practices are seen in their true context, and not merely as hindrances to the economic project of European market-making. The Court, nudged by the Treaty and sometimes by secondary legislation, has ensured EU economic law embraces more than economic concerns. But this does not mean that the balancing of economic and non-economic interests in the name of EU free movement law has become an easy or uncontroversial task of adjudication.

VI. Fundamental Rights and Free Movement

And so in this vein to the place of fundamental rights in EU economic law. This chapter has traced the expansionist trajectory of EU free movement law. Once EU free movement law is revealed to exert such a broad impact that it is likely to affect national measures protecting EU fundamental rights, there arises a tension. Pressure is loaded on the EU – most obviously, the Court – to take account of that fundamental rights context in assessing the justification advanced in support of trade-restrictive national measures. It is in essence the same model as that consid-

---

[41] eg C Newdick, 'Citizenship, Free Movement and Health Care: Cementing Individual Rights by Corroding Social Solidarity' (2006) 43 *CML Rev* 1645.

[42] eg D Dixon, 'The Long Life of Bosman – A Triumph of Law over Experience' (2009) 6(2) *Entertainment and Sports Law Journal* 1.

[43] I used this terminology in 'The EU's porous trade law', delivered as the Institute of European Law's Annual Lecture at the University of Birmingham in November 2010 and I thank those with whom I there had the opportunity to discuss these issues.

[44] I used this terminology in 'Safety Valves in EU trade law', a paper delivered at the University of Zagreb in December 2010 and I thank those with whom I there had the opportunity to discuss these issues.

ered above – EU economic law becomes porous in the sense that measures that appear to conflict with the free movement rules may nevertheless be saved with reference to their role in protecting or promoting fundamental rights. But, important though consumer protection and the legitimate interests of sport may be, the stuff of fundamental rights is more vital again. So the Court of Justice's approach to the justification of trade barriers in the light of their impact on fundamental rights is correspondingly more sensitive. And once again questions arise about the Court's commitment to and understanding of the issues that it accepts in principle as the stuff of possible justification for trade barriers – but with added force.

In *ERT v Dimotiki* the Court for the first time established a clear link between justification for trade barriers and compliance with fundamental rights.[45] It insisted on interpretation of the scope of the freedom to provide services in the light of the general principle of freedom of expression embodied in Article 10 of the European Convention on Human Rights. State restrictions on broadcasting had to be justified with reference to the European Convention (and no adequate justification for the restrictions was forthcoming).

The case law, driven by EU law's ever present ingenious and commercially well-motivated litigants, has grown ever more complex. *Vereinigte Familiapress Zeitungsverlags- und vertriebs GmbH v Heinrich Bauer Verlag* concerned Austrian rules which prevented the use of prize crosswords and puzzles in magazines and newspapers.[46] On the one hand this restricted imports of magazines and newspapers into Austria from (most obviously) Germany where there was no such ban – an impediment to cross-border trade which in addition interfered with German publishers' freedom of expression. On the other hand the Austrian authorities sought to justify their rules with reference to a concern to protect the plurality of the media in Austria. Without such rules, they argued, the much larger German publishers would swallow the Austrian market and deprive it of diverse sources of news and opinion – itself a threat to the vibrancy of democratic contestation.

The Court accepted that maintenance of press diversity may constitute an overriding requirement justifying a restriction on free movement of goods, because such diversity helps to safeguard freedom of expression. As in *ERT*, it connected this explicitly to the protection pursued by Article 10 of the European Convention on Human Rights, which it treated as 'one of the fundamental rights guaranteed by the Community legal order'.[47] On the other hand it observed that 'A prohibition on selling publications which offer the chance to take part in prize games competitions may detract from freedom of expression'.[48] Fundamental rights were therefore engaged on *both* sides of the argument.

---

[45] Case C-260/89 *Elliniki Radiophonia Tileorassi AE (ERT) v Dimotiki Etairia Pliroforissis and Sotirios Kouvelas* [1991] ECR I-2925.
[46] Case C-368/95 *Vereinigte Familiapress Zeitungsverlags- und vertriebs GmbH v Heinrich Bauer Verlag* [1997] ECR I-3689.
[47] Ibid, para 18.
[48] Ibid, para 26.

Resolution of which interest should prevail in the circumstances was reserved to the referring national court – doubtless an unenviably difficult task. But the importance of the ruling lies in the Court's willingness to embed the protection of fundamental rights in the law of free movement. Subsequently in *Herbert Karner GmbH v Troostwijk GmbH* the Court absorbed a sense of priority in the engagement of fundamental rights with economic freedoms.[49] The case concerned the free movement of goods. The Court, dealing with matters of justification, observed that

> [w]hen the exercise of the freedom [of expression] does not contribute to a discussion of public interest and, in addition, arises in a context in which the Member States have a certain amount of discretion, review is limited to an examination of the reasonableness and proportionality of the interference. This holds true for the commercial use of freedom of expression, particularly in a field as complex and fluctuating as advertising.[50]

The Court therefore developed priorities in the wake of free movement law's functional breadth. The likelihood of a Member State being able to justify restrictions on free movement of goods and services which also simultaneously constitute restrictions on freedom of expression is in principle greater where the context of the claim is commercial rather than political.

In *Schmidberger v Austria* the Court was faced with a comparable conflict of competing interests.[51] The Austrian authorities had permitted a protest to block the movement of transport carrying goods through the Brenner Pass. The Austrian failure to intervene was in principle capable of falling within the scope of what is now Article 34 TFEU because it led to an obstacle to trade in goods (for almost 30 hours, while the protest continued). But it was motivated by a concern to protect the freedom of assembly and freedom of expression of those wishing to draw attention to the environmental damage caused by such trade. This, then, was a perfect model of the problem: economic rights clashing with political rights. The Court declared that

> since both the Community and its Member States are required to respect fundamental rights, the protection of those rights is a legitimate interest which, in principle, justifies a restriction of the obligations imposed by Community law, even under a fundamental freedom guaranteed by the Treaty such as the free movement of goods.[52]

Free movement law thus encompasses fundamental rights which conflict – the economic versus the political. One or the other must prevail: these are fundamental rights, but they are not absolute rights. The Court stated that

> [i]n those circumstances, the interests involved must be weighed having regard to all the circumstances of the case in order to determine whether a fair balance was struck between those interests.

---

[49] Case C-71/02 *Herbert Karner Industrie-Auktionen GmbH v Troostwijk GmbH* [2004] ECR I-3025.
[50] Ibid, para 51.
[51] Case C-112/00 *Eugen Schmidberger v Austria*, above n 5.
[52] Ibid, para 74.

The competent authorities enjoy a wide margin of discretion in that regard. Nevertheless, it is necessary to determine whether the restrictions placed upon intra-Community trade are proportionate in the light of the legitimate objective pursued, namely, in the present case, the protection of fundamental rights.[53]

In *Schmidberger*, unlike in *Familiapress*, the Court then proceeded actively to assess the balance. Noting a range of factors[54] it made plain that the Austrian (lack of) action against those conducting the protests constituted no violation of EU law, despite the restrictive effect on cross-border trade in goods.

As a broad summary of the Court's emerging approach, the more sensitive and the more remote from commercial considerations the matters advanced in the context of justification of trade barriers are, the more generous the Court is to the available scope for justification and also to the breadth of the margin of appreciation enjoyed by the regulator – sometimes too, but not always, the more sensitive it is to the authority of the national court to make the final judgement on whether the challenged practices are in fact justified.

A comparable result, but according to slightly different reasoning, may be identified in *Omega Spielhallen*.[55] The case concerned the suppression of games involving simulated killing in Germany on the basis that such practices offended against constitutionally-protected standards of respect for human dignity. The Court treated the matter from the perspective of the free movement of services between Member States: imports from the United Kingdom were impeded. So, was the German intervention justified? The Court was favourably inclined:

> [T]he Community legal order undeniably strives to ensure respect for human dignity as a general principle of law. There can therefore be no doubt that the objective of protecting human dignity is compatible with Community law, it being immaterial in that respect that, in Germany, the principle of respect for human dignity has a particular status as an independent fundamental right.[56]

The structure of this approach to justification is striking. The Court did not construct this as EU free movement law versus German protection of human dignity, but instead as EU free movement law versus *EU* protection of human dignity. The justification was rooted not in German specificity but in EU embrace of a standard of protection comparable with that chosen in Germany (but not found to the same degree in other Member States). So EU law accommodates German anxieties – which, of course, readily puts one in mind of the vital need for a degree of common understanding about the protection of fundamental rights among both EU and national judiciaries not least for fear that the latter may disobey the former if unpersuaded that adequate protection of fundamental rights is on offer at EU level.

---

[53] Ibid, paras 81–82.
[54] Ibid, paras 81–94.
[55] Case C-36/02 *Omega Spielhallen*, above n 6.
[56] Ibid, para 34.

Kadi and Al Barakaat v European Council stands as one of the Court's strongest statements of its determination to treat fundamental rights as embedded in the whole fabric of EU law.[57] The case was not concerned with free movement: it arose in the context of legislative measures 'freezing' individuals' assets pursuant to action taken at the level of the United Nations Security Council, which were challenged for violation of EU fundamental rights standards, in particular for want of regard for the right to be heard, the right to effective legal protection, and the right to property. The Court held that

> [i]t is also clear from the case-law that respect for human rights is a condition of the lawfulness of Community acts (Opinion 2/94, paragraph 34) and that measures incompatible with respect for human rights are not acceptable in the Community (Case C-112/00 *Schmidberger* [2003] ECR I-5659 . . .).[58]

This judgment suggest a shift. The Court here refers to *Schmidberger* in the context of a case which itself had nothing to do with the heartland of economic law, free movement or competition. But the Court fuses rulings dealing with economic law with the more familiar classic fundamental rights context of restraining governmental power that prejudices the position of the individual.

The conclusion may legitimately be drawn from this approach that it is not accurate to depict the protection of fundamental rights by national authorities as permitted *justification* for trade-restrictive measures. That would suggest that economic rights come first, with fundamental rights serving merely as a potential dilution in specific circumstances. *Kadi* can be taken as a claim that there are differently sourced and motivated types of fundamental rights in EU law, but there is no sense of hierarchy. All are on a par. What matters for the resolution of the case is the particular circumstances.

Central to one's assessment of this case law is the calculation of whether the Court is sincerely engaged with the shaping of a mature fundamental rights regime for the EU or whether instead it is simply providing a mask of deference to non-economic concerns in order to promote ever more deeply the project of economic integration – under an understanding that its main obstacle is national courts' defence of national constitutional values. Put another way, is respect for fundamental rights a grudging limit on the vigour of free movement law or is it sincerely embedded within it?

The December 2007 rulings of the Grand Chamber of the Court of Justice in *Viking Line* and *Laval* are the rulings which are most vulnerable to the allegation that, for all the rhetoric of respect for non-economic values, EU free movement law is contaminated by an economic bias.[59] *Viking Line*, stripped down to its core, involved the question whether EU free movement law protected a shipping firm

---

[57] Cases C-402/05 P and 415/05 P *Kadi and Al Barakaat International Foundation v European Council* [2008] ECR I-6351.
[58] Ibid, para 284.
[59] Case C-438/05 *Viking Line*, above n 7; Case C-341/05 *Laval un Partneri Ltd v Svenska Byggnadsarbetareförbundet, and others* [2007] ECR I-11767.

wishing to reflag one of its vessels, the *Rosella*, from the Finnish flag to that of Estonia from collective action by labour unions aimed at deterring corporate migration. The potential losers – Finnish workers; the potential winners – corporate interests seeking lower costs, and Estonian workers. In the longer term, the balancing of winners and losers invites assessment of the type of internal market that is being built: freedom to trade? Freedom to act collectively to compete effectively against corporate power? *Laval*, the second of these rulings, had many similarities and some differences, and arose out of action by Swedish labour unions aimed at blockading worksites owned by Laval, a Latvian company which was employing workers posted to Sweden from Latvia who were not subject to the relatively generous terms and conditions enjoyed by Swedish workers.

The unions are private parties, not public bodies, but the Court has long taken the view that such entities are subject to the Treaty rules governing the free movement of persons, including companies. It did not deviate from that approach. Nor did it find a way to exclude the collective action from the scope of the Treaty on the basis that the EU lacks *legislative* competence in regard to the right of association and the right to strike.[60] The rules of free movement apply even in areas where the EU's legislative reach is exhausted: as explained above, here too the Court was following its own orthodox approach. This left the Court to conclude that it was dealing with a restriction on cross-border economic activity. What mattered was whether the restrictive effects of the collective labour action were *justified*. And here the Court was breaking new ground. It had never before addressed the need to reconcile fundamental (but not absolute) rights in the context of labour disputes. And, as so often, it was forced to do so without any helpful map or priority list in the Treaty.

The Court accepted in principle that the right to take collective action to protect workers is a legitimate interest which justifies a restriction of economic freedoms guaranteed by the Treaty. It added that the European Community, now Union, has 'not only an economic but also a social purpose'.[61] For those fearful of EU free movement law's bite, this is the cheerful part of the judgment. But who actually wins? This is ultimately a matter for the national court before which the litigation had been initiated but the Court of Justice in *Viking Line* explained that that court must ascertain whether the objectives pursued by means of the collective action concern the protection of workers; and that

> even if that action – aimed at protecting the jobs and conditions of employment of the members of that union liable to be adversely affected by the reflagging of the *Rosella* – could reasonably be considered to fall, at first sight, within the objective of protecting workers, such a view would no longer be tenable if it were established that the jobs or conditions of employment at issue were not jeopardised or under serious threat.[62]

---

[60] See now Art 153(5) TFEU.
[61] Case C-438/05 *Viking Line*, above n 7, para 79; Case C-341/05 *Laval*, above n 59, para 105.
[62] Ibid, Case C-438/05 *Viking Line*, above n 7, para 81.

If this test means that it must be checked *in the particular circumstances of this case* whether the collective action is apt to achieve its stated ends of protecting workers' jobs and employment conditions, then the judgment is relatively narrow in its impact – although even here the required assessment of whether the action does not go beyond what is necessary to attain its objective is awkward and threatens unpredictability. If, by contrast, the ruling means that *only* action aimed at protecting the jobs of union members is recognised as capable of being justified under EU law, then the Court has excluded the possibility of more long-term strategic action taken by unions and even the 'political strike' in so far as it impedes cross-border economic activity. That constitutes a dramatic incursion into the permitted scope of collective labour rights. In any event the ambiguity of the Court's judgment is likely to place a deterrent effect on collective labour action – all the more so because of the risk that if action is found to be unlawful, the union may be liable to pay compensation to commercial operators whose business has been caused harm. Exactly this occurred as a result of a subsequent ruling of a Swedish court in the *Laval* litigation, in which it was concluded that discrimination had been suffered by the Latvian company because of Swedish refusal to take account of collective agreements applicable in Latvia.[63] The litigation in *Viking Line* itself was settled out of court shortly after the Court's judgment, but the consequence was a general anxiety that the Court had stumbled into the shaping of collective labour law and policy, an area in which it has little expertise and in which it has adopted a test which significantly favours corporate interests over worker protection.[64] The critiques have covered not only the outcome but also the purpose: to weigh matters of social constitutional law against economic considerations goes beyond the democratic failure of nation states against which free movement law is correctly targeted and asserts, beyond the proper scope of the Treaty, a setting aside of locally-determined welfarist choices.[65] And, disturbingly, the Court did not follow the model regularly preferred in the case law considered above: it left wholly out of account any margin of appreciation apt to permit recognition of local circumstances. This seems inconsistent with previous practice and constitutes the ruling's main weakness.

This section is helpfully finished by brief mention of the illuminating ruling in *Carpenter*.[66] Mrs Carpenter, a national of the Philippines, had entered the United Kingdom on a six months' visa, stayed after its expiry without receiving any extension, and then married Peter Carpenter, a UK national. She was subse-

---

[63] N Reich, 'Laval "Vierter Akt"' (2010) 21 *Europäische Zeitschrift für Wirtschaftsrecht* Heft 12, 454.

[64] *cf* eg L Azoulai, 'The Court of Justice and the Social Market Economy: the emergence of an ideal and the conditions for its realisation' (2008) 45 *CML Rev* 1335; C Barnard, 'Fifty Years of Avoiding Social Dumping? The EU's Economic and Not So Economic Constitution' in M Dougan and S Currie (eds), *Fifty Years of the European Treaties: Looking Back and Thinking Forward* (Oxford, Hart Publishing, 2009); A Davies, 'One Step Forward, Two Steps back? The Viking and Laval cases in the ECJ' (2008) 37 *ILJ* 126.

[65] C Joerges and F Rödl, 'Informal Politics, Formalised Law and the 'Social Deficit' of European Integration: Reflections after the Judgments of the ECJ in *Viking* and *Laval*' (2009) 15 *ELJ* 1.

[66] Case C-60/00 *Mary Carpenter v Secretary of State for the Home Department* [2002] ECR I-6279.

quently served with a deportation order. As a third country national, Mrs Carpenter's rights, if any, were not free-standing but rather derived from her husband. But he was a national of the UK living in the UK. So what role did EU law have? Mr Carpenter ran a business selling advertising space in medical and scientific journals and offering various administrative and publishing services to the editors of those journals. The business was established in the UK, but a significant proportion of the business was conducted with advertisers established in other Member States. Mr Carpenter sometimes travelled to other Member States for the purpose of his business. It was argued that his wife's deportation would require him to go to live with her in the Philippines or separate the members of the family unit if he remained in the United Kingdom. In both cases his business would be affected. The Court agreed this was enough to bring the matter within the scope of EU free movement law. And once it did that, the restrictions – the intended deportation of Mrs Carpenter – had to be justified. They were not. The Court focused on the importance of ensuring the protection of the family life of nationals of the Member States: deportation

> constitutes an interference with the exercise by Mr Carpenter of his right to respect for his family life within the meaning of Article 8 of the Convention for the Protection of Human Rights and Fundamental Freedoms, signed at Rome on 4 November 1950 . . . which is among the fundamental rights which, according to the Court's settled case-law, restated by the Preamble to the Single European Act and by Article 6(2) EU, are protected in Community law.[67]

And so deportation was not justified. It is striking in the judgment how little effort the Court makes to establish a connection between the threatened deportation and the perceived impediment to trade. EU free movement law applies remarkably easily: and when it does protection of fundamental rights immediately becomes part of the assessment.

VII. The Effect of the Lisbon Treaty: 'Softening' EU Trade Law?

The principal argument to be addressed here is whether the amendments made by the Treaty of Lisbon 'soften' the economic focus of free movement law under the Treaty. Or perhaps better, given the explanation of the rising importance attached to fundamental rights in free movement cases advanced in the previous section of this chapter, the issue is whether the Lisbon adjustments *further* soften the economic cutting edge of free movement law. The more one is persuaded that EU free movement law had already been softened by the Court prior to December 2009, the less appeal is attached to the claim that the Lisbon Treaty marks a change

---

[67] Ibid, para 41.

of course. Four aspects of the Lisbon Treaty deserve particular attention. There is some ambiguity involved – and consequently important delegation of interpretative power to the Court.

A. The Charter of Fundamental Rights

The Charter of Fundamental Rights is now binding. This nourishes an argument that its impact is apt to strengthen justification of national practices that impede cross-border trade, where the relevant justification connects to rights or principles enshrined in the Charter. However, even before the Charter was granted formally-binding status, the Court was willing to draw on it in assessing justification of national practices – and it has accepted the adequacy of justification in some cases. *Dynamic Medien*, considered above,[68] is of exactly this type. Certainly the elevation of the Charter to binding status prevented the Court going back on previous willingness to absorb its impact in free movement law – but it is less clear that it constitutes anything new in practice in free movement law.

B. The 'Horizontal Clauses'

According to Article 11 TFEU, 'Environmental protection requirements must be integrated into the definition and implementation of the Union's policies and activities, in particular with a view to promoting sustainable development'. And Article 12 TFEU dictates that 'Consumer protection requirements shall be taken into account in defining and implementing other Union policies and activities'. The argument runs that these mainstreaming or horizontal provisions require that the law of the internal market, and free movement law in particular, shall accommodate environmental and consumer protection concerns and that their promotion by the Lisbon Treaty to the beginning of the TFEU strengthens their role in EU law. Perhaps so: but free movement law has involved taking into account of such concerns for a very long time. *Cassis de Dijon* itself involved assessment of the worth of (rather unconvincing) measures of consumer protection,[69] and environmental protection at national level versus free movement of goods is similarly a long-standing story.[70] Perhaps the Lisbon reforms increase the respect that should be paid to such regulatory concerns but they do not mark a qualitative change in the texture of free movement law.

---

[68] Case C-244/06 *Dynamic Medien*, above n 15.
[69] Case 120/78 *Rewe-Zentrale*, above n 12.
[70] eg Case C-379/98 *Preussen Elektra AG v Schleswag AG* [2001] ECR I-2099.

C. Constitutional Identity

According to Article 4(2) TEU,

> [t]he Union shall respect the equality of Member States before the Treaties as well as their national identities, inherent in their fundamental structures, political and constitutional, inclusive of regional and local self-government. It shall respect their essential State functions, including ensuring the territorial integrity of the State, maintaining law and order and safeguarding national security. In particular, national security remains the sole responsibility of each Member State.

This is the successor to Article 6(3) TEU, which pre-Lisbon provided that 'The Union shall respect the national identities of its Member States'. The new provision is significantly elaborated and could be read as an invitation to show greater respect for national diversity than previously, inter alia, in connection with free movement law's application to national restrictions. But, again, this is by no means a necessary consequence – justification of trade barriers has always been receptive to the possibility of showing just why national peculiarities should be tolerated.

The Court's treatment of Article 4(2) TEU in its 2010 (post-Lisbon) ruling in *Ilonka Sayn-Wittgenstein v Landeshauptmann von Wien* deserves attention.[71] The background, stripped down to a simplified core, is that Austria has a 1919 law abolishing the nobility which, inter alia, does away with titles, whereas Germany has a 1919 law which does away with privileges but allows parts of the noble title to be retained in the surname. Ilonka was adopted in Germany by Lothar Fürst von Sayn-Wittgenstein. In Germany she is Ilonka Fürstin von Sayn-Wittgenstein. In Austria she was advised she must be registered instead as Ilonka Sayn-Wittgenstein. This constituted serious inconvenience to her commercial activity – which involves selling castles. Austria has accordingly restricted the freedom envisaged by Article 21 TFEU. But is it justified? The Court is receptive to Austrian concern, expressed at a constitutional level, to abolish titles in the service of equality of citizens before the law. This is a concern which the Court notes is also recognised under EU law in Article 20 of the Charter. The Court also cites *Omega Spielhallen*:[72] these are sensitive issues, where national authorities are permitted a 'margin of discretion'.[73] It also addresses the place of Article 4(2) TEU:

> [I]n accordance with Article 4(2) TEU, the European Union is to respect the national identities of its Member States, which include the status of the State as a Republic.
>
> In the present case, it does not appear disproportionate for a Member State to seek to attain the objective of protecting the principle of equal treatment by prohibiting any acquisition, possession or use, by its nationals, of titles of nobility or noble elements which may create the impression that the bearer of the name is holder of such a rank. By refusing to recognise the noble elements of a name such as that of the applicant in the

---

[71] Case C-208/09 *Sayn-Wittgenstein*, above n 8.
[72] Case C-36/02 *Omega Spielhallen*, above n 6.
[73] Case C-208/09 *Sayn-Wittgenstein*, above n 8, para 87.

main proceedings, the Austrian authorities responsible for civil status matters do not appear to have gone further than is necessary in order to ensure the attainment of the fundamental constitutional objective pursued by them.[74]

One might plausibly identify a difference between this approach and that adopted in *Omega*. Instead of converting a national constitutional concern into an EU constitutional concern, which was the technique employed in *Omega*, the Court uses Article 4(2) TEU to show concern to respect a specifically *Austrian* concern. One might find a hint here that Article 4(2) TEU is a route to soften free movement law yet further. But more probably this is just a slightly different route to reach the same destination. The outcome is in any event the same: free movement law yields to justified national measures. And in the background is the Court's concern to take seriously sensitive matters of national identity lest national courts intervene unilaterally. That interaction between the EU and national judiciaries, frequently unspoken,[75] offers a rich vein of inquiry. One could readily see the Court of Justice's interpretation of Article 4(2) TEU as a means to open up EU law to national constitutional concerns while still laying formal claim to the supremacy of EU law over national law, in balance with the Bundesverfassungsgericht's concern to open up German law to EU law, while still placing limits on its subjection to EU law in the name of, inter alia, defence of constitutional identity.[76]

D. The (Relegated?) Commitment to Undistorted Competition

Before the entry into force of the Lisbon Treaty on 1 December 2009 it was provided in Article 3(1)(g) TEC that the activities of the EC should include 'a system ensuring that competition in the internal market is not distorted'. Now, post-Lisbon, Article 2 TEU provides only that 'The Union shall establish an internal market'. The commitment to 'a system ensuring that competition is not distorted' has been relegated to a Protocol attached to the Treaties.

A Protocol is legally binding. But it is not inconceivable that it will be argued that shifting the reference to undistorted competition out of the Treaty 'proper' and into a Protocol adjusts the constitutional balance in favour of socially-motivated public regulation at the expense of market competition, and that this should be taken into account in the interpretation of the key economic Articles of the Treaty. All the more so when one appreciates that the Court in the past used the now lost Article 3(1)(g) as a basis for making difficult interpretative choices.[77] This is especially

---

[74] Ibid, paras 92–93.
[75] But not always: cf A Vosskuhle, 'Multilevel Cooperation of the European Constitutional Courts' (2010) 6 *European Constitutional Law Review* 175, for the extra-judicial comments on judicial co-operation by the President of the Bundesverfassungsgericht.
[76] cf *Lisbon*, BVerfG, 2 BvE 2/08, judgment of 30 June 2009. English translation available at www.bundesverfassungsgericht.de/entscheidungen/es20090630_2bve000208en.html.
[77] eg Case C-453/99 *Courage Ltd v Bernard Crehan* [2001] ECR I-6297, para 20.

relevant to competition law[78] but it could also form part of the debate about the application of the free movement rules to sensitive national practices. In particular it could be an argument in favour of 'softening' free movement law.

In *Konkurrensverket v TeliaSonera Sverige*[79] the Court rolled together Article 3(3) TEU, the Protocol and Article 3(1) TFEU in a way that strongly suggests no inclination to be led in a different direction by the Lisbon Treaty's rearrangement of the furniture. However, the ruling was a heartland competition law case, dealing with abusive pricing, and it did not throw up the balancing issues associated with free movement law which will be the real test.

The controversial rulings in *Viking Line* and *Laval*[80] might usefully be assessed from this perspective — not least because the physical shift of the commitment to undistorted competition to a Protocol appears to have been a political trick designed to placate French voters angry at perceived neoliberal trends in the EU of which these cases were widely cited as examples and, in particular, to deny them a referendum on the Lisbon Treaty after their stubborn 'Non' in the referendum on the Treaty establishing a Constitution in 2005. So, the argument now runs, *Viking Line* and *Laval* were driven by a thirst for undistorted competition, which is no longer so constitutionally pressing. And Article 28 of the — now binding — Charter of Fundamental Rights provides, inter alia, that workers have the right to take collective action to defend their interests, including strike action. Moreover, the Treaty now commits the Union to, inter alia, a 'social market' in Article 3(3) TEU.

True, the Lisbon alterations alter the tone of the Treaty, but the Member States were not able to agree definitively to change the heartland of the law of the internal market. Clearly, were one seeking to defend the (trade-restrictive) expression of social and political freedoms before the Court, one would now argue that post-Lisbon the emphasis has shifted: the rise of the 'social market' and the Charter of Fundamental Rights and the relegation of the commitment to undistorted competition all lend support to the claim that pursuit of economic freedom has been legally braked. But the Treaty provisions on free movement have not been changed. Besides, undistorted competition is a commitment found now only in a Protocol, but a Protocol is legally binding. Although there is scope for the Court to adopt an adjusted interpretation of the free movement rules which gives greater weight to justification of practices that tend to inhibit cross-border commercial activity, the Lisbon reforms are too legally 'soft' to *require* that outcome. What is at stake is a possible re-balancing of priorities with consequences sympathetic to social protection, but such an impact is far from guaranteed.[81] Ultimately the Court continues to enjoy a great degree of interpretative autonomy.

---

[78] See eg A Riley, 'The EU Reform Treaty and the Competition Protocol: Undermining EC Competition Law' (2007) *European Competition Law Review* 703.

[79] In Case C-52/09 *Konkurrensverket v TeliaSonera Sverige AB* (ECJ, 17 February 2011), nyr, paras 20–22.

[80] Case C-438/05 *Viking Line*, above n 7; Case C-341/05 *Laval*, above n 59.

[81] cf N Nic Shuibhne, 'Margins of appreciation: national values, fundamental rights and EC free movement law' (2009) 34 *EL Rev* 230; C Semmelmann, 'The European Union's Economic Constitution under the Lisbon Treaty: soul-searching shifts the focus to procedure' (2010) 35 *EL Rev* 516.

The tension between trading freedom and collective labour rights endures post-Lisbon: *Viking Line* and *Laval* remain high-profile. The 'Monti report' of May 2010 – *A New Strategy for the Single Market: at the service of Europe's Economy and Society*[82] – states that

> [t]here is a broad awareness among policy makers that a clarification . . . should not be left to future occasional litigation before the ECJ or national courts. Political forces have to engage in a search for a solution, in line with the Treaty objective [Art 3(3) TEU] of a social market economy.

This seems initially appealing – and yet what sort of solution might be thought politically acceptable? The subsequent Commission Communication issued in October 2010[83] declares that 'Economic freedoms and freedoms of collective action must be reconciled', and advises that likely 'clarification of the exercise of fundamental social rights within the context of the economic freedoms of the single market' can be expected in 2011. But it seems highly improbable that a 'solution' can be extracted through the political process. Even granted a background of broad political consensus and an ability to navigate past the obstacles created by the Court's interpretation of the Treaty, it would be fiendishly difficult to draft a legislative text of a sufficiently concrete nature to prove operationally useful in resolving these collisions between economic rights and political and social interests. And in the EU there is in any event no such consensus: the interests of the Member States with relatively lightly regulated, low-wage economies diverge sharply from those with heavier and more costly regulatory environments. It is hard to expect much more than platitudes and legislative tinkering to emerge from political negotiation. The matter of free movement of patients was mentioned above:[84] it is illuminating that the sensitivity associated with the attempt to reconcile the competing concerns led to the sector being explicitly *excluded* from the Services Directive, Directive 2006/123.[85] So it was no surprise that when the Commission published its Single Market Act in April 2011 there was no suggestion of any breakthrough in addressing the sensitive matter of collective labour action that disturbs the internal market. It was simply (again) announced that

> the Commission will propose legislation applicable to all sectors which will clarify the exercise of freedom of establishment and the freedom to provide services alongside fundamental social rights, including the right to take collective action, in accordance with national law and practices and in compliance with EU law.[86]

---

[82] M Monti. 'A New Strategy for the Single Market: at the service of Europe's Economy and Society' available at: ec.europa.eu/internal_market/strategy/docs/monti_report_final_10_05_2010_en.pdf.

[83] 'Towards a Single Market Act: For a highly competitive social market economy – 50 proposals for improving our work, business and exchanges with one another', COM(2010) 608, available at ec.europa.eu/internal_market/smact/docs/single-market-act_en.pdf.

[84] Case C-372/04 *ex parte Watts*, above n 21.

[85] Directive 2006/123/EC of the European Parliament and of the Council of 12 December 2006 on services in the internal market [2006] OJ L376/36.

[86] Commission, 'Single Market Act: twelve levers to boost growth and strengthen confidence, working together to create new growth' (Communication) COM(2011) 206 final, 17, available at ec.europa.eu/internal_market/smact/docs/20110413-communication_en.pdf.

Legislative paralysis throws the matter on the mercy of free movement law, and the matter of corporate mobility versus collective labour action seems likely to follow this course. Such delegation to the Court ensures that its interpretative choices retain deep political significance in the shaping of the internal market.

VIII. Concluding Remarks

Article 5 TEU provides that 'The limits of Union competences are governed by the principle of conferral'. This entails that 'the Union shall act only within the limits of the competences conferred upon it by the Member States in the Treaties to attain the objectives set out therein'. However, the breadth of the legal order required to make sense of the internal market places immense strain on the practical positioning and policing of these limits. Article 26(2) TFEU dictates that the internal market 'shall comprise an area without internal frontiers in which the free movement of goods, persons, services and capital is ensured in accordance with the provisions of the Treaties', and this requires a set of legal instruments of immense range. And that is how the Treaty is structured. A law of free movement with a broad substantive scope carries with it a need for receptivity to the availability in principle of a broad range of justifications for trade-restrictive practices. And on this model fundamental rights of varying types – political, social, economic – become the stuff of judicial adjudication.

The story told in this chapter demonstrates that the famous insight of Koen Lenaerts from 20 years ago still retains pertinence. He explained that 'There simply is no nucleus of sovereignty that the Member States can invoke, as such, against the Community'.[87] It was to this phenomenon that the Laeken Declaration referred in 2001 in setting out an agenda to be addressed in the reform of the Treaties:[88]

> [T]here is the question of how to ensure that a redefined division of competence does not lead to a creeping expansion of the competence of the Union or to encroachment upon the exclusive areas of competence of the Member States and, where there is provision for this, regions. How are we to ensure at the same time that the European dynamic does not come to a halt? In the future as well the Union must continue to be able to react to fresh challenges and developments and must be able to explore new policy areas.

Inspection of the Lisbon Treaty reveals that there is no silver bullet. Weighing such balances is awkward, but continues to rest with the institutions of the European Union. Protection of fundamental (social, political) rights at national

---

[87] K Lenaerts, 'Constitutionalism and the Many Faces of Federalism' (1990) 38 *American Journal of Comparative Law* 205, 220.
[88] Laeken Declaration on the future of the European Union, available at: european-convention.eu.int/pdf/LKNEN.pdf .

level as a basis for justifying restrictions on (fundamental) economic rights guaranteed by EU law was a preoccupation of the Court before December 2009 and it still is today, in the 'world after Lisbon'. As explained, there are aspects of the Lisbon Treaty that serve to strengthen the argument that free movement law must be more attentive to (in short) non-economic objectives – the Charter of Fundamental Rights, the Treaty's horizontal clauses, defence of constitutional identity and the relegation of the commitment to undistorted competition in the internal market. But one's assessment of the significance of any such potential adjustment depends heavily on whether one reckons the Court in the past to have been sincerely anxious to respect social and cultural concerns expressed through (trade-restrictive) national measures; and any prediction as to the future also entails engagement with Europe's judges, for the ambiguity of the relevant legal material ensures that considerable power has been delegated to the Court to choose between competing interpretations. In my assessment, EU free movement law has always been 'porous';[89] it has always been equipped with 'safety valves'.[90] The Lisbon Treaty does not make a qualitative change to the structure and scope of the law governing free movement.

---

[89] Above n 43.
[90] Above n 44.

2

The Protection of Fundamental Social Rights in Europe after Lisbon: a Question of Conflicts of Interests

CATHERINE BARNARD*

I. Introduction

At first glance, the Lisbon Treaty appeared to be good news for social rights: the incorporation into the Treaty of the Charter of Fundamental Rights with its title on Solidarity, the expansion of the 'horizontal clauses' to include a high level of employment (Article 9 TFEU) and combating discrimination (Article 10 TFEU), and the identification of the objective for the EU of attaining a 'social market economy' all bode well for the EU to have a greater social face. However, this chapter will argue that these changes may in fact add to – or even create – more difficulties for the EU and ultimately for the courts, in fashioning a genuinely 'social dimension' of the EU. Certainly, the Lisbon Treaty offers little by way of guidance for resolving some of the difficulties.

The difficulties can be divided into three. First, there is an increasing proliferation of sources of social rights both at the EU level (horizontally) and vertically at the national and international levels (eg collective bargaining, national law, constitutions, European Convention on Human Rights (ECHR), International Labour Organization (ILO)). How do these levels interact? This problem is exacerbated by the fact that the EU's system of employment protection is far from comprehensive and is dependent, to a large extent, on national labour law traditions to give it flesh. The Posted Workers Directive 96/71 (PWD) is a case in point: it does not prescribe the substance of the rights that posted workers enjoy in the host states. Rather, it identifies in Article 3(1) a list of *national* rules, where they exist, which must be applied to the posted workers.

Secondly, on a micro level there is an increasing number of individual rights that need to be balanced. These rights include not only the traditional employer v workers conflict well known in labour law but also worker v worker (for example,

---

* Professor of European Union Law, Trinity College, Cambridge

the rights of workers from the EU-15 against those in the EU-10; the rights of older workers against those of younger workers, and the rights of the employed against those of the unemployed). As we shall see, the Court of Justice has resorted to the proportionality principle as a tool to help achieve a balance between these rights. However, it will be argued that proportionality may not always be able to provide a clear steer in respect of these fundamental points of difference. We shall examine these sources of tension, drawing examples from two of the most controversial and difficult areas of employment law: the *Viking* and *Laval* case law and the case law on objectively justified retirement age.

Thirdly, on a macro-level, the EU's mandate now extends well beyond attainment of a single market. It now must achieve a 'social market' economy and the promotion of a high level of employment. What happens when these policies conflict? This problem has already been seen in the field of public procurement. The Eurozone crisis has brought the problem home to the public at large. It will be argued that the EU's response to the crisis is in the process of reshaping the current landscape to such an extent that it casts doubt on the objective, set out in Article 151 TFEU, of *improving* living and working conditions.[1]

We shall examine these conflicts in turn.

II. Conflicts of Sources

A. The Problem

In many ways, the EU is a Johnny-come-lately to the whole area of social policy legislation. These were areas already extensively regulated at national level (by both law and collective bargaining) and at international level (particularly by the ILO). The well-known cases of *Viking*[2] and *Laval*[3] illustrate these problems. In resolving the dispute, the Court of Justice applied its classic *EU* single-market approach: it found that the collective action was a restriction on free movement and was thus presumptively unlawful. The strike action could, however, be justified, provided that the trade unions could show that it was taken to protect workers' interests, as narrowly defined, and that the strike action was proportionate, again, as narrowly defined. Part of the subsequent controversy around the decisions concerned the Court's failure to recognise the broader context of the dispute: there was no real engagement with the significance of ILO Convention 87 on freedom of association,

---

[1] Case C-72/91 *Firma Sloman Neptun Schiffahrts AG v Seebetriebsrat Bodo Ziesemer der Sloman Neptun Schiffahrts AG* [1993] ECR I-887, para 26.

[2] Case C-438/05 *International Transport and Workers' Federation and Finnish Seamen's Union v Viking Line ABP and OÜ Viking Line Eesti* [2007] ECR I-10779.

[3] Case C-341/05 *Laval un Partneri Ltd v Svenska Byggnadsarbetareförbundet and others* [2007] ECR I-11767.

although it was referred to, nor was any emphasis placed on the fact that the strike action, in *Viking*, was taken in accordance with the Finnish constitutional right to strike.

Viking and *Laval* thus illustrate in microcosm the broader problems facing the EU in resolving disputes with a social dimension: how to situate itself in a complex legal order. Is it a system based on hierarchy, heterarchy or autonomy? These problems of conflict are not confined to the vertical plane. Even within the EU the Court has struggled to come to terms with potentially conflicting sources, in particular Treaty provisions v legislation and EU legislation v EU legislation. We shall begin by examining these 'horizontal' conflicts before turning to consider the 'vertical' dimension of the problem (EU v Member State and EU v international sources). We shall see that the Lisbon Treaty has provided little by way of template to resolve these conflicts.

B. 'Horizontal' Conflicts of Sources

According to theory, the Treaty prevails over secondary legislation and all pieces of secondary legislation fit neatly together with no risk of conflict between them. We do not live in such a world, and social policy is an area which is particularly affected by such conflicts.

(i) Treaty Provision v Legislation

Laval provides a good example of a conflict between a Treaty rule (the free movement of services which is premised on the principle of home state control) and a Directive (Directive 96/71 on posted workers (PWD), premised on the principle of host state control in respect of those areas governed by Article 3(1) of the Directive). According to the orthodoxy, the Treaty provision should prevail and the Directive declared ultra vires. One of the Court's successes in *Laval* was to marry the Treaty provision with the Directive. In a remarkable process of bootstrapping, the Court was able to use the legal basis of the Directive (free movement of services) to justify interpreting the Treaty in the light of the Directive and, by insisting on strict compliance with the provisions of Articles 3(1) and 3(8), was able to uphold the validity of those provisions of the Directive. But this success came at a price: it meant that host states, like the UK with a territorial approach to their labour law (ie *all* UK labour laws apply to those in the territory who satisfy the personal and temporal scope of the legislation), could no longer justify applying all of their laws to posted workers, despite good industrial relations reasons for so doing.[4] The UK can apply its laws only in those areas listed in Article 3(1) of the Directive. The effect of this is to lower the standards of protection for posted workers working in the UK.

---

[4] C Barnard, 'The UK and Posted Workers: The effect of *Commission v Luxembourg*' (2009) 38 *ILJ* 122.

(ii) EU Legislation v EU Legislation

The argument based on equal treatment of all employees in the name of fairness and good industrial relations highlights another potential source of conflict: how the PWD, which allows a certain number of host state laws to be applied to posted workers, can be reconciled with the Public Procurement Directive 2004/18, which essentially views national labour laws as an impediment to free movement. This issue arose in *Rüffert*.[5] Under the Law of Lower Saxony public (but not private) contracting authorities could award contracts for building works, but only to undertakings and subcontractors which paid the wage laid down in the collective agreements at the place where the service was provided. The question was raised whether foreign posted workers working on such a public contract could actually work for less.

By requiring respect for the German collective agreement by both the domestic and foreigner tenderer, Lower Saxony was complying with the key principle of equal treatment, expressly articulated in Article 2 of Directive 2004/18. This point was noted by the Advocate General,[6] who added that while the aim of public procurement was to meet an identified administrative need for works, services or supplies, 'the award of public contracts also authorises the attainment of other public interest requirements, such as environmental policy or, as in the present case, social objectives'.

However, the Court adopted a different approach. It found that the German law contravened the PWD because the German authorities had failed to comply with the detailed provisions of Article 3(8). In particular, they had failed to declare the collectively agreed pay in the building industry to be universally applicable,[7] with the result that the collectively agreed rules on pay rates could not be applied to the posted workers.[8] The Court added that by requiring undertakings performing public works contracts and, indirectly, their subcontractors to apply the minimum wage laid down by the collective agreement, the German law could impose on undertakings established in another Member State where minimum rates of pay are lower 'an additional economic burden' that is 'capable of constituting a restriction within the meaning of Article [56 TFEU]'.[9] In other words, the application of social provisions constituted a restriction on market access and was presumptively unlawful.

The divergence between the Court and its Advocate General highlights the fundamental problem at the core of the decision: should the Land of Lower Saxony insist on an equal treatment approach (as the Advocate General would suggest) or a single-market perspective (as the Court would suggest)? The effect of the Advocate General's approach would be to allow contracting authorities to impose on contractors all host state labour standards, in the name of equal treatment. The

---

[5] Case C-346/06 *Dirk Rüffert v Land Niedersachsen* [2008] ECR I-1989.
[6] Ibid, para 131.
[7] Ibid, para 26.
[8] Ibid, para 31.
[9] Ibid, para 37.

effect of the Court's approach is that the imposition of German labour standards on the staff of temporary service providers – with the exception of those areas listed in Article 3(1) PWD – is an impediment to market access. The Court's stance therefore significantly restricts the extent to which even minimum terms and conditions can be imposed on posted workers through any procurement regime.

Yet, in reaching this conclusion the Court created its own (reverse) discrimination: domestic service providers (and established service providers exercising their rights under Article 49 TFEU) are subject to all the employment conditions of the procuring state (eg Germany), to the extent this is compatible with the public procurement regime, but out-of-state (eg Latvian) service providers providing services under Article 56 TFEU will not be subject to host state (German) laws, except in the areas listed in Article 3(1) PWD. Not only does this give the out-of-state provider a comparative advantage but it also goes against the objective of 'raising' the labour conditions of posted workers in accordance with Article 151 TFEU.

C. The Vertical Plane

So far we have concentrated on examples of conflicts at the EU level itself. More conflicts arise on the vertical plane. At first sight, perhaps easiest to resolve, at least in terms of the principle of supremacy of EU law, are EU v Member State conflicts (section C(i)). More difficult are EU v international law conflicts (section C(ii)).

(i) EU v Member State Conflicts

(a) EU law v national law

The conflict of EU rules v national law is the bread and butter of the supremacy principle: where national social laws conflict with EU rules, national social provisions are set aside. In cases where national social legislation excluded certain groups (eg transsexuals, gay couples, those associated with a person with a disability[10]) from the scope of protection of the equal treatment legislation, and this conflicted with obligations under the EU Equal Treatment Directive, then the national law was set aside and or subsequently amended to bring national law into line with the Directive. Such an outcome was widely seen as a victory for the evolving social dimension of the EU because it had the effect of *extending* social rights, not diminishing them.

Far more difficult is the situation where general EU law (eg the Treaty provisions on freedom of establishment and the free movement of services, read in conjunction

---

[10] Case C-13/94 *P v S and Cornwall County Council* [1996] ECR I-2143, Case C-276/06 *Tadao Maruko v Versorgungsanstalt der deutschen Bühnen* [2008] ECR I-1757, Case C-303/06 *Coleman v Attridge Law and Steve Law* [2008] ECR I-5603.

with the market access test) is used to strike down *specific* national social rules (eg the right to strike), as in the cases of *Viking* and *Laval*. This problem is exacerbated where the social rules, as we have already seen, are fundamental rights found in the national constitution. Under the supremacy principle the outcome is straightforward: the EU rules prevail. And yet, the Court of Justice needs to exercise care. A number of Constitutional courts have expressed *Solange*[11]-type reservations: if the protection given to fundamental rights at EU level is not as high as at the national level, the national courts may refuse to apply EU law.[12] Many would argue that the effect of *Viking* is to undermine, not to reinforce, the right to strike at national level. If this reasoning is correct then the Court may be laying itself open to a challenge on this basis. Lisbon inevitably failed to address such a threat.

(b) EU v national/subnational collective agreements

All Member States recognise collective agreements as a source of labour law. In some Member States, particularly in the Nordic countries, collective agreements provide the main source of employment rights and the principle of autonomy of the social partners is keenly felt. What happens when this principle comes into conflict with internal market law? This was at issue in *Commission v Germany (occupational pensions)*.[13] A number of local authorities entered into a collective agreement with the trade unions concerning the conversion of earnings into pension savings. The collective agreement identified a limited list of pension providers entrusted with implementing the salary conversion measure. Given the existence of this collective agreement, the local authorities did not issue a call for tenders, as required by Directive 2004/18, with the result that other pension providers were denied the chance to offer their services. The Court noted the need for balance between the competing interests[14] but found that this balance had not been struck on the facts because the effect of the collective agreement was 'to disapply the [public procurement] rules ... completely, and for an indefinite period, in the field of local authority employees' pension saving'.[15]

While, as might be expected following *Viking* and *Laval*, the Court in *Commission v Germany* resolved the question of priority as between (national) collective agreements and (EU) legislation in favour of the EU legislative obligations, it failed to take into account the implicit mandate provided by the Treaties since Maastricht that collective bargaining at national and sub-national (sector/plant) levels should be encouraged, a view implicitly reinforced by the new reference in Article 152 TFEU to the role of the social partners. It was the Maastricht Treaty's encouragement of collective bargaining that prompted the Court in *Albany*[16] to exclude

[11] *Re Wünsche Handelsgesellschaft (Solange II)* [1987] 3 CMLR 225.
[12] For a summary, see P Craig and G De Búrca, *EU Law: Text, Cases and Materials* (Oxford, Oxford University Press, 2011) 268–96 and the references contained therein.
[13] Case C-271/08 *European Commission v Germany (occupational pensions)* [2010] ECR I-7091.
[14] Ibid, paras 44 and 52.
[15] Ibid, para 53.
[16] Case C-67/96 *Albany International BV v Stichting Bedrijfspensioenfonds textielindustrie* [1999] ECR I-5751.

collective agreements from the scope of the competition provision of the Treaty; and in other domains, such as the retirement age case law, the Court has consistently relied on the fact that the mandatory retirement age had been fixed by collective bargaining to justify direct age discrimination.[17]

(ii) EU and International Bodies

While the relationship between national law and EU law has proved difficult, the relationship between the EU and other international bodies, especially the Council of Europe and its organs and the ILO, may still prove more of a challenge, especially where the rules of these bodies differ from national law. The Court has two options: (a) to adopt varying degrees of openness to the international sources, or (b) to assert the autonomy of the EU legal order and implicitly close itself to external influence. While the Lisbon Treaty might appear to mandate the former, practice to-date suggests a preference for the latter.

(a) The openness/accommodation solution

At first sight the openness solution appears the most justifiable. The decisions of the EU are made in the context of an international environment. Its Member States are already signatories to the major international organisations, especially the ILO and the Council of Europe. The Court of Justice should not aim to put itself – and thus the Member States – into conflict with these bodies. Article 151 TFEU also appears to mandate some openness to international bodies due to the reference to the European Social Charter 1961. More generally, the Lisbon Treaty with its obligation on the EU to accede to the ECHR in Article 6(3) TEU and its incorporation of the Charter which makes express reference in Article 52(3) to the ECHR, again appears to recognise the openness of the EU system to these external sources.

But what does openness actually mean? Are these international sources merely an interpretative steer?[18] Or could they go further and take precedence over a conflicting rule at EU level? The significance of this question can be seen by comparing *Viking* with its ECHR analogue *Demir* and *Enerji Yapi-Yol*.[19] As we have seen, in *Viking* the Court adopted an essentially single-market (even Anglo-Saxon) approach and found the strike action to be *unlawful* unless justified and proportionate. By contrast, *Demir* and *Enerji Yapi-Yol* adopt a human rights perspective: strike action is *lawful* and any restrictions on it have to be narrowly construed.

The other striking feature of *Demir* is the extensive reference made by the Court of Human Rights to international sources, particularly the ILO Conventions as

---

[17] Eg Case C-411/05 *Palacios de la Villa v Cortefiel Servicios SA* [2008] ECR I-8531.
[18] Case C-72/91 *Firma Sloman Neptun v Bodo Ziesemer de Sloman Neptun Schiffahrts AG* [1993] ECR I-887, para 26; Case C-438/05 *International Transport Workers' Federation and Finnish Seamen's Union v Viking Line ABP and Oü Viking Line Eesti* [2007] ECR I-10779, para 43.
[19] *Demir and Baykara v Turkey* Application no 34503/97 (ECtHR, 12 November 2008); *Enerji Yapi-Yol Sen v Turkey* Application no 68959/01 (ECtHR, 21 April 2009).

well as to the EU's Charter of Fundamental Rights, to justify the conclusion that the time had come to reverse its previously rather cautious attitude to the scope of Article 11. This suggests that the Court of Human Rights is more open, in fact, to international sources than the Court of Justice. This makes the EU's accession to the ECHR all the more significant from the point of view of protecting social rights.

(b) The autonomy of the EU legal order

Albeit decided in a very different context – terrorist asset freezing – the seminal decision in *Kadi*[20] appears to endorse the opposite perspective: the autonomy of the EU legal order and thus its relative closure to international obligations. To an extent, *Rüffert* appears to support this approach in the social sphere, albeit without express discussion. One of the key documents addressing the interface between public procurement and social obligations is ILO Convention No 94. Yet this measure is not even mentioned by the Court.

D. The Way Forward?

Yet even if the Court wants to shield itself from international law sources, international systems are nevertheless taking an increasing interest in the EU. For example, following a complaint by Balpa (the British Airline Pilots' Association) to the ILO's Committee of Experts on the Application of Conventions and Recommendations that the effect of *Viking* and *Laval* was to expose the unions to crippling damages if they went on strike without complying with the (unclear) terms of the judgments, the Committee observed that it viewed:

> with *serious concern* the practical limitations on the effective exercise of the right to strike of the BALPA workers in this case. The Committee takes the view that the omnipresent threat of an action for damages that could bankrupt the union, possibly now in the light of the *Viking* and *Laval* judgments, creates a situation where the rights under the Convention cannot be exercised . . . The Committee thus considers that the doctrine that is being articulated in these ECJ judgments is likely to have a significant restrictive effect on the exercise of the right to strike in practice in a manner contrary to the Convention.

More recently the ILO issued an information note[21] expressing grave concern about the approach adopted by the Greek government, under the guidance of the EU as part of its stabilisation policy, to limit wage rates for three years. It said:

---

[20] Joined cases C-402 and C-415/05 P *Yassin Abdullah Kadi and Al Barakaat International Foundation v European Council (Kadi I)* [2008] ECR I-6351.

[21] www.ilo.org/public/english/region/eurpro/brussels/downloads/newsletter022011.pdf (last accessed 13 December 2011). See also the European Committee on Social Rights Report in cases brought against Greece in the context of the ESC 1961 No 65/2011 *GENOP-DEI v Greece* and No 66/2011 *GENOP-DEI v Greece*, decisions of 23 May 2012 published 19 Oct 2012.

If, as part of the stabilization policy, a government considers that wage rates cannot be settled freely through collective bargaining, such a restriction should be imposed as an exceptional measure and only to the extent that is necessary, without exceeding a reasonable period, and it should be accompanied by adequate safeguards to protect workers' living standards. A three year period of limited collective bargaining on remuneration . . . constitutes a substantial restriction.

In the same document the ILO also notes that Conventions 98 on collective bargaining and 87 on freedom of association have 'strongly influenced other regional fundamental rights instruments such as the European Social Charter, the European Convention on Human Rights (freedom of association is a part of this) and the EU Charter on Fundamental Rights'. This is a fairly direct criticism of the Court of Justice's closure to international sources of social rights.

In order to protect itself against such criticisms, it is necessary for the Court to revert to a greater openness to other systems. Accession to the Convention will already require that. Openness does not necessarily mean giving supremacy to those systems but the Court should be forced to consider – and explain – why those systems' rules do – or do not – apply in the EU.

III. Conflict of Rights

A. The Conflicts

The second area of conflict in the post-Lisbon world concerns conflict of rights. Traditionally, social rights have been concerned with protecting the interests of the weak against the strong. In the labour law context this has meant protecting workers' rights against the might of the employer and sometimes the state. The EU has played a prominent role in strengthening those rights, particularly in the equality field (with legislation and case law protecting pregnant workers, transsexuals and homosexuals[22]). But the EU has also introduced new conflicts which have proved far more challenging to reconcile.

The first and most obvious is the conflict between the individual rights of the employer to free movement and the collective rights of the trade union workers to strike to protect the interests of their (individual) members. In *Viking* the Court broadly decided in favour of the employer's individual right over the trade union's collective right, albeit that the Court professed to be upholding the right to strike. A second and related conflict concerns the interests of workers from the old Member States and those from the new. These conflicts were, of course, brought into sharp focus by the decisions in *Viking*, and to a greater extent, *Laval* and *Rüffert*. Should workers from the new Member States be able to invoke their

---

[22] See, eg Directive 2006/54 on equal opportunities and equal treatment of men and women in matters of employment and occupation ([2006] OJ L204/23) and Directive 2000/78 establishing a general framework for equal treatment in employment and occupation ([2000] OJ L303/16).

competitive advantage in terms of cheaper labour to win contracts in the old Member States? Should they be able to bring their home state's labour laws with them, or should they be required to respect the ('higher') labour standards in the host state and so not undercut the local labour? As we know, the Court broadly favoured the interests of the new Member States. The refusal by the Member States to incorporate a social progress clause into the Lisbon Treaty, which would have given priority to fundamental social rights over economic rights, as the trade unions had requested,[23] suggests that the Lisbon Treaty has not fundamentally changed the position as set out in *Viking* and *Laval*. However, the inclusion of the phrase 'social market economy' into Article 3(3) TEU[24] might provide a reason for a more genuine attempt at balancing social and economic rights, as Advocate General Cruz Villalon suggested in *Santos Palhota*.[25] How that balancing might be more effectively delivered is considered below.

The equality field also reveals new conflicts. For example, what is the situation when the principle of non-discrimination on the grounds of religion conflicts with the principle of non-discrimination on the grounds of sex or sexual orientation (eg where a religious order refuses to employ a woman or a homosexual)? The Directive does not expressly deal with this conflict, albeit that Article 2(5) says: 'The Directive shall be without prejudice to measures laid down by national law which, in a democratic society, are necessary for . . . the protection of the rights and freedoms of others'.

The area where these conflicts have already been ventilated is in respect of age discrimination. To what extent can employers retain a compulsory retirement age in order to make vacancies available for younger workers? This simple question pits a number of competing rights (young v middle aged v old; employer (for succession planning, managing the workforce) v worker (to stay on in employment)) and competing policies (the interests of insiders (those with a job) v those of outsiders (those without a job)) against one another. Article 6(1) of Directive 2000/78 provides some guidance. It allows *Member States* to:

> provide that differences of treatment on the grounds of age shall not constitute discrimination if . . . they are objectively and reasonably justified by a legitimate aim, including legitimate employment policy, labour market and vocational training objectives, and if the means of achieving that aim are appropriate and necessary.

---

[23] '[N]othing in the Treaty, and in particular neither fundamental freedoms nor competition rules shall have priority over fundamental social rights and social progress'. It adds: 'In case of conflict, fundamental social rights shall take precedence'. ETUC's Resolution adopted on 4 March 2008: www.etuc.org/IMG/pdf_ETUC_Viking_Laval_-_resolution_070308.pdf.

[24] For a discussion of this term, see C Joerges and F Rödl, '"Social Market Economy" as Europe's Social Model?', EUI Working Paper Law No 2004/8, 19 who argue that 'this concept contained an ordoliberal basis which was complemented by social and societal policies, whose aims and instruments were supposed to reply on market mechanisms'. According to Working Group XI on Social Europe (CONV 516/1/03 REV 1 [17]) the objectives should refer to 'social market economy' to underline the link between the economic and social development and the efforts made to ensure greater coherence between economic and social policies.

[25] Opinion of AG Pedro Cruz Villon (5 May 2010) in Case C-515/08 *Criminal proceedings against Vitor Manuel Santos Palhota and others* (CJEU, 7 October 2010), paras 51–53.

Nevertheless, the Court has struggled to balance these competing interests. For example, in *Palacios de la Villa*[26] it found Spanish law, which supported compulsory retirement clauses at age 65 in collective agreements, to be directly discriminatory, but could be objectively justified on the grounds of combating unemployment.[27] The Court said the legitimacy of such an aim of public interest was compatible with Directive 2000/78 and the Treaties, since the promotion of a high level of employment constituted one of the ends pursued by the EU. This aim could, in principle, be regarded as 'objectively and reasonable', justifying 'within the context of national law', as provided for by Directive 2000/78, a difference in treatment on grounds of age laid down by the Member State.[28]

However, in *Andersen*[29] the Court adopted a rather different approach. Danish law provided that an employer, upon dismissal of a salaried employee who had been continuously employed in the same undertaking for 12, 15 or 18 years, had to pay an amount equivalent to one, two or three months' salary respectively. This allowance was not paid where the salaried employee, upon termination of employment, was entitled to receive an old-age pension from a pension scheme to which the employer has contributed. Andersen had worked for his employer for 27 years. He was dismissed unfairly at 63. He decided not to exercise his right to retirement, registering instead as a job seeker. He was denied severance pay. The Court found that the Danish rule could be justified on the ground of facilitating a move to new employment for older employees with many years of service and was generally proportionate, by preventing employers from having to pay double compensation to those who were leaving the labour market and restricting the severance allowance only to those workers who were not entitled to an old-age pension. However, the Court said that in respect of those workers who joined the pension scheme before 50 but wished to waive their right to a pension temporarily in order to continue working, they could not claim the severance allowance, and as a result their interests were unduly prejudiced. Thus, by using the proportionality principle the Court was able to balance the general interests of the system with the interests of the individual. But is proportionality a suitable tool?

B. The Way Forward?

The proportionality principle may well be the tool to help reconcile the competing rights. This is the approach adopted by the German Constitutional Court to

---

[26] Case C-411/05 *Felix Palacios de la Villa v Cortefiel Servicios SA* [2008] ECR I-8531. See also Case C-388/07 *The Queen (on the application of The Incorporated Trustees of the National Council on Ageing (Age Concern England)) v Secretary of State for Business, Enterprise and Regulatory Reform* [2009] ECR I-1569, para 51.
[27] Ibid, para 62.
[28] Ibid, para 66.
[29] Case C-499/08 *Ole Andersen v Region Syddanmark* (CJEU, 12 October 2010) [2011] 1 CMLR 35.

balancing fundamental rights of equal weight. It is called 'practical concordance', an idea attributed to Professor Hesse. According to Donald Kommers:[30]

> Professor Konrad Hesse wrote 'The principle of the constitution's unity requires the optimisation of [values in conflict]: Both legal values need to be limited so that each can attain its optimal effect. In each concrete case, therefore, the limitations must satisfy the principle of proportionality; that is, they may not go any further than necessary to produce a concordance of both legal values'.

He continues:

> In its German version, proportionality is a three-step process. First, whenever Parliament enacts a law impinging on a basic right, the means used must be appropriate (eignung) to the achievement of a legitimate end ... Second, the means used to achieve a valid purpose must have a least restrictive effect (Erforderlichkeit) on a constitutional value. This test is applied flexibly and must meet the standard of rationality. As applied by the constitutional court, it is less than the 'strict scrutiny' and more than 'minimum rationality' test of American constitutional law. Finally, the means used must be proportionate to the end. The burden on the right must not be excessive relative to the benefit secured by the state's objective (Zumutbarkeit). This three pronged test of proportionality seems fully compatible with, if not required by, the principle of practical concordance.

This is the idea that Advocate General Trstenjak seems to have taken on board in *Commission v Germany* (*occupational pensions*). She argued that:

> 188. Therefore, if in an individual case, as a result of exercising a fundamental right, a fundamental freedom is restricted, a fair balance between both of those legal positions must be sought. In that regard, it must be presumed that the realisation of a fundamental freedom constitutes a legitimate objective which may limit a fundamental right. Conversely, however, the realisation of a fundamental right must be recognised also as a legitimate objective which may restrict a fundamental freedom.
>
> 189. For the purposes of drawing an exact boundary between fundamental freedoms and fundamental rights, the principle of proportionality is of particular importance. In that context, for the purposes of evaluating proportionality, in particular, a three-stage scheme of analysis must be deployed where (1) the appropriateness, (2) the necessity and (3) the reasonableness of the measure in question must be reviewed.

She argued that an approach

> characterised by an equal ranking of fundamental rights and fundamental freedoms in which the principle of proportionality serves as the basis for the resolution of conflicts between the exercise of fundamental freedoms and the exercise of fundamental rights would not constitute a fundamental reorientation in the case-law. Instead, this analysis implies a return to the values already inherent in *Schmidberger*.

---

[30] D Kommers, *The Constitutional Jurisprudence of the Federal Republic of Germany*, 2nd edn (University of Chicago Press, 1996) 46. These arguments are developed further in C Barnard, 'A Proportionate response to Proportionality in the field of Collective Action' (2012) 37 *EL Rev* 117.

More surprisingly, she adds that 'In addition, in *Rüffert* one can detect the first signs of a need to qualify the approach taken in *Viking Line* and *Laval un Partneri*'.[31]

There are some signs that this rhetoric had some influence on the Court. It said:

> Exercise of the fundamental right to bargain collectively must therefore be reconciled with the requirements stemming from the freedoms protected by the FEU Treaty, which in the present instance Directives 92/50 and 2004/18 are intended to implement, and be in accordance with the principle of proportionality.[32]

The Court said that reconciling the competing interests entails verification as to whether, when establishing the content of the collective agreement,

> a fair balance was struck in the account taken of the respective interests involved, namely enhancement of the level of the retirement pensions of the workers concerned, on the one hand, and attainment of freedom of establishment and of the freedom to provide services, and opening-up to competition at European Union level, on the other.[33]

It concluded, as we saw above, that a balance on the facts of this case had not been struck (because no procurement process had been undertaken at all) but then outlined a way for a better balance (opening up the tendering process but providing more space for contracting authorities to specify social conditions).[34] What is striking about the case is that the reference to balance is not diluted by any express mention of the market-access approach, nor by the presumption underpinning *Laval* that requiring respect for social standards is unlawful unless justified. Although *Commission v Germany* concerned an interpretation of the public procurement directive and not the Treaties, the Treaty context is evident.[35] It seems that in *Commission v Germany* – a case decided post-Lisbon – the Court implicitly accepted that the economic and social interests are of equal weight and need to be reconciled through the principle of proportionality.[36]

But is proportionality a true panacea? Does it risk being a judicial sleight of hand to legitimise essentially policy decisions? The debate about the merits and demerits of proportionality is neatly summed up by Greer:[37]

---

[31] Opinion of Advocate General Trstenjak (14 April 2010) in Case C-271/08 *European Commission v Germany (occupational pensions)* [2010] ECR I-7091, para 193.

[32] Ibid, para 44.

[33] Ibid, para 52.

[34] See by analogy Case C-160/08 *European Commission v Germany (ambulance)* [2010] ECR I-3713, paras 125–31 where the Court refused to exempt services of general economic interest (SGEIs) (the provision of ambulance services) from the obligations under the public procurement directives.

[35] Eg para 47. See also the Advocate General's opinion, especially paras 183–84. This is discussed further by P Syrpis, 'Reconciling Economic Freedoms and Social Rights – the Potential of Commission v Germany' (Case note) (2011) 40 *ILJ* 222.

[36] In this respect the Court's approach appears to show some signs of convergence with the EU's post-2000 Social Agenda: rather than viewing social policies as a burden on the economy, they are in fact, one of the keys to its success. COM(2000) 379 and COM(2001) 313, 17.

[37] S Greer, '"Balancing" and the European Court of Human Rights: A Contribution to the Habermas-Alexy debate' (2004) 63 *CLJ* 412, 413. See also T Harbo, 'The Function of the Proportionality Principle in EU Law' (2010) *ELJ* 158.

According to the 'hostile' view, [balancing] should be regarded as an irrational and illegitimate renunciation of law in favour of a largely arbitrary judicial discretion, difficult to justify according to the ideals of democracy, respect of human rights, and the rule of law and, therefore ripe for elimination from the legal process. Alternatively, the 'sympathetic' view maintains that, although the current judicial practice of balancing may be difficult both to describe and to defend, the concept of balancing, when properly understood, is neither irrational nor illegitimate.

The principle of proportionality is particularly problematic in the context of industrial relations. The essence of good industrial relations is that basically all workers should be treated the same. It avoids grievances based on perceived favouritism or difference. Yet, proportionality as interpreted by the Court often requires an individual assessment, as *Andersen* (considered above) demonstrates.

The problems with the proportionality review in the social field can be seen in the context of an employer justified default retirement age which a number of employers in the UK wish to introduce following the abolition of the national default retirement age by the Employment Equality (Repeal of Retirement Age Provisions) Regulations 2011.[38] Let's say an employer wants to maintain a default retirement age of 67. Dismissal of an employee at the age of 67 would be direct discrimination but could be justified on the basis of succession planning and intergenerational mobility. Assuming such justifications are compatible with Article 6(1) (considered above),[39] is a blanket retirement age of 67 for all staff proportionate or should the employer take each individual's personal circumstances into account (think of the resource implications of this and the risks that other types of discrimination might occur)?

Many might argue that proportionality does not work at all in some social contexts, notably strike action. The more successful the strike action, the less likely it is to be proportionate. This point has been recognised by the German courts where the proportionality principle is applied but with considerable caution. As Waas has put it:[40]

> Though an *ultima ratio* principle [strike as last resort] is known in the German law on strikes and lock-outs, it is very reluctantly applied by the courts[41] because, among other things, it is regarded as the very aim of a strike to make the employers suffer. As a consequence a strike might only be regarded as 'out of proportion' if it aims at destroying the employer economically.[42]

So can anything be done? Elsewhere I have argued that if, following *Viking*, the proportionality principle must be applied then it is possible to finesse the principle in the field of collective action by focusing on its procedural rather than sub-

---

[38] Employment Equality (Repeal of Retirement Age Provisions) Regulations 2011 (SI 2011/1069).
[39] *cf* C Barnard, 'Retiring Gracefully' (2011) 70 *CLJ* 304. See also *Seldon v Clarkson Wright* [2012] UKSC 16
[40] Private correspondence on file with the author.
[41] Indeed, some argue that following the so-called third 'Warnstreikentscheidung' (warning strike decision) of the BAG (BAGE 58, 364) the BAG has abandoned the *ultima ratio* principle.
[42] See also M Weiss, *Labour Law and Industrial Relations in the Federal Republic of Germany* (Deventer, Kluwer, 1989) 136.

stantive elements (eg, whether national rules on balloting, notice, etc have been complied with) or, more substantively, adding a third limb to the standard two-fold suitability/necessity proportionality test and asking whether the application of the proportionality principle might result in undermining the essence of right being protected, namely the right to strike.[43] This is not a total panacea but at least it is a step in the right direction.

IV. Conflicts of Policies

A. Public Procurement

We turn now to the third area of conflict – conflicts of policies. The EU is no longer merely about creating a single market. It quite possibility has never been merely about the creation of the single market. However, the Lisbon Treaty has now made this clear and the introduction of the horizontal policies make this point explicitly. But what happens when the policies conflict? The field of public procurement provides a good example of the potential conflicts that might arise and how the Court and the legislature have struggled, rather unnoticed by the wider public, to find a balance between competing EU policies.

The General Public Procurement Directive 2004/18 provides that, where the value of a tender exceeds a prescribed minimum, it must be publicly advertised in accordance with the Directive. The Directive's rules must then be satisfied in terms of the detail which can be specified in the tender documents. For the purists, especially those in DG Internal Market, the Directive provides almost no room for non-market factors to be taken into account. In other words, the creation of a level playing-field and the single-market imperative takes precedence over all other interests.[44]

Yet, some Member States – or at least contracting authorities within those states – have recognised that using the purchasing power of the government and other major players is a significant way of achieving social objectives. *Nord Pas de Calais*[45] is a case in point. The case concerned a requirement, when building a school, to use a certain percentage of the workforce from among the unemployed. Was this compatible with the Directive? The 1993 version of the Directive did not appear to provide any room for taking social factors into account in respect of MEAT (the Most Economically Advantageous Tender), one of the two ways for selecting the successful bidder. However, the Court disagreed:

> [T]hat provision does not preclude all possibility for the contracting authorities to use as a criterion a condition linked to the campaign against unemployment provided

---

[43] See further C Barnard, above n 30.
[44] Directive 2004/18/EC on the coordination of procedures for the award of public works contracts, public supply contracts and public service contracts, [2004] OJ L134/114.
[45] Case C-225/98 *European Commission v France* [2000] ECR I-7445.

that that condition is consistent with all the fundamental principles of [Union] law, in particular the principle of non-discrimination.[46]

However, the Court added that such an award criterion had to be expressly mentioned in the contract notice 'so that contractors may become aware of its existence'.[47]

Despite this and other case law, the 2004 amendments to the Public Procurement Directives seem to have made it more difficult to take social factors into account as criteria for the award of a contract. Article 53(1)(a) now provides:

> when the award is made to the tender most economically advantageous *from the point of view of the contracting authority*, various criteria *linked to the subject-matter of the public contract* in question, for example, quality, price, technical merit, aesthetic and functional characteristics, *environmental characteristics*, running costs, cost-effectiveness, after-sales service and technical assistance, delivery date and delivery period or period of completion [can be taken into account] (emphasis applied).

As can be seen, not only must the criteria now be linked to the subject matter of the contract but the tender must be the most economically advantageous from the point of view of the contracting authority. It is hard to argue that a condition relating to the requirement to use the local unemployed is economically advantageous from the point of view of the contracting authority. Moreover, the failure to refer to social matters is exacerbated by the fact that environmental – but not social – characteristics are listed for the first time in Article 53.[48] The Preamble does, however, provide more room for non-economic factors to be taken into account. For example, Recital 46 provides:

> [A] contracting authority may use criteria aiming to meet social requirements, in response in particular to the needs – defined in the specifications of the contract – of particularly disadvantaged groups of people to which those receiving/using the works, supplies or services which are the object of the contract belong.[49]

The one stage at which the Directive does appear to provide room for contracting authorities to specify that social criteria can be taken into account is the performance stage, ie after the contract has been awarded. Article 26 of Directive 2004/18 says:

---

[46] Ibid, para 50.
[47] Ibid, para 51.
[48] Although *cf* the first Recital which says that the 2004 Directive is 'based on the Court of Justice case law, in particular the case law on award criteria, which clarifies the possibilities for the contracting authorities to meet the needs of the public concerned, including in the environmental and/or social area'.
[49] Recent case law shows the extent to which the Court is now prepared to refer to Preambles: see, eg, Case C-307/05 *Del Cerro Alonso v Osakidetza-Servicio Vasco de Salud* [2007] ECR I-7109, para 36. However, recitals have only interpretative value and cannot be used to contradict express provisions in a Directive: Case C-267/06 *Tadao Maruko v Versorgungsanstalt der deutschen Bühnen* [2008] ECR I-1757, para 60.

Contracting authorities may lay down special conditions relating to the performance of a contract, provided that these are compatible with [Union] law and are indicated in the contract notice or in the specifications. The conditions governing the performance of a contract may, in particular, concern *social and environmental considerations* (emphasis applied).

Recital 33 adds that contract performance conditions 'may, in particular, be intended to favour on-site vocational training, the employment of people experiencing particular difficulty in achieving integration, the fight against unemployment or the protection of the environment'. It continues that the requirements can relate to the recruitment of 'long-term job-seekers or to implement training measures for the unemployed or young persons'. However, it adds that 'Contract performance conditions are compatible with this Directive provided that they are not directly or indirectly discriminatory and are indicated in the contract notice or in the contract documents'.

Read together, these provisions suggest that a tender requirement to use 'British workers' (with no reference to the fact that they are currently unemployed) would be directly discriminatory and thus unlawful.[50] Even a requirement drafted in more neutral terms, such as employing 'locally sourced' workers (again with no reference to the fact that they are unemployed), also looks vulnerable because, as the British Office of Government Commerce (OGC) says, 'the local element would not accord with EU principles'.[51] Herein lies the conflict: while the EU is about creating a single market, following Lisbon it is also about, according to Article 9 TFEU, 'the promotion of a high level of employment . . . the fight against social exclusion'.

Article 9 TFEU in fact builds on a long tradition of policies in the field of employment, in particular the EU's Employment Strategy launched in Luxembourg in 1997, the EU's Lisbon strategy launched in 2000[52] and re-launched in 2005 as a strategy for 'Growth and Jobs',[53] and now the EU2020 strategy. A more robust approach towards balancing the competing interests can be found in the Commission's 2010 handbook, 'Buying Social: A Guide to Taking Account of Social Considerations in Public Procurements',[54] which discusses 'Socially responsible public procurement' (SRPP). This refers to

[50] See also S Arrowsmith, *The Law of Public and Utilities Procurement* (London, Sweet & Maxwell, 2005) 1257.

[51] Office of Government Commerce, *Social Issues in Purchasing* (February 2006) 26. See also p 37 'Do not require contractors to employ local people. This would be discriminatory under the EU Treaty'.

[52] Lisbon European Council, Presidency Conclusions, 23–24 March 2000, consilium.europa.eu/ueDocs/cms_Data/docs/pressData/en/ec/00100-r1.en0.htm (accessed 28 March 2009).

[53] See eg European Commission, 'Working together for growth and jobs A new start for the Lisbon Strategy' COM(2005) 24 and the European Council's conclusions, 22 and 23 March 2005, europa.eu/rapid/pressReleasesAction.do?reference=DOC/05/1&format=HTML&aged=0&language=EN&guiLanguage=en (accessed 28 March 2009).

[54] 3 April 2009, available at www.araco.org/infutile/noutatifiec/2009-04-03%20Social%20Considerations%20in%20pp%20-%20sent%20out%20to%20EXTERNAL%20CONSULTATION%20_2_.pdf (accessed 29 June 2009), discussed by CEEP May 2009 pr.euractiv.com/files/09avis11en-social%20considerations%20in%20public%20procurement.pdf (accessed 29 June 2009).

procurement operations that take into account one or several of the following considerations: employment opportunities, decent work, compliance with social and labour rights, social inclusion (including persons with disabilities), equal opportunities, accessibility design for all . . . and wider voluntary compliance with corporate social responsibility (CSR), while observing the principles enshrined in the . . . TFEU and the Procurement Directives.[55]

The handbook then sets out a list of social policies which contracting authorities may take into account, including

> Promoting 'Employment Opportunities' e.g. promotion of youth employment . . . promotion of employment of persons from disadvantaged groups (eg migrant workers, ethnic minorities, religious minorities, people with low educational attainment), promotion of employment opportunities for the long-term unemployed, promotion of employment for old-age unemployed.[56]

If the Court follows the handbook, this suggests that the EU is capable in this field at least to balance a range of conflicting policies.

B. The Eurozone Crisis

While the European Commission handbook envisages that there is space for 'social matters' to be taken into account in a procurement process, it throws up yet further conflicts – of policies and rights, namely the interests of the unemployed as against those in work. The general public has become acutely aware of this tension in the context of the Eurozone crisis. One of the key elements of the EU's plan to recover from the financial crisis is growth, yet it is the least articulated policy in the tsunami of documents, pacts and legislation that have emerged from the various bodies in the EU since the start of the crisis. The traditional tool for delivering speedy growth – devaluation of the currency – is not available to Eurozone Member States. This puts labour law in the front line. It is one of the few areas over which Member States retain competence to regulate and, more realistically at present, to deregulate. The EU seems to be encouraging this view, first through the Euro Plus Pact (EPP) and secondly through the Memorandum of Understanding that states in receipt of an EU/IMF bail-out agree to. Two examples illustrate what is happening in the social field.[57]

First, the EuroPlus Pact (EPP), adopted by the European Council in March 2011, largely as a quid pro quo for the Germans agreeing to the European Stability Mechanism, has four objectives. The provisions under the 'Fostering competitiveness' objective were directly related to labour law and were particularly contested. They provide that

---

[55] ec.europa.eu/social/BlobServlet?docId=6457&langId=en, 7.
[56] Ibid.
[57] See further C Barnard, 'The Financial Crisis and the Euro Plus Pact: A Labour Lawyer's Perspective' (2012) 41 *ILJ* 98.

[e]ach country will be responsible for the specific policy actions it chooses to foster competitiveness, but the following reforms will be given particular attention:

respecting national traditions of social dialogue and industrial relations, measures to ensure costs developments in line with productivity, such as:

review the wage setting arrangements, and, where necessary, the degree of centralisation in the bargaining process, and the indexation mechanisms, while maintaining the autonomy of the social partners in the collective bargaining process;

ensure that wages settlements in the public sector support the competitiveness efforts in the private sector (bearing in mind the important signalling effect of public sector wages).

The proposed monitoring system for wage and productivity levels proved particularly controversial. The original German plan would have achieved this partly by forcing countries to end the indexing of wages to inflation – a move strongly opposed by a number of Member States, in particular Belgium which feared this would undermine its social model.[58] However, the final version does not oblige countries to give up indexing but, if they do not, each government must implement other measures to ensure wages develop in line with productivity.

The second example applies to a bail-out country, Ireland.[59] The Irish government committed itself in the Memorandum of Understanding to cut its national minimum wage by a euro an hour. This decision was justified by the National Recovery Plan 2011–14[60] in the following terms:

Where a NMW is imposed at a level higher than the equilibrium wage rate, unemployment will result. Some workers will be willing to work for a wage lower than NMW but employers are restricted from providing these job opportunities. Other negative effects include:

- Acting as a barrier for younger and less skilled workers to enter the labour force and take up jobs;
- Preventing SMEs from adjusting wage costs downward in order to maintain viability and improve competitiveness; and
- Reducing the capacity of the services sector to generate additional activity and employment through lower prices for consumers.

---

[58] P Hollinger and P Spiegel, 'Cracks over Franco-German Eurozone plan' *FT com*, 4 February 2011. *Cf* Council Recommendation 2011/C 209/01 on the National Reform Programme 2011 of Belgium and delivering a Council Opinion on the updated Stability Programme of Belgium 2011–14 ([2011] OJ C209/1) which identifies the 'system of wage bargaining and wage indexation' as a problem needing reform, a point reiterated in the Council Recommendation 2011/C 217/15 on the implementation of the broad guidelines for the economic policies of the Member States whose currency is the euro ([2011] OJ L217/15), para 5.

[59] See Implementing Decision 2011/77/EU ([2011] OJ L30/34) on granting Union financial assistance to Ireland for a period of three years under the provisions of the Treaty and Regulation (EU) No 407/2010 of 11 May 2010 establishing a European financial stabilisation mechanism. The accompanying Memorandum of Understanding signed on 16 December 2010 and its first update lay down the economic policy conditions on the basis of which the financial assistance is granted. Implementing Decision 2011/77/EU was amended by Implementing Decision 2011/326/EU ([2011] OJ L147/17).

[60] budget.gov.ie/RecoveryPlan.aspx (last accessed 11 Dec 2011).

In addition, collective agreements (properly known as Registered Employment Agreements or Employment Regulation Orders) in the agricultural, catering, construction and electrical contracting sectors have also been repealed. As the National Recovery Plan states:

> Both types of agreements constitute another form of labour market rigidity by preventing wage levels from adjusting. This in turn affects the sustainability of existing jobs and may also prevent the creation of new jobs, particularly for younger people disproportionately affected by the employment crises who form part of the labour force for these sectors.[61]

While a number of these agreements had been around for over 50 years and could result in arbitrary geographical divisions,[62] the removal of the agreements affected some of the lowest paid workers. In recognition of this, the reduction in the minimum wage was, in fact, reversed in the summer of 2011.

C. The Way Forward

The examples taken from the EuroPlus Pact and the Irish MoU illustrate the extent to which EU law is responsible for shaking up systems of national labour law, usually resulting in a lower standard of protection unless powerful forces inside the states, such as the trade unions, are able to work together to prevent this. Some might argue that change is good and that, for too long, these very same forces have sought to promote the interests of insiders (those in jobs) over outsiders (those out of work) and, particularly in times of crisis, this needs to change. They would argue that the EU's mission now should be to provide a reasonable standard of living to those currently out of work by providing employment opportunities, rather than feather-bedding those already in employment. The picture is, however, less straightforward than this. Many of those in work are already 'outsiders' due to their precarious contracts (eg as temps, part-time workers). The reduction in wage protection has a significant effect on this group which tends to be dominated by women and ethnic minorities, all of whom belong to groups which, under Article 10 TFEU, are subject to the EU's obligation to protect against discrimination.

This is where the Lisbon Treaty can and should make a difference. The horizontal provisions in Articles 7–13 TFEU are not merely decorative baubles on the top of the EU Christmas tree. They need to be considered in respect of all decision-making at EU level, and at national level too when national policy makers are acting in the sphere of EU law. While they might not reverse the policy choices themselves, the execution of the policy might well need to be adapted to accommodate some of the horizontal interests.

---

[61] Ibid, p 37.
[62] See the Duffy/Walsh report commissioned by the Irish government in accordance its commitment in the MoU to hold an independent review of the Framework REA and ERO agreements: www.djei.ie/publications/employment/2011/Report_ERO_REA.pdf.

V. Conclusions

The problem identified by this chapter is how to develop an EU-level social policy going forward, a policy which manages to reconcile an ever-expanding range of competing interests, rights and policies many of which are derived from a variety of sources. While no simple formula can produce the 'right' outcome, transparency in decision-making and an articulation of the interests being balanced would provide a good starting point. This is what the Court of Justice called for in *Volker and Schecke*,[63] the first case in which the Court struck down a piece of EU secondary legislation for non-compliance with the Charter of Fundamental Rights. In that case the institutions had to balance the interests of taxpayers, who had a right to be kept informed of the use of public funds, with the rights to privacy of individuals in receipt of public money. The Court said:

> the fact remains that striking a *proper balance* between the various interests involved made it necessary for the institutions, before adopting the provisions whose validity is contested, to ascertain whether publication via a single freely consultable website in each Member State of data by name relating to all the beneficiaries concerned and the precise amounts received by each of them ... [was proportionate] (emphasis applied).[64]

The Court concluded that there was nothing to show that when adopting the legislation

> the Council and the Commission took into consideration methods of publishing information on the beneficiaries concerned which would be consistent with the objective of such publication while at the same time causing less interference with those beneficiaries' right to respect for their private life in general and to protection of their personal data in particular.[65]

The Court therefore rightly refused to second guess the institutions as to what would be a more proportionate response but it did lean on the institutions hard to clarify what they were doing and why. This may be a necessary first step to recognising and balancing social rights and policies in the EU in the post-Lisbon world.

---

[63] See Joined Cases C-92/09 and C-93/09 *Volker and Markus Schecke GbR and Hartmut Eifert v Land Hessen* [2010] ECR I-11063, para 81.
[64] Ibid, para 79.
[65] Ibid, para 81.

3

The Protection of Fundamental Rights within Europe's Internal Market after Lisbon – An Endeavour for More Harmony

SYBE A DE VRIES*

I. Introduction

Fundamental 'human rights' were not mentioned in the original Treaties and it was only later that they came to play a significant role in EU law.[1] The Treaties did, however, contain provisions which are *similar* to fundamental rights, such as the principle of non-discrimination and the principle of equal pay for men and women.[2] But it was not until the adoption of the Maastricht Treaty (1992) that a formal recognition was given to human rights as part of EU law. Later an 'EU Bill of Rights' was set up through the adoption of the Charter of Fundamental Rights, solemnly proclaimed in Nice (2000) but without being granted binding effect. And now the Lisbon Treaty (2009) has entered into force, marking a new phase in the remarkable expansion of fundamental rights protection at the level of the European Union, by inter alia declaring the Charter legally binding. This 'constitutional coming-of-age'[3] of fundamental rights protection, of course, triggers a number of interesting questions. One of these questions concerns the interplay between EU free movement rules and fundamental rights.

Long before the Treaty of Maastricht entered into force, fundamental rights became, through the European Court of Justice's case law, intertwined with

---

* Dr Sybe A de Vries is Jean Monnet Chair in EU Single Market Law and Fundamental Rights at the Europa Institute, Utrecht University. The author would like to thank Wei Pao Chan and Wies Smit for their editing work. This article is partly based on an earlier version and more extensive publication in SA de Vries, X Groussot and G Thor Petursson, *Balancing Fundamental Rights with the EU Treaty Freedoms: The European Court of Justice as 'tightrope' walker* (The Hague, Eleven International Publishing, 2012).

[1] TC Hartley, *The foundations of European Union law: An introduction to the constitutional and administrative law of the European Union*, 7th edn (Oxford, Oxford University Press, 2010) 143.

[2] See PJG Kapteyn, 'Stauder' in TWB Beukers, HJ van Harten and S Prechal (eds), *Het recht van de Europese Unie* (Den Haag, Boom Juridische uitgevers, 2010) 38.

[3] G de Búrca, '16 – The Evolution of EU Human Rights Law' in P Craig and G de Búrca, *The Evolution of EU Law – Second Edition* (Oxford, Oxford University Press, 2011) 481.

common market principles. The development of fundamental rights as general principles of EU law guiding the interpretation of EU law also had ramifications for the common market. More recent cases such as *Schmidberger*, *Viking*, *Laval* or *Omega* make this even more apparent.[4] But these cases show how fundamental rights may clash with the 'fundamental', economic freedoms as well; a conflict that could perhaps be seen as a 'clash of titans' by analogy. The clash of titans is after all a harsh battle characterised by violence, where Perseus, the Greek mythological hero, is finally able to defeat the archaic monsters.

Quite different and stripped of all mythological frills, is Plato's 'more secular' praise for harmony in 'The Republic', where Socrates turns to the final stage in the construction of the just city and the study of the Form of the Good, which has been explained as harmony, order, balance and proportion. The delicate balancing exercise, in which the ECJ has had to engage itself, could be part of the endeavour for closer harmony between these opposing interests. The central question here is whether the balance between protecting fundamental rights and Treaty freedoms has been rightly struck, taking into account the changed EU legal framework. Article 6 TEU underlines the important status fundamental rights have gained in EU law by stating that the Charter of Fundamental Rights of the EU shall have the same legal value as the Treaties; that the 'Union shall accede to the European Convention for the Protection of Human Rights and Fundamental Freedoms' and that 'Fundamental rights, as guaranteed by the European Convention for the Protection of Human Rights and Fundamental Freedoms and as they result from the constitutional traditions common to the Member States, shall constitute general principles of the Union's law'.

In the following the development of fundamental rights as general principles of EU law will be briefly discussed first (Section II). Hereafter a number of examples of cases, in which the Court has had to balance conflicting fundamental rights with fundamental Treaty freedoms, will be given (Section III). The subsequent section contains an assessment of the main Treaty changes due to the Treaty of Lisbon (Section IV). In the last section, the balancing approach of the Court will be assessed.

II. Development of Fundamental Rights as General Principles in the Court of Justice's Case Law: A Classification

The development of fundamental rights at EU level has first taken place in the case law of the European Court of Justice. In the case *Stauder* the ECJ, for the first

---

[4] Case C-112/00 *Eugen Schmidberger v Internationale Transporte und Planzüge v Austria* [2003] ECR I-5659; Case C-341/05 *Laval un Partneri Ltd v Svenska Byggnadsarbetareförbundet and others* [2007] ECR I-11767; Case C-438/05 *International Transport Workers' Federation and Finnish Seamen's Union v Viking Line ABP and OÜ Viking Line Eesti* [2007] ECR I-10779. Case C-36/02 *Omega Spielhallen- und Automatenaufstellungs- GmbH v Oberbürgermeisterin der Bundesstadt Bonn* [2004] ECR I-9609.

time, recognised a fundamental right as a general principle of European law.[5] In this case the question was put to the ECJ whether the requirement that the sale of cheap butter to welfare recipients with a view to reduce the so-called 'butter-mountain' was subject to the condition that the names of the beneficiaries were divulged, was in conformity with the general principles of law. In the *Internationale Handelsgesellschaft* case the ECJ held that 'respect for fundamental rights forms an integral part of the general principles of law protected by the Court of Justice'. Furthermore, the Court referred to the constitutional traditions common to the Member States as source of inspiration. Ever since, the Court has had to pronounce upon various questions raised in different types of cases which concerned fundamental rights. Thereby, roughly speaking, three categories of cases can be discerned.[6]

The first category of cases concerns cases where infringements of fundamental rights by the *EU institutions* were at issue, such as *Stauder* and *Internationale Handelsgesellschaft*.[7] The more recent *Volker and Schecke* case, wherein the Court declared certain provisions of an agricultural regulation invalid as they constituted an unjustified interference with the Charter, is also an example of this category (see below, Section IV.B).[8]

A second category concerns cases where actions by the *Member States* may lead to an infringement of fundamental rights either (i) in implementing EU law, or (ii) in deviating from the free movement rules, or (iii) where Member States invoke fundamental rights as a justification for restrictions on free movement. Regarding (i), this category is relatively well-defined and the least contested and involves the implementation of directives or framework decisions, the application of regulations and the enforcement of EU law.[9]

Regarding (ii) the *locus classicus* is the *ERT* case,[10] the Greek television monopoly case, where the free movement of services was at issue. In this process of justification, Article 10 of the ECHR, the freedom of expression, had to be taken into account. The ECJ found that the public policy, public security and public health derogations must be interpreted and applied in such a way that they respect the general principle enshrined in Article 10 ECHR.

---

[5] Case 29/69 *Erich Stauder v City of Ulm – Sozialamt* [1969] ECR 419.

[6] Compare: Editorial comments, 'The scope of application of the general principles of Union law: An ever expanding Union?' (2010) 47 *CML Rev* 1589, 1590: here a slightly different but still similar classification of situations falling within the scope of the Treaties is made. See also S Prechal, S de Vries and H van Eijken, 'The Principle of Attributed Powers and the Scope of EU Law' in LFM Besselink, FJL Pennings and S Prechal (eds), *The eclipse of the legality principle in the European Union* (Alphen aan den Rijn, Kluwer Law International, 2011) ch 12, 216–18.

[7] Case 29/69 *Stauder*, above n 5; Case 11/70 *Internationale Handelsgesellschaft mbH v Einfuhr- und Vorratsstelle für Getreide und Futtermittel* [1970] ECR 1125.

[8] Cases C-92/09 and C-93/09 *Volker und Markus Schecke GbR and Hartmut Eifert v Land Hessen* [2010] ECR I-11063.

[9] This is also referred to as the Wachauf line of cases: see also the chapter by X Groussot in this book (ch 4); Case 5/88, *Hubert Wachauf v Bundesamt für Ernährung und Forstwirtschaft* [1989] ECR 2609.

[10] Case C-260/89 *Ellinki Radiophonia Tileorassi AE (ERT) v Dimotiki Etairia Pliroforissis and Sotirios Kouvelas* [1991] ECR I-2925.

Regarding (iii), which could be seen as a variation on the foregoing category of cases, Member States may also rely on fundamental rights as a *justification* for restrictions on free movement. *Schmidberger*, *Omega* or *Laval* are examples of cases where the Court accepts that fundamental rights, apart from being used to limit a Member State's action under a derogation, may themselves be relied upon as a derogation from the Treaty freedoms.[11] This category of cases will be analysed in more detail below.

In several cases of the ECJ where fundamental rights played a significant role, the EU dimension – or cross-border link – was less evident or even absent, which raises the question to what extent there is a self-standing obligation under EU law to respect fundamental rights. EU fundamental rights may after all only be invoked, whenever the contested measure comes within the *scope of EU law*. As it is not always clear how the scope of EU law should be defined, this third category of cases is contentious as it may open the door to an 'autonomous' application of EU fundamental rights.[12] In her Opinion in the *Ruiz Zambrano* case Advocate General Sharpston even suggested extending the application of fundamental rights to situations in which the EU is competent to act, whenever there exists an exclusive or shared competence, irrespective of the actual exercise of this competence, or whether a Treaty provision is directly applicable. The Court, however, did not pronounce on the applicability of fundamental rights to this case. Instead, it only referred to Article 20 TFEU, which 'confers the status of citizen of the Union on every person holding the nationality of a Member State', and held that, without hesitation and extensive argumentation, 'citizenship of the Union is intended to be the fundamental status of nationals of the Member States'.[13] Arguably, the enjoyment of – at least certain – fundamental rights could be qualified as crucial for the enjoyment of European citizenship's rights.[14] But it has also

---

[11] Case C-112/00 *Schmidberger*, above n 4; Case C-36/02 *Omega*, above n 4; Case C-341/05 *Laval*, above n 4.

[12] A case which reveals how broad the potential scope of application of EU law can be in respect of fundamental rights' protection is *Karner*. Here the ECJ proceeded with a self-standing test under Article 10 ECHR in reviewing an Austrian law, which was not caught by Article 34 TFEU since it was considered a selling arrangement within the meaning of *Keck*: Case C-71/02 *Herbert Karner Industrie-Auktionen GmbH vTroostwijk GmbH* [2004] ECR I-3025. See for a critical reflection on this case: J Kühling, 'Fundamental Rights' in A von Bogdandy and J Bast (eds), *Principles of European Constitutional Law*, 2nd rev edn (Oxford, Hart Publishing, 2010) 500. In a similar vein, the ECJ decided in *Kücükdeveci* that, due to the mere existence of Directive 2000/78 establishing a general framework on equal treatment in employment and occupation, a German law discriminating on grounds of age fell within the scope of EU law and triggered the EU general principle of non-discrimination on grounds of age: Case C-555/07 *Seda Kücükdeveci v Swedex GmbH & Co* [2010] ECR I-365. The judgment in *Prigge*, which concerned a collective agreement by Lufthansa and its pilots pursuant to which the employment contract for pilots is terminated when they reach 60 years of age, does not only confirm the Court's approach in *Kücükdeveci* but also extends the scope of the Directive and thus the general principle of non-discrimination on grounds of age to actions by social partners: Case C-447/09 *Reinhard Prigge and others v Deutsche Lufthansa AG* (ECJ, 13 September 2011), nyr.

[13] Case C-34/09 *Gerardo Ruiz Zambrano v Office national de l'emploi (ONEm)* (ECJ, 8 March 2011), nyr, paras 40–42. See also H van Eijken and SA de Vries, 'A new route into the promised land? Being a European citizen after Ruiz Zambrano' (2011) 36 *EL Rev* 704.

[14] See also L Azoulai, 'A comment on the Ruiz Zambrano judgment: a genuine European integration' on EUDOCitizenship, available at: eudo-citizenship.eu/citizenship-news/457-a-comment-on-the-ruiz-

been rightly submitted that an all too expansive understanding of the scope of EU fundamental rights protection on the basis of *Ruiz Zambrano* would meet considerable resistance on the part of the Member States; a conflict that the ECJ does not strive for.[15] The more recent judgment in the *Dereci* case seems to reinforce a more hesitant approach of the Court, refusing to extend EU fundamental rights protection through a broad interpretation of the citizenship provisions.[16]

The case law of the ECJ has been based on the recognition of fundamental rights as (unwritten) general principles of EU law. Now the Treaty of Lisbon has entered into force and the Charter of Fundamental Rights has become binding, difficult questions are raised

> about the constitutional interplay between unwritten and written fundamental rights within the Union legal order. Whether the Charter will eventually displace the general principles as the Court's primary reference point; or whether the Court will continue to prefer to rely on its own case law.[17]

This issue will be addressed later (see below, Section IV).

In the following section, the case law of the Court on fundamental rights and fundamental freedoms will be addressed first.

III. The Case Law of the ECJ Regarding Fundamental Rights And Economic Freedoms

It took some time before the Court was confronted with cases where fundamental rights were invoked as justification per se for restrictions on free movement. *Schmidberger* was the first crucial case in which the ECJ was forced to balance the free movement of goods with the protection of fundamental rights. In this section a series of judgments, beginning with *Schmidberger*, will be presented in which the Court has sought to determine the margins of fundamental rights' protection by Member States within the EU internal market framework.

A. *Schmidberger*

Schmidberger is, of course, a famous example of a case where a fundamental right, the right to freedom of expression and assembly, had to be balanced with a

---

zambrano-judgment-a-genuine-european-integration. See also A von Bogdandy, M Kottmann, C Antpöhler, J Dickschen, S Hentrei and M Smrkolj, 'Reverse Solange – Protecting the Essence of Fundamental Rights against EU Member States' (2012) 49 *CML Rev* 489–520.

[15] K Hailbronner and D Thym, 'Case law' (2011) 48 *CML Rev* 1253, 1269–70.

[16] Case C-256/11 *Murat Dereci and others v Bundesministerium für Inneres* (ECJ, 15 November 2011), nyr. See also N Nic Shuibhne, 'Case Law – (Some of) The Kids Are All Right: Comment on McCarthy and Dereci' (2012) 49 *CML Rev* 349–80.

[17] Editorial comments (2010) 47 *CML Rev* 1589, above n 6, 1595.

'fundamental' freedom, the free movement of goods.[18] A *locus classicus* for conflicting rights in EU law.

The case involved a demonstration by environmentalists on the Brenner motorway in Austria, closing the motorway to traffic for nearly 30 hours. Permission for this demonstration was (implicitly) granted by the Austrian authorities. The question was whether the Austrian authorities could be held liable for an infringement of EU law under Article 34 TFEU (the free movement of goods) in conjunction with the principle of Community loyalty as now laid down in Article 4(3) TEU, as the Austrian authorities had not completely banned the demonstration on such an important motorway. According to the Court, thereby referring to its judgment in *Commission v France (Spanish Strawberries)*, the free movement of goods as laid down in Article 34 TFEU was indeed restricted.

But these restrictions were justifiable by the protection of fundamental rights, which form an integral part of the general principles of EU law. The Austrian court (Oberlandesgericht Innsbruck) had explicitly asked whether the free movement of goods should prevail over the fundamental rights at issue. In answering that question the Court held that the freedom of expression and assembly are not absolute – unlike other fundamental rights enshrined in the European Convention on the Protection of Human Rights – and must be viewed in relation to its social purpose. At the same time the ECJ recognised that

> whilst the free movement of goods constitutes one of the fundamental principles in the scheme of the Treaty, it may, in certain circumstances, be subject to restrictions for the reasons laid down in Article 36 of that Treaty or for overriding requirements relating to the public interest, in accordance with the Court's consistent case-law.[19]

Hence, a fair balance between the interests of free trade and freedom of expression must be struck, and Member States enjoy a wide margin of discretion in that regard. According to the ECJ, 'the specific aims of the demonstration are not in themselves material in legal proceedings such as those instituted by Schmidberger'.[20]

The ECJ then sums up a number of factors which make the restriction on the free movement of goods proportionate in the light of the protection of fundamental rights. First, the demonstration took place following a request for authorisation from the national authorities. Secondly, the demonstration took place on a single route, on a single occasion and during a limited period and was thus limited by comparison with the geographical scale and intrinsic seriousness. Thirdly, the purpose of the demonstration was not to restrict trade in goods of a particular type or from a particular source. Fourthly, supportive administrative measures were taken to limit the implications of the demonstration. Moreover, it was, according to the Court, clear that the demonstration did not give rise to a general climate of insecurity, which had a negative effect on trade. Lastly, an outright *ban*

---

[18] Case C-112/00 *Schmidberger*, above n 4.
[19] Ibid, para 78.
[20] Ibid, para 66.

of the demonstration would have led to an unjustifiable interference with the fundamental rights of the demonstrators.[21]

B. *Omega*

Omega was a German company operating the *laserdrome* in Germany, a place used to practice laser games. In a laser game the players try to hit with so called submachine-gun-type laser targeting devices *sensory tags* which are normally fixed to jackets worn by the players, and this equipment and technology were supplied by the British company Pulsar. In other words, we are dealing here with a kind of 'clash of the titans' simulation game with modern weapons in modern times.

But the police of the German State Nordrhein-Westfalen ordered a prohibition of these games as they constituted a danger to public order. Acts of simulated homicide and the trivialisation of violence were contrary to fundamental values prevailing in public opinion. Omega inter alia argued that the order was contrary to EU law, in particular the free movement of services.

The ECJ held that the free movement of services was affected, but could be justified. According to the Court it was clear that the commercial exploitation of games involving the simulated killing of human beings infringed a fundamental value enshrined in the national constitution, namely human dignity. The Court then held that 'the Community legal order undeniably strives to ensure respect for human dignity as a general principle of law'. And

> [t]here can therefore be no doubt that the objective of protecting human dignity is compatible with Community law, it being immaterial in that respect that, in Germany, the principle of respect for human dignity has a particular status as an independent fundamental right.[22]

After having defined human dignity as a general principle of EU law, it went on to assess the proportionality of the German order in the light of the protection of human dignity. According to the Court, the need for and adoption of provisions such as the German prohibition on laser games are not excluded merely because one Member State has chosen a different system of protection than another. In other words, there is no need for one conception which is shared by all Member States as to the way in which the fundamental right is to be protected. And it came – rather quickly – to the conclusion that the German measure corresponded to the level of protection of human dignity which the national constitution seeks to guarantee in the territory of the Federal Republic of Germany.

The particularity of this case is that the Court first defines a typically *German* concept of human dignity as a general principle of *EU* law, and then, while applying the proportionality test, it shows a predominantly Member State-friendly approach.[23]

---

[21] Ibid, paras 84–89.
[22] Case C-36/02 *Omega*, above n 4, para 34.
[23] N Nic Shuibhne, 'Margins of appreciation: national values, fundamental rights and EC free movement law' (2009) 34 *EL Rev* 230, 254.

C. Sayn-Wittgenstein

A case that is similar to *Omega* is the *Sayn-Wittgenstein* case. This fairly unique case involved a refusal by the Austrian authorities to register the name *Fürstin* von Sayn-Wittgenstein. Under the Austrian Law on the abolition of the nobility, which has a constitutional status in accordance with the Federal Constitutional Law, it is prohibited to use titles like 'Fürst' or 'Fürstin'. Ilonka Fürstin von Sayn-Wittgenstein is an Austrian citizen and was formerly named Havel, née Kerekes. After her adoption as an adult by the German Fürst von Sayn-Wittgenstein, she obtained the title 'Fürstin'. The Austrian authorities on adoption granted her with a birth certificate with the name and title she had acquired in Germany. But later on it was established that the title 'Fürstin' could not be registered in Austria under Austrian law. Ilonka von Sayn-Wittgenstein challenged this decision before the Austrian administrative court, which asked whether Article 21 TFEU precludes legislation pursuant to which the competent authorities of a Member State refuse to recognise the surname of an (adult) adoptee, determined in another Member State, in so far as it contains a title of nobility which is not permissible under the (constitutional) law of the former Member State. According to the Court,

> the refusal, by the authorities of a Member State, to recognise all the elements of the surname of a national of that State as determined in another Member State, in which that national resides, and as entered for 15 years in the register of civil status of the first Member State, is a restriction on the freedoms conferred by Article 21 TFEU on every citizen of the Union.[24]

For the justification of this restriction the Austrian authorities referred to the objective of public policy. Regarding this exception ground the ECJ stated that

> the concept of public policy as justification for a derogation from a fundamental freedom must be interpreted strictly, so that its scope cannot be determined unilaterally by each Member State without any control by the European Union institutions ... Thus, public policy may be relied on only if there is a genuine and sufficiently serious threat to a fundamental interest of society.

At this point the Court referred to the *Omega* case (see above). It then continued by stating that

> the specific circumstances which may justify recourse to the concept of public policy may vary from one Member State to another and from one era to another. The competent national authorities must therefore be allowed a margin of discretion within the limits imposed by the Treaty.[25]

---

[24] Case C-208/09 *Ilonka Sayn-Wittgenstein v Landeshauptmann von Wien* (ECJ, 22 December 2010), nyr, para 71.
[25] Ibid, paras 86–87.

The Austrian government had stated that the Law on the abolition of the nobility constitutes implementation of the more general principle of equality before the law of all Austrian citizens and, considering this argument, the Court referred to the Charter of Fundamental Rights, which includes the principle of equality as a general principle of Union law. Interestingly it also, within the context of the proportionality test, referred to Article 4(2) TEU, which states the following: 'The Union shall respect the equality of Member States before the Treaties as well as their national identities, inherent in their fundamental structures, political and constitutional, inclusive of regional and local self-government'. The EU thus recognises and respects the national identity of her Member States, which also encompasses the republican state form.

Two interesting features of this case, which to some extent can be found in the *Omega* judgment as well, are that first the Court explicitly refers to Article 4(2) TEU and appears to be very sensitive to the argument based on the constitutional identity of Austria.[26] And, secondly, there is the rather broad interpretation of the concept of public policy. After all, since cases like *Bouchereau* and *Calfa*[27] one of the conditions that need to be fulfilled in order to successfully rely on public policy is that there must be a genuine and sufficiently serious threat to a fundamental interest of society. This strict requirement is also laid down in Article 27 of Directive 2004/38, the 'Citizenship Directive', which allows Member States to restrict the migration rights of EU citizens only under very limited circumstances.[28] But apparently in some cases the Court is willing to accept a broader reading of the public-policy exception. In the *Josemans* case, for instance, the Court held that

> combating drug tourism and the accompanying public nuisance is part of combating drugs. It concerns both the maintenance of public order and the protection of the health of citizens, at the level of the Member States and also of the European Union.[29]

It can be argued that the ECJ in fact 'fills in' the public-policy exception, which was brought forward by the intervening parties, Belgium, Germany and France, with a rule of reason exception. It is unclear to what extent the public-policy exception could have been invoked as an independent justification ground without involving the fight against drugs as an additional interest.[30]

---

[26] Regarding this see in particular: L Besselink, 'National and constitutional identity before and after Lisbon' (2010) 6 *Utrecht Law Review* 36. See also L Besselink, 'Case Law' (2012) 49 *CML Rev* 671–94.
[27] Case 30/77 *R v Bouchereau* [1977] ECR 1999; Case C-348/96 *Criminal proceedings against Donatella Calfa* [1999] ECR I-11.
[28] Directive 2004/38/EC of the European Parliament and of the Council of 29 April 2004 on the right of citizens of the Union and their family members to move and reside freely within the territory of the Member States [2004] OJ L158/77.
[29] Case C-137/09 *Marc Michel Josemans v Burgemeester van Maastricht* (ECJ (Second Chamber), 16 December 2010), nyr, para 65.
[30] See HJ van Harten and H van Eijken, '"Lookin' for a little green bag..." en de werkingssfeer van het Unierecht' (2011) 4 *Nederlands tijdschrift voor Europees recht* 105, 112.

D. *Dynamic Medien*

Just like in *Omega* and *Sayn-Wittgenstein* the Court in *Dynamic Medien* accepted the Member States' considerable discretion in protecting fundamental rights and fundamental interests vis-à-vis economic freedoms.[31] In this case the dispute concerned the importation of Japanese cartoons called 'Animes' in DVD or video cassette format from the United Kingdom into Germany. The cartoons were examined before importation by the British Board of Film Classification (BBFC). The image storage media bore a BBFC label stating that they may be viewed only by adolescents aged 15 years or older. The German law on the protection of young persons, however, prohibits the sale by mail order of image storage media which have not been examined in Germany in accordance with that Law, and which do not bear an age-limit label corresponding to a classification decision from a higher regional authority or a national self-regulation body ('competent authority'). Dynamic Medien, a company and competitor of the importing company of the Japanese cartoons, started a procedure before the German court, which submitted preliminary questions to the ECJ. The questions were whether such a prohibition is contrary to the free movement of goods and, if so, whether this could be justified.

In examining the justification of the German law the ECJ held that the protection of the rights of the child is recognised by various international instruments and that those international instruments are among those concerning the protection of human rights of which it takes account in applying the general principles of Community law. Furthermore, the Court inter alia referred to the Charter of Fundamental Rights, which provides in Article 24(1) that children have the right to such protection and care as is necessary for their well-being. Regarding the proportionality of the German law and the examination procedure established by the national legislature in order to protect children against information and materials injurious to their well-being, the Court reiterated that

> the mere fact that a Member State has opted for a system of protection which differs from that adopted by another Member State cannot affect the assessment of the proportionality of the national provisions enacted to that end. Those provisions must be assessed solely by reference to the objective pursued and the level of protection which the Member State in question intends to provide. (See also *Omega* and *Sayn-Wittgenstein* above.)[32]

A particularly interesting feature of this case is that, contrary to the *Omega* and *Sayn-Wittgenstein* cases, the ECJ applied the proportionality test in a more procedural fashion in ruling that the examination procedure must be one which is readily accessible, can be completed within a reasonable period, and, if it leads to a refusal, the decision of refusal must be open to challenge before the courts. This has the consequence that Member States in exercising their powers to pursue fun-

---

[31] Case C-244/06 *Dynamic Medien Vertriebs GmbH v Avides Media AG* [2008] ECR I-505.
[32] Ibid, para 49.

damental rights have to take account of principles of good governance.[33] This approach is also clearly visible in other cases where Member States traditionally enjoy broad discretionary powers, like in the field of healthcare or gambling. In the *Watts* case, for instance, which concerned the compatibility of the British system of prior authorisation for medical treatment in another Member State with the free movement of services, the Court held the following:

> [I]n order for a system of prior authorisation to be justified even though it derogates from a fundamental freedom of that kind, it must in any event be based on objective, non-discriminatory criteria which are known in advance, in such a way as to circumscribe the exercise of the national authorities' discretion, so that it is not used arbitrarily. Such a system must furthermore be based on a procedural system which is easily accessible and capable of ensuring that a request for authorisation will be dealt with objectively and impartially within a reasonable time and refusals to grant authorisation must also be capable of being challenged in judicial or quasi-judicial proceedings.[34]

E. *Viking* and *Laval*

The well-known *Viking* and *Laval* cases are of quite a different nature.[35] Viking is a Finnish company that wished to reflag its vessel the *Rosella* under the Estonian flag. The reason for the change was a plan to man the ship with an Estonian crew that could be paid considerably less than the Finnish one. The International Transport Workers' Federation told its affiliates to boycott the *Rosella* and to take other solidarity industrial action. Viking sought an injunction in the English High Court, restraining the ITWF and Finnish Seamen's Union, now threatening strike action, from breaching the free movement of services and freedom of establishment provisions.

Laval was a Latvian company which won a contract to refurbish a school near Stockholm. The Latvian workers earned considerably less than the Swedish workers. The Swedish Labour Union wanted Laval to apply the collective agreement, but it refused, which led to a blockade by the Swedish construction workers of the building site.

In both cases the questions raised by the Swedish and English courts were whether the actions by the trade unions constituted a restriction on the EU economic freedoms, ie the freedom of establishment and the free movement of services, and whether their actions were justifiable. Focusing here on the Court's judgment in *Viking*, the ECJ first held that the right to take collective action, including the right to strike, is a fundamental right forming an integral part of the general principles of Community law. It referred to the European Social Charter,

---

[33] S Prechal, 'Topic One: National Applications of the Proportionality Principle – Free Movement and Procedural Requirements: Proportionality Reconsidered' (2008) 35 *Legal Issues of Economic Integration* 201.

[34] Case C-372/04 *The Queen (on the application of Yvonne Watts) v Bedford Primary Care Trust and Secretary of State for Health* [2006] ECR I-4325, para 116.

[35] Case C-438/05 *Viking*, above n 4; Case C-341/05 *Laval*, above n 4.

the ILO Convention and to the Charter of Fundamental Rights.[36] But the Court also held that the right to strike is subject to certain conditions – it referred to Article 28 of the Charter on Fundamental Rights and to restrictions in national law. It continued by stating that collective action is not excluded from the scope of the free movement provisions and that these provisions can be invoked against actions by trade unions. In other words, these free movement provisions have horizontal direct effect.[37]

It then went on to assess whether collective action can justify restrictions on the freedom of establishment. According to the Court, the right to take collective action for the protection of workers is a legitimate interest which in principle justifies a restriction of one of the fundamental freedoms. The Court stated that the Community has not only an economic, but also a social purpose and that social policy interests must be balanced with the free movement rules.

Although this reference to the social purpose of the Community should not only be seen as merely rhetoric as it may create its own social dynamic in future case law,[38] in assessing the proportionality of the collective action the ECJ leaves little room for the trade unions to justify their actions.[39] The national court must take into account that the right to collective action must serve the protection of workers, that jobs and labour conditions would indeed be under serious threat by reflagging the *Rosella*, that collective action is one of the ways that may serve members' interests, and that account should be taken of less restrictive means before initiating a strike.

IV. Intermezzo: Treaty of Lisbon and the Charter of Fundamental Rights

Nearly all cases that are discussed above had been decided before the Treaty of Lisbon was adopted. The recognition of fundamental rights as general principles of EU law has so far provided sufficient grounds for the ECJ to at least admit these rights as legitimate interests which may justify restrictions on the four freedoms.

But as stated before, the position of fundamental rights in EU law has been given a new impetus by the inclusion of Article 6 TEU. Article 6 of the EU Treaty

---

[36] Case C-438/05 *Viking*, above n 4, para 43.
[37] See S Prechal and S de Vries, 'Seamless web of judicial protection in the internal market?' (2009) 34 *EL Rev* 5.
[38] S Prechal and S de Vries, 'Viking/Laval en de grondslagen van het internemarktrecht' (2008) 11 *Sociaal-Economische Wetgeving* 425, 433.
[39] See J Malmberg and T Sigeman, 'Industrial actions and EU economic freedoms: the autonomous collective bargaining model curtailed by the European Court of Justice' (2008) 45 *CML Rev* 1115, 1130. With regard to the follow-up of, in particular, the *Laval* case, see U Bernitz and N Reich, 'Case No. A 268/04, The Labour Court, Sweden (Arbetsdomstolen) Judgment No. 89/09 of 2 December 2009, Laval un Partneri Ltd. v. Svenska Bygggnadsarbetareförbundet et al' (2011) 48 *CML Rev* 603.

now recognises the binding force of the Charter of Fundamental Rights; it embraces the intention to accede to the European Convention on the Protection of Human Rights and Fundamental Freedoms and codifies the European Court of Justice's case law that fundamental rights shall constitute general principles of Union law. But even before the Treaty of Lisbon (2009) the Charter, since its proclamation in 2000 in Nice, had been – albeit only recently – increasingly relied upon by the EU courts as an authoritative source of fundamental rights.[40] It must be admitted, though, that at first the CJEU was very reluctant to refer to the Charter in its case law on fundamental rights.[41] The question which now looms up is whether the Charter is still merely a codifying document adding little to the existing case law or an autonomous, self-standing source of law generating its own meaning.[42]

A. Content of the Charter

(i) Mixed Approach

Taking a closer look at the Charter it is striking to see that there is no clear distinction between classic political and civil rights on the one hand, and social and economic rights on the other. There appears to be a more 'mixed approach' to fundamental rights in general. Furthermore, some innovative rights and prohibitions are included in the Charter, such as the prohibition on reproductive human cloning, whereas others are not. An example is the protection of minorities. According to Craig and De Búrca 'the Charter could perhaps best be described as a creative distillation of the rights contained in the various European and international agreements and national constitutions on which the ECJ had for some years already drawn'.[43]

The Charter contains seven titles: Title I (Dignity), Title II (Freedoms), Title III (Equality), Title IV (Solidarity), Title V (Citizens' Rights), Title VI (Justice) and Title VII (General provisions governing the interpretation and application of the charter).

Although no clear distinction between classic civil rights and social rights is made, there is a distinction between 'rights' and 'principles'. Article 52(5) states that

> [t]he provisions of this Charter which contain principles may be implemented by legislative and executive acts taken by institutions, bodies, offices and agencies of the Union, and by acts of Member States when they are implementing Union law, in the exercise of their respective powers. They shall be *judicially cognisable only* in the interpretation of

---

[40] cf D Chalmers and G Monti, *European Union law: text and materials: updating supplement* (Cambridge, Cambridge University Press, 2008) 65.
[41] J Morijn, 'Balancing Fundamental Rights and Common Market Freedoms in Union Law: Schmidberger and Omega in the Light of the European Constitution' (2006) 12 *ELJ* 15, 19–20.
[42] cf Chalmers and Monti, *European Union law: text and materials*, above n 40, 69.
[43] P Craig and G De Búrca, *EU Law. Text, cases, and materials*, 5th edn (Oxford, Oxford University Press, 2011) ch 11 'Human Rights in the EU', 395.

such acts and in the ruling on their legality (emphasis added).

This much-debated and contentious provision perhaps seeks to distinguish between 'negatively-oriented civil and political rights and positively-oriented economic and social rights, with a view to rendering the latter largely non-justiciable'.[44] But the impact of this provision may be limited in so far as principles normally have to be further elaborated by the Union and as the courts are not really capable of reviewing such principles extensively.[45] They are sometimes so vaguely formulated that it will be difficult for the Courts to enforce them. The problem, however, remains that it cannot always be deduced from the explanations relating to the Charter of Fundamental Rights which provisions concern rights and which concern principles.

(ii) The Scope of the Charter Vis-à-vis the General Principles of EU Law

According to Article 51 of the Charter, the Charter only applies to acts of Member States when they *implement* EU law. How this condition should be interpreted and how it relates to the application of general principles of EU law still remains unclear. A literal reading of the terms 'implementing EU law' seems to suggest that the scope of application of the Charter is narrower than the scope of application of general principles of EU law which apply to Member States' actions falling within the scope of EU law.

But the explanations relating to the Charter refer to the Court's case law on general principles of EU law instead:

> As regards the Member States, it follows unambiguously from the case-law of the Court of Justice that the requirement to respect fundamental rights defined in the context of the Union is only binding on the Member States when they act in the scope of Union law (judgment of 13 July 1989, Case 5/88 *Wachauf* [1989] ECR 2609; judgment of 18 June 1991, Case C-260/89 *ERT* [1991] ECR I-2925; judgment of 18 December 1997, Case C-309/96 *Annibaldi* [1997] ECR I-7493). The Court of Justice confirmed this case-law in the following terms: 'In addition, it should be remembered that the requirements flowing from the protection of fundamental rights in the Community legal order are also binding on Member States when they implement Community rules . . .' (judgment of 13 April 2000, Case C-292/97 [2000] ECR I-2737, paragraph 37 of the grounds). Of course this rule, as enshrined in this Charter, applies to the central authorities as well as to regional or local bodies, and to public organisations, when they are implementing Union law.

Although the drafting process of the Charter may support a narrow interpretation of the terms 'implementing EU law',[46] the prevailing opinion in literature appears to be that the Charter should not detract from the case law of the Court of Justice

---

[44] Ibid, 398.
[45] R Barents, 'Een grondwet voor Europa (VI): de grondrechten' (2005) 2 *Nederlands tijdschrift voor Europees recht* 39, 44. T Tridimas, *The General Principles of EU Law*, 2nd edn (Oxford, Oxford University Press, 2006) 358–59.
[46] See also Editorial comments (2010) 47 *CML Rev* 1589, above n 6, 1596.

and therefore also be applicable in situations where the Member States do not implement EU law or merely act as agents of the EU, for example, where the fundamental Treaty freedoms are at issue.[47] Even if the Charter were, according to Article 51(1), not to apply to situations where Member States merely act within the scope of EU law, the general principles of EU law and the case law of the Court will. To prevent a dual regime giving rise to arbitrary divergences,[48] it has therefore been argued that, notwithstanding the above mentioned, the scope of application of the Charter should coincide with that of the general principles of EU law.[49]

However plausible this 'solution' may seem, it does not answer the question of what is meant by 'falling within the scope of EU law', triggering the application of fundamental rights; a question that has become even more pertinent now that the Court has considerably extended the reach of general principles of EU law in the *Kücükdeveci* case.[50] In this case the *existence* of a Directive establishing a general framework for equal treatment in the field of employment and occupation, the transposition time for which had expired, was sufficient to bring German legislation on calculation of the notice period for dismissal from employment within the scope of EU law. This had the important consequence that the fundamental right of non-discrimination on grounds of age, which, according to the ECJ, has been given specific expression in the Directive in the domain of employment and occupation,[51] should have been respected by the German legislator. The fact that the German rules did not concern a specific implementation measure of the applicable directive was irrelevant, according to the ECJ; it was sufficient that the matter was governed by the directive.[52] Rather than bringing the Charter and general principles of EU law together, *Kücükdeveci* therefore seems to do precisely the opposite.

The Court will have the chance to clarify the relationship between the Charter and general principles of EU law in the *Yoshida Iida* case.[53] One of the questions from the German court put to the ECJ in this case is whether 'fundamental rights which continue to apply as general principles of Union law under Article 6(3) EU stand autonomously and independently alongside the new fundamental rights laid down in the Charter in accordance with 6(1) EU'. This case is about the rights of a parent, who is a third country national and has custody of a non-dependent child who is a Union citizen, under the Citizenship Directive 2004/38, the Charter

---

[47] K Lenaerts and JA Gutiérrez-Fons, 'The constitutional allocation of powers and general principals of EU law' (2010) 47 *CML Rev* 1629, 1658–60; T Barkhuysen and AW Bos, 'De betekenis van het Handvest van de Grondrechten van de Europese Unie voor het bestuursrecht' (2011) 1 *Jurisprudentie Bestuursrecht Plus* 3, 15–16.

[48] M Dougan, 'The Treaty of Lisbon 2007: winning minds, not hearts' (2008) 45 *CML Rev* 617, 664–65; Lenaerts and Gutiérrez-Fons, 'The constitutional allocation of powers and general principals of EU law', above n 47, 1660.

[49] See also Lenaerts and Gutiérrez-Fons, ibid, 1660.

[50] Case C-555/07 *Kücükdeveci*, above n 12.

[51] Ibid, para 21; see also Case C-447/09 *Prigge*, above n 12, para 38.

[52] Editorial comments (2010) 47 *CML Rev* 1589, above n 6, 1592–93.

[53] Case C-40/11 *Yoshikazu Iida v City of Ulm* (decision of ECJ pending).

of Fundamental Rights and Article 8 ECHR. The case shows similarities with the *Zambrano* case, where, as stated above in Section II, the Advocate General advocated a broad interpretation of Article 51 of the Charter by proposing a more 'federalist approach'.

B. Added Value of the Charter

(i) In General

That the Charter is not merely a codifying document but has an important additional value to the existing fundamental rights which are recognised as general principles of EU law, is, for example, shown by the *Dynamic Medien* case, where the Court expressly referred to the Charter, in particular Article 24 thereof, to justify a new 'mandatory requirement', ie the protection of the child. It has therefore been argued that the Charter 'may contribute significantly to the discovery of general principles'.[54] At the same time, it must be prevented that the Charter is too frequently used as a panacea for problems which are unnecessarily translated into a fundamental rights application.[55]

The *DEB* case may also be evidence of the Charter generating its own meaning. In this case a question was raised by the German Court whether the EU legal principle of effectiveness would preclude a rule of German law which does not allow for the grant of legal aid to a company claiming state liability under EU law. According to the ECJ, the right of a legal person to effective access to justice concerns the principle of effective judicial protection, which is a general principle of EU law stemming from the constitutional traditions common to the Member States, and which has been enshrined in Articles 6 and 13 of the European Convention for the Protection of Human Rights and Fundamental Freedoms.[56] After having analysed the ECHR, which according to the Court does not per se *exclude* the possibility that *legal persons* have a right to effective judicial protection, the ECJ concludes that

> the principle of effective judicial protection, as enshrined in Article 47 of the Charter, must be interpreted as meaning that it is not impossible for legal persons to rely on that principle and that aid granted pursuant to that principle may cover, inter alia, dispensation from advance payment of the costs of proceedings and/or the assistance of a lawyer.[57]

As it is not entirely sure whether the European Convention for the Protection of Human Rights would allow for the possibility to grant legal persons this form of protection, the significance of the Charter is furthermore underlined by the

---

[54] Lenaerts and Gutiérrez-Fons, 'The constitutional allocation of powers and general principals of EU law', above n 47, 1660.
[55] See the Conference Report (annex).
[56] Case 279/09 *Deutsche Energiehandels- und Beratungsgesellschaft mbH (DEB) v Germany* [2010] ECR I-13849, para 29.
[57] Ibid, para 59.

Court's explicit reference to Article 52(3) of the Charter, which does not preclude the grant of wider protection of EU law.[58]

Another case of particular interest here is the above-mentioned *Volker and Schecke* case.[59] This case is about the publication of information on beneficiaries of agricultural aid, which is provided for by an EU Regulation. The Regulation required the publication of the names of the beneficiaries receiving certain agricultural aids. The question was whether this requirement was not contrary to the right to respect of private life (Article 7 of the Charter) and the right to protection of personal data (Article 8(1) of the Charter). The Regulation itself sought to enhance the transparency regarding the use of Community funds in the Common Agricultural Policy.

In assessing the validity of these provisions of the Regulation – which require the dissemination of the information on the beneficiaries of agricultural aid – in the light of fundamental rights, the Court only briefly referred to the European Convention and decided the case by *applying* the Charter instead.[60] Furthermore, the Court had to balance the different interests according to Article 52 of the Charter (see below).

(ii) The Importance of the Charter in the Conflict Between Fundamental Rights and Treaty Freedoms

Although questions remain as to the exact scope of application of the Charter, as to the distinction between rights and principles, and its relationship with the general principles of EU law as developed in the Court's case law, its emphasis on the fundamentality and universality of fundamental rights in EU law cannot be ignored. This should steer the orientation and interpretation of free movement rules in this field as well. Of course, the question remains: *how*? Two preliminary remarks should be made here. First, we have seen that the Charter played a role in recognising a fundamental right as mandatory requirement, which may justify a restriction on free movement (*Dynamic Medien*). And secondly, according to Article 52(1) of the Charter, the exercise of fundamental rights may be limited subject to the conditions, first, that the limitations are provided for by law and, secondly, that the limitations are necessary and proportionate (principle of proportionality). In *Volker and Schecke* this provision was applied by the ECJ, but in the context of an appraisal of an *EU regulation* and its conformity with fundamental rights:

> It follows from the foregoing that it does not appear that the institutions properly balanced, on the one hand, the objectives of ... Regulation No 1290/2005 and of Regulation

---

[58] Ibid, para 35.
[59] Cases C-92/09 and C-93/09 *Volker und Markus Schecke GbR and Hartmut Eifert v Land Hessen*, above n 8.
[60] A Pahladsingh and HJThM van Roosmalen, 'Het Handvest van de Grondrechten van de Europese Unie één jaar juridisch bindend: rechtspraak in kaart' (2011) 2 *Nederlands tijdschrift voor Europees recht* 54, 57.

No 259/2008 against, on the other, the rights which natural persons are recognised as having under Articles 7 and 8 of the Charter. Regard being had to the fact that derogations and limitations in relation to the protection of personal data must apply only in so far as is strictly necessary . . . and that it is possible to envisage measures which affect less adversely that fundamental right of natural persons and which still contribute effectively to the objectives of the European Union rules in question, it must be held that, by requiring the publication of the names of all natural persons who were beneficiaries of . . . aid and of the exact amounts received by those persons, the Council and the Commission exceeded the limits which compliance with the principle of proportionality imposes.[61]

The explicit reference to *limitations* as well as to *proportionality* entails that fundamental rights are – in principle – not absolute, which appears to embrace the Court of Justice's balancing approach (see below).

V. Balancing Free Movement and Fundamental Rights in a New Treaty Context

A. Introduction: Balancing in General

In legal doctrine the question has been raised how in general in cases of conflicting fundamental rights a judge can reach a reasonable and well-motivated judgment. Is there a neutral, objective methodology which the courts can use or apply to prevent value judgments, in which the political and moral conviction of the judge is implied?[62] According to Alexy's 'Law of Balancing' the court should not be afraid of engaging itself in the balancing of conflicting interests. It must be possible to justify the outcome of a case in a rational way by means of a well-motivated judgment. The Law of Balancing has been defined as 'the greater the degree of non-satisfaction of, or detriment to, one principle, the greater must be the importance of satisfying the other'.[63] Alexy's theory departs from the idea that it is not the weight or intrinsic value of a fundamental right or interest that is decisive, but the seriousness of the infringement and the importance of the right in realising general interest; hence the extent to which one principle is infringed for

---

[61] Cases C-92/09 and C-93/09 *Volker und Markus Schecke GbR and Hartmut Eifert v Land Hessen*, para 86, above n 8.
[62] JH Gerards, 'Belangenafweging bij rechterlijke toetsing aan fundamentele rechten', inaugural speech at Leiden University on 4 April 2006, 2, available at media.leidenuniv.nl/legacy/Schriftelijke%20versie%20oratie.pdf.
[63] X Groussot, 'Case C-275/06, *Productores de Música de España (Promusicae) v Telefónica de España SAU*, Judgment of the Court (Grand Chamber) of 28 January 2008, not yet reported – Rock the KaZaA: Another Clash of Fundamental Rights' (2008) 45 *CML Rev* 1745, 1760; R Alexy, *A Theory of Constitutional Rights* (trans J Rivers) (Oxford, Oxford University Press, 2010) 102.

the benefit or satisfaction of another principle.[64]

When it comes to balancing opposing fundamental rights the European Court of Human Rights (ECtHR) generally uses a 'margin of appreciation test'. It has been submitted that the ECtHR generally uses three steps to analyse a conflict between human rights:[65] First, a restriction to a right must be in accordance with or prescribed by law. Secondly, the purpose of the restriction must be within the remit of the legitimate aims prescribed by the article. And, thirdly, the restriction must be necessary in a democratic society. But the ECtHR allows for a wide margin of appreciation for the state when two fundamental rights clash. According to Groussot this appears from settled case law of the ECtHR, such as the *Chassagnou v France* case, where the ECtHR clearly embraced the balancing approach but with a wide margin of appreciation for the states:

> Where these 'rights and freedoms' are themselves among those guaranteed by the Convention or its Protocols, it must be accepted that the need to protect them may lead States to restrict other rights or freedoms likewise set forth in the Convention. It is precisely this constant search for a balance between the fundamental rights of each individual which constitutes the foundation of a 'democratic society'. The balancing of individual interests that may well be contradictory is a difficult matter, and Contracting States must have a broad margin of appreciation in this respect, since the national authorities are in principle better placed than the European Court to assess whether or not there is a 'pressing social need' capable of justifying interference with one of the rights guaranteed by the Convention.[66]

But the certainly delicate and intrusive balancing exercise may be qualified, or even avoided altogether, by the courts.[67] A first example is the technique of *categorisation*, which the courts may use to avoid balancing. Categorisation defines 'bright-line boundaries and then classifies fact situations as falling on one side or the other'.[68] The judge in fact takes away the necessity to engage itself in a balancing exercise. In EU law the classification of certain activities as non-economic by the ECJ, for instance, excludes the applicability of the free movement and competition rules with the important consequence that at the end no balancing is needed. The activity simply falls outside the scope of EU law. The Opinion of Advocate General Bot in *Josemans* may serve as an example of this approach, since, according to him, the Treaty rules on services did not apply to the activities of 'coffee shops' in the Netherlands, which sell soft drugs as well as fizzy drinks and sandwiches. According to the Advocate General the activities related to the sale of soft drugs operate outside the legal economic sphere of the internal market.

---

[64] Groussot, ibid, 1760–62.
[65] JA Sweeney, 'A 'Margin of Appreciation' in the Internal Market: Lessons from the European Court of Human Rights' (2007) 34 *Legal Issues of Economic Integration* 27, 30.
[66] Groussot, 'Rock the KaZaA: Another Clash of Fundamental Rights', above n 63, 1760; *Chassagou and others v France* App nos 25088/94, 28331/95 and 28443/95 (ECtHR, 24 April 1999), para 113.
[67] Gerards, 'Belangenafweging bij rechterlijke toetsing aan fundamentele rechten', above n 62, 7.
[68] KM Sullivan, 'Foreword: The Justices of Rules and Standards' (1992–93) 106 *Harvard Law Review* 22, 59.

The case concerned a Dutch measure preventing non-Dutch nationals from having access to Dutch 'coffee shops' (selling soft drugs).[69] Although the ECJ ruled that the sale of soft drugs did not fall within the scope of application of the Treaty provision on services, since trade in soft drugs is prohibited in all Member States, it did rule that the sale of other products in coffee shops was covered by the Treaty rules on services. As a consequence the measures restricting the sale of these products needed to be justified on grounds of public order. The Court's reasoning in *Josemans* is, in particular in the light of the number of tourists visiting coffee shops in the Netherlands, described as absurd[70] and the outcome of this case can therefore be seen as rather eccentric.

But *categorisation* is not often used by the ECJ as it generally adopts a functional approach, which entails that arguments relating to national competence do not curtail the application of the Treaty freedoms, such as the arguments raised in *Viking* and *Laval* on the fundamental right to strike and collective action.

Another example is the *Grogan* case, which concerned a dispute between the Irish Society for the Protection of Unborn Children (SPUC) and Grogan and other students distributing in Ireland information on abortion clinics in other Member States.[71] One of the questions of the national court was whether medical termination of pregnancy constitutes a service within the meaning of Article 57 TFEU. According to SPUC the provision of abortion could never constitute a service as it is grossly immoral and involves the destruction of the life of a human being. But the ECJ held that these arguments on the moral plane cannot influence the finding that in the Member States where abortion is provided, it is practised legally. Hence it constitutes a service within the meaning of EU law.[72] The distribution of information, however, was considered to constitute a manifestation of freedom of expression and not a service within the meaning of Article 56 TFEU, which meant that the Irish courts were free to prohibit these 'voluntary publications'.[73]

A second concept may be seen as a variation on categorisation and is referred to in legal literature, inter alia by Gerards, as *exclusionary reasons*. This concept implies that it is clear from the aims or intent of the measure, that the restriction on a fundamental right can never be justified.[74] In EU law, for instance, purely economic aims can never justify restrictions on free movement as this would amount to protectionism.[75] But if economic aims are crucial for the realisation of non-economic aims, they will be justifiable. What matters is whether the measure has a protectionist motive or purpose. This, for example, appears to have been the case in the *Spanish Strawberries* case – the forerunner of *Schmidberger* – where

---

[69] See Case C-137/09 *Josemans*, above n 29.
[70] See the chapter by Weatherill in this book (ch 1).
[71] Case C-159/90 *Society for the Protection of Unborn Children Ireland v Grogan and others* [1991] ECR I-4685.
[72] Ibid, paras 16–21.
[73] See also R Lawson, 'The Irish Abortion Cases: European Limits to National Sovereignty?' (1994) 1 *European Journal of Health Law* 167, 173–74.
[74] Gerards, 'Belangenafweging bij rechterlijke toetsing aan fundamentele rechten', above n 62, 12.
[75] Case C-398/98 *European Commission v Greece* [2001] ECR I-7915, para 30.

demonstrations of angry French farmers were intended to protect the sale of French agricultural products.[76] The protest movement

> consisted, inter alia, in the interception of lorries transporting such products in France and the destruction of their loads, violence against lorry drivers, threats against French supermarkets selling agricultural products originating in other Member States, and the damaging of those goods when on display in shops in France.[77]

In other words, the objective of the French demonstrators was, contrary to the demonstrators in *Schmidberger*, to restrict trade in goods and not to manifest their opinion in public.[78]

Another technique that may be used by the courts is a *procedural* test, which entails an examination into the thoroughness of the decision-making procedure and whether procedural guarantees have been taken into account by the regulating state restricting fundamental freedoms or rights. We have seen that the ECJ sometimes uses this technique as part of the proportionality test to review national measures in particularly sensitive areas, such as gambling or healthcare, where Member States have remained primarily competent (see also *Dynamic Medien*, Section III and below, Section V.B).

B. Balancing of Horizontal and Flanking Policy Interests with the Treaty Freedoms

When it comes to balancing opposing interests in *EU law*, the EU Courts and in particular the ECJ have had the most experience with cases where one of the Treaty exceptions to free movement were invoked, or the so-called 'rule of reason', allowing Member States – under certain conditions – to deviate from the rules on free movement whenever a general, non-economic, interest is at issue. These interests can be defined as horizontal and flanking policy interests.[79] Here the principle of proportionality plays a key role.

(i) Three Elements of the Proportionality Principle

The proportionality principle or test usually contains the following three elements:

– There must be a causal connection between the national measure and the aim pursued; the measure is relevant or pertinent;
– There is no alternative measure available which is less restrictive of trade or free movement generally;
– And there must be a relationship of proportionality between the obstacle introduced, on the one hand, and, on the other hand, the objective pursued thereby

---

[76] Case C-265/95 *European Commission v France* [1997] ECR I-6959 *(Spanish Strawberries)*.
[77] Ibid, para 2.
[78] See also Tridimas, *The General Principles of EU Law*, above n 45, 338.
[79] See SA de Vries, *Tensions within the internal market: the functioning of the internal market and the development of horizontal and flanking policies* (Groningen, European Law Publishing, 2006).

and its actual attainment. This is referred to as proportionality *stricto sensu*; meaning that the measure will be disproportionate if the restriction caused is out of proportion to the aim sought by or the result brought about by the national rule.[80]

But the Court rarely applies the third element of proportionality. An example of a case where the Court did question the proportionality *stricto sensu* of a national measure, is the *Danish Bottles* case. A Danish environmental measure stipulated that manufacturers must market beer and soft drinks in re-usable containers only.[81] The containers must be approved by the national agency for the protection of the environment, which may refuse approval of new kinds of containers under certain circumstances. However, these rules were amended in such a way that, provided a deposit-and-return system was established, non-approved containers, except for any form of metal container, could be used for quantities not exceeding 3000 hectolitres a year per producer and for drinks which were sold by foreign producers in order to test the market. The Court held that measures adopted to protect the environment must not

> 'go beyond the inevitable restrictions which are justified by the pursuit of the objective of environmental protection'.
> It is therefore necessary to examine whether all restrictions which the contested rules impose on the free movement of goods are necessary to achieve the objectives pursued by those rules.[82]

Although the ECJ regarded the deposit-and-return system as an indispensable element of the environmental measure, which did not cause a disproportionate infringement of the free movement of goods, it considered the licence requirement and consequential restriction of the quantity of the products, which might be marketed by importers, as disproportionate to the environmental objective pursued. The Court admitted that such a licence requirement contributed to a considerable degree of protection of the environment, as it ensured a maximum of re-use of containers, but nevertheless decided it was disproportionate. The ECJ in effect balanced the level of environmental protection against the restriction on the free movement of goods, thereby reducing the level the Member State could choose.[83] According to Advocate General Slynn in that case there has to be a balancing of interests between the free movement of goods and environmental protection, even if in achieving the balance the high standard of protection sought has to be reduced. Although *Danish Bottles* may have been an isolated case,[84]

---

[80] See JH Jans, 'Proportionality Revisited' (2000) 27 *Legal Issues of Economic Integration* 239.
[81] Case 302/86 *European Commission v Denmark* [1988] ECR 4607 *(Danish Bottles)* citing Case 240/83 *Procureur de la République v Association de défense des brûleurs d' huiles usagées* [1985] ECR 531.
[82] Ibid, paras 11–12.
[83] Ibid, paras 17 and 21.
[84] See the different approach of the Court in Case C-309/02 *Radlberger Getränkegesellschaft mbH and S Spitz KG v Land Baden-Württemberg* [2004] ECR I-11763; see also D Geradin, *Trade and the environment: a comparative study of EC and US law* (Cambridge, Cambridge University Press, 1997) 62.

where environmental product standards are involved, they are subject to a high level of scrutiny by the Court.

Schmidberger can also be seen as a case wherein the Court assessed the proportionality *stricto sensu* of the Austrian measure to allow the demonstration on the Brenner motorway. According to the Court the interests involved must be weighed against all the circumstances of the case in order to determine whether a fair balance was struck between those interests (see below, Section V.D).[85]

(ii) The Impact of the Legitimate Interest and Regulatory Instrument on the Proportionality Test

How intrusive the proportionality text employed by the ECJ will be eventually depends on a number of factors. First, the public interest at stake is relevant. In the field of public health, for instance, the ECJ gives more discretion to the regulating state than in the field of consumer policy. With regard to consumer policy, the more intrusive proportionality test can be explained by the fact that the Court relies on the capacity of the consumer to process information and make informed choices about available products and services.[86] A European notion of an average consumer who is reasonably well informed and reasonably circumspect has developed in the case law. The fact that the consumer is also a beneficiary of the internal market process has allowed the Court to depart from a reasonable level of consumer protection, excluding certain sensitive policy areas like gambling. By contrast, regarding the field of health, it has been argued that the protection of health and life of humans, including healthcare, which is also mentioned by Article 36 TFEU, takes a special position amongst the public interests.[87] Also in the field of gambling, for instance, which is a sensitive policy area from the Member States' perspective, the Court takes a particularly precautionary approach.[88]

Secondly, the regulatory instrument used by the Member State is also relevant for the application of the proportionality principle. National rules on product standards are generally considered to restrict intra-Community trade. The same holds true for measures hindering market access or forming an obstacle to the free movement of workers. Import bans are particularly problematic in the light of the proportionality test. And so are discriminatory measures in the context of services and persons.[89]

---

[85] Case C-112/00 *Schmidberger*, above n 4, para 81; see also X Groussot and G Thor Petursson, 'Balancing as a Judicial Methodology of EU Constitutional Adjudication' in SA de Vries, X Groussot and G Thor Petursson, *Balancing Fundamental Rights with the EU Treaty Freedoms: The European Court of Justice as 'tightrope' walker* (The Hague, Eleven International Publishing, 2012).
[86] De Vries, *Tensions within the internal market*, above n 79, 70; S Weatherill, *EC consumer law and policy* (London, Longman, 1997) 48.
[87] De Vries, *Tensions within the internal market*, ibid, 351.
[88] See Jans, 'Proportionality Revisited', above n 80.
[89] De Vries, *Tensions within the internal market*, above n 79, 353–54.

(iii) Imposing Procedural Requirements on Member States as Part of the Proportionality Test

Apart from these three elements of proportionality, we can also discern another dimension of proportionality, which is of a different nature as it does not focus on the measures as such but on the procedural context. Particularly in certain sensitive areas or areas where Member States are primarily competent, like gambling, culture, public health and healthcare, the Court does not always question the choice of instrument by the state to attain its goals, but instead requires the state to include certain procedural guarantees in its legislation, such as the possibility of judicial review, transparency requirements, procedures which are readily accessible and concluded within a reasonable period of time. The above-mentioned *Dynamic Medien* and *Watts* cases are examples of the more procedural approach by the Court. But even as early as the famous *Reinheitsgebot* case the Court has imposed procedural requirements on Member States.[90]

In the more recent *United Pan-Europe Communications* case the ECJ also took a deferential approach.[91] It regarded Belgian legislation requiring cable operators to broadcast programmes transmitted by certain private broadcasters ('must carry') as constituting a restriction on the free movement of services, but justified on grounds relating to the maintenance of pluralism in the bilingual region of Brussels-Capital. In assessing the justifiability of the Belgian measure, the Court first stated that the maintenance of pluralism as part of a cultural policy is connected with the freedom of expression, which is a fundamental right, and then held that Member States have a wide margin of discretion in protecting this general interest. Within the context of the proportionality test the ECJ held that the legislation was suitable considering the bilingual nature of the Brussels-Capital region. On the question of necessity the ECJ granted broad discretionary powers to the Member State but laid down certain conditions of good governance as these powers must not be used in a manner which diminishes the effectiveness of a fundamental freedom. The state must take account of certain procedural guarantees, such as transparency requirements.[92]

The question has been raised whether procedural requirements should form part of the proportionality test, which is by its very nature concerned with means–ends relationships, or must be seen as general principles of administrative law and good governance.[93]

---

[90] Case C-244/06 *Dynamic Medien*, above n 31; Case C-372/04 *Watts*, above n 34; Case 178/84 *European Commission v Germany* [1987] ECR 1227 (*Reinheitsgebot*); see also Prechal, 'Topic One: National Applications of the Proportionality Principle', above n 33, 203.

[91] C Barnard, *The substantive law of the EU: the four freedoms*, 3rd edn (Oxford, Oxford University Press, 2010) 259.

[92] Case C-250/06 *United Pan-Europe Communications Belgium SA and others v Belgian State* [2007] ECR I-11135, paras 41–47.

[93] Prechal, 'Topic One: National Applications of the Proportionality Principle', above n 33, 216.

C. The Conflict Between Fundamental Rights and Economic Freedoms

(i) The Treaty Freedoms as Fundamental Principles?

The fact that fundamental rights may conflict with the 'economic' Treaty freedoms raises the question as to how the tension between fundamental rights and economic freedoms can actually be seen: as a conflict between two 'constitutional' principles that are both fundamental? There are several arguments which plead in favour of a close nexus between fundamental freedoms and fundamental rights and, accordingly, of treating the Treaty freedoms as fundamental rights. When we look at the four economic freedoms in the case law of the ECJ we can find various references to the fundamental character of the fundamental freedoms.[94] The Court itself uses words like fundamental freedom,[95] one of the fundamental principles of the Treaty,[96] or fundamental Community provision.[97] The 'fundamental nature' of the freedoms can furthermore be deduced from the substantive scope of the Treaty freedoms, which dogmatic foundation is provided for in *Dassonville*, defining measures having equivalent effect to quantitative import restrictions very broadly.[98] The very fact that an indirect and potential effect on trade suffices for the national measure to fall within the scope of Article 34 TFEU, means that citizens have got a far-reaching right to challenge national legislation which they find stands in their way and which restricts their (economic) rights.[99] In a similar vein, Article 34 TFEU has been described as a 'fundamental political right', or as 'subjective public rights'.[100]

The fundamental nature of the Treaty freedoms also appears, although in an indirect fashion, from their institutional dimension, whereby some provisions have (a limited form of) horizontal direct effect.[101] Interesting in this respect is the

---

[94] P Oliver and W-H Roth, 'The Internal Market and the Four Freedoms' (2004) 41 *CML Rev* 407, 407–11.

[95] For instance, Case C-122/00 *Schmidberger* (goods), above n 4; Case C-281/98 *Roman Angonese v Cassa di Risparmio di Bolzano SpA* (workers) [2000] ECR I-4139; Case C-341/05 *Laval* (services), above n 4, and Case C-36/02 *Omega* (services), above n 4.

[96] Case C-265/95 *European Commission v France (Spanish Strawberries)*, above n 76.

[97] See Case C-49/89 *Corsica Ferries France v Direction générale des douanes françaises* [1989] ECR I-4441, para 8: 'As the Court has decided on various occasions, the articles of the EEC Treaty concerning the free movement of goods, persons, services and capital are fundamental Community provisions and any restriction, even minor, of that freedom is prohibited'. See recently the cases which the Commission has started against a couple of Member States regarding the profession of notaries, such as Case C-50/08 *European Commission v France* (ECJ, 24 May 2011), nyr, para 67.

[98] See SA de Vries, 'Dassonville' in Beukers, Van Harten and Prechal, *Het recht van de Europese Unie*, above n 2, 90.

[99] Barnard, *The substantive law of the EU: the four freedoms*, above n 91, 73–74.

[100] MP Maduro, *We the Court. The European Court of Justice and the European Economic Constitution* (Oxford, Hart Publishing, 1998) 81; T Kingreen, *Struktur der Grundfreiheiten des Europäischen Gemeinschaftsrechts* (Berlin, Duncker & Humblot, 1999) 15; see also Oliver and Roth, 'The Internal Market and the Four Freedoms', above n 94, 410.

[101] The *Viking* and *Laval* cases confirm this approach in respect of the freedom of establishment and the free movement of services. It is however not clear how broad the scope of horizontal direct effect is: see also Prechal and De Vries, 'Seamless web of judicial protection in the internal market?', above n 37.

Opinion of Advocate General Maduro in the *Vodafone* case arguing in favour of, more generally, a horizontal application of the free movement rules, as a consequence of which the scope of Article 114 TFEU – the legal basis for internal market legislation – could be extended to the regulation of private behaviour as well. In this case the validity of a Regulation regulating roaming prices in the telecom sector was at issue.[102] The Court, though, did not follow the Advocate General's Opinion on the extensive scope of Article 114 TFEU but took a different and more cautious approach.[103] Rather than extending the scope of Article 114 TFEU to the regulation of private behaviour, the ECJ looked at future distortions of competition and obstacles of trade as a result of divergences between national laws to justify the EU's intervention in roaming prices.[104]

Other arguments to support the fundamental character of the freedoms are that first, the freedoms have played a vital role in building Europe's economic constitution. According to the Ordo-liberal school, which originates from the German town of Freiburg in the 1930s, the constitution should protect the economic freedoms, 'which are as integral to the protection of human dignity, and as indicative of a free society, as political freedoms, which are themselves liberal in nature and which therefore underscore individual economic freedoms'.[105] Secondly, the economic freedoms can often be defined in terms of the freedom to pursue a trade or profession, which is a fundamental right laid down in Article 16 of the Charter of Fundamental Rights.[106] Lastly and very importantly, rights that are implicit in the economic freedoms, such as the right to equal treatment (non-discrimination), the right to move and reside in another Member State, transcend the economic dimension of the free movement rules. The principle of non-discrimination is in fact transformed into a fundamental right to protect individual personality and human dignity.[107]

But there are limits to the application of the Treaty freedoms. In other words, they are not absolute, which is essential as this underlines their relative importance in the Treaty.[108] First, not all market interventions hinder *market access*.

---

[102] Opinion of AG Maduro of 1 October 2009 in Case C-58/08 *The Queen (on the application of Vodafone Ltd and others) v Secretary of State for Business, Enterprise and regulatory reform* (ECJ, 8 June 2010), nyr, paras 19–22; see also the interesting Opinion of AG Trstenjak of 28 March 2012 in Case C-171/11, Fra.bo SpA, in which she pleads for the horizontal direct effect of Article 34 TFEU on the free movement of goods.

[103] Case C-58/08 *Vodafone Ltd and others*, ibid, para 46.

[104] See also M Brenncke, 'Case law' (2010) 47 *CML Rev* 1793.

[105] D Chalmers, 'The single market: from prima donna to journeyman' in J Shaw and G More (eds), *New legal dynamics of European Union* (Oxford, Clarendon Press, 1995) 57.

[106] Prechal and De Vries, 'Viking/Laval en de grondslagen van het internemarktrecht', above n 38, 434.

[107] Ibid, 435.

[108] See for a critical view on the fundamental character of the EU Treaty Freedoms: NJ de Boer, *Justice, Market Freedom and Fundamental Rights: Just how fundamental are the EU Treaty Freedoms? A Normative Enquiry based on the Political Theory of John Rawls into whether there should be a Hierarchy between Fundamental Rights and the Treaty Freedoms* (Europa Instituut Utrecht Student Paper, 2012, at: www.uu.nl/SiteCollectionDocuments/REBO/REBO_RGL/REBO_RGL_EUROPA/Treaty%20Freedoms%20and%20Fundamental%20Rights%20-working%20paper%20-%20Nik%20de%20Boer[1].pdf); see in particular Oliver and Roth, 'The Internal Market and the Four Freedoms', above n 94, 410.

Where national rules address particularly local interests, such as the opening hours for shops or the prohibition of a resale at a loss, the impact of trade must be assumed negligible. This is made clear by the ECJ in its *Keck* judgment.[109] From *Keck* it could be deduced that the legal commitment to free trade appears to entail the abolition of discrimination, or protectionism, but no more.[110] This would mean that the free movement rules primarily serve transnational integration rather than supranational legitimisation. Supranational legitimisation entails that the four freedoms intend 'to complement the national and supranational protection of the individual by fundamental rights and service the purpose of general liberalisation', whereas transnational integration implies that the four freedoms merely serve gaps of protection in cross-border transactions.[111] Hence, supranational legitimisation suggests that the freedoms are rights of individuals serving to safeguard against all undue and disproportionate restrictions of cross-border restrictions.[112] Although a case as *Keck* may be evidence of a more limited scope of the freedoms, its importance must be put into perspective. Not only has the ruling been difficult to apply in practice, its application so far does not extend beyond the free movement of *goods*.

A second limitation to the scope of the fundamental freedoms originates from the concept of 'internal situation' in which the Treaty rules do not apply. In such situations no cross-border link can be established. But the case law is evolving here and a more subtle approach by the ECJ suggests that in some situations EU law may be applicable, even where no cross-border link can be established. Not only the provisions on citizenship, but also the rules on the free movement of goods, most notably the provisions on charges, have been broadly interpreted and applied.[113]

And finally, market integration is not pursued in isolation but must be counterbalanced by social considerations and public interests, which has most recently been 'confirmed' by the concept of social market economy introduced by the Lisbon Treaty. Whereas the internal market originally seemed to be mainly concerned with the abolition of trade barriers, later a broader conception of the

---

[109] See Cases C-267 and C-268/91 *Criminal proceedings against Keck and Mithouard* [1993] ECR I-6097.

[110] De Vries, *Tensions within the internal market*, above n 79, 42.

[111] T Kingreen, 'Fundamental Freedoms' in Von Bogdandy and Bast, above n 12, 532.

[112] Ibid, 532.

[113] Case C-34/09 *Ruiz Zambrano*, above n 13. With regard to tariff barriers: Joined Cases C-485 and C-486/93 *Simitzi v Dimos Kos* [1995] ECR I-2655; Cases C-363/93 and C-407–C-411/93 *René Lancry SA v Direction Générale des Douanes and Société Dindar Confort and others* [1994] ECR I-3957; with regard to Article 34 TFEU: Case C-184/96 *European Commission v France* [1998] ECR I-6197 (*Foie Gras*); Case C-448/98 *Criminal proceedings against Jean-Pierre Guimont* [2000] ECR I-10663; Case C-254/98 *Schutzverband gegen unlauteren Wettbewerb v TK-Heimdienst Sass GmbH* [2000] ECR I-151; with regard to Article 45 TFEU: Case C-281/98 *Angonese*, above n 95: The fact that the Court did not address the 'appreciable Community element' in this case may also reflect an unwillingness to further compromise internal Member State autonomy and sensibilities: See annotation by R Lane and N Nic Shuibhne, 'Case law' (2000) 37 *CML Rev* 1237, 1243; regarding Article 63 TFEU: Cases C-515/99, C-519-524/99 and C-526-540/99 *Hans Reisch and others Grundverkehrslandeskommission des Landes Salzburg* [2002] ECR I-2157.

internal market can be found, conceptualised in more holistic terms, including consumer safety and environmental protection.[114] The realisation of an internal market and the liberalisation of trade are not ends in themselves, but important tools to increase welfare and promote sustainable development.

(ii) Fundamental Rights

Looking at *fundamental rights*, they are, as stated above, at EU level linked to general principles of law, which is confirmed by Article 6(3) TEU. But next to the general principles of EU law, the Charter of Fundamental Rights and the ECHR constitute, according to Article 6 TEU, the sources of EU fundamental rights. Fundamental rights are understood as being at the very core of our understanding of humanity, which do not necessarily need to be codified, are available to any person and could therefore be regarded as different from the free movement rights, which are economic in nature, derive their status from the Treaty and cannot exist outside the EU Treaty.[115] However, as argued above, the economic nature of the freedoms does not as such exclude a fundamental nature of the Treaty freedoms.

Similarly to the Treaty freedoms, fundamental rights are generally not absolute,[116] but can be restricted as well. And this proposition does not only hold true for EU law, but also for national law. Furthermore, Article 52 of the Charter refers to limitations on rights and principles, which must be provided for by law, which must respect the essence of those rights and which must be necessary and genuinely meet objectives of general interest (proportionality test). In other words, the ECJ should employ a proportionality test to assess whether restrictions imposed on fundamental rights are justified.[117]

The Charter of Fundamental Rights, as already observed above, has, since Lisbon, distinguished between rights and principles. *Principles* are, in contrast to *rights*, only judicially cognisable when they have been implemented by legislative or executive acts. The important question is, of course: which of the fundamental rights in the Charter should be regarded as rights and which as principles? And are there fundamental rights which were previously (or according to the ECJ's case law) to be considered as rights but should now be regarded as principles? The answer is probably no, as it is unlikely that the Court will accept a deterioration of fundamental rights' protection just like that. It was put forward by some

---

[114] This developed over time, see: P Craig, 'The Evolution of the Single Market' in C Barnard and J Scott (eds), *The Law of the Single European Market – Unpacking the Premises* (Oxford, Hart Publishing, 2002) 32.

[115] E Spaventa, 'Federalisation Versus Centralisation: Tensions in Fundamental Rights Discourse in the EU' in M Dougan and S Currie, *50 years of the European treaties: looking back and thinking forward* (Oxford, Hart Publishing, 2009) 355.

[116] But a few fundamental rights have a more absolute character, like the freedom from torture, although the recent development of anti-terrorist policies and detention camps have shown that the word 'absolute' can also be put into perspective: see Craig and De Búrca, *EU Law. Text, cases, and materials*, above n 43, 396.

[117] See Cases C-92 and C-93/09 *Volker and Schecke*, above n 8.

Member States, especially the United Kingdom, that Title IV, 'Solidarity', should contain principles which do not have direct effect, rather than rights. But Article 28 of the Charter, which falls under Title IV and includes the right to collective action, is, as discussed above, recognised by the Court in *Viking* and *Laval* as constituting a fundamental right which forms part of the general principles of EU law.[118]

(iii) No A Priori Hierarchy Between Fundamental Freedoms and Fundamental Rights

The point of departure for balancing conflicting fundamental rights with fundamental economic freedoms is, considering the above-made brief analysis, that it is very difficult and not really desirable to establish an a priori hierarchy between fundamental rights and economic freedoms. Although the fundamental freedoms have a fundamental character, they should not be given 'a higher status than that awarded to other fundamental rights and values in the Community legal order'.[119] Yet at the same time the economic origins of the European Union and the freedoms, which continue to remain the backbone – or spine – of the Union, entail that fundamental rights do not prevail over economic freedoms, at least not in the Union model.[120] The statement that in principle no a priori hierarchy exists between fundamental rights and fundamental freedoms alludes to the seeming indivisibility of these rights, which should be equally promoted and protected.[121] But is this affirmed by the EU model where the economic freedoms – at least to a considerable extent – represent the structure of the Union[122] and the corresponding Court's approach in balancing fundamental rights with the Treaty freedoms?

D. Balancing Fundamental Rights and Economic Freedoms

(i) Protection of Fundamental Rights as an Exception to Free Movement

As a preliminary remark it should be observed that the very fact that the restriction on free movement within the internal market was a result of the exercise of a fundamental right in cases such as *Schmidberger* or *Viking* does not influence the finding that the Treaty rules on free movement – the fundamental economic

---

[118] C Barnard, 'EU "Social" Policy: From Employment Law to Labour Market Reform' in P Craig and G De Búrca, *The Evolution of EU Law* (Oxford, Oxford University Press, 2011) 659–60.
[119] Maduro, *We the Court*, above n 100, 166–68.
[120] See also J Dutheil de la Rochère, 'Challenges for the protection of fundamental rights in the EU at the time of the entry into force of the Lisbon Treaty' (2010) 33 *Fordham International Law Journal* 1776, 1787.
[121] See with regard to economic and social rights J Kenner, 'Economic and Social Rights in the EU Legal Order: The Mirage of Indivisibility' in TK Hervey and J Kenner (eds), *Economic and social rights under the EU charter of fundamental rights: a legal perspective* (Oxford, Hart Publishing, 2003) 1–25.
[122] Dutheil de la Rochère 'Challenges for the protection of fundamental rights in the EU', above n 120, 1787.

freedoms – are applicable in the first place. In this sense, the *exercise* of fundamental rights does not escape the scope of application of the Treaty provisions. The arguments raised in *Viking* and *Laval*, ie that, 'according to the observations of the Danish and Swedish Governments, the right to take collective action, including the right to strike, constitutes a fundamental right which, as such, falls outside the scope of Article 43 EC' [now Article 49 TFEU],[123] are therefore exemplary of the confusion that exists regarding the question of whether the EU is competent to act or whether a certain situation falls within the scope of the Treaty. From the case law of the Court it can be deduced that, although certain policy areas are left to the Member States – such as direct taxation, criminal law, certain aspects of social security law, social assistance or public health – this does not mean that national provisions or measures which concern these policy areas can escape the prohibitive rules on free movement of the Treaty.[124]

Yet the Court immediately admits the necessity to reconcile in this context fundamental rights with the Treaty freedoms. The important consequence of this approach is a shift in the burden of proof. Where in *Strasbourg* the proponents of economic rights might have to justify a restriction on human rights, in *Luxembourg* the fundamental, human rights proponents will have to justify their actions; establish that the restriction on free movement is justified on the basis of protecting the fundamental rights. As Brown observed: 'the language of prima facie breach of economic rights suggests that it remains something which is at the heart wrong, but tolerated, which sits rather uneasily with the State's paramount constitutional obligation to protect human rights'.[125] After all, the very fact that the protection of fundamental rights in cases where a conflict with fundamental freedoms arises, must be *justified* in the light of the economic freedoms, could jeopardise the equality or indivisibility of fundamental rights and economic freedoms. Viewed from this perspective the EU may indeed not yet have been fully transformed into a Human Rights Organisation.[126] At the same time, though, the Court has managed to find ways to incorporate fundamental rights in its free movement case law and thus provided for a 'human rights dimension' of the internal market. It will then be essential to establish (i) under what type of exception ground fundamental rights fall, and (ii) the conditions under which fundamental rights can deviate from the Treaty freedoms.

Regarding (i), whether fundamental rights should be qualified as a Treaty exception, as a mandatory requirement or as a self-standing exception ground, which could be placed somewhere in between Treaty exceptions and mandatory

[123] Case C-438/05 *Viking*, above n 4, para 42.
[124] See, eg Case C-158/96 *Raymond Kohll v Union des Caisses de Maladie* [1998] ECR I-1931; Case C-334/02 *European Commission v France* [2004] ECR I-2229; Case C-446/03 *Marks & Spencer plc v David Halsey (HM Inspector of Taxes)* [2005] ECR I-10837; Case C-348/96 *Calfa*, above n 27; Case C-268/06 *Impact* [2008] ECR I-2483. See also Prechal and De Vries, 'Viking/Laval en de grondslagen van het internemarktrecht', above n 38, 435.
[125] C Brown, 'Case C-112/00, *Eugen Schmidberger, Internationale Transporte und Planzüge v. Austria.* Judgment of 12 June 2003, Full Court' (2003) 40 *CML Rev* 1499, 1508.
[126] See in particular the chapter by Douglas Scott in this book (ch 7).

requirements, the case law does not make entirely clear.[127] In *Schmidberger* the Court did not give guidance in this matter but nevertheless seemed to regard fundamental rights as a self-standing category of exception grounds.[128] In *Omega* and *Sayn-Wittgenstein* the Court referred to the concept of public policy, which, though strictly interpreted, could be applied in these cases where Member States enjoy a wide margin of discretion to protect fundamental rights, which have a particularly national constitutional dimension.[129] In *Dynamic Medien* the Court classified the protection of the child as a legitimate interest, which must meet the proportionality requirement.[130] And in *Viking* the Court subsumed the fundamental right to strike under a rule of reason exception ground, ie the protection of workers; rather than examining whether the fundamental right *as such* may justify restriction on free movement.[131] Advocate General Trstenjak in the *Commission v Germany* case stated the following:

> The approach adopted in *Viking Line* and *Laval un Partneri*, according to which Community fundamental social rights as such may not justify – having due regard to the principle of proportionality – a restriction on a fundamental freedom but that a written or unwritten ground of justification incorporated within that fundamental right must, in addition, always be found, sit uncomfortably alongside the principle of equal ranking for fundamental rights and fundamental freedoms.[132]

How fundamental rights are perceived by the Court under the scheme of the justification grounds is important. Discriminatory measures are, after all, in principle only justifiable on the basis of Treaty exceptions, whereas indistinctly applicable measures can also be justified on the basis of the rule of reason, ie mandatory requirements.[133] Although this distinction has become increasingly artificial since the ECJ has in several cases upheld discriminatory laws on the basis of the rule of reason,[134] the Court has never explicitly admitted that the rule of reason could also be applied in case of discrimination.[135] But the fact that a national measure protecting a fundamental right is discriminatory should not be decisive for the applicability of a justification ground in the first place. The increasing weight given to fundamental rights in the Treaty through Article 6 TEU and the binding Charter precisely entails that special account must be taken of fundamental rights

---

[127] Morijn, 'Balancing Fundamental Rights and Common Market Freedoms in Union Law', above n 41, 38–39.
[128] Case C-112/00 *Schmidberger*, above n 4.
[129] See Case C-36/02 *Omega*, above n 4; Case C-208/09 *Sayn-Wittgenstein*, above n 24.
[130] Case C-244/06 *Dynamic Medien*, above n 31, para 42.
[131] Barnard, 'EU "Social" Policy', above n 118, 671; see also T Novitz, 'A Human Rights Analysis of the Viking and Laval Judgments' (2007–08) 10 *Cambridge Yearbook of European Legal Studies* 541, 357; Malmberg and Sigeman 'Industrial actions and EU economic freedoms', above n 39, 1130.
[132] Opinion of AG Trstenjak of 14 April 2010 in Case C-271/08 *European Commission v Germany* [2010] ECR I-7091.
[133] Tridimas, *The General Principles of EU Law*, above n 45, 339.
[134] eg within the field of the environment: Case C-379/98 *PreussenElektra AG v Schhleswag AG* [2001] ECR I-2099 and Case C-2/90 *European Commission v Belgium* [1992] ECR I-4431 (*Walloon Waste*); see also Oliver and Roth, 'The Internal Market and the Four Freedoms', above n 94, 436.
[135] De Vries, *Tensions within the internal market*, above n 79, 370.

in interpreting the provisions on free movement. The Court should thus, more than it has done so far, proceed to consider fundamental rights as self-standing justification grounds, which, similar to the Treaty exceptions of eg Article 36 and 52 TFEU, may allow for the adoption of national discriminatory measures if deemed necessary.[136] Otherwise, the limits caused by the rule of reason on the possibilities to invoke a justification ground would accentuate 'the existence of a hierarchical relationship between fundamental rights and fundamental freedoms' and would seriously jeopardise the idea that no a priori hierarchy exists between them.[137] In a similar vein, the fundamental freedoms can be equated with fundamental rights particularly where they protect equality of opportunity or, in other words, defend the principle of non-discrimination. The fact that mere restrictions of market access are at stake should thus not be decisive for the justification of a fundamental right.

VI. Balancing in the Case Law of the ECJ According to the Proportionality Principle

Regarding (ii), looking at cases like *Schmidberger*, *Omega*, *Sayn-Wittgenstein*, *Dynamic Medien* and *Viking/Laval*, it is apparent that the Court of Justice is *struggling* to find the right test. Overall, the Court has favoured the use of, or 'referred to', a proportionality test. In *Omega*, however, the Court does not only limit its proportionality review of the German ban on laser games to the first element, suitability, but we also discern a rather state-centric approach by the Court, accepting a German particularity of human dignity. After all in the United Kingdom and many other states these laser games are lawful. It has been argued after *Omega* that this decision of the Court is illustrative of the judicial deference in sensitive areas of national constitutional law which lie outside a core or nucleus of shared values and where the ECJ should respect constitutional pluralism.[138] Hence, the ECJ did not wish to impose a common legal conception of human dignity on the Member States. The 'soft' application of the proportionality test employed by the Court allowed the national court to protect a national constitutional standard vis-à-vis the EU interest of free movement. This is referred to as the 'integration model based on value diversity which views national constitutional standards not as being in a competitive relationship with the economic

---

[136] Morijn, 'Balancing Fundamental Rights and Common Market Freedoms in Union Law', above n 41, 39.

[137] See also Opinion of AG Trstenjak in Case C-271/08 *European Commission v Germany*, above n 132, para 185. See for a very critical view on the Court's case law: Spaventa, 'Federalisation Versus Centralisation', above n 115, 343–64.

[138] Lenaerts and Gutiérrez-Fons, 'The constitutional allocation of powers and general principals of EU law', above n 49, 1663.

objectives of the Union but as forming part of its polity'.¹³⁹ And as Germany only wanted to protect its citizens from these laser games, according to Nic Shuibhne, it was protecting its internal constitutional space, without preventing its citizens or companies from moving elsewhere.¹⁴⁰

This approach was endorsed by the Court in *Sayn-Wittgenstein*, where it fascinatingly also referred to Article 4(2) TEU by stating that 'in accordance with Article 4(2) TEU, the European Union is to respect the national identities of its Member States, which include the status of the State as a Republic'.¹⁴¹ By referring to Article 4(2) TEU, the ECJ on the one hand embraces the idea that Member States have considerable leeway in protecting their national constitutional space and identity, yet on the other that national identity is subject to a balancing approach where tensions arise with the economic freedoms.¹⁴²

At the other – far – end of the spectrum, we find cases like *Viking* and *Laval*, which have been criticised for the way in which the ECJ dealt with the right to collective action and the right to strike. Not only is the right to strike in *Viking* subject to the wider goal of worker protection, it must also be assessed under the proportionality test whether no less restrictive means are available; in that sense, the fundamental right may only be a last resort, which may in fact undermine the fundamentality of this social right.¹⁴³ The activist approach of the ECJ could perhaps be best explained by the personal movement rights of EU citizens, which were at stake in *Viking* or *Laval*. And trade unions could easily engage in social protectionism leading to retaliatory measures and eventually to fragmentation. In other words, measures were at issue, albeit socially legitimate, which potentially cloaked protectionism and hence jeopardised the fundamental value of protectionism. At the same time the ECJ may have felt that trade unions should not have such a broad margin of appreciation as Member States have.¹⁴⁴ In *Laval* the ECJ held that trade unions, 'not being bodies governed by public law . . . cannot avail themselves of that provision by citing grounds of public policy in order to maintain that collective action such as that at issue in the main proceedings complies with Community law'.¹⁴⁵ More generally, the fact that private actors are engaged in the protection of public interests is, more particularly within the context of the EU competition rules, seen as problematic.¹⁴⁶ After all, private actors are considered to pursue their own, private, interests first, before considering the 'public at large'. The question is, however, whether such an approach takes due account of the different regulatory instruments used in the Member States to attain public-

---

¹³⁹ Tridimas, *The General Principles of EU Law*, above n 45, 341.
¹⁴⁰ Nic Shuibhne, 'Margins of appreciation: national values, fundamental rights and EC free movement law', above n 23, 252.
¹⁴¹ Case C-208/09 Sayn-Wittgenstein, above n 24, para 92.
¹⁴² A von Bogdandy and S Schill, 'Overcoming absolute primacy: respect for national identity under the Lisbon Treaty' (2011) 48 *CML Rev* 1417, 1425.
¹⁴³ Barnard, *The substantive law of the EU*, above n 91, 259.
¹⁴⁴ Lenaerts and Gutiérez-Fons, 'The constitutional allocation of powers and general principals of EU law', above n 49, 1666.
¹⁴⁵ Case C-341/05 *Laval un Partneri*, above n 4, para 84.
¹⁴⁶ De Vries, *Tensions within the internal market*, above n 79.

policy objectives, like the instrument of self-regulation, and where semi-private or semi-public organisations have regulatory powers; or in Sweden the typically Nordic model of collective bargaining, which leaves the regulation of industrial relations to a large extent to the discretion of the social partners.[147] Shouldn't private actors at least not have the possibility to prove that their behaviour is aimed at realising public-policy aims, and is not merely dictated by self-interest?[148]

Furthermore, whereas in *Omega* and *Sayn-Wittgenstein* the point of departure is constitutional pluralism, in *Viking* and *Laval* the ECJ clearly had a 'transnational mindset seeking to raise standards throughout the EU rather than excluding workers from other Member States'.[149] However, it has also been submitted that for the ECJ, being forced to make political decisions on the legitimacy of social policy choices in a case like *Viking*, it is still essential to gather and process all relevant cultural, economic and social data and that it does, for example, not ignore the fact that strike action in Finland is protected by the Finnish Constitution, or that political strikes are protected in various national systems.[150] But the ECJ took no account of the national traditions and differences in *Viking* or *Laval*.[151] As has been observed in literature, this gives the impression that the Court is inclined to give preference to fundamental rights based on moral or ethical considerations, or on certain essential democratic values and a constitutional system, rather than to rights which are based on economic and social interests.[152]

In the middle – ideally – lies *Schmidberger*, in which, according to Advocate General Trstenjak in her Opinion in case *Commission v Germany* on public procurement and social rights, 'the idea of equal ranking for conflicting fundamental rights and fundamental freedoms was central, which by examination of the proportionality of the opposing restrictions in question, were brought fairly into balance'.[153] According to the Advocate General, in order to ensure an optimum effectiveness of fundamental rights and fundamental freedoms, an analysis based on the proportionality principle would be the best option. But such an analysis should not be confined to an assessment of the appropriateness and necessity of a restriction of a fundamental freedom for the benefit of fundamental rights' protection; it must also include an assessment of whether the restriction on a *fundamental right* is appropriate and necessary in the light of the fundamental freedom.[154] Hence, a type of 'double proportionality test', which in fact can

---

[147] See also Malmberg and Sigeman, 'Industrial actions and EU economic freedoms', above n 39.
[148] De Vries, *Tensions within the internal market*, above n 79, 383.
[149] Lenaerts and Gutiérezz-Fons, 'The constitutional allocation of powers and general principals of EU law', above n 49, 1667; see also Nic Shuibhne, 'Margins of appreciation: national values, fundamental rights and EC free movement law', above n 23, 253: '[I]f a fundamental boundary lens was applied to the internal significance of the social rights at stake, then that might well have defeated the freedoms of establishment and service at issue on a constitutionally enriched plane of analysis'.
[150] Barnard, *The substantive law of the EU*, above n 91, 258.
[151] Malmberg and Sigeman, 'Industrial actions and EU economic freedoms', above n 39, 1130.
[152] Ibid.
[153] Opinion of AG Trstenjak in Case C-271/08 *European Commission v Germany*, above n 132, para 195.
[154] Ibid, paras 189–91.

already be detected in *Schmidberger*, as the Austrian authorities were given the discretion by the ECJ in authorising the demonstration to consider the impact of the protection of the fundamental free movement of goods by banning the demonstration on the fundamental rights of assembly and speech. According to the ECJ, 'the competent national authorities were entitled to consider that an outright ban on the demonstration would have constituted unacceptable interference with the fundamental rights of the demonstrators to gather and express peacefully their opinion in public'.[155]

This proposal bears traces of the third element of the proportionality test, proportionality *stricto sensu*, but without only weighing fundamental rights protection with the free movement of goods, and also the free movement of goods with the interest of fundamental rights protection. It thus reflects a true balancing approach and should therefore be welcomed, as it also comes close to the way in which the ECJ applied the proportionality test in the *Volker and Schecke* case, according to Article 52 of the Charter (see above, Section IV.B). In this way, although balancing by the Court through the application of a *proportionality test* might not always be seen as a true panacea, it can, if properly understood and applied, be a good second-best solution.[156]

VII. Conclusion

So far we cannot find a consistent approach as to how, within the context of EU law, fundamental rights should be balanced with fundamental freedoms. And although this diverging case law may have generated uncertainty and unpredictability,[157] some main lines can be deduced from these judgments. In balancing fundamental rights and fundamental freedoms the Court draws inspiration from its case law on fundamental freedoms and public interests. Where typically national or sensitive interests and values are involved, like 'gambling' or public health, Member States have a greater margin of discretion than in cases where more 'holistic' or universal values, like the protection of consumers, are at issue. The 'good old principle' of proportionality serves here as an instrument to balance the different public interests with the fundamental freedoms.

In a similar vein *Omega* and *Sayn-Wittgenstein* are examples of cases where much leeway is granted to Member States to protect certain fundamental rights, whereas in cases like *Viking* and *Laval*, the possibilities to protect a fundamental, social, right, ie the right to collective action, have been severely limited. From a traditional internal market perspective, looking at the ways in which the ECJ has balanced the Member States' interests with the fundamental freedoms, the

---

[155] Case C-112/00 *Schmidberger*, above n 4, para 89.
[156] See the chapter by Barnard in this book (ch 2).
[157] Barnard 2010, above n 91, 259.

approach to fundamental rights is not surprising. But since we are dealing here with *fundamental* rights as well as considering Article 6 TEU and the binding character of the Charter, the Court must take a more cautious approach, which has the following implications.

First, fundamental rights must be accepted as legitimate interests which in principle allow for discriminatory measures to be upheld. This is essential as fundamental rights and fundamental freedoms must be placed on an equal footing.

Secondly, the Court is inevitably drawn into a balancing exercise. Keeping fundamental rights outside the framework of the four freedoms is no real option. The Court cannot simply refute the *existence* of the fundamental freedoms, as they constitute the core values of European integration.

Thirdly, this does not mean that differences which exist between fundamental rights, between the restrictive nature of the measures seeking to protect these rights, and between the state and private parties relying upon fundamental rights, should not be taken into account at all. It elucidates the more 'hierarchal' approach displayed in *Viking* and *Laval* compared to 'constitutional pluralism', which is said to underpin *Omega* and *Sayn-Wittgenstein*; the ECJ being afraid that the integrity of the EU legal order would be at stake if trade unions were allowed to shield the national labour market from the citizens of new Member States.[158] But, as set out above, the reasoning of the Court is flawed and the Court hardly motivates its judgments. This is essential, especially where cases lead to important political, economic and moral implications. In such 'sensitive' situations, the ECJ may take a step back and resort to principles of good governance instead. The ideal situation – the good example – remains in *Schmidberger*, where the Court managed to employ a balancing exercise without subordinating the fundamental right to the fundamental freedom. Here the Court comes close to the so-called double proportionality test as proposed by AG Trstenjak in *Commission v Germany*.

As a final remark, it must be stated that in the future the Court will be confronted with cases where the Member States' margin of discretion will have to be further defined. Its endeavour for closer harmony to do justice to Plato's praise for harmony order, balance and proportion will therefore continue and not end here.

---

[158] Lenaerts & Gutiérez-Fons 2010, above n 49, 1666.

Part II

The Scope of Fundamental Rights in EU Law

4

The Reach of EU Fundamental Rights on Member State Action after Lisbon

XAVIER GROUSSOT*, LAURENT PECH AND[†]
GUNNAR THOR PETURSSON[††]

I. Introduction

With the entry into force of the Lisbon Treaty on 1 December 2009, the EU Charter of Fundamental Rights (the Charter or EUCFR) has finally become a legally-binding, core element of the Union's legal order and thus the starting point for the Luxembourg judge for assessing the compatibility of a (Member State) measure with EU fundamental rights.[1] The general principles are, therefore, no longer the exclusive guiding norms to ensure the protection of fundamental rights within the EU.[2] This new situation may lead, in fact, to a complex overlapping between the Charter's rights and general principles, particularly if their scope of application is not similar.[3] Arguably, both the general principles and the Charter's rights have similar functions, ie the interpretation of EU law and judicial review of acts of the EU institutions and acts of the Member States falling within the scope of EU law. Also similarly to the Charter's rights (Article 51 EUCFR), the general principles are not unbridled or to use the expression of Sharpston in *Bartsch*, the general principles do not apply in abstract.[4]

The essential problem lies, in fact, in the personal scope of application of EU fundamental rights after the entry into force of the Lisbon Treaty. As a result, before

---

* Professor of EU Law, Lund University.
[†] Jean Monnet Lecturer in EU Public Law, National University of Ireland Galway.
[††] Senior Specialist at the School of Law, Reykjavik University.
[1] See, eg, Opinion of AG Bot of 5 April 2011 in Case C-108/10 *Ivana Scattolon v Ministerio dell'Istruzione, dell'Università e della Ricerca* (ECJ, 6 September 2011), nyr.
[2] Article 6 TEU provides for the Charter and the general principles as Union norms ensuring the protection of fundamental rights in the EU.
[3] At the present time, the material scope of the Charter is wider than the protection afforded by the case law on general principles. Yet in the future the general principles could be relied on to extend the scope *ratione materiae* of the EU fundamental rights.
[4] Opinion of AG Sharpston of 22 May 2008 in Case C-427/06 *Bartsch v Bosch und Siemens Hausgeräte (BSH) Altersfürsorge GmbH* [2008] ECR I-7245, para 69.

reviewing the impact (or lack thereof) of the Lisbon Treaty on the Court of Justice's fundamental rights jurisdiction over Member State action, it may be useful to offer a succinct categorisation of the case law, that is, to specify the different situations where a national measure can be reviewed on the basis of its compliance with EU fundamental rights. Two main categories have been distinguished thus far in relation to general principles:

(i) National measures implementing or applying EU law (*Wachauf* line of cases):[5]

> Member States are bound by EU fundamental rights when they adopt measures to implement regulations or transpose directives or more generally, when they apply national rules whose subject-matter is governed by provisions of EU primary and/or secondary legislation;

(ii) National measures derogating from EU law (*ERT* line of cases):[6]

> Member States are also bound by EU fundamental rights when they invoke reasons of public interest pursuant to EU law to justify a national measure which limits any of the Treaty rights and in particular when they adopt measures which obstruct or which are merely liable to hamper the exercise of EU free movement rights.

Yet the personal scope of the Charter's rights is still very uncertain, particularly due to the wording of Article 51 EUCFR – which states that its provisions are applicable to the Member States 'only when they are implementing Union law' – and the lack, at this time, of any clarifying CJEU case law on its scope of application.[7]

This chapter focuses on the potential 'federalising effect' of the Charter (Section II) as well as the possible impact of its new legally-binding status as regards the 'horizontal' application of EU fundamental rights (Section III). Finally, it offers a classification of the main situations in which EU Fundamental Rights bind the Member States after Lisbon (Section IV). Before addressing these issues related to the reach of EU fundamental rights, let us make clear that the Treaty of Lisbon, by ending the previous patchwork of confusing restrictions imposed on the jurisdiction of the Court of Justice and marginally reforming the law of legal standing for individuals in annulment actions, offers a series of positive changes to the system of remedies and procedures established by the European Treaties.[8] In themselves, however, these jurisdictional and procedural changes have not affected the scope of application of EU fundamental rights as regards measures adopted by Member States, which is not surprising considering that they were essentially motivated by the need to ensure that EU legally-binding measures, save for some limited exceptions, could not escape judicial review.

---

[5] Case 5/88 *Hubert Wachauf v Bundesamt für Ernährung und Forstwirtschaft* [1989] ECR 2609.

[6] Case C-260/89 *Elliniki Radiophonia Tileorassi AE (ERT) v Dimotiki Etairia Pliroforissis and Sotirios Kouvelas* [1991] ECR I-2925.

[7] See, eg, Opinion of AG Trstenjak of 22 September 2011 in Joined Cases C-411/10 and C-493/10 *NS v Secretary of State for the Home Department* (ECJ (Grand Chamber), 21 December 2011).

[8] For further analysis, see L Pech, '"A Union Founded on the Rule of Law": Meaning and Reality of the Rule of Law as a Constitutional Principle of EU Law' (2010) 6 *European Constitutional Law Review* 359, 389 ff.

II. Towards A 'Federal Application' of EU Fundamental Rights?

Legal critics of the Lisbon Treaty often argued against its ratification on the grounds that the transformation of the Charter into a legally-binding document would have a 'federalising effect' which might eventually lead to a situation where the Charter became a 'federal standard'. In other words, the Charter, like the Federal Bill of Rights in the United States, would eventually apply 'irrespective of the subject-matter at issue, that is to say irrespective of whether it falls within federal or State competence'.[9] Koen Lenaerts, now a judge at the European Court of Justice, observed that such a degree of coherence or harmonisation could only be achieved if the Member States would agree to entrust to the Court of Justice the task performed by the US Supreme Court, that of protecting any individual citizen, on the basis of a 'federal' standard of respect for fundamental rights, against any public authority of any kind and in any area of substantive law.[10]

Article 51(1) of the Charter, however, clearly precludes such a 'federal' evolution, as it unmistakably implies that the EU Courts still lack the power to review the compatibility with EU fundamental rights of national rules which fall outside the scope of Union law.

It is well established in the pre-Lisbon case law that the jurisdiction of the Court to review national acts for their conformity with EU fundamental rights is limited to situations where the Member States are acting within the scope of Community/Union law. The purpose of Article 51(1) of the Charter, according to its drafters, was to codify this line of cases.[11] And indeed it provides that

> [t]he provisions of this Charter are addressed to the institutions, bodies, offices and agencies of the Union with due regard for the principle of subsidiarity and to the Member States *only when they are implementing Union law*. They shall therefore respect the rights, observe the principles and promote the application thereof in accordance with their respective powers and respecting the limits of the powers of the Union as conferred on it in the Treaties (emphasis added).[12]

---

[9] K Lenaerts, 'Respect for Fundamental Rights as a Constitutional Principle of the European Union' (2000) 6 *Columbia Journal of European Law* 1, 21.

[10] Ibid, 24.

[11] See Explanations relating to the Charter of Fundamental Rights [2007] OJ C303/17, 32.

[12] For the successive versions of this provision before the adoption of the Charter in 2000, see G De Búrca, 'The drafting of the European Union Charter of Fundamental Rights' (2001) 26 *ELRev* 126, 137 (the author judiciously observes that the 'somewhat tedious tracing of the convoluted path taken by what might seem like a fairly innocuous "horizontal" clause, from its earliest and reasonably strict interpretation by the secretariat's guideline, through several broader intermediate formulations, and reverting ultimately to an even stricter version, illustrates an emergent reluctance to commit the Member States to observing the norms of the Charter other than in the cases which are most closely linked to the European Union where the Member States have little or no autonomy'). One should also note that the 2000 text of Article 51(1) has been subject to additional amendments initiated by some and agreed by all the Member States in the context of the two intergovernmental conferences that took place before the signing of the Constitutional Treaty and its successor, the Treaty of Lisbon. Some were

Article 51 contains a second paragraph, which further provides that 'The Charter does not extend the field of application of Union law beyond the powers of the Union or establish any new power or task for the Union, or modify powers and tasks as defined in the Treaties'. In a similar vein, Article 6(1) TEU further reiterates that the Charter's provisions 'shall not extend in any way' EU competences 'as defined in the Treaties'. These provisions mostly confirm beyond any doubt that the Charter cannot, *in itself*, offer a legal basis for the EU to legislate and thereby extend, according to the awkward formulation used in the Explanations, 'the range of Member State action considered to be "implementation of Union law"'.[13] Because Article 51(2) is essentially concerned with the legislative competence of the EU, it will not be subject to further analysis. However, it is important to point out that 'a prohibited national action may be interpreted by the ECJ as falling within the scope of application of EC law without the Community necessarily having legislative power to act in that field'.[14]

Before returning to Article 51(1), one should perhaps explain why most national governments were keen to have such a provision inserted in the Charter in the first place. To put it concisely and at the risk of over-simplification, national representatives from some influential countries such as the United Kingdom were concerned that the European Court of Justice might be tempted to emulate the US Supreme Court.[15] Indeed, in the first half of the twentieth century, the US Supreme Court decided, on its own initiative, to 'incorporate' the federal Bill of Rights through an expansive interpretation of the Fourteenth Amendment into the US Constitution.[16] To refer to a single American judgment previously men-

---

minor: 'agencies' and 'offices' were added to the list of EU authorities subject to the Charter; some were purely stylistic ('the Treaties' logically replaced in 2007 the previous reference to 'the Constitution'). In fact, the only significant change was the insertion of the following phrase before the signing of the Constitutional Treaty: 'and respecting the limits of the powers of the Union as conferred on it in the other parts of the Constitution'. No substantive amendment to Article 51(1) was tabled before the signing of the Lisbon Treaty, which would seem to suggest that Member States were happy with the rather strict albeit relatively ambiguous phrasing used regarding the reach of EU fundamental rights on Member State action.

[13] Explanations to the CFR, above n 11, 32.

[14] G De Búrca, 'The Principle of Subsidiarity and the Court of Justice as an Institutional Actor' (1999) 36 *Journal of Common Market Studies* 217, 221. This view is clearly backed up by the European Court of Justice's case law, which has constantly rejected any correspondence between legislative competence and judicial competence (the 'interpretative authority' of the Court). In other words, EU fundamental rights may bind national authorities even in areas where the EU lacks the positive power to legislate and the scope of EU law should not therefore be conflated with the areas where the EU has been given permission to act. For an interesting discussion of how the Court may at times undermine the principle of allocated powers through a flexible definition of the reach of EU law, see S Prechal, S de Vries and H van Eijken, 'The Principle of Attributed Powers and the 'Scope of EU Law' in LFM Besselink, FJL Pennings and S Prechal (eds), *The Eclipse of the Legality Principle in the European Union* (Alphen aan den Rijn, Kluwer Law International, 2011) 213 ff.

[15] See eg Lord Goldsmith, 'The Charter of Rights – a brake not an accelerator' (2004) 5 *European Human Rights Law Review* 473 (the author welcomes Article 51(1) as it makes clear that Member States are only affected when they act to implement Union law and that the Charter, accordingly, does not impose new obligations on them when they act within national competence).

[16] Particularly important is the first paragraph of the fourteenth amendment, which was passed in 1868 after the conclusion of the Civil War. It reads as follows: 'No State shall make or enforce any law

tioned when examining the European *Rutili* case, in the 1925 case of *Gitlow v New York*, the US Supreme Court finally decided that through the Fourteenth Amendment, a plaintiff is entitled to rely on the right to free speech protected by the First Amendment to challenge the constitutionality of a State law which made it a crime to advocate the violent overthrow of government.[17] This came as a relative surprise as the Supreme Court initially held the Bill of Rights to apply only to the Federal Government, which meant that the Federal courts could not prevent enforcement of State laws restricting the rights guaranteed in the Bill of Rights.[18] The most important point here is that since *Gitlow*, the Supreme Court has allowed, on the basis of the Fourteenth Amendment, for the progressive expansion of the federal Bill of Rights' scope of application to all State norms even when the States act within their *own* sphere of competence. Thanks to this arguably radical reinterpretation of the federal constitutional text, the US Supreme Court has built a unified constitutional order as regards respect for fundamental rights.

Irrespective of the merits of such 'federal' harmonisation in the field of fundamental rights, Article 51(1) of the Charter would appear to prohibit the European Court of Justice from conferring upon itself the power to review Member States' actions on the basis of a federal standard of respect for fundamental rights in areas *outside* the scope of EU law. An 'American' evolution to be achieved by judicial activism seems, therefore, virtually impossible. As a matter of fact, Article 51(1) appears to narrow the pre-Lisbon reach of EU fundamental rights, as it explicitly provides that the Member States must respect these rights *only* when they are implementing Union law.[19]

One may wonder, however, whether this is one of the various drafting deficiencies pointed out by numerous scholars.[20] Indeed, the formula cited above contradicts the well-established principle since *ERT* that EU fundamental rights bind the Member States whenever they act within the scope of EU law, which includes situations where the Member States seek to justify national measures derogating from EU law by reasons of public interest.[21] One swift look at the so-called explanations seems to suggest that the drafting deficiency thesis is accurate but also suggests that those who drafted Article 51(1) did not fully understand the arguably opaque case law of the Court as regards its jurisdiction to review national acts for their conformity with EU fundamental rights:

which shall abridge the privileges or immunities of citizens of the United States; nor shall any State deprive any person of life, liberty, or property, without due process of law; nor deny to any person within its jurisdiction the equal protection of the laws'.

[17] *Gitlow v People of the State of New York* 268 US 652 (1925).

[18] For further analysis and references, see the highly critical and by now classic study of the Supreme Court's judicial activism by R Berger, *Government by Judiciary – The Transformation of the Fourteenth Amendment*, 2nd rev edn (Indianapolis, Liberty Fund, 1997).

[19] G De Búrca, 'The drafting of the European Union Charter of fundamental rights' (2001) 26 *EL Rev* 126, 137.

[20] For a neat overview, see M Dougan, 'The Treaty of Lisbon 2007: Winning Minds, Not Hearts' (2008) 45 *CML Rev* 617, 663.

[21] B de Witte, 'The Legal Status of the Charter: Vital question or non-issue?' (2001) 8 *Maastricht Journal of European and Comparative Law* 81, 85.

As regards the Member States, it follows unambiguously from the case-law of the Court of Justice that the requirement to respect fundamental rights defined in the context of the Union is only binding on the Member States when they act in the scope of Union law (judgment of 13 July 1989, Case 5/88 *Wachauf* [1989] ECR 2609; judgment of 18 June 1991, Case C-260/89 *ERT* [1991] ECR I-2925; judgment of 18 December 1997, Case C-309/96 *Annibaldi* [1997] ECR I-7493). The Court of Justice confirmed this case-law in the following terms: 'In addition, it should be remembered that the requirements flowing from the protection of fundamental rights in the Community legal order are also binding on Member States when they implement Community rules . . .' (judgment of 13 April 2000, Case C-292/97 [2000] ECR I-2737, paragraph 37 of the grounds). Of course this rule, as enshrined in this Charter, applies to the central authorities as well as to regional or local bodies, and to public organisations, when they are implementing Union law.[22]

Without being too harsh, it seems fair to say that these explanations reflect a 'concoction of formulations',[23] as they offer a mixture of various formulas used by the Court of Justice and refer not only to situations where the Member States 'act in the scope of Union law' to 'implement Community rules' but also to the obligation to respect fundamental rights 'in the context of the Union'.

The unclear and, one may add, not perfectly accurate nature of the explanations is highly unfortunate. Article 6(1) TEU, as amended by the Lisbon Treaty, provides indeed that 'due regard' is to be had to the explanations relating to the Charter, and referred to in the Charter itself, when interpreting the rights, freedoms and principles laid down in the Charter. This Treaty provision – which was not particularly imperative as Article 52(7) of the Charter had been amended by the Member States in 2004 to provide that the explanations 'shall be given due regard by the courts of the Union and of the Member States' – suggests that the EU courts as well as national courts must rely on them when interpreting any of the rights, freedoms and principles protected by the Charter even though they do *not* as such have the status of law. With respect to Article 51(1) of the Charter, this means that the Court of Justice ought to rely on relatively ambiguous explanations that yet seem to suggest that this provision does not mean what it actually says because it does not reflect the intent of its drafters. It will therefore be for the Court of Justice to eventually remedy what we also consider to constitute an 'inadvertent omission'.[24] And even if one is of the view that the narrow and inaccurate formulation used in Article 51(1) does in fact reflect the deliberate intention of its drafters to reduce the Court of Justice's scope of review of national measures on fundamental rights grounds,[25] we submit that the explanations demonstrate at the very least that this was not a goal entertained by most members of

---

[22] Explanations to the CFR, above n 11, 32.
[23] L Besselink, 'The Member States, the National Constitutions, and the Scope of the Charter' (2001) 8 *Maastricht Journal of European and Comparative Law* 68, 76.
[24] FG Jacobs, 'Human Rights in the European Union: The Role of the Court of Justice' (2001) 26 *EL Rev* 331, 338.
[25] See De Witte, 'The Legal Status of the Charter', above n 21, 86.

the body which adopted the explanations and the text of the Charter in October and December 2000 respectively.

In any event, the pre-Lisbon case law of the Court shows that the Court is not 'inclined to reduce the scope of its jurisdiction over Member State action for compliance with fundamental rights',[26] and in particular, that the Court has shown no particular restraint when referring to provisions of the Charter in ERT-type situations.[27] The post-Lisbon case law of the Court also offers at least one significant judgment concerning Article 51(1). In *DEB*, national legal provisions which made it impossible for legal persons to avail themselves of legal aid, were held not to be compatible with the principle of effective judicial protection, as enshrined in Article 47 of the Charter. In the context of this case, the Court noted that 'Article 51(1) of the Charter states that the provisions thereof are addressed to the Member States when they are implementing EU law'.[28] As noted above, Article 51(1) actually provides that provisions of the Charter are addressed to the Member States *only* when they are implementing EU law. It is too early to say if this is another example of inadvertent omission. The Court did not – regrettably for us – further discuss Article 51(1) as the dispute clearly fell within the scope of this provision to the extent that the plaintiff alleged that it had suffered a loss on account of the delayed transposition in Germany of two directives and was therefore pursuing a claim before a national court, by which it was seeking to establish state liability for infringement of EU law. Another remarkable but not surprising aspect of that judgment is that the Court, when faced with explanations that did not 'provide any clarification'[29] as regards the word 'person' used in the first two paragraphs of Article 47 of the Charter, decided that legal persons are not excluded from the scope of that article on the basis of its own interpretation of several provisions of the Charter and its examination of the case law of the European Court of Human Rights.

Lastly, a recent and controversial judgment must be mentioned, although it does not directly address the scope of application of the Charter but rather the impact of Article 20 TFEU, which confers the status of citizen of the Union on every person holding the nationality of a Member State. In the case of *Zambrano*,[30] the main issue was whether two married asylum seekers from Columbia residing in Belgium could be granted residence and work rights under EU law once they became parents of two children who acquired Belgian nationality. All the Member

---

[26] P Craig and G De Búrca, *EU Law: Text, Cases, and Materials*, 4th edn (Oxford, Oxford University Press, 2008) 402.

[27] Case C-438/05 *International Transport Workers' Federation and Finnish Seamen's Union v Viking Line ABP and OÜ Viking Line Eesti* [2007] ECR I-10779, para 43 and Case C-341/05 *Laval un Partneri Ltd v Svenska Byggnadsarbetareförbundet* [2007] ECR I-11767, para 90.

[28] Case C-279/09 *DEB Deutsche Energiehandels- und Beratungsgesellschaft mbH v Bundesrepublik Deutschland* (ECJ, 22 December 2010), nyr, para 30.

[29] Ibid, para 39.

[30] Case C-34/09 *Gerardo Ruiz Zambrano v Office national de l'emploi (ONEm)* (ECJ, 8 March 2011), nyr. See also Case C-256/11 *Murat Dereci and Others v Bundesministerium für Inneres* (ECJ, 15 November 2011), nyr.

States that submitted observations defended the view that the applicant's situation could not trigger the application of EU law because the children had never left Belgium. In other words, since there was no identifiable cross-border element, it was argued that this situation should be considered as falling outside the scope of Union law even though no one denied that the applicant's children enjoyed the status of EU citizens. In line with the recommendation of Advocate General Sharpston, the Court disagreed: It first held that Article 20 TFEU precludes *national* measures which have the *effect* of depriving EU citizens of the genuine enjoyment of the substance of the rights conferred by virtue of their status as EU citizens. Because a refusal to grant a right of residence and a work permit to a third country national with dependent minor children in the Member State where those children are nationals and reside has such an effect, the Court decided that it was irrelevant that the children never exercised their right to free movement within the territory of the Member States. Belgium's decision therefore fell within the scope of Union law.

More than the outcome, which is very much in line with pre-Lisbon case law,[31] this case is particularly significant because it raises the question of the scope of application of EU citizenship/fundamental rights that are not constrained by Article 51(1) of the Charter because they are guaranteed by other provisions of EU law or are recognised as general principles of EU law. In a particularly remarkable Opinion, Advocate General Sharpston meticulously addresses the question of whether EU fundamental rights can be invoked as free-standing rights against a Member State. The Advocate General naturally knew that the case law of the Court quite clearly indicates that private parties cannot rely on EU fundamental rights when the facts of the relevant case do not trigger the application of other provisions of EU law. In the absence of 'some link' with EU law, the relevant national measure cannot be said to fall within the scope of Union law or (to paraphrase Article 51(1)) to be implementing Union law. For the Advocate General, however, the time has come to clearly spell out what 'the scope of Union law' means for the purposes of EU fundamental rights protection, and her own suggestion is to make

> the availability of EU fundamental rights protection dependent neither on whether a Treaty provision was directly applicable nor on whether secondary legislation had been enacted, but rather on *the existence and scope of a material EU competence*. To put the point another way: the rule would be that, provided that the EU had competence (whether exclusive or shared) in a particular area of law, EU fundamental rights should protect the citizen of the EU *even if such competence has not yet been exercised*.[32]

After reviewing the advantages of such an approach, Sharpston nonetheless concludes that

---

[31] See in particular Case C-200/02 *Kunqian Catherine Zhu and Man Lavette Chen v Secretary of State for the Home Department* [2004] ECR I-9925.

[32] Opinion of AG Sharpston of 30 September 2010 in Case C-34/09 *Ruiz Zambrano*, n 30 above, (ECJ, 8 March 2011), para 163.

[m]aking the application of EU fundamental rights dependent solely on the existence of exclusive or shared EU competence would involve introducing an overtly federal element into the structure of the EU's legal and political system. Simply put, a change of the kind would be analogous to that experienced in US constitutional law after the decision in *Gitlow v New York* . . . A change of that kind would alter, in legal and political terms, the very nature of fundamental rights under EU law. It therefore requires both an evolution in the case-law and an unequivocal political statement from the constituent powers of the EU (its Member States), pointing at a new role for fundamental rights in the EU.[33]

The judgment of the Court, however, does not address this fundamental issue. In fact, it does not even acknowledge it, which reinforces the view whereby the *Wachauf*/*ERT* line of cases is there to stay. In other words, the Lisbon Treaty has not transformed EU fundamental rights into free-standing rights that can be invoked in any situation to challenge national measures.

To conclude on the alleged federal effect of the Charter, a cursory reading of the Charter easily confirms that it has not empowered the Court of Justice to review any provision of national law in the light of the fundamental rights it lays down. Even in areas where the EU can legislate, the reach of the fundamental rights enshrined in the Charter is not boundless. As explained above, Article 51(1) confirms beyond any doubt that national authorities, when acting *outside* the scope of EU law, are *not* bound by its provisions. In other words, it is still a condition for EU courts in exercising their jurisdiction that the relevant national measure falls within the scope of Union law. While this notion of 'scope' may be viewed as fairly ambiguous, it is simply wrong to affirm that natural and legal persons, following the entry into force of the Lisbon Treaty, have gained the right to institute judicial proceedings on the basis of any provision of the Charter, in any situation, against any national (or EU) public authority. If anything, the Charter may be criticised for apparently narrowing the pre-Lisbon reach of EU fundamental rights law as it includes a provision which appears to suggest that the national authorities must respect EU fundamental rights *only* when they are implementing Union law. One may only hope that the Court will eventually remedy the drafting deficiencies of the Charter on this point. What is nevertheless crystal-clear is that the Charter cannot enable the European Court of Justice to function in a way similar to the operation of the US Supreme Court, that is, to define a 'federal' standard against which *all* national rules may be evaluated and eventually set aside. Viewed in this light, the so-called 'opt-out' Protocol[34] secured by the UK and Poland serves no useful

---

[33] Ibid, paras 172–73.

[34] Protocol No 30 ([2010] OJ C83/313) was devised in order to satisfy the British government's 'wish . . . to clarify certain aspects of the application of the Charter' (Recital 8 of the Protocol). However, Protocol No 30 does not render the Charter wholly inapplicable in those countries – it does not preclude individuals from invoking the Charter's provisions before British and Polish courts – and is not therefore, strictly speaking, an 'opt-out' protocol but rather a de facto interpretative declaration. For a recent confirmation of this view by the Court of Appeal in England and Wales: See *R (on the application of NS) v Secretary of State for the Home Department*, 12 July 2010 [2010] CA Civ 990 (the fundamental rights set out in the Charter can be relied on as against the United Kingdom and the

legal purpose, as the Charter already made clear that it does not in itself 'extend the ability' of the Court of Justice, or any British or Polish court 'to find that the laws, regulations or administrative provisions, practices or action of Poland or of the United Kingdom are inconsistent with the fundamental rights, freedoms and principles that it reaffirms'.[35] The crucial and final point is that fundamental rights guaranteed by national constitutions and/or the ECHR are complemented, not superseded by the Charter. Whilst one may legitimately express some concerns over the possibility of future judicial activism and a federal interpretation of the Charter, the Court of Justice, if only for 'diplomatic' reasons,[36] is unlikely to let the fundamental rights 'genie' get out of the bottle.

III. Towards an Increased Application of EU Fundamental Rights in 'Horizontal' Situations?

The landmark *Kücükdeveci* judgment, issued on 19 January 2010, suggests that similarly to the general principles of EU law, provisions of the Charter are capable of affecting legal relations between private parties.[37] The so-called horizontal effect of certain EU law provisions – the right to rely on these provisions in the context of legal proceedings between private parties – was made clear in *Defrenne II* where the Court held that the Treaty principle of equal pay for male and female workers for equal work, now laid down in Article 157 TFEU, applies not only to the action of public authorities, but also extends to all agreements intended to regulate paid labour collectively, as well as to contracts between individuals.[38] The

first-instance judge erred in holding otherwise). Interestingly, the Master of Rolls subsequently made a reference to the Court of Justice (see Case C-411/10 *NS v Secretary of State for the Home Department*) asking inter alia whether a decision made by a Member State under the relevant regulation falls within the scope of EU law for the purposes of Article 6 TEU and/or Article 51 of the Charter, and assuming that such a decision falls within the scope of EU law, whether Protocol No 30 has any effect in respect of the duty of the UK to observe EU fundamental rights when implementing EU law.

[35] Article 1(1) of the Protocol. It must be said that this provision only restates the obvious as the Charter itself provides that it does not and cannot be relied on to extend the powers of EU institutions, including the Court of Justice, but it does so in an incredibly awkward manner by referring in particular to the puzzling notion of ability rather than the traditional notion of jurisdiction. And generally speaking, this provision will *not* preclude the Court of Justice from ruling that UK or Polish rules or practices are contrary to EU fundamental rights which are guaranteed as general principles of Union law or which are further developed by other provisions of EU law.

[36] It must be remembered that the US Supreme Court's 'legal coup' took place in rather unique historical circumstances – the persistent segregationist practices in Southern States – which required, in turn, a revolutionary expansion of the scope of the US Bill of Rights.

[37] For more developments on the concept of direct and indirect horizontal effects of EU fundamental rights, see M Safjan and P Miklaszewicz, 'Horizontal Effect of the General Principles of EU Law in the Sphere of Private Law' (2010) 18 *European Review of Private Law* 475.

[38] Case 43/75 *Gabrielle Defrenne v Société Anonyme Belge de Navigation Aerienne (SABENA)* (*Defrenne II*) [1976] ECR 455, para 39. See also Case C-281/98 *Angonese v Cassa di Risparmio di Bolzano* [2000] ECR I-4139, para 36 and the analysis offered by AG Bot in his Opinion of 7 July 2009 in Case C-555/07 *Seda Kücükdeveci v Swedex GmbH & Co KG* [2010] ECR I-365, para 85.

ability to invoke the principle of equal pay means that in proceedings between private parties national courts must declare void any contractual agreements or collective regulations which have an element of discrimination based on sex. The *Defrenne II* ruling has generally been welcomed if only because it ensures respect for the principle of hierarchy of norms and is consistent with the Court's role as the guardian of the rule of law.[39]

The question we shall now focus on is whether the legally-binding status of the Charter may increase the opportunities for individuals to invoke EU fundamental rights in the context of legal proceedings between private parties. Advocate General Bot, in the concluding paragraph of his Opinion in *Kücükdeveci*, offered an interesting prediction:

> [G]iven the ever increasing intervention of Community law in relations between private persons, the Court will, in my view, be inevitably confronted with other situations which raise the question of the right to rely, in proceedings between private persons, on directives which contribute to ensuring observance of fundamental rights. Those situations will probably increase in number if the Charter of Fundamental Rights of the European Union becomes legally binding in the future, since among the fundamental rights contained in that charter are a number which are already part of the existing body of Community law in the form of directives.[40]

The Advocate General, unfortunately, does not further explain why one should expect the number of instances where EU fundamental rights may be applied in horizontal situations to increase post-Lisbon Treaty. The sole argument proposed would appear to be that some of the Charter's rights have been further specified by a series of directives. One may wonder if this is not also true of most general principles of EU law. The Charter does, however, increase the visibility of the rights it contains and may therefore lead more applicants and their counsel to seek to rely on them or at the very least, to test their cognisability. Yet it remains to be seen whether they will do so in the context of proceedings between private persons.

But let us return to the issue of the immediate impact of the *Kücükdeveci* case in relation to the horizontal application of the fundamental rights enshrined in provisions of the Charter. This judgment may not, however, be understood without first considering its immediate predecessor: the *Mangold* case, in which the Court was asked to clarify the horizontal application of rights laid down in directives.

In *Mangold*, the main legal issue was whether the fixed-term contract concluded under German law by a 56-year-old man with a private employer was incompatible with the principle of non-discrimination on grounds of age as laid down in Directive 2000/78[41] because it authorised, without restrictions, the conclusion of fixed-term

---

[39] D Simon, 'SABENA is dead, Gabrielle Defrenne's case is still alive: the old lady's testament . . .' in MP Maduro and L Azoulai (eds), *The Past and Future of EU Law – The Classics of EU Law Revisited on the 50th Anniversary of the Rome Treaty* (Oxford, Hart Publishing, 2010) 269.
[40] Opinion of AG Bot in Case C-555/07 *Kücükdeveci*, above n 38, para 90.
[41] Council Directive 2000/78/EC of 27 November 2000 establishing a general framework for equal treatment in employment and occupation [2000] OJ L303/16.

employment contracts for all workers over the age of 52. An important aspect of the case is that the period prescribed for transposition of that directive had not yet expired as far as Germany was concerned. It was already clear by then that a Member State to which a directive is addressed may not, during the period prescribed for transposition, adopt measures that may seriously compromise the attainment of the result prescribed by the directive.[42] But it was far from certain whether this reasoning could be applied in the context of horizontal situations such as the one in *Mangold*. After noting that Directive 2000/78 does *not* itself lay down the principle of equal treatment in the field of employment and occupation, the Court ruled that the principle of non-discrimination on grounds of age, which the Directive promotes by laying down a general framework for combating discrimination on that basis, must instead be regarded as a general principle of EU law derived from various international instruments and the constitutional traditions common to the Member States. As a result, for the Court, there is no need to further discuss the absence of transposition in Germany, as the 'observance of the general principle of equal treatment, in particular in respect of age, cannot as such be conditional upon the expiry of the period allowed to the Member States for the transposition'[43] of this directive. The question rather becomes whether the contested German provision falls within the scope of Union law. Provided that it does and that a reference is made to the Court for a preliminary ruling, it is well established that the Court must provide all the criteria of interpretation needed by the national court to determine whether the German provision is compatible with this general principle of law. In this case, the Court did accept that the national legislation at issue aimed to implement Directive 1999/70.[44] Therefore, it was reasonable to conclude that the national measure fell within the scope of EU law in accordance with the *Wachauf* line of cases. But *Mangold* could arguably also be read as an *ERT*-style derogation case, as the controversial national measure constituted an exception to the principle of non-discrimination on grounds of age. National derogations from this principle are, however, permitted by the Directive itself as long as the Member State shows that the national legislation is objectively justified under EU law.[45]

In any event, the Court was not convinced that the German legislation was objectively justified, as Germany failed to show that fixing an age threshold is objectively necessary to favour the integration into working life of unemployed older workers, and held that EU law precludes any provision of national law, such as the one at issue, that authorises the conclusion of the fixed-term employment contracts. With respect to our topic of inquiry, the most significant aspect of this

---

[42] Case C-129/96 *Inter-Environnement Wallonie ASBL v Région Wallonne* [1997] ECR I-7411, para 45.

[43] Case C-144/04 *Werner Mangold v Rüdiger Helm* [2005] ECR I-9981, para 76.

[44] Ibid, para 75. Directive 1999/70/EC of 28 June 1999, concerning the framework agreement on fixed-term work concluded by ETUC, UNICE and CEEP [1999] OJ L175/43.

[45] See Article 6(1) of the Directive: 'Member States may provide that differences of treatment on grounds of age shall not constitute discrimination, if, within the context of national law, they are objectively and reasonably justified by a legitimate aim, including legitimate employment policy, labour market and vocational training objectives, and if the means of achieving that aim are appropriate and necessary'.

case is that it clearly spells out that the general principles of Union law, including fundamental rights, can be relied on in the context of legal disputes between private parties when they are further developed in directives regardless of whether the deadline for transposition of the directives had passed or not. This has an important practical consequence, as the Court of Justice also indicated that it is the responsibility of the national court hearing a dispute involving the principle of non-discrimination in respect of age, to provide the legal protection which individuals derive from rules of Union law to ensure that those rules are fully effective, even if this means setting aside any provision of national law which may conflict with EU law.[46]

This reasoning has been subject to severe criticism essentially because it would undermine the coherence of the doctrine of direct effect by allowing for the horizontal direct effect of provisions of non-implemented directives whereas the Court has consistently ruled that a directive, being formally addressed to Member States, cannot of itself impose obligations on an individual and cannot therefore be relied on as such against an individual.[47] Some scholars have nonetheless welcomed the *Mangold* decision by considering that it is not shocking that general principles of EU law can have direct effect and thus can be relied upon in relationships of a purely civil nature.[48] Moreover, the Court did not suggest that the principle of non-discrimination in respect of age, as a general principle of Union law, had 'real' horizontal direct effect.[49] In other words, 'a national court, hearing a dispute involving private parties only, cannot disapply, at their expense, provisions of national law which are in conflict with a directive'.[50] The Court of Justice merely indicated that a private party may rely on the principle of non-discrimination on grounds of age – a general principle of EU law – whenever the national legislation falls with the scope of EU law due to its close tie with EU secondary legislation. As such and not as a self-sufficient norm, the general principle can be relied upon before a national court in order to challenge the validity of national legislation conflicting with it. Where the challenge is deemed to be well founded and the national legislation cannot be interpreted so as to conform with the general principles of EU law, the national court must set aside the provision of national law at issue so as to guarantee the full effectiveness of the general principle. *Mangold* is therefore about *invocabilité d'exclusion*.[51] The 'coherence' of the doctrine of direct effect, or rather, the rule whereby a directive cannot be relied on as such against an

---

[46] Case C-144/04 *Mangold*, above n 43, para 77. See, to that effect, Case 106/77 *Amministrazione delle Finanze dello Stato v Simmenthal SpA* [1978] ECR 629, para 21.

[47] See eg Editorial Comments, 'Horizontal Direct Effect – A Law of Diminishing Coherence' (2006) 43 *CML Rev* 1.

[48] J Jans, 'The Effect in national Legal Systems of the Prohibition of Discrimination on Grounds of Age as a General Principle of Community Law' (2007) 34 *Legal Issues of Economic Integration* 53, 66.

[49] Ibid, 62: the Court did not say that the prohibition of age discrimination, as a general principle of Union law, has real horizontal effect. It merely said that this general principle of EU law can be relied on before a national court in order to challenge the validity of national legislation conflicting with it.

[50] Opinion of AG Tizzano of 30 June 2005 in Case C-144/04 *Mangold*, above n 43, para 122.

[51] See Jans, 'The Effect in national Legal Systems of the Prohibition of Discrimination on Grounds of Age as a General Principle of Community Law', above n 48, 62.

individual, remains unaffected as in *Mangold*, the directive disappears behind the general principle of EU law that the directive merely, dare we say, implements.

We will not discuss whether the Court was right to regard the principle of non-discrimination on grounds of age as a general principle of EU law, given that it would be difficult to derive it from the constitutional traditions common to the Member States.[52] One may simply point out that the Charter explicitly prohibits discrimination on this ground.[53] More importantly, the potential for increased horizontal application of Charter rights in the light of *Kücükdeveci* should now be considered.

In *Kücükdeveci*, the Court of Justice had first to determine whether national rules regarding calculation of the notice period for dismissal from work fell within the scope of Union law and, were this the case, whether they were compatible with the general principle of non-discrimination on grounds of age. As regards the first problem, the Court noted that in contrast to the situation in *Bartsch*,[54] the allegedly discriminatory conduct occurred after the expiry of the transposition deadline of Directive 2000/78:

> On that date, that directive had the effect of bringing within the scope of European Union law the national legislation at issue in the main proceedings, which concerns a matter governed by that directive, in this case the conditions of dismissal.[55]

The Court does not even seem to require that the disputed national rules should constitute a measure specifically adopted to implement Directive 2000/78. Rather, the mere expiry of the transposition deadline is enough to bring within the scope of Union law any national measure that has a bearing on the area(s) governed by the Directive. This means that while the national rule at issue does not explicitly seek to implement Directive 2000/78, because it affects the conditions of dismissal of employees, it must therefore be regarded as a measure falling within the (material) scope of the Directive and therefore of Union law. What is also striking in *Kücükdeveci* is that there is no reference to *Wachauf*. It might be 'that the Court albeit silently and thus not terribly helpfully still conceived the situation in *Kücükdeveci* as being of implementation, albeit in a rather broader manner than in *Bartsch*'.[56] If this view is correct, it would confirm the view defended in this

---

[52] For some critical views, see Opinion of AG Mazák of 15 February 2007 in Case C-411/05 *Félix Palacios de la Villa v Cortefiel Servicios SA* [2007] ECR I-8531.

[53] Article 21(1): 'Any discrimination based on any ground such as age or sexual orientation shall be prohibited'.

[54] Case C-427/06 *Bartsch*, above n 4. A decision that once again deals with social policy and the (non-implemented) Directive 2000/78 in Germany and where the Court accepted to hold that in the circumstances of the case, the national guidelines at issue did *not* constitute a measure implementing Directive 2000/78. In other words, the matter fell outside the scope of EU law and, therefore, the general principle of EU law could not be used by the CJEU to review the national legislation since, using the words of Advocate General Sharpston, the general principles do not apply in abstract. A close link is in fact needed between the national legislation and the general principle enshrined in the Directive.

[55] See Case C-555/07 *Kücükdeveci*, above n 38, para 25.

[56] Editorial Comments, 'The Scope of Application of the General Principles of Union Law: An Ever Expanding Union?' (2010) 47 *CML Rev* 1589, 1593 (fn 26).

paper that the *Wachauf*-style review of national measures may be applied in a large number of situations, including horizontal national proceedings where their subject-matter falls within the scope of Union law by virtue of a piece of EU secondary legislation.

The approach taken by the Court of Justice as regards the scope of application of Union law in *Mangold*, *Bartsch* and *Kücükdeveci* has been recently reaffirmed in *Römer*, a Grand Chamber judgment delivered on 10 May 2011 and which concerns the application of the principle of non-discrimination on grounds of sexual orientation in the context of social policy.[57] The applicant claimed that, for the calculation of his pension under the relevant national rules, he ought to be treated in the same manner as a married, not permanently separated, pensioner. However, the Court was not convinced that EU law governed the applicant's situation. With reference to *Bartsch* and *Kücükdeveci*, the Court held that neither (ex) Article 13 EC (now Article 19 TFEU) nor Directive 2000/78 allows a situation such as that at issue in the proceedings before the Court to be brought within the scope of Union law in respect of the period *prior* to the expiry of the deadline for transposing that directive.[58]

In the wake of *Kücükdeveci* and to summarise, one should distinguish between two main situations where national legislation regulating horizontal situations may fall within the scope of EU law in relation to Directive 2000/78: Before and after the expiry of the transposition deadline. In the latter scenario, any national measure that concerns a matter governed by the directive falls within the scope of Union law (*Kücükdeveci*). In the former scenario, to fall within the scope of Union law, the relevant national measure must either specifically implement the directive (*Bartsch*) or fall within the scope of EU law by virtue of another piece of EU law (*Mangold*). In the end, it follows from this line of case law that the application of the general principles of EU law is closely tied to EU secondary legislation[59] and, therefore, it appears clear to us that the general principles of EU law do not apply in abstract; that the directives are not merely 'decorative rules' and that the CJEU is in fact cautious when applying directives and general principles of law simultaneously.[60]

One additional important related issue to address is whether this line of cases (*Wachauf*-style horizontal situations) should only be limited to non-discrimination on grounds of age or may also apply to other general principles of EU law and in particular the fundamental rights that may be simultaneously enshrined in the

---

[57] Case C-147/08 *Jürgen Römer v Freie und Hansestadt Hamburg* (ECJ, 10 May 2011), nyr.
[58] Case C-55/07 *Kücükdeveci*, above n 38, paras 60–63.
[59] E Muir, 'Of Ages in – And Edges of – EU Law' (2011) 48 *CML Rev* 39, 56.
[60] Many Advocates General are sceptical about the *Mangold* reasoning and have urged the Court to be extremely cautious when dealing with directives enshrining general principles. Accordingly a reckless approach might lead, using the words of AG Ruiz-Jarabo Colomer, to a situation where the directives constitute mere 'decorative rules'. See, eg, the Opinion of AG Mázak in Case C-411/05 *Palacios de la Villa*, above n 52, para 133 ff, and Opinion of AG Ruiz-Jarabo Colomer in Cases C-55 and C-56/07 *Michaeler, Subito GmbH, and Volgger v Amt für sozialen Arbeitsschutz, Autonome Provinz Bozen* [2008] ECR I-3135, para 21 ff.

Charter.[61] In the words of Advocate General Kokott, 'it remains to be seen whether the Court will extend such horizontal direct effect to other general legal principles'.[62] One may wisely suggest that the Court think twice before extending the *Kücükdeveci* approach to areas beyond those governed by EU anti-discrimination law where the (general) principle of equal treatment naturally logically enjoys a special standing.[63] This would however suggest that the principle of equal treatment is in a preferred position amongst fundamental rights and this is not a position we would advocate. Similarly, we submit that most if not all provisions of the Charter, whilst they are primary aimed at protecting individuals against public authorities, are all capable of being directly effective in the context of judicial proceedings between individuals.[64] If anything, the case law of the European Court of Human Rights indicates that many of the rights guaranteed by the European Convention on Human Rights can affect relations between private individuals.[65] By contrast with the legal position of the European Convention in the national legal systems, one cannot usefully invoke provisions of the Charter where the national measure or action being challenged falls outside the scope of Union law, as this chapter has made clear.[66] To put it differently, the scope *ratione personae* of the rights contained in the Charter is similar to the general principles of EU law. However, the material scope of application of the Charter is broader. When one adds this to the more highly visible nature of the Charter, one cannot exclude that claimants and their counsel may not seek on a more regular basis to test the applicability of the Charter's rights in the context of 'horizontal' litigation.[67]

---

[61] See Case C-73/07 *Tietosuojavaltuutettu v Satakunnan Markkinapörssi Oy and Satamedia Oy* [2008] ECR I-9831. In this case, the European Commission relied on the general principle protecting the right to privacy in relation to a non-implemented directive.

[62] Opinion of AG Kokott of 6 May 2010 in Case C-104/09 *Roca-Álvarez v Sesa Start Espana ETT SA* (ECJ, 30 September 2010), nyr, para 55.

[63] See Muir, 'Of Ages in – And Edges of – EU Law', above n 59, 56.

[64] An alternative approach would be to deny the horizontal application of the Charter's rights as its Article 51 provides that they are only addressed to the EU institutions and the Member States (when they implement EU law) and instead, recognise the horizontal direct effect of the general principles of EU law as in the *Kücükdeveci* case.

[65] For further discussion of the *Drittwirkung* effect of the provisions of the ECHR, see eg P van Dijk et al (eds), *Theory and Practice of the European Convention on Human Right*, 4th edn (Antwerpen, Intersentia, 2006) 15 ff.

[66] For a recent example, see Case C-434/09 *Shirley McCarthy v Secretary of State for the Home Department* (ECJ, 5 May 2011), nyr (the sole status of EU citizen is not sufficient to trigger the application of EU law where the EU citizen has not exercised his right of free movement and is not subject to measures having the effect of depriving him of the genuine enjoyment of the substance of the rights associated with his status as a Union citizen, or of impeding the exercise of his right to move and reside freely within the territory of the Member States).

[67] In a recent Opinion delivered on 8 September 2011, AG Trstenjak argued for the lack of horizontal effect of the Charter's rights. As argued in this chapter, we disagree with such a stance (See Opinion of AG Trstenjak of 8 September 2010 in Case C-282/10 *Maribel Dominguez v Centre informatique du Centre Ouest Atlantique and Préfet de la région Centre* (ECJ, 24 January 2011), nyr.

IV. 'New' Classification of the Main Situations in Which EU Fundamental Rights Bind the Member States

The potential for an increased horizontal applicability of EU fundamental rights, following the new status of EU primary law acquired by the Charter post-Lisbon Treaty, would seem to justify a new classification with respect to the main situations in which EU fundamental rights bind the Member States. The traditional assumption is that EU fundamental rights cannot bind private parties but are only applicable in vertical situations, that is, in the context of litigation between a private party and a public authority. As previously explained, we believe that two main vertical situations can be distinguished: Member States are bound by EU fundamental rights either when they implement or derogate from provisions of EU law, the notions of implementation and derogation having been broadly understood by the Court of Justice. We further submit that the horizontal effect of EU fundamental rights ought to be taken into account and assessed in the light of the *Wachauf* and *ERT* lines of cases. Accordingly and as will be explained below, it would appear appropriate to distinguish between two further situations: a situation of *Wachauf à l'horizontale* and a situation of *ERT à l'horizontale*.

	National measures implementing EU law	National (including private) measures derogating from EU law
Vertical situation: Dispute between a private party and a state authority	*Category 1: Wachauf-type situations* ■ *Wachauf* [1989] ■ *Klensch* [1986] ■ *Bosphorus* [1996] ■ *Molenheide* [1997] ■ *Lindqvist* [2003] ■ *Rundfunk* [2003] ■ *BookerAquaculture* [2003] ■ *Steffensen* [2003] ■ *Eiterköpfe* [2005] ■ *DEB* [2010] ■ *NS* [2011]	*Category 2: ERT-type situations* *ERT* [1993] ■ *Familiapress* [1997] ■ *Carpenter* [2002] ■ *Baumbast* [2002] ■ *Schmidberger* [2003] ■ *Omega* [2004] ■ *Sayn-Wittgenstein* [2010] ■ *Ruiz-Zambrano* [2011] ■ *Dereci* [2011]
Horizontal situation: Dispute between private parties	*Category 3: Wachauf à l'horizontale* ■ *Mangold* [2005] ■ *Kücükdeveci* [2010]	*Category 4: ERT à l'horizontale* *Defrenne II* [1975] ■ *Bosman* [1995] ■ *Angonese* [2000] ■ *Karner* [2004] ■ *Viking* [2007] ■ *Laval* [2007]

A. Reliance on EU Fundamental Rights against National State Authorities (Categories 1 and 2)

Traditionally, the various situations in which EU fundamental rights may be relied upon to challenge national measures have been regrouped into two broad categories. The first category concerns the review of national measures implementing EU law by the European Court of Justice (previously referred to as the *Wachauf*-style review of Member State measures). It is submitted that this category covers all national measures that concern the implementation – broadly understood – of EU secondary legislation, be it directives[68] or regulations.[69] In other words, a national measure should fall within the scope of Union law wherever it is linked to the application, enforcement or even the sole interpretation of EU secondary legislation.[70] If so, the national measure must be compatible with the requirements of the protection of fundamental rights in the Union legal order.

Where national measures derogate from EU free movement rules, including the specific EU citizenship provisions of the TFEU, the Court of Justice has also jurisdiction to review their compatibility with EU fundamental rights. This has been referred to as the *ERT*-style review of Member State measures, as the Court held in *ERT* that where the Member States rely upon the derogations provided for in what is now the TFEU, to justify national rules which affect the exercise of any of the EU's fundamental freedoms, the national rule at issue must be *interpreted* in the light of the general principles of Union law and in particular of fundamental rights, and must obviously be compatible with them.[71] This was clearly confirmed in the *Familiapress* judgment where the Court made clear that *ERT*-style review of national measures also applies where Member States rely upon the range of the so-called public interest justifications or mandatory requirements developed through the case law of the Court to justify non-discriminatory measures derogating from provisions of EU law.[72]

In *Schmidberger*,[73] the Court addressed a different hypothesis: Faced with a national measure derogating from EU rules on the free movement of goods but

---

[68] Case C-101/01 *Criminal proceedings against Bodil Lindqvist* [2003] ECR I-12971, paras 84–87.

[69] Case C-84/95 *Bosphorus Hava Yollari Turizm ve Ticaret AS v Minister for Transport*, [1996] ECR I-3953, para 19.

[70] In our view, the cases of *Booker Aquaculture* (Cases C-20/00 and 64/00 *Booker Aquaculture and Another v The Scottish Ministers* [2003] ECR I-7411) and *Joachim Steffensen* (Case C-276/01 [2003] ECR I-3735) should also be understood in the light of *Wachauf*. This judgment is in fact quoted in both cases though the cases do not deal in the strict sense with the implementation of directives but rather with their application. In *Booker Aquaculture*, the Court of Justice had to assess the breach of the right to property in connection with to the absence of compensation concerning an implemented directive whereas the Court of Justice emphasised that procedural safeguards concerning rights of the defence should be respected when implementing a directive in *Steffensen*.

[71] See Case C-260/89 *ERT*, above n 6, paras 43–44.

[72] See Case C-368/95 *Vereingte Familiapress Zeitungsverlags und Vertreibs GmbH v Heinrich Bauer Verlag* [1997] ECR I-3689.

[73] See Case C-112/00 *Eugen Schmidberger Internationale Transporte und Planzüge v Austria* [2003] ECR I-5659.

justified by the need to protect freedom of assembly, the Court agreed that national authorities may seek to justify a measure derogating from an EU economic fundamental freedom on the ground that it is necessary to protect fundamental rights guaranteed in the Union legal order. For the Court, since both the Union and its Member States are required to respect fundamental rights, the protection of those rights may also be understood as an overriding requirement relating to the public interest, 'which, in principle, justifies a restriction of the obligations imposed by Community law, even under a fundamental freedom guaranteed by the Treaty such as the free movement of goods'.[74] In other words, not only do EU fundamental rights constitute limits on the Member States' regulatory autonomy, but Member States may also seek to rely on them against other EU law norms and in particular, when they need to justify national measures interfering with EU free movement rights.[75]

In any event, the most important point regarding the *ERT* line of cases is that any national measure which negatively affects one of the four EU fundamental freedoms – free movement of goods, persons, services and capital – automatically falls within the scope of Union law and as such, it must be shown to be compatible with EU fundamental rights or be justified with reference to EU fundamental rights. The recent case of *Sayn-Wittgenstein* also confirms the validity of an additional point made above: national measures derogating from EU (non-economic) citizenship provisions must be treated similarly to national measures derogating from EU (economic) free movement rights. In this rather entertaining case opposing the Austrian Princess of Sayn-Wittgenstein against the Austrian state regarding the Austrian Law on the abolition of the nobility, the Court nevertheless concluded the dispute fell within the substantive scope of EU law as it involved EU primary law, ie, Article 21 TFEU, thanks to the Princess who made also use of the freedom to move to and reside in another Member State (Germany), albeit the Court did confirm that the rules governing a person's surname and the use of titles of nobility are matters within the competence of the Member States.[76] What is particularly worth noting about this case is that the Court confirmed that any national measure interfering with EU citizenship rights can be treated as a 'standard' national restriction on EU economic free movement rules.[77] In other words,

---

[74] Ibid, para 77.

[75] This approach was confirmed in *Omega* (Case C-36/02 *Omega Spielhallen- und Automatenaufstellungs- GmbH v Oberbürgermeisterin der Bundesstadt Bonn* [2004] ECR I-9609). There is, however, a minor difference with the case of *Schmidberger* to the extent that the Court decided that the fundamental right at stake, the principle of respect for human dignity, should be treated as being part of the public policy exception already provided for in the EC Treaty. The end result was nonetheless the same: Respect for human dignity can justify a restriction of EU free movement rights and in *Omega*, the national restrictive measure was found compatible with EU law because it did not go beyond what was necessary to attain the objective pursued by the competent authorities, ie the objective of protecting human dignity.

[76] Case C-208/09 *Ilonka Sayn-Wittgenstein v Landeshauptmann von Wien* (ECJ, 22 December 2010), nyr.

[77] Ibid, paras 37–40. The Court noted that the Princess (Fürstin) engaged in a professional activity in Germany providing services to recipients in one or more other Member States and she was therefore also in a position to argue a violation of the freedom to provide services (Article 56 TFEU).

in both situations, they may be justified on public policy grounds only if they are necessary for the protection of the interests which they are intended to secure and only if those objectives cannot be attained by less restrictive measures.[78] In the end, this case reflects the thin dividing line between economic (Article 56 TFEU) and non-economic provisions (Article 21 TFEU) of the TFEU.[79] For the CJEU, though the rules governing a person's surname and the use of titles of nobility are matters within the competence of the Member States, the matter fell within the scope of EU law since EU primary law was applicable in the case at issue.

B. *Wachauf à l'horizontale* and *ERT à l'horizontale* (Categories 3 and 4)

Provided that the contested national measure falls within the scope of Union law, a private party may seek to rely on EU fundamental rights against another private party. Cases such as *Mangold*,[80] *Bartsch*[81] and *Kücükdeveci*[82] may be said to apply the *Wachauf*-style review of Member State measures in the context of 'horizontal' judicial proceedings. In all of these cases, EU law was relevant because the national measures at issue were concerned with the implementation of EU secondary legislation and the private plaintiffs all sought to obtain from courts that they set aside the national measures on the grounds that their EU fundamental rights were affected in the context of legal proceedings against private employers. The extension of the *Wachauf*-style review to horizontal situations requires us to look beyond a narrow definition of the state, since individuals are not responsible for the implementation – broadly understood – of EU law. However, proceedings between private parties can in fact create a situation that concerns in essence the same question, ie the (correct) application of EU legislation. It should also be kept in mind that such proceedings can never be completed without the involvement of the judiciary and in that sense the state is always present, in horizontal situations.

In the fourth and final category distinguished above (*ERT à l'horizontale*), cases such as *Viking* and *Laval* and also *Bosman* have been included. These cases oppose natural or legal persons (regulatory bodies, trade unions, economic operators) and offer striking examples where free movement claims conflict with defences grounded in fundamental rights.[83] In other words, these cases call for an eminently difficult

---

[78] The Court found the Austrian legislation to comply with these requirements. Indeed, and similarly to the situation in *Schmidberger*, the Austrian refusal to recognise on public policy grounds the surname of a national which has been obtained in another Member State and contains a title of nobility is essentially justified in the name of the principle of equality before the law of all Austrian citizens, a principle which the EU legal system strives to protect as well as a general principle of law which is also enshrined in Article 20 of the Charter of Fundamental Right (paras 88–89).

[79] Case C-208/09 *Sayn-Wittgenstein*, above n 76.

[80] Case C-144/04 *Mangold*, above n 43.

[81] Case C-427/06 *Bartsch*, above n 4.

[82] Case C-555/07 *Kücükdeveci*, above n 38.

[83] Case C-71/02 *Herbert Karner Industrie-Auktionen GmbH v Troostwijk GmbH* [2004] ECR I-3025, paras 48–53.

reconciliation between EU fundamental rights and EU fundamental freedoms. In *Bosman*, the Court went as far as to accept that private parties themselves can rely on EU derogatory clauses to justify national measures derogating from EU free movement rules, and the issue of the public versus private nature of the litigious national rules is irrelevant with respect to the scope and content of the justifications put forward before the Court of Justice.[84] However, it goes without saying that private parties are less likely to put forward 'public order' justifications as, by their very nature, they are intended to be invoked solely by the state when it has to defend national restrictions.[85]

Whilst one may reasonable contend that the *Viking* and *Laval* judgments are no models of clarity, they strongly indicate that the Court of Justice has firmly put the right to take collective action, enshrined in Article 28 of the Charter and invoked by trade unions in these two cases, within the 'methodology of justifications' already quite well honed in the case law of the Court in respect of vertical relations. Unsurprisingly, the Court also confirmed that for the restrictions on the freedom to provide services of the relevant undertakings, following threatened or actual boycott actions undertaken by the trade unions, to be compatible with EU law, they must be justified by overriding reasons of public interest such as the protection of the workers of the host Member State against possible social dumping, and must not go beyond what is necessary in order to attain the objective being pursued by the trade unions. Therefore, it appears that there is nothing in principle preventing a private party from invoking any of the justifications already provided for in EU primary law or recognised by the case law of the Court as reasons of public interest.

V. Concluding Remarks

To sum up, EU fundamental rights bind the Member States when their measures or actions can be said to fall within the scope of EU law. This is normally the case whenever they enact measures to implement EU law (*Wachauf* line of cases) or adopt measures that constitute derogations from provisions of EU law (*ERT* line of cases). In this latter situation, EU fundamental rights may either be relied upon to interpret and review the legality of the national derogating measure or, by contrast, to justify it when it conflicts, for instance, with EU economic and

---

[84] Case C-415/93 *Union royale belge des sociétés de football association ASBL v Jean-Marc Bosman* [1995] ECR I-4921, para 86.

[85] See C Barnard, 'Derogations, Justifications and the Four Freedoms: Is State Interest Really Protected?' in C Barnard and O Odudu (eds), *The Outer Limits of European Union Law* (Oxford, Hart Publishing, 2009) 278. This conclusion can be supported by the view of the Court in *Spanish Strawberries* where the Court states that the Member States retain 'exclusive competence as regards the maintenance of public order and the safeguarding of internal security': Case C-265/95 *European Commission v France* [1997] ECR I-6959, para 33 (*Spanish Strawberries*).

non-economic free movement rights. We suggested above that two parallel categories can also be usefully distinguished: EU fundamental rights may indeed become relevant in 'horizontal' situations, that is, in the context of judicial disputes between private parties. We have therefore four main scenarios as regards the European Court of Justice's jurisdiction to review national measures for compliance with EU fundamental rights. It is argued that this classification applies both to Charter rights and general principles of Union law since, as discussed above, we do consider that Charter's rights may be applied to horizontal situations in specific circumstances. As regards this last point, it appears clear that the reach of fundamental rights after Lisbon clearly depends also on the future relationship between Charter rights and general principles of Union law. If the Charter's rights are not given the same personal scope of application as the general principles, then the general principles, due to their pervasive gap-filling character, can easily be used to evade the (potential) limited scope of the Charter. This situation should be avoided if only for ensuring the coherence of fundamental rights' protection within the European Union.

5

An End to the Possibilities – on Horizontal Liability in *Laval* and the Limits of Judicial Rights Protection

MARTIN MÖRK*

I. Introduction[1]

On 2 December 2009, one day after the Lisbon Treaty entered into force, the Swedish Labour Court concluded that Swedish trade unions had violated Article 49 EC (Article 56 TFEU) by taking collective action against Laval un Partneri Ltd – a Latvian company posting Latvian workers to Sweden.[2]

The finding was hardly surprising. Two years earlier, the European Court of Justice (ECJ) had settled the matter in the now infamous *Laval* case,[3] pronouncing in its own abstract way, that Article 49 EC precluded trade unions from taking collective action in circumstances such as the ones at hand.

Somewhat more surprising was the Labour Court's finding with regard to the question of liability. Clarifying that Swedish law did not allow for the trade unions to be held liable as against Laval for a breach of Article 49 EC, the Labour Court determined, without referring a question on the matter to the ECJ, that EU law required such a remedy.

---

* Head of Litigation, The Swedish Equality Ombudsman. The views expressed are the author's personal views and do not necessarily reflect those of the Equality Ombudsman.

[1] I wish to thank Ulf Bernitz for providing the inspiration for this chapter. In addition, I am indebted to Jan Komárek, Ida Otken Eriksson, Emmanuel Slautsky and Karin Wistrand for comments on earlier drafts. The usual disclaimer applies.

[2] Judgment of the Labour Court (Arbetsdomstolen) No 89/2009 of 2 December 2009 in Case No A 268/04 *Laval un Partneri Ltd v Svenska byggnadsarbetareförbundet et al*. For case comments, see U Bernitz and N Reich, 'Case No. A 268/04, The Labour Court, Sweden (Arbetsdomstolen) Judgment No. 89/09 of 2 December 2009 in *Laval un Partneri Ltd v Svenska byggnadsarbetareförbundet et al*' (2011) 48 *CML Rev* 603; M Rönmar, 'Laval returns to Sweden: The Final Judgment of the Swedish Labour Court and Swedish Legislative Reforms' (2010) 39 *ILJ* 280; A Kruse, 'Arbetsdomstolens dom i Laval – lojal tillämpning av EG-rätten eller vågad egen tillverkning?' (2010) *Europarättslig tidskrift* 381.

[3] Case C-341/05 *Laval un Partneri Ltd v Svenska Byggnadsarbetareförbundet and othersl* [2007] ECR I-11767.

In support of this conclusion the Labour Court, more or less trailing the ECJ's reasoning in *Francovich*,[4] inter alia referred to the effectiveness of EU law and the principle of loyalty 'according to which a breach of Community law should lead to effective sanctions to prevent such breaches'. Moreover, the Labour Court invoked a general EU law principle of liability that was applicable in horizontal situations. This principle, the Labour Court held, supporting itself mainly on *Francovich*, *Courage v Crehan*,[5] *Manfredi*[6] and *Raccanelli*,[7] must apply whenever Treaty provisions creating rights for individuals were found to be directly effective in a horizontal fashion:

> Liability for damages on an EC law basis has in the case law of the European Court of Justice been extended to situations in which a private party claims rights in accordance with EC law as against another private party. In order for liability for violations of EC law to exist between private parties, the EC legal rules violated must have direct effect on the national level, thereby creating rights for individuals that national courts are to protect. In addition, it is required that the direct effect is also applicable in relationships between private parties, so called horizontal direct effect.[8]

As for the conditions for determining whether the collective actions were such as to trigger liability under the principle, the Labour Court drew inspiration from the *Francovich* line of case law on non-contractual liability. Although the Labour Court expressed reservations as to whether the same conditions should apply to state and private party infringements, the Court in the end still applied the sufficiently serious breach criterion to the trade union action:

> [T]he Labour Court concludes that the actions of the trade unions at issue, the industrial actions, according to the preliminary ruling of European Court of Justice constituted a serious violation of the Treaty, as they were in conflict with a fundamental principle in the Treaty, the freedom to provide services. Although the right to take industrial action is also recognised by the EC as a fundamental right, the industrial actions in question, despite their objective of protecting workers, were held to be unacceptable as they were not proportionate. The Labour Court finds the stance of the ECJ in these issues to mean that there is a sufficiently clear violation of EC law in this case. The conditions for liability are thus met.[9]

In an interesting side remark, the Labour Court noted that whether or not the Swedish state also could be held liable was 'a question which should not affect the assessment of the Labour Court'.[10] In that context, the Labour Court pointed to

---

[4] Cases C-6/90 and 9/90 *Andrea Francovich and Danila Bonifaci and others v Italy* [1991] ECR I-5357.
[5] Case C-453/99 *Courage Ltd v Bernard Crehan* [2001] ECR I-6297.
[6] Cases C-295/04 to C-298/04 *Vincenzo Manfredi v Lloyd Adriatico Assicurazioni SpA and others* [2006] ECR I-6619.
[7] Case C-94/07 *Andrea Raccanelli v Max-Planck-Gesellschaft zur Förderung der Wissenschaften eV* [2008] ECR I-5939.
[8] Case No A 268/04 *Laval*, above n 2, 34.
[9] Ibid, 42.
[10] Ibid.

the ruling in the *Lehtinen* case,[11] in which the ECJ stated that Community law did not preclude that an individual was held liable in addition to the Member State.

The Labour Court did not content itself with laying down a new tort action directly based on EU law. By setting aside the very provision permitting the collective action in the first place (!) the Labour Court proceeded to establish an additional tortious breach of the applicable Swedish law. For the two breaches Laval was awarded exemplary (ie punitive) damages of approximately SEK 550,000. As the trade unions were considered to have lost the proceedings they were also ordered to pay Laval's legal costs of about SEK 2,100,000.

The ruling presents an extraordinary example of a national court of last instance demonstrating loyalty to EU law and its methods. In the same vein however, the judgment is also an illustration of the potential dangers inherent in some of these methods. The obvious remark in this respect concerns the discovery of a general EU law principle of liability applicable both in vertical and horizontal relationships. General principles of EU law have traditionally been discovered in Luxembourg and it is difficult to know what one is to make of sightings made elsewhere. In the absence of authoritative statements from the ECJ, the legal status of such principles must be considered as rather uncertain.

However, it would be too easy to discredit the outcome of the case solely by pointing to this weakness in the Labour Court's reasoning. Couldn't the Labour Court have arrived at the same conclusion without the support of the dubious principle? Wouldn't it have been possible to lay down the liability simply by referring to the duty to protect Laval's rights in an effective manner? After all, the principle of effective rights protection has been recognised in the EU legal order for a long time. In the words of the ECJ,

> the principle of effective judicial protection is a general principle of [EU] law stemming from the constitutional traditions common to the Member States, which has been enshrined in Articles 6 and 13 of the European Convention for the Protection of Human Rights and Fundamental Freedoms . . . and which has also been reaffirmed by Article 47 of the Charter of fundamental rights of the European Union.[12]

Article 47 of the Charter states that '[e]veryone whose rights and freedoms guaranteed by the law of the Union are violated has the right to an effective remedy before a tribunal'. Furthermore, Article 19(1) TEU provides that 'Member States shall provide remedies sufficient to ensure effective legal protection in the fields covered by Union law'.

The sophisticated claim, advanced by Bernitz and Reich, is that the horizontal damages remedy was indeed called for to cover a lacuna in effective rights protection.[13] In the following, I shall investigate this claim. As my focus will be on the requirement of effective rights protection, I shall remain agnostic with

---

[11] Case C-470/03 *AGM-COS.MET Srl v Suomen valtio and Tarmo Lehtinen* [2007] ECR I-2749.
[12] Case C-432/05 *Unibet (London) Ltd and Unibet (International) Ltd v Justitiekanslern* [2007] ECR I-2271, para 37.
[13] Bernitz and Reich, 'Case No. A 268/04', above n 2, 615.

respect to the existence of a general liability principle applicable in horizontal relations.

II. The *Laval* Case in the ECJ – Some Brief Points of Departure

Considering the vast amount of literature sparked by the *Laval* case (and its spiritual sibling *Viking*[14]), both the factual circumstances and the details of the ECJ's reasoning should be well known.[15] The following points are however central to the discussion to follow.

(i) The exercise of the fundamental right to take collective action in Sweden is guaranteed by the Swedish Constitution[16] and the law incorporating the European Convention on Human Rights (by virtue of Article 11 of the Convention).[17] The specific regulation of the exercise of the right to take collective action follows from the Swedish legislation, which entails rather specific rules on how and when industrial action may be resorted to.[18]

(ii) As confirmed by the Labour Court, the collective actions were lawful according to the applicable Swedish law. For that reason, the Swedish Police refused to stop the blockades when called to do so by Laval. Moreover, in December of 2004, prior to the ruling of the ECJ, the Labour Court rejected Laval's application for interim relief on the basis that there was no probable cause for the claims that the Swedish legislation and the collective actions where contrary to EU law.[19] Thus, on the Labour Court's own preliminary assessment, the Swedish legislation was in conformity with EU law.

---

[14] Case C-438/05 *International Transport Workers' Federation and Finnish Seamen's Union v Viking Line ABP and OÜ Viking Line Eesti* [2007] ECR I-10779.

[15] See eg B Bercussion, 'The Trade Union Movement and the European Union: Judgment day' (2007) 13 *ELJ* 279; L Azoulai, 'The Court of Justice and the Social Market Economy: the Emergence of an Ideal and the Conditions for its Realization' (2008) 45 *CML Rev* 1335; N Reich, 'Free Movement v. Social rights in an enlarged Union – the Laval and Viking cases before the ECJ' (2008) 9 *German Law Journal* 125; J Malmberg and T Sigeman, 'Industrial actions and EU economic freedoms: The autonomous bargaining model curtailed by the European Court of Justice' (2008) 45 *CML Rev* 1115; ACL Davies, 'One Step Forward, Two Steps Back? The *Viking* and *Laval* cases in the ECJ' (2008) 37 *ILJ* 126; S Prechal and S de Vries, 'Seamless Web of Judicial Protection in the Internal Market' (2009) 34 *EL Rev* 5; K Apps, 'Damages Claims Against Trade Unions After Viking and Laval' (2009) 34 *EL Rev* 141; N Hös, 'The Principle of Proportionality in the *Viking* and *Laval* cases: An appropriate standard of judicial review?' (2009) EUI Working Papers Law 2009/06, available at cadmus.eui.eu/bitstream/handle/1814/11259/LAW_2009_06.pdf?sequence=1.

[16] Instrument of Government (Regeringsformen (1974:152)) c 2, s 14 (at the time of the *Laval* ruling: c 2, s 17).

[17] The Act (1994:1219) on the European Convention for the Protection of Human Rights and Fundamental Freedoms.

[18] The Act (1976:580) on Co-Determination.

[19] Decision of the Labour Court (Arbetsdomstolen) No 111/2004 of 22 December 2004 in Case No A 268/04 *Laval*, above n 2.

(iii) The ECJ found the Swedish legislation permitting the collective actions against Laval to be discriminatory. Whereas collective action aimed at replacing Swedish collective agreements was prohibited, the same law allowed the right to be exercised against employers already bound by collective agreements with foreign trade unions.
(iv) From the ECJ's ruling it follows that the trade unions had violated article 49 EC in two respects: first, by taking collective action pursuant to the discriminatory legislation mentioned above, and secondly, by taking collective action to support demands going beyond the so-called minimum core of protection as outlined in the Directive on the Posting of Workers.[20]
(v) The proportionality test the ECJ applied to the trade union action in *Laval* was a strict one, assessing whether the action itself went beyond what was necessary to protect the interest of workers.[21]

In the following, and as far as it is possible, the focus will not be on whether the ECJ's ruling made sense, but whether holding the trade unions liable was indeed *required* under the doctrine of effective rights protection.

III. A Requirement Based on Effective Rights Protection?

A justification based on the principle of effective rights protection takes the rights of the individual as the starting point. The corresponding duty to protect the rights in question falls upon the state. It is the state that is to guarantee the availability of effective remedies for rights violations. But against whom should such remedies be made available?

On a pure rights-based reading, the answer is simple. The remedies should be granted against whomever it would be effective to grant them against. As a matter of principle, if effective rights protection would require a remedy against an individual, there is a claim against the state that it should provide for it.[22] Neither Article 19(1) TEU nor Article 47 of the Charter of Fundamental Rights specify anything regarding against whom the remedy should be directed.

---

[20] Directive 96/71/EC of the European Parliament and of the Council of 16 December 1996 concerning the posting of workers in the framework of the provision of services [1997] OJ L18/1.

[21] Apps, 'Damages Claims Against Trade Unions After Viking and Laval', above n 15, 143. For a detailed discussion, see Hös, 'The Principle of Proportionality in the *Viking* and *Laval* cases', above n 15.

[22] See eg AP Komninos, 'New Prospects for Private Enforcement of EC Competition Law: *Courage v Crehan* and the Community Rights to Damages' (2002) 39 *CML Rev* 447, 472; M Dougan, *National Remedies Before the Court of Justice: Issues of Harmonisation and Differentiation* (Oxford, Hart Publishing, 2004) 60. See also: W van Gerven, 'Of Rights Remedies and Procedures' (2000) 37 *CML Rev* 501, 519 and more generally on the issue of horizontal liability, N Reich, 'Horizontal Liability in EC law: Hybridization of Remedies for Compensation in Case of Breaches of EC Rights' (2007) 44 *CML Rev* 705.

As long as the state in this context is identified with the legislature, the duty to provide an effective remedy does not pose any specific problems. In a constitutional democracy adhering to the rule of law, it is the task of the legislature to pass legislation protecting rights in both horizontal and vertical relationships, ideally enabling the requisite remedies and procedures in a clear and predictable fashion.

However, knowing that the legislature at times fails to foresee, ignores or even refuses to acknowledge the need for redress in certain situations, courts may, as a matter of EU law, be required as entities of the state to step in and provide for an effective remedy to protect the individual. Since 'ought' is taken to imply 'can', the requirement of effective rights protection silently confers great power to the courts. In order to restrain this power, the requirement must be limited.

A. The *Unibet* limitation

The first important limitation of the requirement of judicial effective rights protection is that national courts are not obliged to create new remedies as long as the ones already existing under national law provide sufficient relief.[23]

One must bear in mind that an act whereby a new remedy is created by a court is an extraordinary event both in the EU and the national legal orders. One need only to think of the controversy stirred up by the Court of Justice, when the Court in *Francovich* 'discovered' a new all-European principle of non-contractual Member State liability for violations of EU law.

For a long time it was also held that EU law, in view of national procedural autonomy, did not require the creation of new remedies at all.[24] This restriction led to a general confusion as to where the line should be drawn between the adaptation of an existing remedy and the creation of a new one.[25] As Arnull has pointed out, the ruling in *Unibet*[26] constituted a significant development in this respect, establishing that the interest of effective rights protection may require national courts to lay down new remedies.[27]

In *Unibet*, two internet gaming companies (the applicants) established in Malta and the UK respectively, launched court proceedings against the Swedish state, claiming that Swedish gaming legislation infringed Article 49 EC by prohibiting the advertisement of their services. The applicants sought a declaratory ruling concerning non-contractual liability, and, in addition, a declaration that the companies should be able to advertise their services in Sweden notwithstanding the prohibition. The latter motion was clearly inadmissible as it entailed a free-

[23] Case C-432/05 *Unibet*, above n 12, paras 41–42.
[24] Case 158/80 *Rewe-Handelsgesellschaft Nord mbH and Rewe-Markt Steffen v Hauptzollamt Kiel* [1981] ECR 1805.
[25] A Arnull, 'The Principle of Effective Judicial Protection in EU law: An Unruly Horse?' (2011) 36 *EL Rev* 51, 55.
[26] Case C-432/05 *Unibet*, above n 12. The author represented the Chancellor of Justice of Sweden (the Swedish State) in the national court proceedings. The opinions are the author's personal and do not necessarily reflect those of the Chancellor of Justice or the Swedish state.
[27] Arnull, 'The Principle of Effective Judicial Protection in EU law', above n 25, 56.

standing form of judicial review prohibited by the Swedish Constitution.[28] The applicants, however, claimed their interests in effective rights protection required the court to allow for the motion. In response, the Swedish state held that no such remedy was required, inter alia pointing to the possibility to have the compatibility of the legislation assessed within the framework of the liability claim.

The matter eventually reached the Swedish Supreme Court, which made a reference to the Court of Justice. The Supreme Court asked whether a freestanding judicial review of national legislation was required when the national legislation could be reviewed within the framework of other available remedies.

In its response, the Court of Justice stated that the Treaty was not intended to create remedies other than the ones already laid down by national law, except in situations where it would be 'apparent from the overall scheme of the national legal system in question that no legal remedy existed which made it possible to ensure, even indirectly, respect for an individual's rights under Community law'.[29]

When assessing the available remedies in the Swedish system, the Court concluded that there was no need for a freestanding action. The Unibet companies could have the question of the EU law conformity of national legislation assessed as a preliminary issue within the framework of their damages claim. Furthermore, they had the option of applying for an exemption from the application of the prohibition from the Swedish government. A refusal to grant such an application could be challenged in court.

Whilst the ruling clarifies that EU law may indeed require new remedies to be established, it also sets a high threshold for such a requirement to be triggered. It must be *apparent* that no legal remedy existed in national law that could ensure, *even indirectly*, the respect for an individual's rights under EU law.

The threshold of an apparent gap in the remedial system can only be motivated by constitutional concerns. Much like the discovery of general principles of law, the perception of gaps is a politically, and therefore constitutionally, charged ontological activity. Holding that an unregulated situation is a gap in the system entails a claim that the situation ought to be regulated. Considering that there may be valid reasons for the lack of regulation, there may be fundamental disagreement as to whether there is a gap or not (and hence whether a court may be authorised to fill it).[30]

The notion of gaps in the remedial system represents a supreme challenge in this respect. Determining the presence of a gap is not only a matter of scrutinising the types of remedies available, but also of assessing their effectiveness. Considering the vagueness of the criterion of effectiveness, there is a risk that some courts will

---

[28] The Swedish Constitution only empowers courts to set aside provisions in conflict with higher norms in the context of a concrete dispute (c 11, s 14 of the Instrument of Government).

[29] Case C-432/05 *Unibet*, above n 12, paras 41–42.

[30] The difference between what is seen as a gap and what is merely treated as an unregulated situation may be illustrated by the disparity of the Court's findings in Case C-13/94 *P v S and Cornwall County Council* [1996] ECR I-2143 and Case C-249/96 *Lisa Jacqueline Grant v South-West Trains Ltd* [1998] ECR I-621. See also Hartley, who draws a distinction between 'true gaps' and 'intended gaps' in TC Hartley, *Constitutional Problems of the European Union* (Oxford, Hart Publishing, 1999) 44 f.

see gaps, where others will not. Demanding that the gap be apparent signals that national courts should refrain from creating new remedies if there is any room to consider the existing remedies to be sufficient. Furthermore, establishing *indirect protection* as the standard to measure the effectiveness of existing remedies narrows the scope for new remedies even further.

B. A Gap in the Protection?

What is then the relevance of the *Unibet* limitation to the horizontal liability established by the Swedish Labour Court in the *Laval* case? Remember, the claim was that the effective protection of Laval's rights required the remedy, ie that there was a gap in the protective system. Indeed, the Labour Court stressed that there was no possibility under national law to hold the trade unions liable. But why would suing the state not be an option for Laval? Would a damages action against the state really be an *apparently* ineffective remedy?

There are two arguments concerning the *Francovich* action that will be addressed here. The first one is that the state had no responsibility for what actually happened, and, the second, that suing the state would therefore be apparently ineffective.

This would potentially draw a link between *Laval* and cases like *Walrave*[31] *Bosman*,[32] and *Angonese*[33] where horizontal direct effect was found to apply to 'associations or organizations not governed by public law' creating obstacles through 'the exercise of their legal autonomy' when 'regulating gainful employment in a collective manner'. A problem in this respect is that whereas there is a strong claim that the state indeed had very little to do with the infringements in those cases, the same does not apply to the actions of the trade unions in *Laval*. By analogy with *Bosman*, trade unions could, at least in some Member States, perhaps be likened to autonomous sporting associations when they regulate the market through collective agreements. However, when they take industrial action, they are more like athletes, playing by the rules laid down by the state.[34] Whereas the state has no responsibility whatsoever to ensure that sporting associations and research institutions can actually discriminate individuals, the state does have a duty to provide stable and predictable conditions for the exercise of fundamental rights. The right to take collective action as well as the conditions that apply to its exercise is by necessity provided for by law. As a matter of fact, the right to take collective action against out-of-state employers with existing foreign collective agreements had been specifically introduced in Swedish legislation in the 1990s to allow unions to tackle the phenomenon

---

[31] Case 36/74 *BNO Walrave and LJN Koch v Association Union cycliste internationale, Koninklijke Nederlandsche Wielren Unie and Federación Española Ciclismo* [1974] ECR 1405.

[32] Case C-415/93 *Union Royale Belge des Sociétés de Football Association ASBL v Jean-Marc Bosman* [1995] ECR I-4921.

[33] Case C-281/98 *Roman Angonese v Cassa di Risparmio di Bolzano SpA* [2000] ECR I-4139.

[34] See also Apps, 'Damages Claims Against Trade Unions After Viking and Laval', above n 15, 147; Davies, 'One Step Forward, Two Steps Back?', above n 15, 136.

of social dumping. Considering the involvement of the state and the fundamental rights element, the *Laval* case has more in common with *Schmidberger*[35] than it does with *Walrave*, *Bosman* and *Angonese*.

In *Schmidberger*, Austrian authorities granted a permission for/decided not to ban an environmental manifestation on the Brenner motorway, as it was lawful under Austrian law. The demonstration lasted 30 hours and prevented traffic from crossing the border from Italy to Austria. A German transport company sued the Austrian state for *Francovich* damages. The Court of Justice found the demonstration to be caught by Article 28 EC (now Article 34 TFEU), but that the restriction was deemed justified due to the legitimate interest of Austria not to violate the demonstrators' fundamental rights of expression and assembly.

The ruling demonstrates that the Austrian state was seen to have a responsibility for allowing the manifestations. Why would the same not apply to the Swedish state in *Laval*? Just as the Austrian legislation expressly permitted the demonstrations, Swedish legislation expressly permitted the collective actions. Furthermore, in view of the fundamental rights aspect, the Austrian authorities saw no possibility to ban the demonstration much in the same way the Swedish Police refused to take action against the trade unions.

Considering these similarities, it appears difficult to claim that the Austrian state in principle was responsible in *Schmidberger*, while denying such responsibility for the Swedish state in *Laval*. And if one should accept that a damages action could legitimately have been brought against the Swedish state, there would not be any gap in the protection of Laval's rights – provided of course this remedy would not be *apparently* ineffective.

This last caveat brings us to the second line of argumentation for the inaptness of *Francovich* liability. This position accepts the underlying responsibility of the state, but questions the effectiveness of suing the state in the particular context of the *Laval* case. At the core of the argument lies the difficulty of establishing a violation for state inaction in relation to individual parties. The authorities cited in this context are the *French Strawberries* case (also known as the *Spanish Strawberries* case)[36] and *Schmidberger*.[37] Important to note here, is that these two cases are not as similar as they may seem at a first glance. In *French Strawberries*, France was held to have violated Article 30 of the EC Treaty (now Article 34 TFEU) by a long-term failure to act against French farmers engaging in unlawful violent acts directed at the trade in imports of fruits and vegetables. In *Schmidberger*, the demonstrations on the Brenner highway were not only lawful under Austrian law, but also subject to special constitutional protection. There is arguably an important distinction to draw between, on the one hand, failing to act against behaviour that is unlawful under national legislation and, on the other hand, failing to act against a prima facie lawful exercise of fundamental rights, or as the Court acknowledged in *Schmidberger*,

---

[35] Case C-112/00 *Eugen Schmidberger, Internationale Transporte und Planzüge v Austria* [2003] ECR I-5659.
[36] Case C-265/95 *European Commission v France* [1997] ECR I-6959 (*Spanish Strawberries*).
[37] Prechal and De Vries, 'Seamless Web of Judicial Protection in the Internal Market', above n 15, 22.

it is not in dispute that by that demonstration, citizens were exercising their fundamental rights by manifesting in public an opinion which they considered to be of importance to society; it is also not in dispute that the purpose of that public demonstration was not to restrict trade in goods of a particular type or from a particular source. By contrast, in *Commission* v *France* . . . the objective pursued by the demonstrators was clearly to prevent the movement of particular products originating in Member States other than the French Republic, by not only obstructing the transport of the goods in question, but also destroying those goods in transit to or through France, and even when they had already been put on display in shops in the Member State concerned.[38]

Further, and more importantly, whereas *Schmidberger* could equally be conceived of as a case of state action, the same does not apply to *French Strawberries*.[39] French legislation neither allowed nor protected the actions in question. Moreover, French authorities never authorised the obstructions and the attacks.

Why is this important? Well, upon closer scrutiny *Laval* proves to be more like *Schmidberger* than *French Strawberries*. The actions of the trade unions were authorised by Swedish legislation and protected under the Swedish Constitution. The Swedish trade unions were thus more like the organisers of a lawful demonstration, than an angry bunch committing criminal acts. Just like *Schmidberger*, *Laval* is thus more a case of state action than of the state's failure to act. To assess the effectiveness of the *Francovich* liability option in the context of state inaction therefore seems less appropriate.

If *Laval* sought damages, the available option was suing the state for having enacted permissive rules that were deemed discriminatory by the Court of Justice. In addition, it should be noted that when the Labour Court was first seised of the case, it rejected an application for interim relief, thus potentially causing the damages. It is far from obvious that such a claim would have been unsuccessful. The claim that effective rights protection required a new remedy to be established by the Labour Court can therefore not be sustained under the *Unibet* criterion. It was not *apparent* that Laval's interests in effective rights protection could not have been properly seen to within the framework of a *Francovich* liability action. On this reading there was no gap in the remedial system and hence no requirement for the Labour Court to lay down a new remedy.

However, suppose for the sake of the argument that there had been no clear legislative basis for the trade union action and that the only violation that could be brought against the state would be a claim of state inaction. Would that really change the picture in a drastic way? Would such conditions render the *Francovich* option apparently ineffective as a means of rights protection? Prechal and De Vries have, for example, pointed to the difficulty of requiring the Member States to interfere with labour relations.[40] Translated into the language of the *Francovich* doctrine, this means that not only would it be difficult to establish a breach, but it

---

[38] Case C-112/00 *Schmidberger*, above n 35, para 86.
[39] The referring court seems to have understood the case as a case of legislative or administrative default. Ibid, para 22.
[40] Prechal and De Vries, 'Seamless Web of Judicial Protection in the Internal Market', above n 15, 22.

would be even more strenuous to meet the threshold of a sufficiently serious breach required for state liability. If we recall, in *Brasserie du Pêcheur and Factortame* the Court outlined that for the purposes of assessing whether a sufficiently serious breach is at hand:

> The factors which the competent court may take into consideration include the clarity and precision of the rule breached, the measure of discretion left by that rule to the national or Community authorities, whether the infringement and the damage caused was intentional or involuntary, whether any error of law was excusable or inexcusable, the fact that the position taken by a Community institution may have contributed towards the omission, and the adoption or retention of national measures or practices contrary to Community law.[41]

Generally speaking there is a wide margin of discretion for the Member States to assess whether or not to use force to interfere with the exercise of a fundamental right. In *Schmidberger* the Court stated:

> [T]aking account of the Member States' wide margin of discretion, in circumstances such as those of the present case the competent national authorities were entitled to consider that an outright ban on the demonstration would have constituted unacceptable interference with the fundamental rights of the demonstrators to gather and express peacefully their opinion in public.[42]

In the specific – and rather construed – context of a *Francovich* case based on state inaction in *Laval*, ie in the absence of clear provisions permitting the collective actions, the wide margin of discretion enjoyed by the Swedish authorities would probably save the Swedish state from being held liable for inaction.[43] But would this really discount the *Francovich* remedy as ineffective to the extent that it would be justified to hold the trade unions responsible instead? If you cannot actually hold the state liable, why should you be able to attack the private parties?

The only possible argument would be that such an action could be more effective. But the only reason it could be more effective is if it would be possible to apply different and stricter criteria to the trade unions than to the state itself. But then the effectiveness of the remedy would depend on the criteria, and not on who, so to speak, the real tortfeasor is. And why should it be possible to hold trade unions to a stricter standard than one would hold a Member State? If it is a difficult task for Member States to assess the appropriate balance between fundamental rights and fundamental freedoms, would it not be fair to assume it to be daunting for a private party?

Unfortunately, many things suggest that these important concerns were ignored by the Swedish Labour Court. We know that the trade unions were held to stricter criteria than would have been the state. The trade unions were not

---

[41] Cases C-46/93 and C-48/93 *Brasserie du Pêcheur SA v Germany and The Queen v Secretary of State for Transport, ex parte Factortame Ltd and others* [1996] ECR I-1029, para 56.

[42] Case C-112/00 *Schmidberger*, above n 35, para 89.

[43] See also Prechal and De Vries, 'Seamless Web of Judicial Protection in the Internal Market', above n 15, 22.

awarded much in terms of margin of appreciation. The proportionality test applied by the ECJ was the narrow one.[44] Against this background it was easier for the Labour Court to determine the existence of a sufficiently serious breach than if the case had concerned state inaction. In this determination no scope was allowed for considering the breach an excusable error in law. This appears too stringent. One should recall that when charged with the question of interim relief, the Labour Court had itself deemed the legislation and the collective actions to be prima facie in conformity with EU law.

If the outcome could be justified solely by reference to the interest of protecting Laval's rights because of the ineffectiveness of a *Francovich* remedy, then in principle the transport company in *Schmidberger* would have a similar claim for an effective damages remedy against the organisers of the Brenner Pass demonstration. If the strict standards laid down by the ECJ in *Laval* had been applied to the demonstrations, a national court could easily have established that the demonstrations were disproportionate infringements of Schmidberger's rights to the cross-border transport of goods on a highway (the demonstrators did not have to block the traffic, the demonstrations lasted too long, they should not have been planned in conjunction with a bank holiday etc).

The attentive reader will perhaps remark that the free movement of goods provision lacks horizontal direct effect and, furthermore, that environmental organisations could be distinguished from both sporting associations and trade unions. But such critique is beside the point when discussing the question of whether the protection of individual rights *as a matter of principle* requires a remedy against other private parties, in situations where an action against the state is available.

From a principled rights–remedies perspective, national courts would have just as much of a duty to provide effective remedies to compensate companies in Schmidberger's position as they would Laval. One cannot at the same time hold that what is good enough for Schmidberger (ie *Francovich* damages) is not good enough for Laval. Put simply, *Francovich* damages are either effective as a remedy or they aren't. Again, should we consider it effective enough to protect Schmidberger, we must consider it sufficiently effective to protect Laval.

I should stress that we are only talking about this in terms of effective rights protection in the context of the limitations applicable to the requirement of the judicial creation of new remedies. There should be no question that seeking damages from the trade unions was more effective for Laval in this particular case than trying to hold the state liable for inaction or even legislative error.[45] The only point I am making is that this does not matter as long as a damages action against the state would be effective enough.

As already stated, there may be other arguments for a direct remedial action against the trade unions, notably the general interest of effectiveness that lies in

---

[44] Apps, 'Damages Claims Against Trade Unions After Viking and Laval', above n 15, 143. For a detailed analysis, see Hös, 'The Principle of Proportionality in the *Viking* and *Laval* cases', above n 15.

[45] The trade unions in question were financially stable. In other circumstances, an action against the state may have appeared more attractive.

sanctioning violations of EU law. As we have seen, the Labour Court did cite such reasons for its ruling. But those are reasons not specifically connected to the interest of effective rights protection. For Laval, the interest of effective rights protection was sufficiently satisfied, and there was thus no gap to be filled.

What then about equivalence? Could not the *Unibet* limitation and the 'gap' reasoning be bypassed altogether by referring to the existing option in Swedish law to hold trade unions liable for breaches of Swedish legislation? This would perhaps be a potential avenue had the Swedish legislation in question not so clearly established that what the trade unions did was not tortious. The very legislation that permitted damages to be awarded against trade unions also specified that what the trade unions did in *Laval* was not sanctioned by liability. In those circumstances, one cannot hold that a horizontal remedy existed for similar claims without doing violence to the notion of comparison. In the comparable situation in which an industrial action is taken pursuant to permissive legislation later found to violate the Swedish constitution, there simply would be no way in which the trade union could be held liable.

In fact, the only remedy available in Sweden in *Laval*-like circumstances was the possibility to turn to the state for *Francovich* damages for a legislative breach. Any development from this order of affairs would have had to pass the *Unibet* test.

Important to note in this context is that EU law did not prevent the Labour Court from establishing a new damages action. The *Unibet* limitation only specifies the situations in which the creation of new remedies is required as a matter of EU law – it does not prohibit their creation in other instances. In those other instances, it is a matter for the national courts to determine whether or not they are authorised under national law to establish new remedies. As long as we are speaking of new remedies against the state, there are no particular reasons why EU law should prevent national courts from creating them. Those new remedies will in general promote the effectiveness of EU law without harming individual interests. However, when the new remedies sought are damages actions against other private parties, things become more complicated. As I shall argue in the following, there may even be situations in which EU law should restrict national courts from establishing new remedies.

IV. Further Limits to the Requirement in Horizontal Situations?

Basic to the notion of the rule of law is that the subjects of the law should be able to be guided by it. According to the Court of Justice,

> [t]he principle of legal certainty is a fundamental principle of Community law which requires, in particular, that rules should be clear and precise, so that individuals may

ascertain unequivocally what their rights and obligations are and may take steps accordingly.[46]

The predictability aspect is of special importance when there is a risk for sanctions. The Court has held that 'with regard to the principle of legal certainty, this requires in particular that rules involving negative consequences for individuals should be clear and precise and their application predictable for those subject to them'.[47]

The ruling of the Swedish Labour Court entailed the granting of exemplary damages which has a strong element of sanction. This raises issues concerning retroactivity, legitimate expectations and legal certainty for the future.

A. Retroactivity or Legitimate Expectations?

One of the central tenets of the rule of law is the prohibition on retroactive sanctions. No-one should be subjected to sanctions for actions not prohibited at the time they were taken. If a negative consequence is attached to a certain behaviour this should be known beforehand. When it comes to legal development in the judicial sphere however, the concept of retroactivity is sometimes difficult to apply. The EU legal system operates under the fiction that the preliminary rulings of the ECJ clarify the meaning of the law *ex tunc*. In theory there is thus no problem of retroactivity when the ECJ in a *Laval*-like fashion delivers a ruling laying down a thitherto unknown prohibition. In practice, there is a clear ex post facto problem, but the issue is elegantly conceptualised as a matter of legitimate expectations.

The value assigned to such expectations has in some rare instances prompted the Court to limit the effect of its rulings, thus slightly disturbing the fiction of the permanence of meaning. In *Defrenne* the Court famously limited the effects in time of its ruling concerning the horizontal direct effect of the principle of equal pay for equal work.

> [I]mportant considerations of legal certainty affecting all interests involved, both public and private, make it impossible in principle to reopen the question as regards the past. Therefore, the direct effect of Article 119 [EEC Treaty] cannot be relied on in order to support claims concerning pay periods prior to the date of this judgment, except as regards those workers who have already brought legal proceedings or made an equivalent claim.[48]

---

[46] Case C-344/04 *The Queen (on the application of International Air Tranport Association and European Low Fares Airline Association) v Department for Transport* [2006] ECR I-403, para 68; Case 169/80 *Administration des douanes v Société anonyme Gondrand Frères and Société anonyme Garancini* [1981] ECR 1931; Case C-143/93 *Gebroeders van Es Douane Agenten BV v Inspecteur der Invoerrechten en Accijnzen* [1996] ECR I-431, para 27; Case C-110/03 *Belgium v European Commission* [2005] ECR I-2801, para 30.

[47] Case C-17/03 *Vereniging voor Energie, Milieu en Water (VEMW) and others v Directeur van de Dienst uitvoering en toezicht energie* [2005] ECR I-4983, para 80.

[48] Case 43/75 *Gabrielle Defrenne v Société anonyme belge de navigation aérienne (Sabena)* [1976] ECR 455, paras 74–75.

Interesting to note is that the legal certainty for the employers of workers who had already brought proceedings, was not considered as important as the certainty of other employers. This breach of equal treatment under the law was probably at least in part due to the interest of maintaining an impetus for private parties to continue to raise points of EU law. If such parties would not benefit from a clarification of the interpretation of EU law, the interest in private enforcement would be scant.

In *Denkavit*, the ECJ clarified that it was for the Court alone to decide upon temporal restrictions of an interpretation.[49] In practice, this means that a national court cannot take the legitimate expectations of private parties into consideration unless the ECJ has said so. Considering the negative consequences for some employers accepted in *Defrenne*, the conclusion would probably apply in the remedial sphere as well. However, should the new horizontal remedy sought have a punitive aspect – such as the exemplary damages awarded in the Swedish *Laval* case – matters may be different. Indeed, the Court may see reason to acknowledge that the requirement of effective rights protection under EU law should not be used to motivate new sanctions of private behaviour ex post facto.

Such a development would at the very least be called for in areas where the private party in question has acted in accordance with express permissions laid down in national law. We can recall that, just like the demonstrators in *Schmidberger*, the trade unions in *Laval* relied on the authority of national law. Holding private parties liable in such situations is arguably a greater infringement on legal certainty than in instances where the action in question has not previously been expressly deemed permissible by the national legislature.

Punishing private parties for relying on national law will inevitably undermine the action-guiding function of this law. It will send a signal that national legislatures are not to be trusted, and that private parties, in order to avoid liability, had better second-guess them before acting. Moreover, it removes the incentive for national legislatures to pass new national legislation in conformity with EU law. If in the end, national legislation cannot signal with authority whether an action will entail a risk of sanction or not, why bother passing it?

This critique should, at least in part, be reminiscent of that directed against the *Mangold* ruling.[50] As is well known, in that case the Court found that a general principle of prohibition of discrimination on grounds of age produced exclusionary effects in horizontal relations requiring provisions not in conformity with the principle to be set aside. The fact that the deadline for implementation of the Equal Treatment Directive had not expired was of no consequence. The principle existed independently of the Directive and did not need to be implemented in national law to be applicable.

Aside from the controversy surrounding the discovery of the general principle as such, the ruling was seen to disregard the legal certainty considerations underlying

---

[49] Case 61/79 *Amministrazione delle finanze dello Stato v Denkavit italiana Srl* [1980] ECR 1205, para 18.
[50] Case C-144/04 *Werner Mangold v Rüdiger Helm* [2005] ECR I-9981.

the Court's post-*Marshall* case law,[51] which denies that directives could have horizontal direct effect.[52] Although the exclusionary effect of the general principle in *Mangold* can be distinguished from the substitution effect that would be at hand should the Equal Treatment Directive have been granted direct horizontal applicability, the negative effects on legal certainty cannot. As Advocate General Mazák phrased it in his Opinion in *Palacios de la Villa*,

> what is to my mind decisive, in particular with due respect to the principle of legal certainty, is whether the legal position of an individual is affected to his detriment as a result of the invocation of a directive, regardless of whether, technically, that adverse effect was brought about by the mere exclusion of the conflicting national provision in question or in consequence of its substitution by the directive.[53]

That the *Mangold* ruling entailed a legal development injurious to the legitimate expectations of private parties was also confirmed by the German Constitutional Court when given the last word in the *Mangold* saga. The Bundesverfassungsgericht (BVerfG) held that a person who had relied on national German law prior to a *Mangold*-type ruling from the ECJ, would have a claim against the German state to be compensated for the violation of his or her legitimate expectations flowing from national law:

> It is hence possible in order to ensure the constitutional protection of legitimate expectations in constellations of the retroactive inapplicability of a law as a result of a ruling by the Court of Justice to grant compensation domestically for a party concerned having trusted in the statutory provision and having made plans based on this trust. The Union's liability law also assigns to the Member State responsibility for a statute which violates Union law and hence reduces the burden on the citizen.[54]

The solution pointed to by the German Constitutional Court does in many respects appear ingenuous. It recognises that national legislation can give rise to legitimate expectations, and clarifies that a breach of these expectations may be serious enough so as to render the state liable. Importantly, it acknowledges the final responsibility of the state vis-à-vis individuals to ensure that the law of the land can be trusted. Perhaps this model of state liability is the solution to the problem of the ad hoc creation of a horizontal damages action? Should a private party be held horizontally liable despite having acted in accordance with national law, any damages paid could later on be compensated by the state. But why should the state have to pay for the consequences of a legislative inconformity that would

---

[51] Case 152/84 *M Helen Marshall v Southampton and South-West Hampshire Area Health Authority* [1986] ECR 723, para 48; Case C-91/92 *Paola Faccini Dori v Recreb Srl* [1994] ECR I-3325, para 20; Case C-201/02 *The Queen (on the application of Delena Wells) v Secretary of State for Transport, Local Government and the Regions* [2004] ECR I-723, para 56.

[52] See especially, Opinion of Advocate General Mazák of 15 February 2007 in Case C-411/05 *Félix Palacios de la Villa v Cortefiel Servicios SA* [2007] ECR I-8531.

[53] Ibid, para 126.

[54] *Honeywell*, BVerfG, 2 BvR 2661/06, judgment of 6 July 2010, para 85. Official translation published on the web page of the Federal Constitutional Court (Bundesverfassungsgericht): www.bundesverfassungsgericht.de/entscheidungen/rs20100706_2bvr266106en.html.

have been incapable of engendering liability had an action been brought against the state under the *Francovich* doctrine? It is plain that the error of the national legislature in *Mangold* was excusable and could not constitute a sufficiently serious breach. Holding the state liable in those circumstances may seem a good idea to the private parties affected, but how does one justify it to the tax payer?

More importantly, even if the German solution could fully remedy the losses flowing from a ruling from the ECJ and an ensuing horizontal damages action, it fails to address the main rule of law concern ensuing from the *Laval* case – legal certainty for the future. While this may be less of a problem in the age discrimination cases due to the advent of clear and precise national implementation legislation, matters are different concerning the right to take collective action post-*Laval*.

B. Proportionality Instead of Proportionate Law?

The general prohibitions of restrictions laid down in the free movement provisions do not have a clear and precise scope. They say more about what the law ought to be in a general fashion than about what officials and judges – and hence by implication private parties – ought to do in a concrete case.[55] They are directed to the regulator, and not to the actor. In that sense they can legitimately be seen as binding on private parties when laying down rules, eg regulating gainful employment in a collective fashion. For governing individual action however, the prohibitions on restrictions are too unclear and imprecise to fulfil any guiding function.[56] They simply state that restrictions ought to be forbidden. Considering the broad scope of the market access test, it means that almost anything could be forbidden, as almost anything could be an obstacle.[57]

At the level of justification, determining whether an individual action – or for that matter an inaction – could be justified as a proportionate restriction is bound to be more like dancing in the dark than threading a well-lit path of reason. The public interest derogations are not adapted to the motivations of private parties. Moreover, whereas the test of proportionality serves a function in the assessment of law as such, the standard is not fit for guiding private action in a direct way.[58] A general rule stating that one shall not infringe the rights and freedom

---

[55] F Laporta, whose distinction between 'ought to be' norms and 'ought to do' norms I make use of here, holds that 'ought to be' norms express an ideal state of affairs, whereas 'ought to do' norms state a desired action to be taken. My information on Laporta's theory stems from the account provided by Aarnio in A Aarnio, *Reason and Authority: a treatise on the dynamic paradigm of legal dogmatics* (Aldershot, Dartmouth, 1997) 181 f.

[56] See also Prechal and De Vries, who in this respect make a distinction between the prohibiton of restrictions and the prohibition of discrimination, of which the latter according to the authors has become clear enough to be applied directly in horizontal situations (at least with respect to direct discrimination), in Prechal and De Vries, 'Seamless Web of Judicial Protection in the Internal Market', above n 15, 18.

[57] Ibid.

[58] Regarding the difficulty of applying the proportionality test in the context of collective action, see Bercusson, 'The Trade Union Movement and the European Union', above n 15, 304.

of others in a disproportionate fashion appears attractive, but what would it mean in actuality?

When proportionality is relied on to guide individual action it becomes a rule of law problem. Law should be clear and predictable so as to remove the necessity to go to court. However, a law that is unclear requires court action for clarity and is therefore costly, unpredictable and thus fundamentally ineffective *qua* law. In the words of Derrick Wyatt 'courts should be used as courts, not law shops'. Prescribing proportionality as the standard for private party action would indeed turn courts into proportionality machines, clarifying the meaning of proportionality at each pull of the lever.[59]

Of course one cannot avoid proportionality. There will be irreconcilable conflicts in individual cases that can only be acceptably resolved by a reference to proportionality. But one should not in general rely on it to govern the actions of individuals. If one is to take legal certainty seriously, private parties need to be governed by proportionate law, not proportionality.

But would there not be a way the proportionality test could be made more certain? Lenaerts (who was adjudicating both *Laval* and *Viking*) and Gutiérrez-Fons have proposed that the legality of the actions of private parties should be determined on the basis of their mind-set, even suggesting that the outcome in *Laval* and *Viking* would have been different had there been no protectionist elements present:

> [H]ad the Scandinavian trade unions in *Laval* and *Viking* reacted to cheaper labour coming from the Baltic States with a transnational mindset, perhaps seeking to raise standards throughout the EU rather than seeking to exclude workers from other Member States, the ECJ might have been more sympathetic to their claims.[60]

The drawback with this particular view is that it is indeed a difficult task to assess the mind-set, ie the mental and emotional processes of a private party, in particular if that private party happens to be an organisation. How could one possibly gauge whether an organisational demand for equal pay for equal work for foreign workers is actually aimed at excluding them from the labour market? And how would one determine whether an organised consumer boycott directed at services from another Member State is protectionist or not? Including an assessment of the mind-set of private parties in the proportionality test does not seem to promote the value of legal certainty.

Relying on proportionality becomes specifically problematic when the exercise of a fundamental right is at stake. Because without legal certainty, the right becomes difficult to exercise, especially if there is a risk of a sanction and high court costs. In the context of the right to take collective action this chilling effect has been confirmed by the ILO's expert committee in the UK *Balpa* affair. The

---

[59] See also Hös, 'The Principle of Proportionality in the *Viking* and *Laval* cases', above n 15, 15 f with regard to the German experience of using the proportionality test in labour disputes.

[60] K Lenaerts and JA Gutiérrez-Fons, 'The Constitutional Allocation of Powers and General Principles of EU Law' (2010) 47 *CML Rev* 1629, 1666 f.

committee stated that the 'omnipresent threat of an action for damages that could bankrupt the union, possible now in the light of the *Viking* and *Laval* judgements, creates a situation where the rights under the Convention cannot be exercised'.[61]

By attaching a new sanction to the disproportionate exercise of a fundamental right, the national court is indirectly regulating the right, thereby creating a situation of uncertainty liable to impede its free exercise in the future. Such uncertainties could normally be handled by new legislation providing more clarity while drawing a more proportionate balance between the competing interests. The regulation of fundamental rights is, however, subject to specific constitutional constraints in both the Member States and the EU, rendering the adoption of new legislation difficult. In the case of the right to take collective action, the competence of the EU to harmonise the matter is expressly excluded.[62]

There is thus a considerable risk that the establishing of a new damages action against a private party could produce a permanent situation of uncertainty whereby that party could no longer safely exercise a fundamental right. In those situations, like the one that was at hand in the Swedish Labour Court after the ECJ's ruling, EU law should neither require nor allow the judicial creation of a horizontal damages action.

V. Conclusion

In the present chapter, I have investigated the isolated claim that the Swedish Labour Court's ruling in *Laval* was called for to fill a gap in the protective system – ie whether *as a matter of effective rights protection,* the Labour Court was legally obliged to provide Laval with a horizontal damages action.

I have argued that such a claim cannot be sustained in the light of the high threshold that applies to the duty for national courts to create new remedies. In situations where private parties infringe free movement law by exercising fundamental rights pursuant to national law, the availability of a damages action against the state must be seen to provide sufficient relief. The potential difficulty of actually holding the state liable in those instances cannot on its own justify that private parties should face the risk to be held liable under less stringent criteria.

On a more general note, I have also questioned whether EU law should allow national courts to establish horizontal remedies in a way that risks violating the basic rule of law standards. In particular, I have pointed to the problem of creating new horizontal damages actions with a punitive element having an ex post facto effect in situations where private parties have relied on express permissions in national law. Finally, I have voiced concern that the free movement provisions

---

[61] International Labour Conference (99th session) Report of the Committee of Experts on the Application of Conventions and Recommendations, Report III (Part 1A) (Geneva 2010) 209.
[62] Art 153(5) TFEU.

and the proportionality test fail to provide the clarity and precision necessary to guide individual action. In the specific context of fundamental rights, this uncertainty coupled with a threat of damages risks producing a situation wherein a fundamental right cannot be exercised.

6

Horizontal Effects of Private Rights Vested by Union Law on Damages to be Paid by Another Private Party: The *Laval* Case as Model

ULF BERNITZ*

I. Introduction

As is well-known, European Union law acknowledges certain private rights to be applicable horizontally, ie, in relations between private parties. These rights have to be respected and enforced in the national law of the Member States.[1] However, it is still far from clear what is required in this regard and Union law seems to be in a state of evolution.[2] This is the case not least in relation to the possibilities for a private party to claim damages against another private party who has acted contrary to what is required by a Union right protecting private parties. The right to

---

* Ulf Bernitz is Professor of European Law at Stockholm University, as well as Senior Research Fellow at St Hilda's College, University of Oxford.

[1] As expressed by the ECJ in the *Francovich* case (para 31): 'It should be borne in mind at the outset that the EEC Treaty has created its own legal system, which is integrated into the legal systems of the Member States and which their courts are bound to apply. The subjects of that legal system are not only the Member States but also their nationals. Just as it imposes burdens on individuals, Community law is also intended to give rise to rights which become part of their legal patrimony. Those rights arise not only where they are expressly granted by the Treaty but also by virtue of obligations which the Treaty imposes in a clearly defined manner both on individuals and on Member States and the Community institutions'. Joined Cases C-6 and C-9/90 *Francovich and Others v Italy* [1991] ECR I-5357.

[2] See, inter alia, S Prechal and S de Vries, 'Seamless web of judicial protection in the internal market?' (2009) 34 *EL Rev* 5; N Reich, 'The Interrelation between rights and duties in EU law: Reflections on the state of liability law in the multilevel governance system of the Union: Is there a need for a more coherent approach in European private law?' (2010) 29 *Yearbook of European Law* 122; D Leczykiewicz, 'Private party liability in EU law: In search of the general regime' (2009–10) 12 *Cambridge Yearbook of European Legal Studies* 257; A Ward, 'National and EC remedies under the EU Treaty: Limits and the role of the ECHR' in C Barnard and O Odudu (eds), *The Outer Limits of European Union Law* (Oxford, Oxford University Press, 2009) 329; A Ward, 'Damages under the EU Charter of Fundamental Rights' (2011) 12 *ERA Forum* 589. See also the contributions in this volume of C Barnard (ch 2), X Groussot (ch 4), M Mörk (ch 5) and S de Vries (ch 3).

claim damages is of particular importance, as it is often the only remedy available in all those cases where an intrusion on a protected right has taken place.

Against this background, it is interesting to study the well-known, albeit controversial *Laval* case. In this case, based on the ruling by the European Court of Justice (ECJ),[3] the Swedish Labour Court decided in its final judgment that the trade union had to pay damages to Laval based directly on the finding that the trade union had taken industrial action interfering with Laval's right to free movement of services under Article 56 TFEU.[4] Based on detailed reasoning, the Labour Court found this Treaty provision on free movement to include a right to damages in a horizontal relation between private parties.

In this chapter it will be argued that private rights protected by Union law in horizontal relations entail a right to claim damages from private parties, albeit the law is in an early stage of development. It is important to distinguish State liability under the *Francovich* doctrine and liability of private parties. They constitute two different types of responsibility to which different legal principles apply. The notion of a 'sufficiently serious breach' is shaped for the particular position of Member State organs implementing and applying Union law and does not fit as a delimitation of the liability of private parties in horizontal damages cases. However, a certain delimitation is desirable to avoid liability of private parties for *minor* breaches of Union law, eg, by adopting the test 'sufficiently clear'.

II. Private Rights Protected by Union Law

Which are these private rights protected by Union law? Largely, there are two types of such rights. The first are those rights which have developed gradually under the Treaty case law, eg, the right not to be discriminated against, the right to establish and conduct a business, the right to work in other Member States, the right to trade in goods within the Union and the right to provide services within the Union. To mention an example, the prohibition of discrimination based on nationality between workers of the Member States (Article 45(2) TFEU) is applicable to contracts between individuals and enforceable against private parties.[5] Normally, these rights are subject to different types of limitations and restrictions and might have to be balanced against conflicting rights. However, all of them

---

[3] Case C-341/05 *Laval un Partneri Ltd v Svenska Byggnadsarbetareförbundet et al* [2007] ECR I-11767.
[4] 'Arbetsdomstolens domar (Judgments by the Labour Court) 2009, no 89 of 2 December 2009'. Available in English translation (unofficial) in M Rönnmar (ed), *Labour Law, Fundamental Rights and Social Europe*, Swedish Studies in European Law, vol 4 (Oxford, Hart Publishing, 2011) 227; U Bernitz and N Reich, 'Case No. A 268/04, The Labour Court, Sweden (Arbetsdomstolen) Judgment No. 89/09 of 2 December 2009, Laval un Partneri Ltd. v. Svenska Byggnadsarbetareförbundet et al.' (2011) 48 *CML Rev* 603; A Kruse, 'Arbetsdomstolens dom i Laval – lojal tillämpning av EG-rätten eller egen vågad tillverkning?' (2010) *Europarättslig Tidskrift* 381.
[5] Case C-281/98 *Roman Angonese v Cassa di Risparmio di Bolzano SpA* [2000] ECR I-4139, para 34.

contain a protected core.⁶ The right of individuals to rely on the directly effective provisions of the Treaty would be impaired if individuals were unable to obtain redress when their rights are infringed by breach of EU law.⁷ In addition, Union law recognises the right for private parties to claim damages from other private parties which have engaged in restrictive practices unlawful under Union competition law.⁸

Another type of protected rights is those private rights which have been established under the Charter of Fundamental Rights of the EU, having the status of primary law since 1 December 2009. It seems clear from the wording of the Charter and its references to the Convention for the Protection of Human Rights and Fundamental Freedoms (ECHR) that it does not only take in vertical relations between Union institutions and national authorities applying Union law, on the one side, and private parties on the other but to a certain extent also horizontal relations between private parties.⁹ To what extent the latter is the case is rather uncertain at present, but it seems justified to point, as examples, to articles such as Article 7 on Respect for private and family life, Article 8 on Protection of personal data, Article 11 on Freedom of expression and information, Article 12 on Freedom of assembly and of association, Article 17 on the Right to property, Article 21 on Non-discrimination, Article 24 on the Rights of the child and Articles 27 and following on Workers' rights.

Hopefully, in some years' time, the Court of Justice will have been able to clarify different aspects of the legal status of the Charter, including inter alia to what extent it covers horizontal relations between private parties. To the extent the Charter is found to do so, its provisions have to be enforceable against private parties; otherwise the protected rights would mostly remain on paper. On this point the Charter is silent but Article 52(3) states that in so far as the Charter contains rights which correspond to rights guaranteed by the ECHR, the meaning and scope of those rights shall be the same as those laid down in the Convention. As is well-known, Article 13 of the ECHR states the right to an effective remedy and Article 41 of the ECHR gives the Strasbourg Court the power to afford just compensation to the injured party. According to Article 52(3) of the Charter, Union law is not prevented from offering more extensive protection than the

---

⁶ See eg A Hartkamp, 'The effect of the EC Treaty in private law: On direct and indirect horizontal effects of primary Community Law' (2010) 18 *European Review of Private Law* 527, M Safjan and P Miklaszewicz, 'Horizontal effect of the general principles of EU law in the sphere of private law' (2010) 18 *European Review of Private Law* 475, P Cabral and R Neves, 'General principles of EU law and horizontal direct effect' (2011) 17 *European Public Law* 437.

⁷ Joined Cases C-46 and C-48/93 *Brasserie de Pêcheur SA v Germany and The Queen v Secretary of State for Transport, ex parte Factortame Ltd and others* [1996] ECR I-1029 para 20.

⁸ Cases C-453/99 *Courage Ltd v Bernard Crehan* [2001] ECR I-6297 and C-295–C-298/04 *Vincenzo Manfredi and others v Lloyd Adriatico Assicurazioni SpA et al* [2006] ECR I-6619.

⁹ Although AG Trstenjak in her Opinion in the *Dominguez* case argued for the lack of horizontal effect of the Charter's rights: Opinion of AG Trstenjak of 8 September 2010 in Case C-282/10 *Maribel Dominguez v Centre informatique du Centre Ouest Atlantique and Préfet de la région Centre* (ECJ, 24 January 2012), nyr. Groussot disagrees with this point of view: see his contribution in ch 4 of this volume on 'The Reach of EU Fundamental Rights on Member State Action after Lisbon'.

ECHR. Although we need to wait for the emerging case law of the ECJ, most likely the right to claim damages will play a key role in future in the safeguarding of the application of the provisions of the Charter.

The right to damages is linked to the general Union law principles on the assessment of damages. These principles have been developed in relation to State liability for breach of Union law obligations, primarily in the *Francovich* case[10] and the *Brasserie du Pêcheur* and *Factortame* cases.[11] However, they express general principles on the law of damages common to the legal systems of the Member States. It is to be assumed these principles would be guiding ones also in cases concerning the duty to pay damages under Union law in horizontal relations between private parties. Thus, the reparation of loss or damage must be commensurate with the loss or damage sustained so as to ensure the effective protection for the parties' rights.

In the absence of relevant Union law provisions, it is for the domestic legal system of each Member State to set the criteria for determining the extent of reparation, but those criteria must not be less favourable than those applying to similar claims or actions based on domestic law and must not be such as in practice to make it impossible or excessively difficult to obtain reparation. The damages granted must not be limited in such a way that they exclude loss of profit by individuals. The award of exemplary damages pursuant to a claim or action founded on Union law is possible if such damages could be awarded pursuant to similar claims founded on domestic law. However, the injured party must show reasonable diligence in limiting the extent of the loss or damage, or risk having to bear the damage himself.[12]

III. A Brief Note on the *Laval* Case in the ECJ

In December 2007, the ECJ delivered its judgment in the *Laval* case on a collective action taken by the dominant Swedish trade union in the building sector (Byggnads) against a Latvian company based in Riga (Laval) which had posted workers in Sweden to work on building sites but had refused to enter into a collective agreement with Byggnads. The action included sympathy actions by other unions and took the form of a blockade of a building site in the town of Vaxholm near Stockholm where Laval's Latvian workers were engaged in rebuilding a school-house. The action prevented the delivery of goods onto the site and included the cutting off of the supply of electricity and picketing, causing difficulties for the Latvian workers to enter the site. The action forced Laval to stop work-

---

[10] See above n 1.
[11] See above n 7.
[12] The principles mentioned were pronounced by the ECJ in the joined *Brasserie de Pêcheur* and *Factortame* cases, paras 82–89, above n 7.

ing on the site and somewhat later the town of Vaxholm requested the contract to be terminated.

Laval brought proceedings before the Swedish Labour Court (Arbetsdomstolen) against Byggnads and a collaborating union, seeking a declaration that the blockading and the sympathy actions were illegal and an order that such action should cease. It also sought an order that the unions pay compensation for the damage suffered. The Labour Court referred the case to the ECJ after the main hearing on the issue of the legality under EU law of the industrial action taken, but not on the issue of compensation for the damage caused.[13]

The judgment by the ECJ in the *Laval* case is often studied in conjunction with the *Viking* case decided in the same month.[14] The *Viking* case, referred for a preliminary ruling from the Court of Appeal in London, was about an international collective action aiming at deterring the Viking Line from reflagging its large ferry, *Rosella*, from the Finnish flag to that of Estonia. The two cases have much in common: the clashes between the right to free movement guaranteed in the Treaty as invoked by firms in the 'new' Member States (Latvia, Estonia) offering services in the EU market at lower wage costs on the one hand, and established collective labour law and practices of workers with a generally higher wage level in 'old' Member countries like Sweden and Finland on the other.[15]

In the *Laval* case Byggnads argued, supported by the Swedish and Danish governments, that the right to take collective action, including the right to strike, fell outside the scope of Article 56 TFEU (ex Article 49 TEC) on free movement of

---

[13] Laval's request for an interim injunction in order to stop the ongoing industrial action was rejected by the Labour Court.

[14] Case C-438/05 *International Transport Workers' Federation and Finnish Seamen's Union v Viking Line ABP and OÜ Viking Line Eesti* [2007] ECR I-10779. In the *Viking* case, the ECJ was focusing on the freedom of establishment (Article 49 TFEU, ex Article 43 TEC).

[15] On the ECJ judgments in *Laval* and *Viking* see, inter alia, the comments by J Malmberg and T Sigeman, 'Industrial Actions and EU Economic Freedoms: The Autonomous Collective Bargaining Model Curtailed by the European Court of Justice' (2008) 45 *CML Rev* 1115; N Reich, 'Free Movement v. Social Rights in an Enlarged Union – the Laval and Viking Cases before the ECJ' (2008) 9 *German Law Journal* 125; N Reich, 'Fundamental Freedoms vs. Fundamental Rights: Did *Viking* get it wrong?' (2008) *Europarättslig Tidskrift* 851; C Kilpatrick, 'Laval's regulatory conundrum: collective standard setting and the Court's new approach to posted workers' (2009) 34 *EL Rev* 844; K Apps, 'Damages claims against trade unions after Viking and Laval' (2009) 34 *EL Rev* 141; P Rodière, 'Les arrêts Viking et Laval, le droit de grève et le droit de négociation collective' (2008) *RDT eur* 47; ACL Davies, 'One Step Forward, Two Steps back? The Viking and Laval cases in the ECJ' (2008) 37 *ILJ* 126; L Azoulai, 'The Court of Justice and the social market economy: The emergence of an ideal and the conditions for its realization' (2008) 45 *CML Rev* 1335; N Hös, 'The principle of proportionality in the *Viking* and *Laval* cases: An appropriate standard of judicial review?' *EUI Working Papers Law* 2009/06; S Prechal and S de Vries, 'Seamless web of judicial protection in the internal market?' (2009) 34 *EL Rev* 5; 'Workshop Papers on Viking & Laval' (2007–08) 10 *Cambridge Yearbook of European Legal Studies*; S Deakin, 'Regulatory Competition after Laval' (2008–09) 11 *Cambridge Yearbook of European Legal Studies* 581; R O'Donogue and B Carr, 'Dealing with Viking and Laval: From Theory to Practice' (2008–09) 11 *Cambridge Yearbook of European Legal Studies* 123; C Barnard, 'EU "Social" Policy: From Employment Law to Labour Market Reform' in P Craig and G de Búrca (eds), *The Evolution of EU Law* (Oxford, Oxford University Press, 2011) 641, in particular 664 ff; Ö Edström, 'The Right to Collective Action – in Particular the Right to Strike – as a Fundamental Right' in *Labour Law, Fundamental rights and social Europe*, Swedish Studies in European Law, vol 4, 57; T Sigeman, 'Fackliga stridsåtgärder mot gästande tjänsteföretag – EG-rätten förtydligad' (2008) *Svensk Juristtidning* 553.

services. This far-reaching argument – the supremacy of collective labour law – was not accepted by the ECJ. It recognised the right to take collective action as a fundamental right in European law but held that its exercise does not fall outside the scope of the provisions of the Treaty. The exercise had to be reconciled with the requirements related to other rights protected under the Treaty and in accordance with the principle of proportionality. The Court stated:

> Although the right to take collective action must therefore be recognised as a fundamental right which forms an integral part of the general principles of Community law the observance of which the Court ensures, the exercise of that right may none the less be subject to certain restrictions. As is reaffirmed by Article 28 of the Charter of Fundamental Rights of the European Union, it is to be protected in accordance with Community law and national law and practices.[16]

The Court underlined that the freedom to provide services is one of the fundamental principles of the Union and confers rights on individuals which the national courts must protect.[17] The Court found restrictions of that freedom to be warranted only if justified by overriding reasons of public interest and, if that is the case, the restriction must be suitable for securing the attainment of the objective it pursues and not go beyond what is necessary to attain it.[18]

The ECJ reached very clear conclusions in the *Laval* case, more so than in most preliminary rulings. The Court ruled that a trade union was precluded under the circumstances from attempting by means of collective action in the form of a blockade to force a service provider in another Member State to sign a collective agreement. It also found the trade unions were precluded from taking collective action against undertakings in other Member States.

IV. The Swedish *Laval* Case on the Awarding of Damages

After receiving the judgment of the European Court, the Swedish Labour Court recommenced the proceedings in the *Laval* case and held a new trial, focusing on the damage claims.[19] Laval claimed economic damages in the amount of SEK 1,420,000 (about € 150,000) and exemplary damages totaling SEK 1,350,000 (about € 140,000).

As the Labour Court had not included any questions on the issue of the right to damages in its referral to the ECJ, it had to assess the legal bases for the liability to pay damages for violations of EU law without guidance from the ECJ on this

---

[16] *Laval un Partneri Ltd v Svenska Byggnadsarbetareförbundet and others*, above n 3, para 91.
[17] Ibid, para 97.
[18] Ibid, para 101.
[19] The *Viking* case was settled out of court. Viking Line reflagged the *Rosella* to Sweden instead of Estonia.

point. On the whole the Labour Court ruled in favour of Laval and awarded it exemplary damages in the total amount of SEK 550,000 (about € 60,000) and ordered the unions to pay Laval's litigation costs totalling around SEK 2,100,000 (about € 230.000).[20] It is the normal rule in Swedish procedural law that the losing party has to pay the litigation costs.

It is most interesting to study the very comprehensive reasoning of the Labour Court. It started by mentioning basic principles of EU law, in particular the loyalty principle (now Article 4(3) TEU), the state liability according to the *Francovich* doctrine and the general EU law principle of effectiveness. The Court continued:

> Liability for damages on an EC law basis has been extended in the case law of the European Court of Justice to situations in which a private party claims rights in accordance with EC law as against another private party. In order for damage liability for violations of EC law to exist between private parties, the EC legal regulations that are violated must have direct effect on the national level, and therewith, create rights for the individual that the national courts have to protect. Thereto is required that direct effect is also applicable in the relationship between the two private parties, 'horizontal direct effect'.

The Court noted that Article 56 TFEU (ex Article 49 TEC) on free movement of services is viewed as having direct effect[21] and that the same applies to Article 49 TFEU (ex Article 43 TEC) on the right of establishment[22] and Article 101 TFEU (ex Article 81 TEC) on restrictive agreements (citing the *Courage v Crehan* and *Manfredi* cases).[23] In particular, the Court observed the *Raccanelli* judgment of the ECJ in 2008.[24] That case concerned an Italian doctoral candidate who was found to have been discriminated against economically by a private research institution (the Max-Planck-Gesellschaft, MPG) in Germany due to nationality. The ECJ found this private institution had to observe the EU principle of non-discrimination in relation to workers. The Labour Court cited the conclusion reached by the ECJ:

> In the event that the applicant . . . is justified in relying on damage caused by the discrimination to which he has been subject, it is for the referring court to assess, in the light of the national legislation applicable in relation to non-contractual liability, the nature of the compensation which he would be entitled to claim.[25]

The Labour Court found Article 56 TFEU on free movement of services to have direct effect in the relationship between the labour unions and Laval. The court did not find any explicit support in the case law of the ECJ for the proposition that

---

[20] Exemplary damages play an important role in Swedish labour law. Section 55 of the Co-Determination Act states: 'In assessing whether, and to what extent, a person has suffered loss, consideration shall also be given to such person's interest in compliance with statutory provisions or provisions in the collective bargaining agreement and to factors other than those of purely economic significance'.
[21] The Court referred to para 97 in the *Laval* judgment of the ECJ.
[22] The Court referred to para 58 in the *Viking* judgment of the ECJ.
[23] Above n 8.
[24] Case C-94/07 *Raccanelli v Max-Planck-Gesellschaft zur Förderung der Wissenschaften eV* [2008] ECR I-5939.
[25] Ibid, para 52.

an individual is to pay damages on an EU law basis to another individual upon violation specifically of Article 56. However, referring in particular to the area of competition law and the *Raccanelli* case, the Labour Court concluded there has been established a general principle within EU law that damages may be awarded between private parties upon a violation of a treaty provision that has horizontal direct effect. The Labour Court found it sufficiently clear that the industrial actions taken in the case had violated EU law. The Court concluded the proper effect of EU law would be jeopardised unless the unions could be ordered to pay compensation to Laval for the injuries it could prove to have suffered as result of the action taken by the unions.

In the following part of the judgment the Labour Court considered which law on tort liability should be applicable. The Court stated as starting point:

> EC law does not . . . designate any specific procedural or tort law regulations that are to be applied in the event of a violation of EC law. There is an absence . . . of regulations in Swedish law that are directly applicable in situations such as the case at hand. The Labour Court consequently must, against the background of the Swedish legislation, after setting aside conflicting Swedish law or reconstructing such, determine the type of compensation that the Company has the right to claim.

Citing *Marshall*,[26] the Labour Court noted that economic compensation must be adequate in the sense that it provides complete compensation for the actual harm that has been caused by the violation of EU law that has occurred. Citing the *Suomen valtio and Lehtinen* case,[27] the Court noted that according to the principle of equivalence, national tort law must not discriminate EU based claims in comparison with comparable claims based on domestic law. The Court also noted its own earlier decision where exemplary damages had been awarded in a case of violation of EU non-discrimination law through analogous application of the principles of Swedish tort law.[28] Reminding itself of the *Brasserie du Pêcheur* and *Factortame*[29] cases the Court found EU tort liability normally to have retroactive effect. In its reasoning the Labour Court combined general principles of EU law with the application of national rules on compensation.[30]

Considering the facts of the case, the Labour Court found Laval had not been able to prove any economic loss. On this point, the Court seems to have applied a remarkably strict standard. However, as mentioned already, exemplary damages were awarded, about € 60,000. The Labour Court found the industrial actions taken constituted clear violations of EU law. According to established Swedish case law, developed by the Labour Court, high demands are placed on the labour market organisations when it comes to investigating, with exactitude and care,

---

[26] C-271/91 *M Helen Marshall v Southampton and South-West Hampshire Area Health Authority* [1993] ECR I-4367.
[27] C-470/03 *AGM-Cos.MET Srl v Suomen valtio and Tarmo Lehtinen* [2007] ECR I-2749.
[28] Arbetsdomstolens domar 2002 No 45.
[29] Above n 7.
[30] This methodology is commented and discussed in U Bernitz and N Reich, above n 4, (2011) 48 *CML Rev* 603, 611 ff under the heading 'Hybridization of remedies'.

whether a planned industrial action is not prohibited by a possibly arising duty to maintain industrial peace. The Court found that the same view ought to be applied when it comes to those impediments that EU law can potentially lay down.

The Swedish Labour Court is the court of first and last instance in collective agreement cases. However, Byggnads applied to the Swedish Supreme Court for relief for substantive defect, a kind of extraordinary remedy applicable only if a judgment is found to be manifestly wrong. The Supreme Court dismissed the application and did not state any reasons of its own on issues of European law.[31]

V. An Assessment of the Critique of *Laval* with Regard to the Right to Damages

The decision by the Swedish Labour Court in the Laval case to order the trade union to pay damages to Laval must be characterised as advanced and very loyal to European law, but in my opinion the judgment was well founded, even if the law in the area is uncertain.[32] It represents an important step in securing the functioning of the rights to free movement under Union law against actions by other private parties that intrude on those rights without justification by such overriding reasons of public interest that constitute sufficient justification according to Union case law.

However, this position is not taken by everyone. A strong critique of the decision by the Swedish Labour Court to award damages is presented in this volume in the chapter by Martin Mörk. He makes an elegant presentation of the possible counter-arguments but I do not share his conclusions. It is not possible to discuss here all the different aspects which have been brought into the fore by him but some important points deserve attention.

Since the entry into force of the Lisbon Treaty the Charter of Fundamental Rights constitutes an important point of departure. As was pointed out by the ECJ in the *Laval* case, the Charter recognises in its Article 28 the Right of collective bargaining and action as a fundamental right. It states:

> Workers and employers, or their respective organisations, have, in accordance with Union law and national laws and practices, the right to negotiate and conclude collective agreements at the appropriate levels and, in cases of conflicts of interest, to take collective action to defend their interests, including strike action.

It follows directly from the text of the Charter article cited that collective actions have to be taken '*in accordance with Union law*'. Thus, as the courts did in the

---

[31] Nytt Juridiskt Arkiv (NJA) 2010, Notice no 30.
[32] See, inter alia, *Wyatt and Dashwood's European Union Law* (Oxford, Hart Publishing, 2011) 314, referring to AG van Gerven in case C-128/92 *HJ Banks & Co Ltd v British Coal Corporation* [1994] ECR I-1209 and Case C-281/98 *Roman Angonese v Cassa di Risparmio di Bolzano SpA* [2000] I-4139.

Laval case, the right to take collective action has to be reconciled with the requirements relating to other rights of private parties which also enjoy protection under Union law.[33] It would not have been correct, as is often suggested, to have given the collective action taken by Byggnads some kind of unconditional priority. Moreover, the fact that collective actions constitute a fundamental right within the wider EU fundamental rights system indicates that the general system of remedies within Union law, including the possibilities to claim damages, should be applicable also to unlawful collective actions. Combining the Lisbon Treaty, the Charter and the rights connected to free movement earlier developed in the case law, the EU has developed an economic constitution based on an intricate system of individual rights and duties to which legal remedies are attached and where it is the task of the courts to draw the lines and maintain a delicate balance between conflicting rights. This 'economic community of rights' has been emerging for some time but has been made very visible by the two judgments of the ECJ and the Swedish Labour Court in *Laval*. This constitutionalised economic system is alien to traditional Scandinavian legal theory and also to British legal thinking, but given its firm Treaty basis the system seems here to remain. It will be for the Court to strike the intricate balance between the different, sometimes conflicting individual rights and duties.[34]

Martin Mörk discusses in his chapter the relation between Member State responsibility under the *Francovich* doctrine and the responsibility of private parties under Union law. He favours state responsibility. It is known that Byggnads has not directed claims for damages against the Swedish State in relation to the *Laval* case. Whether such claims could have been successful will not be discussed here, but as pointed out by the ECJ in its *Laval* judgment there were obvious deficiencies in the Swedish implementation of the Posting of Workers Directive.[35] The Directive[36] provides two different methods to secure the terms offered to posted workers in order to avoid wage dumping. The methods are state regulation of minimum rates of pay or the state declaring collective agreements universally applicable (*erga omnes*). Sweden had decided not to introduce any of these methods, as they were considered unwarranted interventions into the freedom of the parties on the labour market to negotiate agreements. In its criticism of Sweden, the ECJ characterised the missing provisions as the nucleus of mandatory rules for the protection of posted workers in the host country.

In my opinion, it is important not to mix up Member State responsibility following from the *Francovich* principles and the responsibility of individual parties under Union law having horizontal effect. These are two different kinds of

---

[33] On this balance, AG Cruz Villalón in Case C-447/09 *Reinhard Prigge, Michael Fromm and Volker Lambach v Deutsche Lufthansa AG*, judgment of 13 September 2011, nyr, paras 41–46.

[34] Case C-70/10 *Scarlet Extended*, nyr, provides an example, balancing the intellectual property protection of copyright under Article 17(2) of the Charter and the right to conduct a business under Article 16 of the Charter, see in particular paras 43 to 46.

[35] Ibid, paras 73 ff.

[36] Directive 96/71/EC, [1997] OJ L18/1 concerning the posting of workers in the framework of the provision of services.

responsibility to which different legal principles apply and should be treated separately. The criteria for state liability, primarily the requirement of a 'sufficiently serious breach' have been developed in the case law of the ECJ in *Francovich* and subsequent cases with regard to the specific role and function of State organs in implementing EU law.[37] The whole notion of 'sufficiently serious breach' is shaped to fit the particular position of Member State organs in their specific function implementing Union law. It is obvious that private parties, eg labour unions, are in quite a different position. To the extent Union law is binding and horizontally applicable Union law should be observed by private parties in the same way as they have to observe the national law of the Member States. Private parties do not enjoy any 'margin of appreciation' whether or not they have to observe Union law.

Does this mean that a private party is liable under Union law having horizontal effect for every minor breach of its obligations towards another private party and obliged to pay full compensation? The general principles for the assessment of damages, as expressed by the ECJ, were mentioned in Section II of this chapter. When it comes to the question about minor breach it is interesting to note that the Swedish Labour Court gave at least a partial answer in its *Laval* judgment by using the test *sufficiently clear*. The Court stated:

> [T]he Labour Court finds that the actions of the Labour Unions at issue, the industrial actions, in accordance with the European Court of Justice's preliminary ruling, constitute a serious violation of the Treaty, as they were in conflict with a fundamental principle in the Treaty, the freedom to provide services. Even if the right to take industrial actions has also been recognised by the EC as a fundamental right, it was found that the actual industrial actions, despite their objective of protecting workers, are not acceptable as they were not proportionate. The Labour Court finds that the stance of the ECJ in these issues entails that there is a violation of EC that is sufficiently clear. The requisite of damage liability therefore exists.

It remains to be seen if the ECJ will accept the test 'sufficiently clear' or something similar, but a certain delimitation of the scope of the liability along these lines seems advisable.

Another line of criticism in Martin Mörk's chapter deals with the vagueness of the law and the lack of sufficient legal predictability. This is certainly a point worth attention. However, Union law is still a young legal system in a state of development. With regard to the *Laval* case we need to keep two important factors in mind. First, a new fundamental provision on Right of collective bargaining and action was brought into the Union legal system as Article 28 of the Charter with only a minimum of surrounding legal framework. Secondly, as mentioned above, Sweden had chosen, when implementing the Directive on Posted Workers, to omit the crucial part of the directive on protection against wage dumping without

---

[37] In particular the *Brasserie du Pêcheur* and *Factortame* cases, see above n 3 and case C-352/98 P *Laboratoires pharmaceutiques Bergaderm SA, in liquidation, and Jean-Jacques Goupil v European Commission* [2000] ECR I-5291.

supplying an alternative. In reality, in the *Laval* case the legislators had left it to the courts to solve the problems and shape the law within the general Union law framework. The *Laval* judgments have pushed the law forward quite substantially in relation to the protection of private rights in horizontal relations, in particular with regard to the possibilities to claim damages. The model of reasoning used in this regard by the Swedish court is well worth close attention.

Part III

The Constitutional Dimension of Fundamental Rights

7

The Court of Justice of the European Union and the European Court of Human Rights after Lisbon

SIONAIDH DOUGLAS-SCOTT*

I. Introduction

The Lisbon Treaty introduced some major changes to the nature of fundamental rights protection in the European Union, which affect the nature of its relationship with the European Convention on Human Rights (ECHR). Article 6 TEU, as amended, ensures the binding, primary law status of the Charter of Fundamental Rights (CFR), as well as creating a new legal basis for the EU to accede to the ECHR. Article 6(3) TEU also confirms the status of fundamental rights emanating from the ECHR and constitutional traditions of the Member States as general principles of EU law. In particular, the now binding legal status of the CFR and provision for EU accession to the ECHR will affect the relationship between the Court of Justice of the European Union (ECJ) and the European Court of Human Rights (ECtHR), which is the subject of this chapter. It will also further complicate what is an already complex relationship between these two institutions. The key question will be whether these further changes wrought by Lisbon will do anything to improve fundamental rights protection in Europe, or, by adding further layers of complexity, obscure and problematise human rights in the European legal space. This chapter falls into two parts. First, it examines the present position; the nature of the existing relationship between these two institutions, following the commencement of the Lisbon Treaty changes, but prior to the EU's accession to the ECHR. In the second part, it examines the issue of accession and how this is likely to affect these courts.

---

* Professor of European and Human Rights Law, Lady Margaret Hall, University of Oxford.

II. The Situation Prior To EU Accession to the ECHR

Presently, the European Union is not a party to the ECHR and therefore not directly bound by it. However, the ECHR is still of relevance for the Luxembourg courts and the ECtHR can still be concerned with the EU. They can engage in the following ways set out below.

A. Jurisdictional Issues

Although the EU is not a party to the ECHR, the Strasbourg Court still possesses the jurisdiction to determine cases which involve the EU and EU law. The various modalities are briefly discussed.

(i) No Remedy for Direct Actions Against the EU in Strasbourg

As the EU is presently not a contracting party to the ECHR, it cannot be held directly responsible for violations of the Convention caused by EU primary or secondary law or other EU activities. Any complaint directed against the EU in the ECtHR is inadmissible, as established, for example, by the *CFTD* case.[1] Nor will an applicant be successful in Strasbourg if they attempt to proceed against all of the EU Member States as jointly liable for EU action.[2] An illustration is provided by the *Connolly*[3] case, in which the applicant's complaint in Strasbourg was that, in an earlier action in the Luxembourg Court, his request to submit written observations to the Advocate General had been denied. He therefore proceeded against all the (then) EU Member States of the ECHR, claiming a violation of Article 6 ECHR. However the Strasbourg Court rejected his complaint as inadmissible, holding that EU Member States could only be held responsible where there was an act of some sort on their territory. Other than this, EU action would not be attributed to the Member States and thus did not fall into their jurisdiction under Article 1 ECHR.

(ii) Member State Liability May However be Established if it is Responsible for an Act or Omission Related to the EU on its Territory

However, the ECtHR has held that the EU's Member States may be responsible, and jurisdiction under Article 1 ECHR established, for human rights violations

---

[1] *CFTD v European Communities* App no 8030/77 (1978) 13 DR 213. Also *M & Co v Federal Republic of Germany* App no 13258/87 (1990) 64 DR 138.

[2] Unless the act takes the form of an action taken by Member States on their own territory – see below.

[3] *Connolly v 15 Member States of the European Union* App no 73274/01 (ECtHR, 9 December 2008). The earlier action T-163/96 *Connolly v European Commission* [1999] ECR II-463 had concerned Connolly's employment dispute with the European Commission over his dismissal for the publication of his book, *The Rotten Heart of Europe* which had criticised the EMU project.

originating in EU law where an act takes place on their territory. The much discussed and highly significant *Bosphorus*[4] case illustrates this. In *Bosphorus*, Ireland had impounded an aircraft as required by an EC regulation, which was based on a UN Security Council Resolution. Because the aircraft was impounded by Irish authorities on Irish territory, the ECtHR found that the applicant was within Ireland's jurisdiction according to Article 1 of the ECHR. As a result, Ireland could be held responsible for any violation of the ECHR which thereby arose, regardless of whether the act or omission was a consequence of domestic law or of the necessity to comply with international legal obligations. However, in this case, the ECtHR found Ireland not liable and no violation to have taken place on the following grounds. First, the ECtHR established the existence of a *presumption* by which, *so long as* an international organisation 'is considered to protect fundamental rights . . . in a manner which can be considered at least equivalent to that for which the Convention provides' the Court will presume that a state has acted in compliance with the Convention, where the state had no discretion in implementing the legal obligations flowing from its membership of the organisation (emphasis applied).[5] Secondly, the Court held that this presumption could, however, be rebutted where the protection in the particular case was regarded as 'manifestly deficient'.[6] However, the protection in the *Bosphorus* case was not found to have been manifestly deficient.

The *Bosphorus* establishment of a presumption for the EU of 'equivalent protection' of human rights has attracted much criticism. First, it has been questioned as to why the EU should benefit from such a presumption at all?[7] No Member State of the ECHR benefits from such a presumption. Secondly, there is the criticism that the application of the presumption of equivalence, rebuttable only by the 'manifestly deficient' protection of rights, leads to a low, abstract standard of human rights review, rather than being based on the concrete circumstances of the case. In *Bosphorus*, there was no separate review on the facts of the case, leading to very harsh results.[8] As the concurring judges pointed out in *Bosphorus*, this was 'in marked contrast to the supervision generally carried out

---

[4] *Bosphorus Hava Yollari Turizm Ve Ticaret Anonim Sirketi v Ireland* (2006) 42 EHRR 1. See also *Matthews v UK* (1999) 28 EHRR 361, in which the ECtHR held that transfer of competence from a Member State to the EU will not necessarily absolve state responsibility under the ECHR (*Matthews* at para 22).

[5] *Bosphorus v Ireland* (above n 4), paras 155–56.

[6] Ibid, para 156.

[7] Furthermore, it is to be noted that in *Cooperatieve Producentenorganisatie van de Nederlandse Kokkelvisserij UA v Netherlands* App no 13645/05 (ECtHR, 20 January 2009) the ECtHR held that the *Bosphorus* presumption applied not only to the measures taken by a Member State when implementing legal obligations flowing from its membership of the EU, but also to the procedures followed within EU, including the procedure before the ECJ and the question whether those proceedings afforded equivalent guarantees of fairness.

[8] Namely, Bosphorus was unable to run its airline, and lost 3 years out of a 4-year aircraft lease. As it stated in argument, this was the only aircraft which had been impounded under the sanctions regulations

under the European Convention on Human Rights'.[9] However, the roots of the *Bosphorus* presumption have a traceable pedigree. In *M & Co v Germany*,[10] the now defunct European Commission of Human Rights held that a transfer of powers to an international organisation by a Member State would not be incompatible with that state's obligations under the ECHR, providing that, within the international organisation, fundamental rights would receive 'equivalent protection'. This judgment of the European Commission seemed to have been influenced by the similar doctrine developed by the German Bundesverfassungsgericht in its *Solange II* case.[11] Furthermore, as is well known, the Luxembourg Court, in its case law on fundamental rights, has long relied on the ECHR, and the jurisprudence of the Strasbourg Court, even though it had no obligation to do so.[12] This specificity, namely the ECJ's willingness to adhere to the ECHR and Strasbourg case law, may help explain why the ECtHR formulated the equivalence test.

(iii) Member State Discretion Regarding EU Law

A contrast should, however, be made between *Bosphorus*-type situations, in which Member States are implementing EU acts in which they have no discretion, and those cases, such as the implementation of directives, in which room for manoeuvre and discretion is given to the Member States as to how they choose to implement EU Law. Here, states may be subject to the jurisdiction of the ECHR in their own right. In *Cantoni*[13] in 1996, the Court reviewed a French law which implemented the Medicines Directive, without feeling inhibited by the fact that it derived from EC law. Cases such as those involving the application of the European Arrest Warrant in the Member States are likely to raise further complex issues of the intermingling of EU and national law.[14]

[9] Joint concurring opinion of judges Rozakis, Tulkens, Traja, Botoucharova, Zagrebelsky and Garlicki at para 4. Judge Ress, in a separate concurrence, warned that the concept of Convention compliance by international organisations should not be seen as a step toward the creation of a double standard. Nor did he believe that the presumption of compliance should prevent a case by case review.

[10] *M & Co v Federal Republic of Germany* (1990) 64 DR 138, decided in 1990 (in which the applicant was claiming breach of the right to a fair trial under Article 6 ECHR in the course of the execution of an ECJ judgment in a competition case). The European Commission found that the EC legal system did provide equivalent protection and deemed the action inadmissible; see also *Heinz v Parties to European Patent Convention* (1994) 76A DR 125, where a similar approach was taken.

[11] Case No 2 BvR 197/83 (BVerfG) BVerfGE 73, 339 (Neue Juristische Wochenschrift (NJW) 1987, 577) (22 October 1986).

[12] See eg S Douglas-Scott, 'A Tale of Two Courts' (2006) 43 *CML Rev* 629 for further elaboration of this.

[13] *Cantoni v France* ECHR 1996-V 52. In fact, *Cantoni* is notable for the fact that the ECtHR found the case admissible notwithstanding the fact that France had implemented the relevant directive almost word for word into national law. *Cantoni* has been interpreted as a 'warning shot' by Spielmann (the Luxembourg judge at the Court of Human Rights), coming as it did soon after the ECJ's own Opinion 2/94 which held that the EU had no legal basis to accede to the ECHR – Spielmann, 'Jurisprudence des jurisdictions de Strasbourg et de Luxembourg dans le domaine des droits de l'homme: conflits, incohérences et complémentarité' in P Alston, M Bustelo and J Heenan (eds), *L'Union européenne et les droits de l'homme* (Brussels, Bruylant, 2001) 805.

[14] Nor have national courts been troubled by the European Arrest Warrant's origins in EU law, when reviewing and even annulling national measures implementing it – see eg German Constitutional

B. Mutual Influence

Aside from the jurisdictional issues discussed in the last section, whereby the two systems are forced to confront each other's existence, there is another way in which the two courts acknowledge each other and cooperate. This is where, as a matter of choice, they cite the other's case law, even in cases where there is no jurisdictional overlap.[15] The ECJ has not in the past claimed to be bound by the ECtHR but the relationship between the Courts has been generally friendly. In *Moustaquim*, the ECtHR referred to the EU as a 'special legal order'.[16] Callewaert has recently referred to the 'Unionisation' of the ECHR and the 'Conventionalisation' of the EU.[17]

The Luxembourg courts refer to Strasbourg more frequently than does Strasbourg to Luxembourg. Such references are made on a considerable variety of issues, eg on freedom of expression in *Familiapress*, or on the right to a fair trial in *Pupino*.[18] As early as 1970, the ECJ had acknowledged that the EEC was bound by fundamental rights and, in the absence of a Community catalogue, it had to find a source for those rights. The ECHR (along with national constitutions) was an obvious source. The ECJ first explicitly mentioned the ECHR in *Rutili*[19] in 1975 (shortly after France joined the ECHR) and thereafter referred to specific articles in the Convention – between 1975 and 1998 the ECHR was cited in over 70 judgments of the Luxembourg Court.[20] The ECJ in the past stated that the ECHR was not binding but a 'source of inspiration'. What this meant was not clear.[21]

Court decision (BVerfG, NJW 58 (2005), 2289). See also the discussion below regarding the co-respondent mechanism for EU accession to the ECHR.

[15] For the growing academic literature on this, see eg, D Spielmann, 'Human Rights Case-Law in the Strasbourg and Luxembourg Courts: Conflicts, Inconsistencies and Complementarities' in P Alston, *The EU and Human Rights* (Oxford, Oxford University Press, 1999). See also S Peers, 'The European Court of Justice and the European Court of Human Rights' in E Orucu (ed), *Judicial Comparativism in Human Rights Cases* (UKNCCL 2003); L Scheeck, 'Solving Europe's Binary Human Rights Puzzle. The Interaction between Supranational Courts as a Parameter of European Governance', Questions de Recherche/Research in Question No 15 – October 2005 Centre d'études et de recherches internationales (Sciences Po); S Douglas-Scott, 'A Tale of Two Courts', above n 12; G Harpaz, 'The European Court of Justice and Its Growing Relation With The European Court of Human Rights: The Quest for Enhanced Reliance, Coherece and Legitimacy' (2009) 46 *CML Rev* 105; C Timmermans, 'The Relationship Between The European Court of Justice and The European Court Of Human Rights' in A Arnull, C Barnard, M Dougan and E Spaventa (eds), *A Constitutional Order of States: Essays in Honour of Alan Dashwood* (Oxford, Hart Publishing, 2011).

[16] *Moustaquim v Belgium* (1991) Series A no 193 (ECtHR, 18 February 1991), at para 49.

[17] Johan Callewaert, '"Unionisation" and "Conventionalisation" of Fundamental Rights in Europe' in J Wouters, A Nollkaemper and E De Wet (eds), *The Europeanization of Public International Law: The Status of Public International Law in The EU And its Member States* (The Hague, TMC Asser Press, 2008).

[18] Case C-368/95 *Vereinigte Familiapress Zeitungsverlags- und vertriebs GmbH v Heinrich Bauer Verlag* [1997] ECR I-3689; C-105/03 *Criminal proceedings against Maria Pupino* [2005] ECR I-5285.

[19] Case 36/75 *Rutili v Ministre de l'Interiori* [1975] ECR 1219.

[20] E Guild and G Lesieur, *The European Court of Justice on the European Convention on Human rights. Who said what, when?* (London/The Hague/Boston, Kluwer Law International, 1998).

[21] However, accession to the ECHR will make it directly binding on the EU, and see also below regarding the CFR and its now binding nature.

Whenever a court treats a legal source as a persuasive authority rather than a precedent this can reduce certainty, broadening the legal arguments which can acceptably be taken into consideration, but the controversial nature of persuasive authority can be seen in the arguments in the US Supreme Court over whether it is permissible to cite and draw upon foreign precedents.[22] Notwithstanding, some jurists see ECJ jurisprudence as having progressively incorporated the ECHR into EU law over time. Jacqué, for example, describes the *Pupino* case as 'an excellent example of direct incorporation'.[23]

Yet citation of Strasbourg *jurisprudence* in Luxembourg is a relatively recent phenomenon, commencing in the late 1980s with the Opinions of Advocates General, and only occurring as late as 1996 in the case of the Court of Justice itself. Indeed the ECJ's first reference in *P v S*[24] was made, somewhat ironically, after it had denied, in its *Opinion 2/94*,[25] that the EU had the competence, as the treaties then stood, to accede to the ECHR. While the earlier references made to Strasbourg tended to be brief and unexpansive, more recent references engage more with Strasbourg jurisprudence and tend to be more reliant on it as a ground of justification. In *Kadi*,[26] which concerned alleged fundamental rights violations by EU measures implementing UN Security Council measures which blacklisted alleged terrorists, considerable reference was made to Strasbourg case law, perhaps in an attempt to bolster the authority of the ECJ judgment.[27]

The Strasbourg Court has less frequently cited Luxembourg case law. Although there are many cases in which *parties* have raised Luxembourg case law, the Court of Human Rights does not cite Luxembourg very frequently in its own legal opinions, and most of those in which it has done so have been recent references. This is not surprising. Strasbourg is the specialist human rights court and for a long time there was little in the way of Luxembourg human rights jurisprudence for it to consider. However, it is to be expected that, now that the Charter of Fundamental Rights (CFR) has become binding, there will be a growth of fundamental rights case law in the ECJ, and more scope for the ECtHR to cite its cases.

Strasbourg has certainly made reference to the Charter on a good number of

---

[22] For specific examples of judicial parochialism, see that of US Supreme Court Justice Scalia in the juvenile death penalty case of *Roper v Simmons* – 'More fundamentally, however, the basic premise of the Court's argument – that American law should conform to the laws of the rest of the world – ought to be rejected out of hand', Justice Scalia, *Roper v Simmons* 543 US 551, 125 SCt 1183, 1226 (2005).

[23] JP Jacqué, 'The Accession of the European Union to the European Convention on Human Rights and Fundamental freedoms' (2011) 4 *CML Rev* 995, 1000.

[24] Case C-13/94 *P v S and Cornwall County Council* [1996] ECR I-2143. Ironically, the reference was to the ECtHR's decision in *Rees v United Kingdom* (1986) Series A no 106, in which that Court held that the UK's refusal to allow a transsexual to change their birth certificate following gender reassignment surgery did not breach Article 8 ECHR – which could hardly been seen as a victory for human rights.

[25] *Opinion 2/94* [1996] ECR I-1759.

[26] Joined Cases C-402/05 P and C-415/05 P *Yassin Abdullah Kadi and Al Barakaat International Foundation v European Council and European Commission* [2008] ECR I-6351.

[27] See also now App no 10593/08 *Youssef Nada v Switzerland* (ECtHR, 23 March 2011) in which a challenge was brought in the ECtHR against a national measure implementing a UN Security Council blacklisting resolution..

occasions, and carefully followed its evolving status. Indeed, the ECtHR confirmed the Charter's status as an authority long before it received any mention by the ECJ.[28] More recently, in *Neulinger and Shuruk*, the Strasbourg Court noted that the Charter 'became legally binding with the entry into force of the Lisbon Treaty'.[29] In *Scoppola (No 2)*,[30] the Strasbourg Court used Article 49 of the Charter to revise its case law on Article 7 ECHR, and also cited the ECJ's *Berlusconi*[31] judgment as authority for the retroactive application of the more lenient penalty under Article 7 ECHR.[32]

Other dissents and concurrences in the ECtHR have made use of the Charter – for example, in *Martinie v France*, a concurrence of three judges suggested that certain aspects of the right to a fair trial should be 'fundamentally reviewed' in light of Article 47 of the Charter.[33]

Therefore, although from the perspective of the ECtHR, the CFR might be viewed as part of an international treaty (namely the Lisbon Treaty) applicable to only 27 out of its 47 Council Of Europe Member States, the Strasbourg Court has shown, on the whole, an openness to the Charter and a willingness to review its case law in the light of it.

Arguably, the quality of the ECJ's case law regarding fundamental rights has profited to a great extent from this parallelism in interpretation. The fact that the ECtHR, too, increasingly refers to the ECJ's case law helps to create a uniform human rights standard in Europe.

An oft-cited fear when it comes to the relationship between the ECHR and EU is that of development of diverging standards between the two transnational courts, due to their concurrent human rights jurisdiction. However, the ECHR has been recognised by the ECJ as an integral part of EU law for nearly 40 years and there has not been a case in which the ECJ has *deliberately* gone against Strasbourg's interpretation of the ECHR. The usually cited cases of conflict – eg *Hoechst* and *Orkem* – are not evidence for this – but rather examples of instances where there was either no, or no clear authority, from Strasbourg on the issue – and notably in *Roquette*, the ECJ took trouble to reverse its earlier decision in *Hoechst* in the light of subsequent Strasbourg case law.[34]

---

[28] *Christine Goodwin v UK* (2002) 35 EHRR 18.
[29] *Neulinger and Shuruk v Switzerland* App no 41615/07 (ECtHR (Grand Chamber), 6 July 2010) para 55.
[30] *Scoppolla v Italy* App no 1024/03 (ECtHR (Grand Chamber), 17 September 2009).
[31] Cases C-391/02 and C-403/02 *Criminal proceedings against Silvio Berlusconi and Others* [2005] ECR I-3565.
[32] Several dissenting judges were highly critical of the majority's decision in *Scoppola* (Partly Dissenting Opinion of Judge Nicolaou, joined by Judges Bratza, Lorenzen, Jociené, Villiger and Sajó), concluding that the majority opinion had 're-written' Article 7 ECHR 'to accord with what they consider it ought to have been'. The dissent did not make explicit reference to the Charter, but the strong uneasiness of the dissent with the majority judgment might indicate an unwillingness of those judges to use the Charter as a means to enhance ECHR rights.
[33] *Martinie v France* (2006) 42 EHRR 15.
[34] Joined cases 46/87 and 227/88 *Hoechst AG v European Commission* [1989] ECR 2859 modified in Case C-88/99 *Roquette Frères SA v Direction des Services Fiscaux du Pas-de-Calais* [2000] ECR I-10465 at paras 23 and 29. However, for the view that the ECJ has not completely brought its case law in line

Since 1998, the judges and court officials of the ECJ and the ECtHR have been meeting on a regular, but not formally institutionalised basis. This cooperation, however, is not based on a legal duty to cooperate, but merely on comity. Indeed, in the past, friction has been noted between the EU and the COE, evidence of a fear that the EU might seek to usurp or marginalise[35] the COE's role in the human rights field – a fear which was specifically addressed in the Juncker report.[36]

However, in the *Declaration on Article 6(2) TEU* appended to the Lisbon Treaty, the Conference noted the existence of a regular dialogue between the two Courts and stated that 'such dialogue could be reinforced when the Union accedes to [the] Convention'.[37] Therefore, the Courts are under a political obligation to continue with that dialogue and even intensify it. And, in the words of a judge of the ECJ, 'The influence the one exerts on the other is mutual and real'.[38]

(i) Greater Dialogue as a Result of the Lisbon Treaty

But, notwithstanding this provision, greater dialogue between the two Courts is in any case likely, as a consequence of the entry into force of the Lisbon Treaty, for two reasons. First, the competences of the ECJ have been extended by Lisbon to cover a number of areas very relevant from a human rights point of view. For example, the former Third Pillar, now incorporated into Title V TFEU on the Area of Freedom, Security and Justice, was previously excluded from most of the jurisdiction of the Luxembourg Court, whereas now, after a transitional period of five years,[39] the ECJ will have full jurisdiction. Given the proliferation of measures adopted by the EU in this area, which is increasing with the Stockholm Programme,[40] there will surely be

---

with that of the ECtHR see W Weiss, 'Human Rights in the EU: Rethinking the Role of the European Convention on Human Rights After Lisbon' (2011) 7 *European Constitutional Law Review* 64, 77.

[35] Elsewhere the fear that the EU is becoming an 'Empire' has been expressed, partly due to an aggressive application of its rules to its neighbours, evidencing imperial politics – see J Zielonka, *Europe as Empire* (Oxford, Oxford University Press, 2007).

[36] In this report, Prime Minister Jean-Claude Juncker proposed that a working rule be established, according to which 'the decisions, reports, conclusions, recommendations and opinions of [the Council of Europe] monitoring bodies: 1. will be systematically taken as the first Europe-wide reference source for human rights; 2. will be expressly cited as a reference in documents which they produce'. Jean-Claude Junker, Council of Europe/European Union: 'A Sole Ambition for the European Continent', *Report to the Heads of State and Government of the Member States of the Council of Europe* (11 April 2006), see also *Memorandum of Understanding Between the Council of Europe and the European Union*, CM(2007) 74 (10 May 2007); See also P Drzemczewski, 'The Council of Europe's Position with Respect to the EU Charter of Fundamental Rights' (2001) 22 *Human Rights Law Journal* 14.

[37] Declaration on Article 6(2) of the Treaty on European Union: 'The Conference agrees that the Union's accession to the European Convention for the Protection of Human Rights and Fundamental Freedoms should be arranged in such a way as to preserve the specific features of Union law. In this connection, the Conference notes the existence of a regular dialogue between the Court of Justice of the European Union and the European Court of Human Rights; such dialogue could be reinforced when the Union accedes to that Convention'.

[38] Timmermans, 'The Relationship Between The ECJ and The ECtHR', above n 15, 153. Notably, this interaction also gave rise to the *Joint Communication* of judges Costa and Skouris regarding accession of the EU to the ECHR – see further below.

[39] On this see Protocol no 36 to the Lisbon treaty on transitional provisions, Article 10.

[40] Council of the European Union, *The Stockholm Programme – An open and secure Europe serving and protecting the citizens* (Brussels, 2 December 2009) 3.

more litigation relevant from a human rights perspective in the Court of Justice, and in particular, more litigation potentially subject to an overlap of competences between the two European Courts. Consequently, there will be a need for a greater dialogue, given that more questions will arise in Luxembourg as to the correct interpretation of a number of ECHR provisions.

C. Charter of Fundamental Rights Now Binding

A further reason why dialogue between the two Courts is likely to increase as a result of Lisbon is that the CFR has come into force and has primary law status, and the ECJ is already applying the Charter more frequently. In a *Joint communication from Presidents Costa and Skouris*[41] it was observed that the CFR has rapidly become of primary importance in the recent case law of the ECJ. The Communication noted that, in the period from 1 December 2009, to early 2011, the CFR had been cited in some 30 judgments. Thus, the Charter has now become the departure point text for the ECJ's assessment of fundamental rights, and it would seem that, where the European Convention and the case law of the Strasburg Court are cited and drawn upon, this will only be in cases where there is no existing authority from the ECJ on a particular issue. For example, in *Schecke and Eifert*[42] the ECJ assessed the validity of the regulations at issue in the light of the provisions of the Charter[43] as the primary basis for judicial review, stressing the equivalence of protection of the Charter and the European Convention under Article 52(3) CFR.

The Charter has borrowed about half of its rights from the ECHR. One of its general provisions, Article 52(3), states that, to the extent that rights in the Charter are borrowed from the Convention, they are to be given the same meaning and content as they have in the European Convention.[44] This was underlined by the Joint Communication of judges Costa and Skouris which suggested a 'parallel interpretation' of such rights.[45] So the Charter itself establishes a strong link between its own fundamental rights and the Convention, and Article 52(3) aims to maintain consistency between the rights of the CFR and the ECHR. This provides another reason for the Court of Justice, when applying the Charter, to maintain contact with the Strasbourg Court and its jurisprudence. Therefore, Article

---

[41] Delegations from the ECtHR and the ECJ met on 17 January 2011 – Joint communication from Presidents Costa and Skouris, press release no 75 issued by the Registrar of the ECtHR on 27 January 2011, www.echr.coe.int .

[42] Joined Cases C-92/09 and C-93/09 *Volker und Markus Schecke GbR and Hartmut Eifert v Land Hessen* [2010] ECR I-11063.

[43] And in which, notably, the ECJ did not discuss the temporal applicability of the Charter, despite the fact that the disputes at issue had occurred before the entry into force of the Treaty of Lisbon.

[44] Art 52(3) 'In so far as this Charter contains rights which correspond to rights guaranteed by the Convention for the Protection of Human Rights and Fundamental Freedoms, the meaning and scope of those rights shall be the same as those laid down by the said Convention. This provision shall not prevent Union law providing more extensive protection.'

[45] Joint Communication at para 1.

52(3) provides for the ECHR a minimum standard of human rights in the EU and also leads the EU to be indirectly bound by the ECHR, as it must always be followed when restricting fundamental rights in the EU, to ensure the EU maintains the same level of protection. Indeed, Weiss goes as far as to suggest that Article 52(3) 'materially incorporates the core norms of the Convention into EU law'. Weiss also contends that Article 52(3) gives the relevant provisions of the ECHR the same status as EU primary law since the CFR has the same legal value as the treaties, and should also share the qualities of direct effect and primacy regarding domestic law.[46]

Yet which rights of the ECHR are at issue here? The wording of the CFR is not identical to that of the ECHR, nor are the rights protected therein identical. For example, Article 6 CFR – the right to liberty and security of the person – is expressed in one clause, whereas in Article 5 ECHR it is expressed in five. However, a list of corresponding rights can be found in the official explanations[47] relating to the Charter, which, although they do not have the status of law, according to Article 52(7) of the Charter, 'shall be given due regard by the Courts of the Union and the Member States' when interpreting the Charter. But there is still room for uncertainty.

It should also be highlighted that the wording of Article 52(3) CFR does not make express reference to the ECtHR's case law. Only the ECHR itself is mentioned. Might Article 52(3) nonetheless be interpreted as containing such a reference, in which case it is arguable that the case law of the ECtHR itself would bind the ECJ when interpreting the relevant provisions of the CFR? On the one hand, it would seem unlikely that the drafters of Article 52(3) intended merely to refer to the then 50-year-old text of the ECHR, and not the ECtHR ongoing jurisprudence, particularly given the ECtHR's dynamic interpretation of the ECHR as a 'living instrument'.[48] The official explanations regarding Article 52(3) explicitly mention the case law. They state that

> [t]he meaning and scope of the guaranteed rights are determined not only by the text of those instruments, but also by the case law of the European Court of Human Rights and by the Court of Justice of the European Union.

Further, the Preamble to the EU Charter is phrased in a similar manner and also refers to the case law of the ECtHR and the ECJ.[49]

On the other hand, if the case law of the ECtHR were binding, this would mean that the ECtHR's human rights case law became part of EU law. Further, Article 52(7) CFR only postulates a duty to *duly regard* the Charter's Official Explanations and thus seems to suggest merely a duty to 'duly regard' the ECtHR's case law.

---

[46] Weiss, 'Human Rights in the EU' (above n 34) at 64 and 71. However, the claim for direct effect of CFR provisions is questionable, at least in the case of some of its provisions, given the lack of drafting of some of its articles in terms of principles rather than rights.
[47] Explanations relating to the Charter of Fundamental Rights [2007] OJ C303/17.
[48] Eg *Tyrer v United Kingdom* (1978) Series A no 26 at 15–16, para 31.
[49] Recital 5 of the Preamble of the Charter refers, inter alia, to 'rights as they result ... from ... the case-law of the Court of Justice of the European Union and of the European Court of Human Rights'.

Therefore it might seem that there is little case for arguing that ECJ interpretations of the EU Charter must strictly follow that case law of the ECtHR.[50] Indeed, if the ECtHR's case law were to bind the ECJ this would introduce a doctrine of stare decisis more typical of Common Law, and unknown to EU law, as well as threatening the autonomy of the ECJ's interpretations of EU law.[51] The Strasbourg Court is not bound by its own judgments, nor does the ECHR provide that the national courts of the contracting parties to the Convention be bound by its decisions. Article 46 ECHR states that Court judgments are only binding inter partes. However, in *J McB v LE* the ECJ appeared to suggest that where Charter rights are derived from ECHR rights, the ECJ should follow the clear judgments of the ECtHR.[52] So, at the very least, a close link between the case law is established.

D. Conclusions to Section II

To date, the ECtHR has not condemned a decision of the Luxembourg Court as violating fundamental rights. Furthermore, it is in the ECJ's interests to align its fundamental rights jurisprudence with Strasbourg, or at least to maintain it as a minimum standard, in order to legitimise its own institutional position, especially given the challenge to its authority by some national courts, such as the German Constitutional Court.[53] The saga of the EU Arrest Warrant and the declaration of invalidity of its national implementing measures in Germany[54] and elsewhere, on grounds of failure to protect fundamental rights sufficiently, illustrate the threat to the ECJ and EU from national constitutional courts where it is believed that inadequate protection has been given to fundamental rights. The avowal of a strong protection of human rights has been a means for the Luxembourg court to maintain and increase its authority and the primacy and constitutional autonomy of EU law, as witnessed in the *Kadi* decision.

On the other hand, where it is possible,[55] EU law may also present advantages to litigants over actions in Strasbourg. Unlike under the ECHR, where the applicant must exhaust all domestic remedies in order to get a hearing in Strasbourg, applicants may get a ruling from Luxembourg by way of a preliminary reference from a domestic court. Domestic courts also have the power to set aside national measures which conflict with EU human rights law – which provides a much

---

[50] Further, it should be noted that there were various unsuccessful attempts to include an explicit reference to the ECtHR's case law during the Convention.
[51] On which see below.
[52] Case C-400/10 PPU *J McB v LE* (ECJ, 5 October 2010), nyr.
[53] In *Mannfred Brunner v European Union Treaty* [1994] 1 CMLR 57 on the compatibility of the Maastricht treaty with the German Basic law, the German Constitutional court held that it retained the competence to review EU measures which violate fundamental rights.
[54] For the German Constitutional Court decision see BVerfG, NWJ 58 (2005), 2289.
[55] The Charter of Fundamental Rights does not apply universally but only in relation to EU law. Article 51(1) Charter reads: 'The provisions of this Charter are addressed to the institutions, bodies, offices and agencies of the Union with due regard for the principle of subsidiarity and to the Member States only when they are implementing Union law'.

faster remedy than a Strasbourg lawsuit and subsequent enforcement by the COE Committee of Ministers. Cases such as *Pupino* and *Kadi* illustrate that the ECJ is willing to use its human rights jurisdiction and apply Strasbourg case law to Member States directly. Thus, even those Member States in which the status of precedents from the European Court of Human Rights is still unclear can be forced to apply it, giving the Convention added strength through EU law. For example, section 2 of the UK Human Rights Act 1998 only requires the UK courts to 'take into account' Strasbourg jurisprudence, denying it any status as binding precedent. In Germany, the Constitutional Court has not required the strict application of ECtHR case law, even in cases directly brought against Germany.[56] Therefore, ECHR rights could be strengthened through their enforcement as fundamental EU rights in the Member States of the EU. To the extent that rights are enforced through the EU, this could result in a harmonisation of the ECHR in the EU, rather than the more differentiated impact and dissemination, particularly due to the application of its 'margin of appreciation' doctrine, it has to date received through the Strasbourg institutions.

Furthermore, as EU competence has increased, so has its human rights competence,[57] with a possible corresponding decline in Strasbourg jurisdiction which is restricted to Member States' domestic law – an ever-dwindling field. The CFR contains many more rights, and a far more up to date catalogue, than the ECHR. Further, according to Article 52(3) CFR, the Charter may offer more extensive protection than the ECHR. There is also the possibility of applying fundamental rights as general principles of law under Article 6 TEU, in new and potentially radical ways, as the principle of non-discrimination on grounds of age, applied in the *Mangold* case,[58] illustrates. If EU competences continue to grow, the ECHR could be rendered redundant at least as far as its EU members are concerned.[59] Strasbourg is currently overloaded, and suffering from a very large backlog of applications, particularly from the newer Member States. Therefore, all sorts of possible consequences for the two institutions follow from the now binding nature of the CFR, introduced by the Lisbon Treaty.

---

[56] See, on this, *Decision of the German Federal Constitutional Court*, 2 BvR 1481/04 of 14 October 2004; *Kazim Görgülü v Germany* (ECtHR, 26 February 2004). See also the English case *R v Horncastle and others* [2009] UKSC 14, regarding concerns as to the Strasbourg Court's ability to understand the English hearsay rule.

[57] See, for example, AG Sharpston's call for a 'seamless protection of fundamental rights under EU law in all areas of exclusive or shared EU competence' – apparently even in cases in which EU competence has not even been exercised – in Case C-34/09 *Gerardo Ruiz Zambrano v Office national de l'emploi (ONEm)* (ECJ, 8 March 2011), but contrast the subsequent cases Case C-434/09 *Shirley McCarthy v Secretary of State for the Home Department* (ECJ, 5 May 2011) and C-256/11 *Murat Dereci and others v Bundesministerium fur Inneres* (ECJ, 15 November 2011).

[58] Case C-144/04, *Werner Mangold v Rudiger Helm* [2005] ECR I-9981; also Case C-555/07 *Seda Kücükdeveci v Swedex GmbH & Co KG* [2010] ECR I-365.

[59] For the suggestion that EU states should withdraw from the ECHR see AG Toth, 'The European Union and Human Rights: The Way Forward' (1997) 34 *CML Rev* 491; also HG Schermers' early fear expressed in 'The European Communities under the ECHR' (1978) 1 *Legal Issues of European Integration* 1. See also A Williams, 'Burying, not praising the European Convention on Human Rights: a provocation' in N Walker, J Shaw and S Tierney (eds), *Europe's Constitutional Mosaic* (Oxford, Hart Publishing, 2011).

III. Accession of the EU to the ECHR

Although accession of the EU (or formerly the EC or EEC) to the ECHR had been considered, and was the subject of much discussion, in the past, it was never achieved.[60] The Lisbon Treaty now provides a legal basis for the EU to accede to the ECHR. There would be many advantages in EU accession to the ECHR. A formal linking of the EU and ECHR could be seen as underlining EU concern with human rights, and also eliminate charges of double standards, based on the criticism that whereas the EU requires all of its Member States to be members of the ECHR, it is not itself a member. EU accession to the ECHR would also alleviate the situation in which individuals may find themselves when faced by possible breaches of the ECHR by EU institutions, with no external supervision or remedy in Strasbourg, given the present situation in which, unless EU law has been implemented by some Member State act, there is no possible action in Strasbourg.[61] Accession would therefore satisfy a perceived need for external judicial supervision of EU institutions, especially given the large growth of EU agencies and competencies in, eg, the field of criminal law. Accession could also help address the critique of the German Constitutional Court, in its *Solange* case law,[62] that EU protection of fundamental rights is inadequate.

However, for some time, a specific obstacle to EU accession was the Luxembourg Court's *Opinion 2/94*[63] on whether the then Community had the power to accede to the European Convention. In that *Opinion* the ECJ held that, as EC law then stood, the Community had no competence to accede to the ECHR as there was no adequate legal basis in the Treaty for accession, rejecting the argument that the 'implied powers' clause of then Article 308 EC might serve as a base. Therefore, accession could only be brought about by way of Treaty amendment. Article 6(2) of the TEU, as amended, has removed that obstacle,[64] providing a legal basis for EU accession, reading as follows: '2. The Union shall accede to the European Convention for the Protection of Human Rights and Fundamental Freedoms. Such accession shall not affect the Union's competences as defined in the Treaties.'

---

[60] For example, the European Commission issued a Memorandum in April 1979 on 'The Communities becoming a signatory of the European Convention on Human Rights' as an initial step towards consolidating human rights protection in the Community – *Bulletin of the European Communities*, supplement 2/79.
[61] See discussion above in Section II.
[62] eg *Solange I* decision, 29 May 1974, BVerfGe, 37, 271.
[63] *Opinion 2/94 on Accession of the EC to the ECR* [1996] ECR I-1759 taken under then Article 308(6) of the EC treaty.
[64] Although it is conceivable that the ECJ might give another Opinion on a new Accession Agreement, finding it incompatible with EU law – See F Jacobs, 'The Internal Legal Effects of the EU's International Agreements and the Protection of Individual Rights' in A Arnull et al, *A Constitutional Order of States*, above n 15, 153.

It was also necessary for the ECHR to be amended, and a new Article 59(2), introduced by Protocol 14 to the ECHR, makes provision for the accession of the EU.[65]

A. How?

Therefore Article 6(2) of the TEU now makes it an obligation for the EU to accede to the ECHR.[66] This does not, however, mean that accession is by any means a simple affair. Given the particular characteristics of the EU, and its singular nature as a *sui generis* international organisation rather than a state, accession will prove challenging. The Council of Europe and its institutions are not designed with supra-national entities in mind. The following questions had already been canvassed in the course of previous attempts to urge EU accession, namely: who would represent the EU in the Strasbourg Court?; and would non-Member States of the EU have a right to bring proceedings against the EU in the ECtHR? The requirement for exhaustion of domestic remedies under the Convention could also lead to extended litigation if EU law were at issue and preliminary rulings had already been made to Luxembourg. The accession process must take account of these challenges as well as the complicated procedures for accession required by EU law set out below.

Accession must follow the long and complex mandatory procedure that governs all EU agreements with third countries and international organisations, set out in Article 218 TFEU. For such an agreement to be concluded, Article 218 sets a requirement of unanimity in the Council, the consent of the European Parliament (by a two-thirds majority) and its ratification in all EU[67] and COE Member States.

Further, it is probable that one or more Member States will ask the ECJ for an opinion under Article 218(11) TFEU on whether the accession treaty is compatible with EU law. There may also be concern or objections raised by some non-EU COE Member States. Therefore the accession process is likely to take several years. Notwithstanding this, the Stockholm Programme of the Council of the EU urged that 'the rapid accession of the EU to the European Convention on Human Rights is of key importance'.

The COE Committee of Ministers adopted, on 26 May 2010, ad hoc terms of reference for the Steering Committee for Human Rights (referred to in the documents as CDDH) to draft, in collaboration with the EU, a legal instrument for the

---

[65] The new Article 59(2) ECHR reads: 'The European Union may accede to this Convention'. But accession must be ratified by all COE Member States.

[66] Jacobs notes the oddity of imposing an obligation on the EU to accede when fulfillment of that obligation is not solely in the hands of the EU itself, but also its Member States and COE non-EU Member States. Jacobs suggests that it might have been preferable for Article 6(2) TEU to have been drafted in terms of the EU 'using its best endeavours to accede'. Jacobs, above n 64, 152.

[67] Some of which, including the UK following the coming into force of EU Act 2011 in September 2011, may require a referendum under their constitutional law provisions.

accession of the EU to the ECHR.[68] For the EU itself, the Council of the EU adopted on 4 June 2010 a Decision authorising the European Commission to negotiate an agreement for the EU to accede to the Convention.[69] Official negotiations started in early July 2010. A Working Party, formed of a 'committee of experts' (mainly officials) from Member States of both the EU and ECHR, was appointed to produce a draft of an accession document. Notably, the ECJ itself issued a 'discussion document' on EU accession,[70] and the Court's own position is of great interest, given that it may well be asked by some Member States to give an Opinion on the compatibility of EU accession to the ECHR with EU law. In July 2011, a final version of the draft legal instruments on the Accession of the European Union to the ECHR was adopted,[71] and the ensuing discussion is based on this document.

However, it should be stressed that the term 'final' is misleading here, as this document is only the basis for further discussion among the Member States and will be subject to detailed scrutiny and further changes. Already, by a meeting of COREPER in October 2011, some Member States had expressed reservations as to the content of the proposed Draft Accession Agreement, and it had become clear that the EU could not express a unanimous position on the draft. Subsequent meetings were held in order to identify possible solutions to accommodate these concerns.

The objections raised by Member States to the Draft Agreement so far (ie up to early 2012) concern issues such as the scope of the accession of the EU to the ECHR, the non-affectation of the Member States' competences as a result of the accession, the extent of application of the co-respondent mechanism and the exercise of voting rights of the EU and its Member States in the Committee of Ministers when supervising the execution of judgments against the EU by the ECtHR. However, by late 2012 negotiations had restarted and representatives of the EU and of the 47 ECHR states (the Group 47+1) met to agree on the text of a final accession agreement.[72] Once this final agreement has been reached, the ratification process can commence, although it is probable that ECJ will first be asked for its Opinion as to whether the agreement is compatible with the EU Treaties.'

There has been some criticism of the lack of transparency of aspects of the proceedings (in particular with regard to the EU) – for example, the Council decision authorising the Commission's negotiating mandate was confidential and therefore not open to parliamentary scrutiny – a feature that came under strong criticism in

---

[68] CM/Del/Dec(2010)1085, of 26 May 2010.
[69] The decision is based on Article 6(2) TEU, Article 218(8) TFEU, Protocol 8 and Declaration 2 to the Lisbon Treaty.
[70] Curia.europa.eu/jcms/jcms/p.6428/
[71] CDDH-UE(2011) 16 fin. However, the UK Lord Chancellor, and Minister for Justice, Kenneth Clarke, in his oral evidence on 7 September 2011 to the House of Commons European Scrutiny Committee on the topic of EU Accession to the ECHR and the EU Charter, emphasised that this document had no binding legal status whatsoever, and was simply the first step in starting the complex negotiations (HC 1492-i).
[72] See eg Council of Europe meeting report 47+1 (2012) R02.

the UK Parliamentary European Scrutiny Committee.[73] NGOs also urged for the widest possible consultation, and Amnesty International expressed concern that 'the absence of civil society's participation and the lack of democratic scrutiny of the negotiations may give rise to questions about the overall process and result in gaps in human rights protection'.[74]

With accession, the EU would become the 48th signatory of the ECHR. The EU would be represented by its own judge at the European Court of Human Rights in Strasbourg, and would have to comply with judgments of this court in cases brought against it.

B. Problems?

There were several problematic aspects of accession highlighted by the Council Presidency in February 2010.[75] The following two proved particularly challenging and will be discussed in further detail below, namely:

- the question of the most appropriate manner to ensure that the accession complies with the conditions laid out in the Treaties and their Protocols (in particular Protocol No 8 relating to Article 6(2) of the TEU), which required both the preservation of EU competences and of the interpretive monopoly of the ECJ in the interpretation of EU law.
- the advisability of a 'co-defendant' mechanism, ensuring that in certain cases both the EU and the Member State concerned may, where appropriate, be parties in any proceedings before the European Court of Human Rights.

(i) Preserving the Autonomy of the EU Legal Order

In *Opinion 1/91* and *Opinion 1/00*,[76] the ECJ held that the EU had no competence to enter into international agreements that would permit a court other than the Luxembourg court to make binding determinations about the content or validity of EU law. The Court in *Kadi* also strongly underlined the autonomous nature of EU law, particularly with regard to fundamental rights. The Lisbon Treaty itself introduced further provisions which expressly require that the Accession Agreement should be drafted in such a way that autonomy of EU law is not undermined, namely:

---

[73] See UK Parliamentary briefing paper *EU Accession to the European Convention on Human Rights*, SN/IA/5914, 22 March 2011, at 11, and oral evidence of Kenneth Clarke to European Scrutiny Committee (HC 1492-i).

[74] Amnesty International, 'Recommendations to the EU Hungarian Presidency' (2011).

[75] See also T Lock, 'EU Accession to the ECHR: Implications for Judicial Review in Strasbourg', (2010) 35 *EL Rev* 777–98, and 'Walking on a tightrope: the draft accession agreement and the autonomy of the EU legal order' (2011) 48 *CML Rev* 1025 for a thorough treatment of accession issues; J-P Jacqué, 'The Accession of the European Union to the European Convention on Human Rights and Fundamental freedoms' (2011) 48 *CML Rev* 995, 1000.

[76] *Opinion 1/91 (EEA Agreement)* [1991] ECR I-6079, *Opinion 1/00 (European Common Aviation Area)* [2002] ECR I-3493, see also *Opinion 1/09* of the ECJ finding the Draft agreement on Community Patent Court incompatible with EU law (ECJ, 8 March 2011).

- *Article 6(2) TEU* provides that accession 'shall not affect the Union's competences as defined in the Treaties'.
- *Article 1 of Protocol No 8* provides that the Accession Agreement must 'make provision for preserving the specific characteristics of the Union and Union law'.
- *Article 2 of Protocol No 8* provides that accession 'shall not affect the competences of the Union or the powers of its institutions'.
- *Article 3 of Protocol No 8* provides that the Accession Agreement must not affect Article 344 TFEU, which requires that disputes concerning the interpretation or application of the EU Treaties must be settled only in accordance with the provisions of the Treaties.

Unfortunately, this Protocol fails to elaborate on what are the 'specific characteristics of the EU and its laws'. Therefore its scope is unclear. However, it seems clear that, if the ECtHR were to determine for itself issues of EU law, then this would violate the holdings of *Opinions 1/91* and *1/00* and threaten the autonomy of the EU legal order. The Accession Agreement will also have to ensure that EU Member States will continue to be bound by Article 344 TFEU.[77]

However, under the ECHR, and the case law of the ECtHR, it has been established that it is primarily for the national courts to interpret and apply matters of domestic law. Domestic remedies must be exhausted (under Article 34 ECHR) to ensure that national courts have had a chance thoroughly to consider the matter. Once the action comes to Strasbourg, the ECtHR does not rule on the validity of national law but on its compatibility with the ECHR in a concrete case. The same procedures would apply if the EU became a member, and therefore, the interpretive autonomy of the ECJ should not be threatened.

Notwithstanding, a major concern throughout the negotiating of the Draft Accession Agreement was whether, by the time a challenge was brought to an EU action in the ECtHR, the ECJ would have had a chance to rule on all issues of validity of EU law which might give rise to a violation of the ECHR. If not, the ECJ's interpretive monopoly under *Foto-Frost* and Article 19(1) TEU[78] would be at risk. The problem stems from the fact that most EU litigation is brought in the national courts rather than by way of a direct action in the EU courts (partly because of the rather restrictive standing rules under Article 263 TFEU) giving rise to a danger that such an action might be determined and finalised in the national courts without the ECJ having had a chance to pronounce on the issue. The decision whether or not to make a preliminary reference to the ECJ lies in the hands of the national courts under Article 267 TFEU, and they may decide not to do so, or find the

---

[77] This also means that, while non-EU COE Member States of the ECHR may bring an action against the EU post accession, EU states will not be able to bring an inter party case against the EU in the ECtHR, since Article 344 TFEU bars them from using such other international means of dispute.

[78] Case 314/85 *Foto-Frost v Hauptzollamt Lübeck-Ost* [1987] ECR 1129. Article 19(1) TEU states as follows: 'The Court of Justice of the European Union shall include the Court of Justice, the General Court and specialised courts. It shall ensure that in the interpretation and application of the Treaties the law is observed'.

matter to be *acte clair*; or refer only on some aspects of a particular case.[79] Therefore there exists a danger that accession to ECHR could undermine the autonomy of EU law. Several possible solutions were suggested to this problem. In their *Joint communication*, judges Costa and Skouris suggested that a specific procedure should be put in place, to ensure that the ECJ could carry out internal review before the ECtHR carried out its external review.[80] Timmermans discusses the possibility of the Commission having a power to request the ECJ to rule on the compatibility of an EU act with fundamental rights once a claim is lodged by an individual before the ECtHR. A further suggestion was that a separate action might be brought against a Member State for failing to make a preliminary reference.[81] In such a case, the ECtHR would rule only on this violation, not on alleged violation of ECHR by the EU. Others suggested a soft law solution, based on urging national courts to make more preliminary references to Luxembourg.

The procedure adopted by the Draft Final Agreement is as follows:

> Article 3(6): In proceedings to which the European Union is co-respondent, if the Court of Justice of the European Union has not yet assessed the compatibility with the Convention rights at issue of the provision of European Union law as under paragraph 2 of this Article, then sufficient time shall be afforded for the Court of Justice of the European Union to make such an assessment and thereafter for the parties to make observations to the Court. The European Union shall ensure that such assessment is made quickly so that the proceedings before the Court are not unduly delayed. The provisions of this paragraph shall not affect the powers of the Court.

Notably, however, the Draft Final Agreement does not specify how this 'opportunity' is to be afforded, nor who should bring the issue before the ECJ. The matter seems to be left to the EU itself to be worked out. But should this procedure take the form of a preliminary ruling, and what would the effect of such a ruling be? Would

---

[79] Indeed, as the ECJ itself ruled in the *IATA* case, the very fact that the validity of an EU measure was challenged in a national court was not sufficient to require a preliminary reference. Case C-344/04 *International Air Transport Association and European Low Fares Airline Association* [2006] ECR I-403, para 28. Notably, in *Ullens de Schooten and Rezabek v Belgium* Application nos 3989/07 and 38353/07 (ECtHR, 20 September 2011) the ECtHR held that the ECHR does not guarantee the right to have a case referred to the ECJ for a preliminary ruling. This was the first case in which the ECtHR ruled on the commensurability with Article 6 ECHR of a refusal by a national court to make a preliminary reference to the ECJ, and is therefore highly relevant, given the future accession of the EU to the ECHR. The ECtHR did not, however, exclude that the refusal to refer a question might, under certain circumstances, affect the fairness of the proceedings – if, for example, national courts refused to give reasons for the refusal, particularly where the applicable law permitted such a refusal only in exceptional circumstances, or if the *CILFIT* guidelines were not correctly applied by a court of last instance (namely, those of Case C-283/81 *Srl CILFIT and Lanificio di Gavardo SpA v Ministry of Health* [1982] ECR 3415 in which the ECJ held that in order for a court of last instance to reject a request for a reference, the issue must be 'irrelevant', or the EU provision in question must already have been interpreted by the ECJ, or the correct application of EU law must be 'so obvious as to leave no scope for any reasonable doubt').

[80] Joint communication, above n 41.

[81] See Draft Council Decision authorising the Commission to negotiate the Accession Agreement of the EU to the ECHR: 'Involvement of ECJ regarding the compatibility of legal acts of the Union with fundamental rights' (para 11 of the Negotiating directives) Presidency Delegations, Brussels, 2 June 2010, 10568/10, which discusses these proposals.

it require amendment of the treaty provisions on the Court's jurisdiction? This is presently unclear. The explanations to the Draft Final Agreement note that an accelerated procedure before the ECJ already exists and that the ECJ has been able to give rulings under that procedure within six to eight months, but do not make any further specification as to the form of the ruling. However, Article 3(6) does make it clear that this procedure may only be used for those cases where the EU itself is a party, or joined as a co-respondent.[82]

(ii) The Introduction of a New Co-respondent Mechanism

A further complication is that of *who* should be held responsible in Strasbourg for human rights violations in the context of EU law, and whether there is a need to introduce a 'co-respondent' mechanism, which would allow the joint participation of the EU and of the EU Member States concerned.

A large part of EU law is implemented by its Member States, and, therefore, it will seem logical for the applicant to proceed against the sate. Yet, cases such as *Bosphorus* reveal that the Member States will sometimes have no choice or discretion as to whether, or how, an action emanating from the EU is implemented. In such cases, the root of the problem lies with the EU measure, rather than the Member State. A further and distinct challenge is that of primary EU law, normally the Treaties, which it is not possible for EU institutions themselves to amend. If primary law itself is found to breach human rights, then the Member States would have to be joined as parties, as they would ultimately have to amend the Treaties to remedy the situation. Therefore, EU accession prompts tricky questions as to how the responsibility between the Member States and the EU should be split.

This issue was raised in Article 1(b) of Protocol No 8 to the Lisbon Treaty which requires the Accession Agreement to make provision: 'in particular with regard to: . . . the mechanisms necessary to ensure that proceedings by non-Member States and individual applications are correctly addressed to Member States and/or the Union as appropriate'.

Therefore a key question is *who* will be the '*appropriate*' addressee. In the negotiation of the Draft Accession Agreement, this issue proved controversial, especially with NGOs such as Amnesty International,[83] who feared that the adoption of a co-respondent mechanism could work against individual applicants, by being overly complex in terms of law, or prejudicing their chances of success if they failed to proceed against the correct party. In particular, they expressed concern at an earlier version of the Draft Agreement, which required only a 'substantial link' with EU law in order for both Member States and the EU to be joined. The fear was that in cases where EU law requires the mutual recognition by states of each

---

[82] See below for discussion of the co-respondent mechanism.
[83] See eg Informal Working Group on the Accession of the European Union to the European Convention on Human Rights (CDDH-UE) Submission by the AIRE Centre and Amnesty International, AI Index: IOR 61/003/2011.

other's laws (as in the case of the execution of European Arrest Warrants) it could be difficult to assess whether fault lay with the EU or a state, and that executing states would in any case have no discretion not to comply with EU law in order to observe human rights.[84] Such difficulties have already been illustrated by cases in which asylum seekers have been transferred, under the requirements of EU law, from one state to another in which it was claimed that detention conditions did not satisfy minimum standards under the ECHR.[85] It had appeared that, under EU law, the principle of mutual trust would rule out any assessment by surrendering courts of the requesting Member State's compliance with fundamental rights.[86] However, in 2011, in *NS v Home Secretary* and *ME and Others v Refugee Applications Commissioner*, following the Opinion of AG Trstenjak, the ECJ held that the obligation to interpret the Asylum Regulation 343/2003 in a manner consistent with fundamental rights precluded the operation of a conclusive presumption of fundamental rights compliance by the Member State primarily responsible for examining an asylum application.[87] This leads to a very complex interplay of EU law, national law and fundamental rights law of the CFR and ECHR. Therefore, the danger is that an overbroad application of the co-respondent mechanism would place an unnecessary burden on applicants, given that there exist many cases in which a 'substantial link' might be said to exist with EU law.

Article 3 of the Draft Accession Agreement deals with this matter. It requires the insertion of a new paragraph at the end of Article 36 ECHR, stating that:

> 4. The European Union or a Member State of the European Union may become a co-respondent to proceedings by decision of the Court in the circumstances set out in the

---

[84] For example, the lack of a proportionality test in the EAW Framework Decision raises complex legal issues and has been criticised because of the large number of requests for extradition for minor offences. Poland, for example, on account of the strict adherence of its prosecutors to the doctrine of legality, has issued a large amount of EAWs for minor offences. However, it might prove hard to devise a proportionality test in keeping with the spirit of judicial co-operation and mutual trust which underpins the Framework Decision on the EAW, and the time-limits which are central to its operation.

[85] For this see eg *MSS v Belgium and Greece* (ECtHR (Grand Chamber), 21 January 2011.

[86] For example, in Case C-491/10 PPU *Aguirre Zarraga v Pelz* (ECJ, 22 December 2010), nyr, the German court asked the ECJ to clarify whether a receiving judge might exceptionally refuse to recognise a judgment certified under Article 42 of Regulation 2201/2003. However, the ECJ held that the principle of mutual trust requires courts of the Member State of origin to have the exclusive authority to ensure that their judgments comply with Articles 24 of the Charter, and, consequently, Article 42 of the Regulation, based on the assumption that Member States' respective national systems are '*capable of providing an equivalent and effective protection of fundamental rights*'. This judgment appears to posit a non-rebuttable presumption of equivalent and effective human rights protection. Yet *MSS v Belgium* (and now recent ECJ Opinion of the Advocate General in *NS* – see below) might be seen as challenging this.

[87] '[T]he Member States, including the national courts, may not transfer an asylum seeker to the "Member State responsible" within the meaning of Regulation No 343/2003 where they cannot be unaware that systemic deficiencies in the asylum procedure and in the reception conditions of asylum seekers in that Member State amount to substantial grounds for believing that the asylum seeker would face a real risk of being subjected to inhuman or degrading treatment within the meaning of Article 4 of the Charter', Joined Cases C-411/10 *NS v Secretary of State for the Home Department* and C-493/10 *ME and others v Refugee Applications Commissioner and Minister for Justice, Equality and Law Reform* (ECJ, 21 December 2011), nyr.

Agreement on the Accession of the European Union to the Convention for the Protection of Human Rights and Fundamental Freedoms. A co-respondent is a party to the case. The admissibility of an application shall be assessed without regard to the participation of a co-respondent in the proceedings.

Article 3(5) of the Draft Accession Agreement also states that 'A High Contracting Party shall become a co-respondent only at its own request and by decision of the Court'. Article 3 also appears to take into account some of the objections voiced by NGOs. It no longer refers to a 'substantial link' with EU law, but now – the new – Article 3(2) rather states that:

> Where an application is directed against one or more Member States of the European Union, the European Union may become a co-respondent to the proceedings in respect of an alleged violation notified by the Court if it appears that such allegation calls into question the compatibility with the Convention rights at issue of a provision of European Union law, notably where that violation could have been avoided only by disregarding an obligation under European Union law.

This appears to cover a *Bosphorus*-type situation, in which a state could only avoid a breach of the ECHR by violating EU law itself. However, the problem with this wording is that it would require the ECtHR to determine what in fact were the obligations of the state under EU law, and such a determination could violate the autonomy of EU law. A provision, such as that of Article 3(6) enabling the ECJ itself to first to determine this matter, is therefore crucial.

Article 3(3) Draft Agreement appears to concern EU primary law and provides that:

> Where an application is directed against the European Union, the European Union Member States may become co-respondents to the proceedings in respect of an alleged violation notified by the Court if it appears that such allegation calls into question the compatibility with the Convention rights at issue of a provision of the Treaty on European Union, the Treaty on the Functioning of the European Union or any other provision having the same legal value pursuant to those instruments, notably where that violation could have been avoided only by disregarding an obligation under those instruments.

This would involve cases where an applicant raises the issue of compatibility of EU primary law with the ECHR. Primary EU law may only be altered through a Treaty amendment following the procedure set out in Article 48 TEU, which usually requires the consent of, and ratification by, all EU Member States, so it cannot be remedied by EU institutions acting alone, so it would be necessary to join the Member States as co-respondents.[88] Once again, however, if the ECtHR were itself to determine whether a claim involved an issue of primary or secondary law this might violate the autonomy of EU law. Indeed, certain Member States had earlier

---

[88] Nor can issues of primary law be solved by a Member State acting alone – see also *Matthews v United Kingdom* (1999) 28 EHRR 361, in which the UK experienced great difficulties in remedying a violation ultimately attributable to EU primary law.

argued that primary law should be excluded from the scope of ECtHR review.[89] Therefore, once again, the provision of a mechanism whereby the ECJ can first make a ruling is critical. Further, the Draft Accession Agreement does not state how liability of co-respondents is to be apportioned, but the Explanations attached state that in case of a violation, co-respondents would normally be jointly liable.

(iii) Other Issues of Accession

There exist other challenges of accession, which will be briefly mentioned, as space prevents more than a short treatment.

(a) *Bosphorus* presumption

One such problem will be the *Bosphorus* 'presumption of equivalence', discussed earlier in this chapter. This presumption has been keenly criticised and there is speculation as to whether the presumption should survive the EU's accession to the ECHR. Why should the ECHR privilege the EU in this way, raising a prospect of one set of standards for states and another for the EU, especially given that (notwithstanding the now binding nature of the CFR) there are still dimensions of the EU's protection of fundamental rights which remain less effective than those of its Member States – for example, access to the ECJ is still limited, even under the amended Article 263 TFEU. Given that the accession of the EU to the ECHR would alter the relationship between the two Courts, reserving the last word for the ECtHR, rather than maintaining the present situation of co-operation and comity, it is arguable that, post accession, Strasbourg should apply a more rigorous, concrete review to EU acts, rather than the abstract test of equivalence of *Bosphorus*. Yet, on the other hand, it could also be argued that the presumption of equivalence reflects the specific, *sui generis*, situation of the EU legal order, as maintained and acknowledged in Protocol No 8 of the Lisbon Treaty, and that accession should not change this, nor the *Bosphorus* presumption. So it is difficult to predict with any certainty what will become of *Bosphorus* post accession.

(b) Scope of EU accession

Article 6(2) posits a duty for the EU to accede to the ECHR, but what of the ECHR's protocols? Should these also be included in the accession? Given that not all protocols have been ratified by all EU Member States, the prospect of EU accession to all of them would appear unlikely. Yet, in the course of negotiations, the European Parliament and EU Commissioner Reding[90] had expressed a preference for the ratification at the very least of all protocols dealing with rights in

---

[89] Notably the French government, see eg French Senate, 'Communication de M Robert Badinter sur le mandate de négociation' (E5248) 25 May 2010, at: www.senat.fr/europe/r25052010.html#.

[90] See speech by Commissioner Reding, 'The EU's accession to the European Convention on Human Rights: Towards a stronger and more coherent protection of human rights in Europe' (Brussels, 18 March 2010).

CFR. However, Article 1 of the Draft Accession Agreement provides only for the EU to accede to the First Protocol (which includes, inter alia, the right to property, the right to vote and the right to education) and Protocol 6 (abolition of the death penalty in time of peace), but, interestingly, not Protocol 13, which abolishes the death penalty in all circumstances.

(c) The EU judge and voting in the Committee of Ministers

From the terms of the Draft Agreement, it appears that the role and workload of the EU judge should not be restricted to cases related to the EU. The judge appointed in respect of the European Union is to have equal status to the other judges. The European Parliament is to participate in the procedure for election, sending a delegation to participate in the Parliamentary Assembly of the COE, whose size will be equal to the highest number of representatives to which a state is entitled under the statute of the Council of Europe.[91] According to Article 7 Draft Accession Agreement, the EU 'shall be entitled to participate in the Committee of Ministers', and has the right to vote, in certain circumstances. Some rather convoluted paragraphs set out these procedures, which are designed to deal, in particular, with the problem of bloc voting by EU Member States (who are required by EU law to act in a co-ordinated manner) at the expense of non-EU ECHR contracting parties.[92]

It is also established, under Article 8, Draft Accession Agreement, that the EU will contribute toward the COE expenditure related to the functioning of the ECHR.

IV. Conclusions

Accession by the EU to the ECHR, rendering EU law subject to review in Strasbourg, will have a more direct impact on EU law, and, by extension, EU Member State law, than under the pre-accession position, whereby rulings of the ECtHR apply in principle only at state or governmental level. Further, the binding nature of the Charter, and its injunction to have regard to ECtHR case law, will mean that decisions of the Strasbourg Court, which do not have direct or *erga omnes* effect in EU Member States, will in fact attain such effect when followed by the Court of Justice in its judgments.

On the one hand, this situation is likely to provoke a closer scrutiny of Strasbourg judgments, and of the interpretive practices used by the Strasbourg

---

[91] For this, see Article 6 'Election of Judges', Draft Accession agreement.
[92] See Article 7(1) and (2) Draft Accession Agreement. EU law sometimes requires the EU and its Member States to co-ordinate their actions and votes similarly in international organisations, so the Accession Agreement sets out special voting procedures in order to avoid the 27 EU Member States automatically outvoting other COE members in the execution of judgments and friendly settlements in cases involving the EU.

Court. There has been concern expressed at both the Court's 'margin of appreciation' doctrine and of its assertion of a Member State 'consensus' in high-profile cases. The consensus doctrine derives from the Court's perception that the ECHR is a 'living instrument',[93] which requires an evolutive interpretation. Such a dynamic interpretation allows the Court to depart from previous decisions 'in order to ensure that the interpretation of the Convention reflects societal changes and remains in line with present-day conditions',[94] which should be determined by an enquiry as to whether a European 'consensus' exists on the matter at issue. As the finding of a European consensus is often crucial to the determination of whether, or to what extent, a right is protected by the ECHR, and will also determine whether a margin of appreciation should be accorded to a state, the consensus doctrine is extremely important.

Yet there has been much criticism of the application of a 'European' standard in recent years, and of the way in which it seems to have been applied to reduce Member State autonomy. A case which has come under particular fire is that of *Hirst v United Kingdom (No 2)*,[95] in which the ECtHR held that the UK's total denial of voting rights to prisoners violated the right to vote in the First Protocol to the ECHR,[96] in spite of the absence of any European consensus on the issue.[97] In particular, the legitimacy of a uniform 'European' standard has been questioned in cases which involve the balancing of rights, rather than a straightforward violation of one right: for example, in a conflict between the right to privacy and freedom of expression as in the *von Hannover* case,[98] which provoked much criticism in Germany, which the ECtHR had found to be in breach of the applicant, Princess Caroline's, privacy rights, by insufficiently protecting them against press intrusions.

In January, 2010, at a seminar to mark the official opening of the judicial year of the ECHR, a UK judge, Lady Justice Arden, delivered a paper entitled: 'Is the Convention Ours?' about the respect shown by Strasbourg for the role of national institutions, which she explained as being, 'really a call for judicial restraint by the Strasbourg Court, and a sharing by it of its responsibilities for judging whether a breach of human rights has occurred', and continuing that 'subsidiarity, includ-

---

[93] *Tyrer v United Kingdom* (1978) 2 EHRR 1, para 31.
[94] See *Inze v Austria*, Series A no 126 (ECtHR, 28 October 1987).
[95] *Hirst v United Kingdom (No 2)* [2005] ECHR 681; see also *Greens and MT v United Kingdom* [2010] ECHR 1826. However, in January 2012, in a paper published in *The Independent*, the President of the ECtHR, Nicholas Bratza, expressed his disquiet at the attacks on *Hirst* in the following terms: 'It is particularly unfortunate that a single judgment of the court on a case relating to UK prisoners' voting rights, which was delivered in 2005 and has still not been implemented, has been used as the springboard for a sustained attack on the court and has led to repeated calls for the granting of powers of Parliament to override judgments of the court against the UK, and even for the withdrawal of the UK from the convention'. (Nicolas Bratza: 'Britain should be defending European justice, not attacking it', www.independent.co.uk/opinion/commentators/nicolas-bratza-britain-should-be-defending-european-justice-not-attacking-it-6293689.html).
[96] Article 3 of Protocol 1 to the European Convention on Human Rights.
[97] Five of the dissenting judges in *Hirst* criticised the Court for its extensive reference to the Canadian Supreme Court and the South African Constitutional Court, in contrast to 'only summary information concerning the legislation on prisoners' right to vote in the Contracting States'.
[98] *von Hannover v Germany* [2004] ECHR 294, (2005) 40 EHRR 1.

ing the margin of appreciation, is a concept the Strasbourg Court should strengthen in its jurisprudence'.[99] Lady Justice Arden's comments reveal a more general dissatisfaction with some Strasbourg rulings. The Interlaken Declaration of 19 February 2010 by the High Level Conference on the Future of the European Court of Human Rights reflects this disquiet by inviting the ECHR to 'avoid reconsidering questions of fact or national law that have been considered and decided by national authorities, in line with the ECHR's case-law'.[100]

These problems will be exacerbated if the loosely-applied doctrines of consensus and margin of appreciation of the Strasbourg case law are applied through and in the very different context of EU law. If there is to be parity of membership, it would seem that the EU, too, should be able to benefit from a margin of appreciation in certain circumstances, but just what should those circumstances be? Also, how to place the EU in the context of a European consensus when the EU is, by its very nature, singular, *sui generis*, and different? EU law provokes fundamental rights issues in a different way from the national context and the way in which they are pleaded in the ECtHR. Even within EU law, fundamental rights issues arise in a differentiated way. For example, much of the litigation involving fundamental rights in the General Court concerns competition law, and requires societal and economic interests enforced through competition law to be balanced with the fundamental rights of companies. However, when undertakings claim the right against self-incrimination, or the presumption of innocence, then the specific context of EU competition law might require a different approach to these protections than when they are claimed by individuals in the ECtHR.[101] On the other hand, fundamental rights litigation in the ECJ often raises issues of a different and complex nature, in which the claim is that the Member States have not complied with EU fundamental rights standards, or even, on the contrary, where a Member State claims a reliance on a fundamental right as a defence to an alleged violation of an EU fundamental freedom. How the ECHR margin of appreciation might accommodate these complexities of EU law remains to be resolved. One such way might be through the maintenance of the *Bosphorus* presumption, which acknowledges the specificity of the EU. However, this approach would bring other problems and the criticism already discussed earlier in this chapter.

It is undoubtedly the case that an increase of fundamental rights monitoring and activities through EU law would be seen as highly undesirable by some, as

---

[99] The Rt Hon Lady Justice Arden DBE, *Is The Convention Ours?* (January 2010): www.judiciary.gov.uk/Resources/JCO/Documents/lj-arden-european-court-human-rights-29012010.pdf; also in the context of a reassessment of Strasbourg jurisprudence in the UK, see the Coalition Government's Commission on a UK Bill of Rights (Hansard HC vol 523 Pt 120, 959 16 Feb 2011).

[100] High Level Conference on the Future of the European Court of Human Rights, *Interlaken Declaration*, 19 February 2010; also *Izmir Declaration* on the Future of the European Court of Human Rights, 7 June 2011.

[101] So, for example, in the 2006 case of *SGL Carbon* (C-308/04 P *SGL Carbon v European Commission* [2006] ECR I-5977) Advocate General Geelhoed suggested that, 'It is not possible simply to transpose the findings of the European Court of Human Rights without more to undertakings', also noting that case law from other jurisdictions, such as that under the US 5th Amendment right against self-incrimination, could not be invoked by companies.

limiting state autonomy, as well as lacking in democratic legitimacy. The adoption and coming into force of the EU Act in the UK in 2011, which makes ratification of future amendments to the TEU and TFEU subject to approval by referendum, reveal a suspicion of any potential transfers of power from states to the EU – as do the legal challenges and ensuing careful scrutiny by, eg, the German Constitutional Court, of each EU rehaul and transfer of sovereignty brought about by treaty change. Existing critiques of the ECtHR and a demonstration of the desire to 'bring rights home' in the context of Strasbourg also reveal a reluctance to allow European regional authorities any greater competence in the human rights field. The UK has expressed strong reservations about the draft Final Accession Agreement due to its fear of further erosion of Member State competences by the EU.[102] In January 2012, the UK Prime Minister, David Cameron, gave a speech[103] in Strasbourg to the Parliamentary Assembly of the Council of Europe, urging the European Court of Human Rights to concentrate on serious abuses of human rights. He also maintained that the Court had, in some cases, been too ready to substitute its judgment for that of 'reasonable national processes'. This speech was part of Britain's attempt, during its six month presidency of the Council of Europe, to outline a series of reforms to streamline the work of the ECtHR.

Notably, however, on the same day (25th January 2012) representatives of the Parliamentary Assembly of the Council of Europe and the European Parliament urged national governments – namely the UK and France – not to stand in the way of the EU signing up to the ECHR, and issued a joint statement, maintaining, inter alia, that:

> EU accession to the convention is also needed to fully ensure consistency in the work of the Strasbourg and Luxembourg courts. This is a vital first step towards creating a 'common European space' for human rights, and has the full backing of both the European Parliament and the Parliamentary Assembly of the Council of Europe.
>
> We are therefore deeply concerned that the accession process – which is a legal obligation for the EU under the Lisbon Treaty – is currently being sidetracked by political objections from the UK, and to a lesser extent France.
>
> We cannot risk this process being derailed, as failure to fully incorporate the EU could serve to weaken the existing European system for human rights protection which has been put in place by the Council of Europe over the last 60 years and is envied worldwide.
>
> Intense negotiations since June 2010 show that the complex technical and legal issues involved in this process can be resolved. What is needed now is clear and unequivocal political commitment on the part of all 27 EU Member States.[104]

Such an unequivocal commitment may be some time in coming. The potential increase in EU human rights litigation following on from the binding nature of

---

[102] See above n 70.

[103] A full text of the speech is available here: www.number10.gov.uk/news/european-court-of-human-rights/ .

[104] assembly.coe.int/ASP/NewsManager/EMB_NewsManagerView.asp?ID=7351.

the Charter has already been noted, as well as the advantages that EU litigation may appear to present over Strasbourg, and concomitant danger of marginalisation of Strasbourg. Yet if the ECJ is seised of a greater number of human rights cases, this prompts a stricter scrutiny of its own capacity to become a human rights court. However, the transformation of the EU from Internal Market to human rights organisation cannot be achieved merely by the assertion of some new, majestic-sounding Treaty provisions declaring the EU's values,[105] the amendment of Article 6 TEU by the Lisbon Treaty, or by the ordering of human rights at the pinnacle of EU law in just one case, *Kadi*, and the speculations of some Advocates General.[106] Nor can human rights be developed in the most substantive, comprehensive and aspirational of ways through a court-led, instrumental means, in which human rights are pursued by those most able to afford to litigate them – which, in the case of the EU, are usually corporate concerns (thus justifying the transformation of 'human' into 'fundamental' rights).[107] And to date, it has been the ECJ which has played the leading role in developing fundamental rights law within the EU. Much more work has to be done, and, in any case, the question must be asked – to what extent *should* we look to the EU as a human rights organisation?

There is much, then, to be resolved, and EU accession to the ECHR is by no means straightforward. We may expect these issues to occupy the field of European human rights law for some time to come. For the time being, complexity appears to be the most notable feature of European human rights law.

---

[105] Article 2 TEU, in its post-Lisbon version, makes reference to the values of the EU.

[106] See Joined Cases C-402 and 415/05 P, *Yassin Abdullah Kadi and Al Barakaat International Foundation v European Council and European Commission* [2008] ECR I-6351; AG Maduro in *Centro Europa 7*, interpreted the provisions for fundamental rights in Article 6 TEU as ensuring that 'the very existence of the European Union is predicated on respect for fundamental rights' (a statement which was notably not adopted by the ECJ) and an 'existential requirement' which aimed to situate the EU beyond market constitutionalism (Case C-380/05 *Centro Europa 7 Srl v Ministerio delle Comunicazioni* [2008] ECR I-349, para 19).

[107] For further reflections of this nature see S Douglas-Scott, 'The EU and Human Rights after the Treaty of Lisbon' (2011) 11 *Human Rights Law Review* 645.

8

Competing Rights?

IAIN CAMERON*

I. Introduction

In this chapter, I examine the issue of rights competition between the EU Charter on Fundamental Rights and Freedoms (the Charter), the European Convention on Human Rights (ECHR) and national rights catalogues. To begin with, some caveats are in order. This issue involves three different legal disciplines: EU law, European human rights law and domestic constitutional law. It is obviously helpful if one is an expert in all of these. I am less of an expert in EU law compared to the other two disciplines, and this is reflected in the relative space I devote to the different aspects of rights competition. Constitutional lawyers naturally tend to have a national perspective.[1] The examples I choose to illustrate constitutional issues, and the rights interaction between EU law, the ECHR and a national constitution, are mainly taken from the Swedish system. Finally, the complex tripartite relationship between national systems for the protection of human rights, and the two semi-autonomous and complementary European systems is continually developing. The Court of Justice of the European Union (CJEU) has only recently begun to apply the Charter as a legally-binding document. The terms of accession of the EU to the ECHR are still being discussed.[2] The present chapter does not and cannot hope to deal with all aspects of this tripartite relationship, but seeks only to raise a number of interesting issues relating to it.

Treatment of the issue of rights competition involves saying something first, very briefly, about how rights can compete. I then examine, again very briefly, the way in which rights protection is constructed in the three systems and how each deals with 'intra-system' rights competition. I proceed to look at how each system

---

* Professor, Faculty of Law, University of Uppsala. This written version of my paper builds upon the oral version, delivered at the conference organised at the University of Oxford on 11 March 2011. I have, however, taken the liberty of developing several points on the basis of the subsequent discussions at the conference. The law is generally stated as it was at the time of the lecture. However, in some particularly pertinent matters I have included references to subsequent legal developments.

[1] In my case, I have a double perspective: both British and Swedish constitutional law. But neither system (nor any other EU Member State's system) can be called 'typical' for the EU.

[2] A draft agreement on accession was published in July 2011, but certain Member States later raised objections to it.

has dealt with interaction with the other systems and the issue of 'extra-system' rights competition before turning to the subject of how the systems may interact in the future. I close with a number of concluding remarks.

II. How Can Rights Compete?

What do I mean by 'competing rights'? Robert Alexy argues that rights are of a 'principle' character, and that one has a competition between them when a situation arises where both are applicable, but one cannot advance both rights simultaneously.[3] A precondition of a competition is that the rights in question are at the same hierarchical level. This is a formal criterion: it is not the same thing as the way that a right is formulated. Some rights competitions might seem easier to solve because one of the rights is formulated in absolute terms. For example, a few ECHR rights – notably Article 3 prohibiting torture, or inhuman and degrading treatment and Protocols 5 and 13, prohibiting the death penalty – are expressed in absolute terms. It is not permissible for example to balance the interest in obtaining important national security information against the right not to be tortured. But even with absolute rights, balancing comes into play, namely at the initial determination whether the absolute right is applicable at all.

When competition between rights on the same hierarchical level arises it is solved in three different ways: subordination of right A to right B; subordination of right B to right A; or balancing of rights A and B.

A distinction can be made between the situation when a right is subject to limits (such as national security or the prevention of crime), and the situation in which two rights compete. In the former situation, one begins with the right and then subjects it to limits. However, in both cases, there are competing social values (or public goods) to be balanced, eg integrity and the fight against crime, or freedom of assembly and maintenance of public order. For Alexy, the 'right' is the *result* of the balancing exercise between these social values. Thus, states A and B may both protect 'freedom of expression' under constitutional law, but the content of these rights may be very different – even if both A and B are democratic 'rights respecting' states.[4]

The fact that states A and B give different contents to the social values of freedom of expression and integrity, and approach the task of reconciling these social values, if they come into competition with one another, is not a problem per se (although it can mean that comparisons between these two states risk being superficial). What is a problem, however, is when the *same* state is subject to *different* rights catalogues which each can give a different content to a right, and the

---

[3] R Alexy, *A Theory of Constitutional Rights* (trans J Rivers) (Oxford, Oxford University Press, 2002).
[4] This distinction is more difficult to make when a right is formulated in such a way that a limit can be made on it 'for the protection of [unspecified] rights and freedoms of others'. See further below, text at n 16.

final word on the content of one or more of these catalogues is not under its control. One can call this situation one of competing *interpretations* of rights, but for reasons which will become apparent, this way of putting it underplays the conflict involved.

Alexy's theory on balancing is not uncontroversial.[5] But he does not contend that his theory describes (or prescribes) how courts other than the German constitutional court (Bundesverfassungsgericht, BVerfG) should approach the task. I mention it now only because it puts balancing values at the centre of human rights protection,[6] and as such is a useful introduction to the discussion in the present chapter.

III. The Swedish Approach to Dealing with Rights

In Sweden, the courts have historically had a relatively limited role to play in protecting constitutional rights. The Swedish chapter on constitutional rights was added more or less as an afterthought in 1976. There is thus no strong judicial tradition of protection of constitutional rights to which the ECHR (incorporated in 1995) and the Charter can easily be 'fitted in'. There is no constitutional court in Sweden (or in any of the Nordic states). Instead, all courts and (something which is exceptional in international comparison) all administrative authorities, may engage in constitutional review. Until 1 January 2011 this was subject to a requirement that the conflict between a statute, or an ordinance, and the Constitution be 'manifest' before the courts could refuse to apply the statute or ordinance. This 'manifest' requirement has now been removed.

The legislative process is a crucial part of the system of rights protection.[7] It is usually open and relatively long, and expert opinions are usually taken properly into account. The travaux préparatoires to legislation are usually extensive and provide detailed guidance for the courts. The judges are also involved in the legislative process in that Bills are usually sent to an expert body, the Council of Legislation, consisting of a group of senior judges, who examine both the technical drafting aspects, their coherence with other relevant legislation and their constitutionality. In the circumstances, Swedish judges are usually able to trust the

---

[5] Habermas, in particular, has criticised it in J Habermas, *Between Facts and Norms* (Cambridge, Cambridge University Press, 1996).
[6] See also M Kumm, 'Constitutional Rights as Principles: on the structure and domain of constitutional justice' (2004) 2 *International Journal of Constitutional Law* 574 and T Scanlon, 'Adjusting Rights and Balancing Values' (2002) 74 *Fordham Law Review* 1477. One can also argue that what we call human rights are really a conglomerate of different rights, and are more properly seen as 'rights to a state of being', N MacCormick, *Institutions of Law: An Essay in Legal Theory* (Oxford, Oxford University Press, 2007).
[7] See generally I Cameron, 'Protection of Constitutional Rights in Sweden' [1997] *Public Law* 488–512 and T Bull, 'Judges without a Court – Judicial preview in Sweden' in T Campbell (ed), *Sceptical Essays on Human Rights* (Oxford, Oxford University Press, 2010).

'institutional competence'[8] of the legislator, which is almost always in a better position to design systems of legal regulation compared to the type of ad hoc examinations a court is capable of doing.[9] What the judges have to do is fine-tune the systems.

At the risk of over-simplification, constitutional interpretation has been a 'bottom-up' interpretation in Sweden: an administrative authority's regulations are usually deemed to be in accordance with the government ordinance, which is almost invariably deemed to be authorised by the statute providing for the delegation of authority. The statute, in turn is hardly ever not deemed to be in accordance with the Constitution. This pragmatic method of judicial interpretation (which means concrete specific norms being preferred whenever possible over abstract general norms) is certainly convenient when a court has to deal with many cases, as the lower courts have to do. However, respect for the democratic principle, and institutional competence, certainly buttresses it.

Most Swedish writers consider that the courts are correct to take a limited view of their norm-creative role. The lack of constitutional review is seen as evidence of the healthy functioning of the democratic system. Certainly, at the end of the day, if the political process cannot ensure compliance with the Constitution, then no court mechanisms will be able to stand long against pressures to limit constitutional rights.

So far, there has been very little tension between the legislature and the government on the one hand, and the courts on the other, as to which should have the 'last word' on the legitimacy of a particular policy. Thus, it is unlikely that the constitutional change mentioned above will significantly increase the amount of constitutional review in Sweden. As explained further below, however, the ECHR and now the Charter, mean that the courts are slightly more often going to be called upon to engage in constitutional review.

The rights in the Instrument of Government (IG) Chapter 2 can be divided into 'absolute', 'strong relative' and 'weak relative' rights. Modification of 'absolute' rights requires constitutional amendment. This category consists of rights under the Freedom of the Press and Freedom of Expression Acts (covering the print and broadcast media respectively) as well as a few other rights (freedom from torture, from the death penalty, etc). Having said this, constitutional amendment is relatively simple in Sweden, requiring only a simple majority, voting twice on a Bill in Parliament, with an intervening general election. The relative rights are 'strong' (those listed in IG 2:20) when they can be restricted by statute, only as long as certain material and procedural conditions are fulfilled (necessity in a democratic society, etc). They are 'weak' when they can be restricted simply by statute, or even by subordinate legislation. The content of most of these weak rights in Chapter 2, eg intellectual property rights or the right to collective strike

---

[8] *cf* CA Gearty, *Principles of Human Rights Adjudication* (Oxford, Oxford University Press, 2004).
[9] I would argue that even a court such as the CJEU which has extensive expertise to call upon is in a much worse position in this regard compared to a properly functioning legislature.

action, is usually defined by ordinary legislation and so are 'constitutional' only in the most formal sense.

Traditionally, the freedoms of expression and information have enjoyed strong protection in Sweden. Both of these rights are also mechanisms of political control, and constitutional protection of these rights predates the advent of parliamentary democracy (and therefore long before 1976, when the other rights were added).[10] Protection of personal integrity was only added to IG Chapter 2 in 2011.[11]

As regards the ECHR, it is incorporated at the level of statute. There is, however, a constitutional provision, IG 2:19, which provides that statutes or ordinances may not conflict with the ECHR. This gives the ECHR a status, in practice, between a statute and the Constitution.

The Charter has, by virtue of section 2 of the Act of Accession, the status it has under EU law, meaning supremacy over national law.[12]

An implicit condition for the courts to show deference to the legislature, when it decides both whether a restriction in a right is necessary, and how to draw balances between competing rights, is that there is a fairly high level of rationality in public and parliamentary debate. Sweden has not been totally free from media-fanned moral panics, irrational fears of terrorism, and other causes of repressive criminal and criminal procedure legislation. But, I think it is fair to say that – so far – the legislature has deserved the trust put in it: the actual enjoyment of human rights in Sweden is relatively high.

As the job of balancing competing interests is done by the legislature, there have been very few cases in which the courts have considered that intra-system rights competition exists. The paucity of cases can also be partly explained by the need for a concrete dispute to exist[13] before the courts can take up an issue, and the existence of non-judicial mechanisms of rights protection, in particular the Ombudsman. One relevant case is *NJA 2001 s 409*, although arguably even this is more a case of extra-system competition, as it concerned Swedish implementation of EU directives on protection of personal information. This concerned the prosecution of a person for naming and criticising a banker on a website devoted to criticism of banking foreclosures of businesses in the wake of the Swedish financial crisis in the early 1990s. The (clumsy) Swedish implementation of the relevant directives meant that any publication of such personal information without consent was prohibited. However, the Supreme Court reconciled this with

---

[10] A recent illustration of the preference of transparency over integrity is the fact that the Swedish government intervened in the *Volker* case, dealt with below, in an unsuccessful attempt to get the CJEU to rule that the disclosure requirements were valid.

[11] Particular aspects of this were already protected. IG 2:6 (proposition 2009/10:80) now provides that 'everyone is vis-à-vis the state protected against significant interferences with personal integrity, if this occurs in the absence of consent and involves surveillance or monitoring an individual's personal relations'.

[12] Law (1994:1500) on the Accession of Sweden to the European Union. Although Swedish acceptance of the supremacy of EU law is itself subject to a '*Solange*' reservation, expressed in the constitutional provision which authorises the Act of Accession, IG 10:6.

[13] Code of Judicial Procedure, Chapter 13, section 2.

freedom of expression on the internet by emphasising the exception provided for 'journalistic' purposes in the directive and by giving an extensive ECHR-conform interpretation to what is meant by 'journalism'.

IV. The Approach of the ECtHR to the Protection of Rights Under the ECHR

Like the Swedish courts, the European Court of Human Rights (ECtHR) only takes up concrete disputes, brought by an actual (or at least, potential) victim.[14] The ECtHR has – up until relatively recently – determined only the declaratory issue of whether or not the ECHR has been breached, and if it has, what, if any, compensation the victim should obtain. Otherwise, cases 'return' to the national legal order for implementation.

There is no formal rights hierarchy set out in the ECHR. Having said this, the ECtHR has repeatedly referred to certain articles – Articles 2, 3, 4 and 5(1) – as containing 'core rights'. Moreover, in practice, a hierarchy exists, in that the ECtHR's enormous backlog has forced it to adopt a priority policy as regards dealing with applications.[15]

Rights set out in the ECHR are formulated differently. A few are expressed in absolute terms, others in relative terms. Within the latter category, some, such as Articles 8–11, are subject to specific limitation clauses, similarly but not identically worded. Some rights have been found to be implicit, such as the right of access to court (implied in Article 6) and thus subject to implicit limits. Some rights are regarded as implicitly alienable (eg access to court) whereas some are explicitly non-derogable.

When the ECtHR has been faced with a situation in which two rights have been said to compete, it has sometimes employed the principle of *lex specialis* and the international law principle that a treaty must be interpreted as a whole. For example, it has stated that Article 11 is a *lex specialis* in relation to Article 10. Once the decision has been reached that the 'main' right has not been violated, discussion of the 'subsidiary' right is cut short.[16]

---

[14] There is the possibility of more abstract reviews in the context of inter-state complaints. One of the reform proposals which has been discussed for the ECtHR is the possibility of giving advisory opinions to national supreme and constitutional courts.

[15] www.echr.coe.int/NR/rdonlyres/DB6EDF5E-6661-4EF6-992E-F8C4ACC62F31/0/Priority_policyPublic_communication_EN.pdf. The first three categories, in order of significance are: urgent applications (in particular risk to life or health of the applicant, or other circumstances linked to the personal or family situation of the applicant); applications raising questions capable of having an impact on the effectiveness of the Convention system; and applications raising an important question of general interest and applications which on their face raise as main complaints issues under Arts 2, 3, 4 or 5(1) of the Convention.

[16] See, eg *Johnston and others v Ireland* (1986) Series A no 112, where the Court stated that the case was about Art 12, not Art 9.

The ECtHR has not been consistent, however. For example, it has also stated on occasion that overlapping rights should be interpreted together, eg that Article 11 cases concerning freedom of demonstration should be seen in the light of the overarching right set out in Article 10.[17]

The limitation clauses to the rights set out in Articles 8–11 include the 'protection of the rights and freedoms of others'. This enables the ECtHR to factor in the interest in, eg, protecting personal integrity when dealing with freedom of expression, or vice versa, without having to find an explicit competition between these two rights.

V. The Approach of the CJEU to the Charter

The Charter consists of four sections, and contains a large number of rights in 50 articles, civil, political, economic and social.[18] The Charter is an ambitious document compared to the ECHR, and many national rights catalogues. The method of drafting, a convent consisting of national delegations of parliamentarians, favoured 'rights inflation'. The Charter groups rights together under different abstract headings, but does not provide for a formal hierarchy between them. The Charter contains a general limitation clause (Article 52).[19]

The Charter applies to EU institutions, but, more controversially, also to the Member States when acting within the scope of EU law. The two primary examples of the latter situation are where a national body acts as the agent of the EU[20] and where a national body acts under national legislation which derogates from an EU norm.[21] As the boundaries of EU law are indeterminate, so too are the boundaries of the Charter.

Review by the CJEU with the possible result of annulling EU legislation for violation of the Charter is seen by some as less controversial compared to review which has the (indirect) effect of making Member States' legislation in violation of Charter rights inapplicable.[22]

---

[17] See eg *Young, James and Webster v United Kingdom* (1981) Series A no 44, para 57; *Ezelin v France* (1991) Series A no 202, para 37.

[18] Charter of Fundamental Rights of the European Union [2000] OJ C364/1.

[19] Article 52(1) provides: 'Any limitation on the exercise of the rights and freedoms recognised by this Charter must be provided for by law and respect the essence of those rights and freedoms. Subject to the principle of proportionality, limitations may be made only if they are necessary and genuinely meet objectives of general interest recognised by the Union or the need to protect the rights and freedoms of others'. For discussion, see S Peers, 'Taking Rights Away? Limitations and Derogations' in S Peers and A Ward (eds), *The European Union Charter of Fundamental Rights* (Oxford, Hart Publishing, 2004).

[20] Case 5/88 *Hubert Wachauf v Bundesamt für Ernährung und Forstwirtschaft* [1989] ECR 2609.

[21] Case C-260/89 *Ellinki Radiophonia Tileorassi AE (ERT) v Dimotiki Etairia Pliroforissis and Sotirios Kouvelas* [1991] ECR I-2925.

[22] See, eg JHH Weiler, 'Fundamental Rights and Fundamental Boundaries' in *The Constitution of Europe: 'Do the New Clothes Have an Emperor?' and Other Essays on European Integration* (Cambridge, Cambridge University Press, 1999).

Unlike the ECtHR, the CJEU has a legislative will to discern. However, the EU negotiating process means that the end result can be vague, deliberately or by default. As is well known, this can give the CJEU considerable influence over the content of secondary legislation when this comes to be interpreted and applied.

Unlike the Swedish courts and the ECtHR, most of the work of the CJEU when it comes to interpreting rights is done in the form of (abstract) preliminary rulings. However, the preliminary ruling does not determine the case, which returns to the national legal order for resolution.

At the time the Charter was made binding law, the Member States attempted to limit the potential for the Charter to expand EU competences,[23] as well as to limit the interpretative power of the CJEU concerning the vaguer rights set out in the Charter.[24]

The CJEU referred to the Charter occasionally before it became binding law. Since the entry into force of the Lisbon Treaty, the CJEU has employed the Charter both as primary law and as interpreting general principles of EU law. There can be different reasons for this, but one of these is the Polish opt-out of the Charter.

Specific EU legislation may have to satisfy other standards set out in the Treaties and the general principles of EU law developed by the CJEU. Thus, the CJEU's protection of important values is not limited to those set out in the Charter.

One of the occasions so far in which the CJEU has explicitly dealt with the issue of competing rights within the Charter is the *Volker* case.[25] It concerned an EU regulation requiring publication on the internet of the names of the recipients of EU common agricultural policy subsidies and the sums they received. The right under Article 42 of the Charter to access to documents (and Article 41, to good administration) was thus set against the right of personal integrity (Article 8). The CJEU found that the underlying reason for transparency was the minimisation of fraud, and this could be secured without identifying recipients. It thus annulled this part of the regulation.

---

[23] Art 6(1) of the TEU provides in a relevant part that 'The provisions of the Charter shall not extend in any way the competences of the Union as defined in the Treaties'.

[24] Art 52(5) provides that 'The provisions of this Charter which contain principles may be implemented by legislative and executive acts taken by institutions, bodies, offices and agencies of the Union, and by acts of Member States when they are implementing Union law, in the exercise of their respective powers. They shall be judicially cognisable only in the interpretation of such acts and in the ruling on their legality'.

[25] Joined Cases C-92/09 and C-93/09 *Volker und Markus Schecke GbR and Harmut Eifert v Land Hessen* [2010] ECR I-11063. See also Case C70/10, Scarlet Extended SA v Société belge des auteurs, compositeurs et éditeurs SCRL (SABAM), (CJEU) 24 November 2011 nyr.

VI. The Approach of the ECtHR to National Protection of Rights

How has the ECtHR handled the issue of reviewing *national* balancing of competing rights? The ECHR is a minimum standard of rights protection (Article 53). It is complementary to the national mechanisms. Procedurally this is reinforced by the requirement that national remedies be exhausted before recourse is allowed to the ECtHR. Although the ECtHR frequently emphasises the subsidiarity principle, the task of the ECtHR is to determine in a concrete case whether the respondent state fulfills the minimum standards of the Convention. It thus measures national law against an international law standard. In doing so, the ECtHR follows the traditional international law principle that national law, even national constitutional law, does not justify non-compliance with international obligations.[26] Under international law, any branch of government, including the courts, is capable of breaching international law and giving rise to international responsibility.[27]

However, the Convention system is a mix, at times an uneasy mix, of an international court dispensing individual justice to complainants and a constitutional court dealing with classes of dispute. Its constitutional nature has grown in recent years.[28] Part of the reason for this is that the ECHR is incorporated into the national law of the 47 contracting parties. The ECtHR has made it clear that a corollary of the exhaustion of domestic remedies rule is that the ECtHR expects that it is possible for a complainant to raise the substance of a Convention issue at the national level.

For the above reasons, and because there is often a material overlap between constitutional and Convention rights, the ECtHR is continually being put in the position of 'reviewing' national courts' rights-balancing exercises.

A good example of the Court's approach here is a series of Austrian cases involving criminal convictions, or civil restraining orders on the printed and broadcast media for damage to reputation or for using another person's image (photograph) without permission. In many of these cases the Court has found violations of the ECHR.[29] The Court has sought to strike a balance between publishing information about a person's private life and press freedom. It has tended

---

[26] See Art 26, Vienna Convention on the Law of Treaties, signed Vienna, 23 May 1969, entered into force 27 January 1980, 1155 UNTS 331.
[27] See, eg *Robert E Brown Claim (United States v Great Britain)* (1923) 6 RIAA 120.
[28] See, eg Greer, who notes a change in the Court's raison d'être, to expressing 'an abstract constitutional model for the whole continent and to promote convergence in the deep structure and function of public institutions': S Greer, *The European Convention on Human Rights: achievements, problems and prospects* (Cambridge, Cambridge University Press, 2006) xv. See also E Bates, *The evolution of the European Convention on Human Rights: from its inception to the creation of a permanent court of human rights* (Oxford, Oxford University Press, 2010).
[29] *News Verlags GmbH & Co KG v Austria* App no 31457/96 (ECtHR, 11 January 2000); *Krone Verlag GmbH & Co KG v Austria* App no 34315/96 (ECtHR, 26 February 2002); *Osterreichischer Rundfunk v Austria* App no 35841/02 (ECtHR, 7 December 2006).

to find that politicians and other public figures have voluntarily put themselves under public scrutiny and so must tolerate more 'fair comment'. They are thus entitled to less protection for personal integrity.

Unlike a national constitutional court, the ECtHR has no legislature as a counter-part. The ECtHR does not have one national will to discern and so it is not easy to determine the 'right' level of 'counter-majoritarianism'. The potential scope for 'interference' by the ECtHR in states' domestic policies is huge. It tries to steer a course between subsidiarity and intervention to uphold minimum European standards. Its activities are against the backdrop of 47 different legal cultures (several of them with major structural failings from the perspective of the *Rechtsstaat*). States with poor human rights records have tended to regard the ECHR as a vitally important safeguard of human rights (when it rules against other states) and a collection of irritating, unaccountable and ignorant foreigners (when it rules against themselves).

The ECtHR examines national law as part of the context of the case. As is well known, the mechanism the ECtHR applies when it wants to avoid conflicts with national rights conceptions is the margin of appreciation.[30] Generally speaking where the Court finds a 'common European conception' this in general justifies a narrow margin of appreciation. The Court is not usually sympathetic to arguments that 'everyone else has got it wrong'.[31] The question is whether the ECtHR shows special respect for *constitutional* rights provisions or the judgments of constitutional or supreme courts interpreting constitutional rights catalogues. The evidence is not consistent. There are cases where violations have been found anyway.[32] On the other hand, there are cases in which the constitutional nature of the restriction appears to have been weighed in.[33]

It would also appear that some of the cases where a wider margin has been granted relate to balancing rights. In any event, the ECtHR has stated that when it

---

[30] So much has been written about the margin of appreciation that I will content myself to referring to two recent interesting contributions to the debate, J Christoffersen, *Fair Balance: A study of proportionality, subsidiarity and primarity in the ECHR* (Dordrecht, Nijhoff, 2009) and Y Arai-Takahashi, 'Disharmony in the Process of Harmonisation? – The Analytical Account of the Margin of Appreciation Doctrine as an Interpretive Device of the ECHR' in C Andersen and M Andenas (eds), *Theory and Practice of Harmonisation* (Cheltenham, Edward Elgar, 2011).

[31] The UK occasionally makes this argument, see *S and Marper v UK* App nos 30562/04 and 30566/04 (ECtHR, 4 December 2008).

[32] eg *Demir and Baykara v Turkey* App no 34503/97 (ECtHR, 12 November 2008) [2008] ECHR 1345. This is also an example of Charter influence on content of an ECHR right, below. See further *Wizerkaniuk v Poland* App no 18990/05 (ECtHR, 5 July 2011) and the ECtHR's initial rejection of the BVerfG's approach to balancing integrity/expression in *von Hannover v Germany* App no 59320/00 (ECtHR, 24 June 2004) [2004] ECHR 294 (later 'clarified' in *von Hannover (No 2) v Germany* App nos 40660/08 and 60641/08 (ECtHR, 7 February 2012).

[33] See *Leyla Sahin v Turkey* App no 44774/98 (ECtHR, 29 June 2004) (Turkish constitutional requirement of secularism and ban on wearing headscarfs at university), *Dogru v France* App no 27058/05 and *Kervanci v France* App no 31645/04 (ECtHR, 16 December 2008) (laïcité and ban on wearing headscarfs at schools), *A, B and C v Ireland* App no 25579/05 (ECtHR, 16 December 2010) (constitutional rights of the foetus/unborn child, where the Court also referred to a 'firmly held' moral view amongst the population in Ireland).

comes to the questions of finding whether there is a right at national law,[34] and of balancing rights,[35] it should usually defer to the views of the national authorities.

VII. National Protection of Human Rights and the Role this Gives to the ECHR and the ECtHR

Every European state, apart from the UK, has a national catalogue of rights. The incorporated ECHR is thus meant as a complementary system of protection in every state apart from the UK. The incorporated Convention has only the status that national law gives it and in most cases, this means an ordinary statute. Thus, a national court will usually have to prefer a constitutional right over a Convention right, if there is an irreconcilable conflict between these.[36]

The actual effect the incorporated ECHR has on the national legal order varies considerably, depending upon a number of different factors.[37] In Sweden, the courts have referred more often to the ECHR than they have to the rights in IG Chapter 2. This can be largely explained by the fact that, until 1 January 2011 there was no constitutional equivalent to Article 6 ECHR – the right which the Swedish courts have felt most comfortable with interpreting and applying.

The main means by which the ECtHR case law affects Swedish law is through the principle of treaty-conform construction. As mentioned earlier, the Swedish courts are reluctant to engage in constitutional review. Where a litigant wishes to argue that Swedish law, or its application in a particular case, is contrary to the ECHR, the Swedish courts want 'clear support' for this in ECtHR case law. This is seldom forthcoming, one notable exception being *NJA 2005 s 805* where an evangelical pastor was acquitted of the crime of incitement to hatred (which was otherwise proven) on the basis that his highly insulting words (against homosexuals)

---

[34] 'Where ... the superior national courts have analyzed in a comprehensive and convincing manner the precise nature of the impugned restriction, on the basis of the relevant Convention case-law and principles drawn therefrom, this Court would need strong reasons to differ from the conclusion reached by those courts by substituting its own views for those of the national courts on a question of interpretation of domestic law ... and by finding, contrary to their view, that there was arguably a right recognised by domestic law', *Roche v UK* App no 32555/96 (ECtHR, 2005-X) para 120.

[35] 'Where the balancing exercise between those two rights has been undertaken by the national authorities in conformity with the criteria laid down in the Court's case-law, the Court would require strong reasons to substitute its view for that of the domestic courts': *Axel Springer AG v Germany* App no 39954/08 (ECtHR, 7 February 2012) at para 88 referring, inter alia, to *Palomo Sánchez and Others v Spain* App nos 28955/06, 28957/06, 28959/06 and 28964/06 (ECtHR (Grand Chamber), 12 September 2011) para 57.

[36] The (in)famous statement to this effect by the BVerfG in BVerfGE 111, 307, following the *Görgülü* case is correct from a constitutional perspective. For a Swedish case on this point, see *RÅ 2006 ref 87*, the Convention right to private life could not be used to avoid revealing the results of personality tests used in a recruitment process which were covered by the constitutional right of access to official documents.

[37] See generally the essays on reception in H Keller and A Stone Sweet, *A Europe of rights: the impact of the ECHR on national legal systems* (Oxford, Oxford University Press, 2008).

were uttered from the pulpit and were thus entitled to a special protection for religious speech.

The national legislator and/or the national courts have to take the ECHR and ECtHR judgments seriously for it to have a real impact in national law. The ECtHR just like the CJEU, has tried to enlist the domestic courts in the enforcement of the (incorporated) ECHR, inter alia, by emphasising that its judgments have an '*erga omnes*' effect and so are 'applicable' in all the contracting parties.[38] Other developments increasing the constitutional elements in the ECtHR are the advent of 'general' Article 46 judgments, and the pilot judgment procedure.

But an ECtHR judgment in favour of a given applicant cannot unconditionally be 'applied' in a subsequent case brought by the same applicant before a national court. The ECtHR judgment determines the issue: has the respondent state violated the Convention? It is then up to the national authorities (operating in accordance with the national division of powers between the legislature, executive and judiciary)[39] to decide what effect this determination can be given at national law. To take a German example to illustrate this, in *Görgülü v Germany*[40] the ECtHR decided that the Federal Republic of Germany violated the ECHR by failing to allow the unmarried father of a child to be heard in legal proceedings before the child was given away for adoption. The father then brought proceedings before the German courts wanting custody over the child to be given to him. When the German appeal court failed to do so, he brought proceedings before the BVerfG. The BVerfG stated that

> if ... the Strasbourg Court establishes that there has been a violation of the Convention, and if this is a continuing violation, the decision of the Strasbourg Court must be taken into account in the domestic sphere: that is, the responsible authorities or courts must discernibly consider the decision and, if necessary, justify comprehensibly why they nevertheless do not follow the international interpretation.[41]

It is important to understand that the margin of appreciation means that the ECtHR adjudicative process results in an accumulation of *principles* rather than the *rules* (albeit at a high level of abstraction) which can emerge from the adjudicative process before a national constitutional court.[42]

Nonetheless, the distinction between national case law creating rules and international case law creating principles should not be overplayed. Moreover, the above-mentioned separation between the international and national issues may not be so easy to apply in practice. The Convention principles can become

---

[38] See eg *Opuz v Turkey* App no 33401/02 (ECtHR, 9 June 2009) para 163.

[39] The ECtHR has in the past paid insufficient attention to the values of democracy and the separation of powers when it has considered the rule of law concept. However, in some areas (in particular, secret surveillance) the ECtHR has now begun to insist on *statutory* regulation of the area as a whole. See eg *Association for European Integration and Human Rights and Ekimzhiev v Bulgaria* App no 62540/00 (ECtHR, 28 June 2007) paras 75–77.

[40] *Kazim Görgülü v Germany* App no 74969/01 (ECtHR, 26 February 2004).

[41] BVerfG 111, 307 (324).

[42] S Greer, '"Balancing" and the European Court of Human Rights: A Contribution to the Habermas-Alexy Debate' (2004) 63 *CLJ* 412, 424.

national law rules when they are concretised by national courts. Rights are defined in abstract terms and, precisely because of the restraint exercised by the ECtHR, there may be little guidance for a national court in a concrete case from the ECtHR's case law as to whether the Convention forbids, or permits, or obliges, a given law or practice. At the same time, the national court is supposed to (and will want to) decide the case and solve the problem, without having to let it go to Strasbourg. Thus, a national court often has a large measure of discretion in how *it* uses the incorporated Convention, especially in new situations. In countries where the constitution and the legal culture give judges considerable power – such as the UK – the Convention can give them a potent weapon to go against the will of the national legislature or executive.

The heavy attack the ECtHR is currently experiencing from certain politicians and sections of the media in the UK should be understood from this double perspective: it is both a criticism of foreign 'interference' with the UK Parliament and of judicial interference in government policy-making.

VIII. The Role National Protections of Constitutional Rights Play Under the Charter

The Charter, like the ECHR, is meant to be a minimum level of protection, not to be interpreted as restricting or adversely affecting human rights binding upon the EU or all the Member States by virtue of international agreements (including the ECHR) or by the Member States' constitutions (Article 53).

However, as is well known, the position of the CJEU is that national law, including national constitutional law, is subordinate to EU law and that only the CJEU may set aside EU law.

National rights serve as inspiration for the CJEU in developing the content of the general principles of EU law. Whereas the CJEU initially referred to the common constitutional traditions of the Member States, in *Omega* it accepted a restriction on the free movement of services based on a specifically German conception of human dignity.[43] In this respect one can also note that Article 4(2) TEU requires the Union to respect the Member States' 'national identities, inherent in their fundamental structures, political and constitutional'.

The Charter contains an explicit provision designed to minimise conflicts between Charter articles and national constitutional rights, namely Article 52(4)

---

[43] Case C-36/02 *Omega Spielhallen- und Automatenaufstellungs-GmbH v Oberbürgermeisterin der. Bundesstadt Bonn* [2004] ECJ I-9609 concerning restrictions on free movement of services (in this case, war games using toy guns employing lasers) paras 37–38. See also C-208/09, *Ilonka Sayn-Wittgenstein v Landeshauptmann von Wien* (ECJ, 22 December 2010) para 87 'the specific circumstances which may justify recourse to the concept of public policy may vary from one Member State to another and from one era to another. The competent national authorities must therefore be allowed a margin of discretion within the limits imposed by the Treaty'.

which provides that 'In so far as this Charter recognises fundamental rights as they result from the constitutional traditions common to the Member States, those rights shall be interpreted in harmony with those traditions'. However, how this is to be interpreted is up to the CJEU. Like the ECtHR, the job of the CJEU is to evaluate whether national law meets other standards, in this case, the standards of EU law. The starting point of the CJEU when it comes to national rights protection is that restrictions on the four freedoms and other requirements of the internal market must be justified, but that the protection of fundamental rights is a legitimate basis for restriction of a fundamental EU freedom.[44] Thus, the CJEU has begun in the opposite direction from either the ECtHR or a national court exercising a power of constitutional review.[45] Both of these courts start from the human right and then determine whether a public good, eg free movement of services, justifies a restriction in the right in the circumstances.

Such an approach can be illustrated by the *Schmidberger* case, concerning a 30-hour demonstration on an Austrian motorway which the authorities permitted to go ahead, with the result that transporters of perishable goods – allegedly – suffered losses. Putting a road hauler's interests in transporting tomatoes on the same, or a higher, level than freedom of assembly might seem strange, or even distasteful, to some. On the other hand, the treaties were – prior to the Charter obtaining legal force – the only 'constitutional' law the CJEU had to go on. Besides, as already noted, for those who do not hold with metaphysics all rights give expression to and can be reduced to societal 'interests' or 'values'. Practically speaking, even if man cannot live by tomatoes alone, one can argue that achieving and maintaining the right to transport tomatoes over national boundaries has contributed at least as much to the welfare of Western Europeans since WW II as has achieving and maintaining the traditional civil and political rights (and certainly involved less shedding of blood).

Apart from *Schmidberger*, I will note four other cases where the CJEU took up the issue of national rights balancing. All have been extensively discussed, so these need only be mentioned here. In *Carpenter*[46] the CJEU stated that it is for the national court to assess whether the national law was proportionate to the aim and whether the objective could be achieved by measures less restrictive of both the four freedoms and EU human rights. *Promusicae*,[47] concerned the refusal by a Spanish internet provider (Telefónica) to disclose to an organisation, Promusicae, acting on behalf of its members who were holders of intellectual property rights,

---

[44] Case 112/00 *Eugen Schmidberger, Internationale Transporte und Planzüge v Austria* [2003] ECR I-5659, para 75.

[45] Moreover, as Peers notes, the structure of reasoning of the ECJ regarding limitations in human rights is not the same as that of the ECtHR (beginning with the accordance with the law and followed where applicable with a two or three pronged proportionality test), Peers 2004, above n 19.

[46] Case C-60/00 *Mary Carpenter v Secretary of State for the Home Department* [2002] ECR I-6279.

[47] Case C-275/06 *Productores de Música de España (Promusicae) v Telefónica de España SAU* [2008] ECR I-271. For commentary see X Groussot, 'Case C-275/06, *Productores de Música de España (Promusicae) v. Telefónica de España SAU*, Judgment of the Court (Grand Chamber) of 28 January 2008, not yet reported – Rock the KaZaA: Another Clash of Fundamental Rights' (2008) 45 *CML Rev* 1745.

personal data relating to the use of the internet by means of connections. Both parties to the national proceedings relied upon transposed EU directives. The CJEU stated that when transposing the relevant directives, the Member States must

> take care to rely on an interpretation of the directives which allows a fair balance to be struck between the various fundamental rights protected by the Community legal order. Further, when implementing the measures transposing those directives, the authorities and courts of the Member States must not only interpret their national law in a manner consistent with those directives but also make sure that they do not rely on an interpretation of them which would be in conflict with those fundamental rights or with the other general principles of Community law, such as the principle of proportionality.[48]

The third and fourth cases, *Laval*,[49] and *Viking Line*[50] concerned collective action by unions to avoid 'social dumping' which had the effect of limiting the freedom of establishment and intra-EU trade in services. In both cases, the CJEU recognised the right to strike as a fundamental EU right, but stated that it had to be balanced against other fundamental interests. According to some authors, these cases signal a more interventionist approach on the part of the CJEU.[51]

One can note in this connection that CJEU judgments have, even more so than those of the ECtHR, affected the national constitutional balance of power. This is because the CJEU has made it clear that a national measure (even one protecting human rights) involving a restriction in an EU freedom must be subject to national judicial review.

IX. The Role the Charter and the Protection Afforded by the CJEU Play in the ECHR and Vice Versa

This section can be kept relatively brief because it is the subject of another chapter in this volume.[52] For the ECtHR, the Charter plays several roles. First and foremost, it serves as the mechanism of protection of rights at the EU level, making it – hopefully – unnecessary for the ECtHR to intervene. As is well known, the ECtHR signalled in the *Bosphorus* case that this situation holds 'so long as' the EU guarantees an equivalent level of rights protection. The *Bosphorus Airways* test[53]

---

[48] Case C-275/06 *Productores de Música de España (Promusicae) v Telefónica de España SAU*, ibid, para 68.
[49] Case C-341/05 *Laval un Partneri Ltd v Svenska Byggnadsarbetareförbundet and others* [2007] ECR I-11767.
[50] Case C-438/05 *International Transport Workers' Federation and Finnish Seamen's Union v Viking Line ABP and OÜ Viking Line Eesti* [2007] ECR I-10779.
[51] See eg the chapter by Barnard in the present volume (ch 2).
[52] See eg the chapter by Douglas Scott in the present volume (ch 7).
[53] *Bosphorus Hava Yollari Turizm ve Ticaret Anonim Sirketi v Ireland* App no 45036/98 (ECtHR, 30 June 2005).

– intervening only if the gaps in EU rights protection are manifest – is favourable to the EU. It must change when the EU becomes a party to the ECHR. There is no *legal* reason for treating the EU more favourably than a state. This test should be replaced by the margin of appreciation doctrine.[54]

Since *Bosphorus*, the ECtHR has been 'in' the arena of EU law on a number of occasions – apparently to the irritation of at least some of the judges in the CJEU. In particular, the case of *MSS v Belgium and Greece* deserves mention.[55] The Court found that, notwithstanding the Dublin Convention on return of refugee seekers to the first EU state they entered, the discretion to return which Belgium nonetheless retained under the Dublin Convention meant that it continued to bear responsibility for breaches of the ECHR (in this case, for deporting asylum seekers to inhuman or degrading conditions in Greece). The case can be criticised, from an EU perspective, for undermining the principle of mutual trust, fundamental for relying upon the principle of mutual recognition. But in my view it is a welcome, indeed, overdue, 'reality check'. There was little basis for mutual trust in this particular situation. The case illustrates very well that some form of external rights control of the EU is necessary.

The ECtHR case law is not only negative for the CJEU. It has had, inter alia, the positive effect of forcing the EU Member States to accept an expansion of CJEU competence to deal with the specific issue of targeted sanctions adopted under the Common Foreign and Security Policy (a gap in protection which would otherwise have 'let the ECtHR in').

In fact, the interplay between the CJEU/ECtHR and their respective human rights catalogues works on several levels. The Charter has already had other important effects in the case law of the ECtHR. It has served as an aid to the interpretation of the Convention and as an inspiration to change its earlier practice so as to harmonise ECHR protection levels with that of the Charter.[56]

As regards the role the ECHR is likely to play in the Charter before and after EU accession to the ECHR, as with the situation as regards national constitutional rights, in addition to Article 53, the Charter contains an explicit provision designed to minimise conflicts between the ECHR and Charter articles.[57] As the

---

[54] Others, eg, Peers, 'Taking Rights Away? Limitations and Derogations', above n 19, 168, have come to the same conclusion.

[55] *MSS v Belgium and Greece* App no 30696/09 (ECtHR, 21 January 2011).

[56] See, eg *Demir and Baykara* App no 34503/97, above n 32, regarding the right to take collective action; *Sergey Zolotukhin v Russia* App no 14939/03 (ECtHR, 10 February 2009), regarding *ne bis in idem*, examined further below; *Schalk and Kopf v Austria* App no 30141/04 (ECtHR, 24 June 2010) (right of single sex couples to marry) and *Bayatyan v Armenia* App no 23459/03 (ECtHR, 7 July 2011) (conscientious objection to military service).

[57] Art 52(3) provides that 'In so far as this Charter contains rights which correspond to rights guaranteed by the [ECHR], the meaning and scope of those rights shall be the same as those laid down by the said Convention. This provision shall not prevent Union law providing more extensive protection'. See, however, the Opinion of Advocate General Cruz Villalón on 12 June 2012 in Case C 617/10 *Åklagaren v Hans Åkerberg Fransson*. Cruz Villalón considered that, as some states had made reservations to certain rights in the ECHR, these could not have the same scope as the equivalent rights in the Charter. Reasons of space prevent me from going further into this controversial issue.

text of the ECHR is vague, the commentary to the Charter, moreover, makes it clear that the ECtHR's interpretation of the ECHR should prevail.

Two brief points can be made here. The first is that the ECHR is a partial list of rights. The Charter's list is very much longer. In many cases, ECtHR case law has interpreted the text of the ECHR so as to provide a scope similar to the explicit Charter protection (eg data protection has been interpreted as being a part of Article 8 ECHR). However, there are several Charter rights which do not (yet) have an ECHR equivalent. Two examples will suffice to illustrate. Article 3(3) of the Charter (dignity of the human person) explicitly lists eugenic practices as forbidden. Article 42 of the Charter protects freedom of information, whereas under the ECHR, the ECtHR has only given this instrumental protection, insofar as it exists under Article 8.[58]

Secondly, when the EU accedes to the ECHR, it is likely to have a status similar to that of any other international treaty binding upon the EU, namely a status above that of secondary EU legislation, but under the EU 'constitution' (including the Charter).

As regards the approach of the CJEU to the ECtHR, much can be said. It suffices here to say that the CJEU has – broadly – adapted its case law to take divergent case law of the ECtHR into account. In the *Hoechst* case, the CJEU took the position that the protection of the 'home' in Article 8 ECHR did not extend to business premises, but in *Niemietz* the ECtHR stated that under certain circumstances it can.[59] The CJEU later corrected its case law to come into line with *Niemietz*.[60]

X. Factors Indicating and Encouraging Rights Competition

Why should there be any competition between the courts responsible for applying their respective human rights catalogues? Simply put, it is because these courts were established to do different things, and thus will use their respective rights catalogues in different ways. A constitutional/supreme court protects the rights of the citizen against encroachment, the ECtHR is to give an international 'second opinion' on the need for a particular national measure restricting rights, and the CJEU was established to safeguard (which can mean *promote*) the constitutive EU treaties.

---

[58] *Társaság a Szabadságjogokért v Hungary* App no 37374/05 (ECtHR, 14 April 2009).
[59] Cases 46/87 and 227/88 *Hoechst AG v Commission* [1989] ECR 2859; *Niemietz v Germany* (1992) Series A no 251-B, 16 EHRR 97.
[60] Case C-94/00 *Roquette Frères SA v Directeur général de la concurrence, de la consommation et de la répression des fraudes, and European Commission* [2002] ECR I-9011.

More specifically, the first point I would make concerns why there might be competition between the Convention and/or the Charter on the one hand and a national human rights conception on the other. A right expresses a community standard, and different political communities have different standards. As Weiler puts it, they establish 'fundamental boundaries'.[61] Ascertaining the relative weight of two opposing rights involves looking into substantive moral justifications.[62] Moreover, the political functions a right serves in one system may argue for giving it preference over another right. For example, to return to the *Volker* case, one can argue that there are other values in favour of publication, inter alia, the fostering of democratic debate: the fact that rich landowners receive huge sums of money in Common Agricultural Policy (CAP) subsidies is well known. It is probably fair to say that not only the Swedish government, but the great majority of the Swedish population would disagree with this particular balancing exercise conducted by the CJEU.

One sort of restriction in a right might be regarded as acceptable by the majority in one EU state – indeed, desirable – whereas in another it is regarded by the majority as unacceptable. There is undoubtedly a large measure of agreement in EU states on the content of 'core' rights framed in unconditional terms, such as the prohibition of torture or the death penalty. But there is considerable evidence that there are significant differences among the populations in EU states as regards the values which underlie relative (limitable) rights. For example, the sociological data contained in the World Values Survey (WVS) is graphically demonstrated in simplified form in the so-called Inglehart-Welzel Cultural Map of the World.[63] All the Nordic states (together with the Netherlands) are placed in a 'modernist' group with high 'scores' both on feelings of security (the population is not so worried about the state, or other threats) and on rationality/secularism. Interestingly, Sweden is the most 'extreme' country within this group, so much so that in the latest, sixth, wave of the WVS, the graph had to be extended, because Sweden was off the scale. This data must naturally be used with caution, but it can provide important clues as to why different states draw different right/restriction balances. For example, the variance in attitudes towards security/survival contra integrity would explain the very different approaches taken in the UK and Sweden as regards tolerance of CCTV (Closed-Circuit Television).

I think it is clear that there are fundamental boundaries between EU states, and that these concern *both* the content of certain rights balances, and which organ of the state has primacy to draw these balances (the courts/parliament).

The second point concerns to what extent these fundamental boundaries should continue to exist. In other words, how willing should the ECtHR and the CJEU be to impose minimum European standards notwithstanding contrary positions taken on rights by national legislatures and national supreme/constitutional courts? Here one can draw an analogy with rights protection in federal systems. Where a court

---

[61] Weiler, 'Fundamental Rights and Fundamental Boundaries', above n 22.
[62] Thanks to Yutaka Arai-Takahashi for useful comments on this point.
[63] www.worldvaluessurvey.org/wvs/articles/folder_published/article_base_54.

exercising a power of constitutional review in such a system is seised of the issue whether the legislation or practice of a component state violates the federal legislation or practice, it has several possible alternatives. It can decide that the federal legislation or practice sets a *uniform* standard which has been violated or not violated, or it can decide that the federal legislation or practice sets a *minimum* standard that has been violated or not violated. Subsidiarity/democracy argues in favour of minimum standards and thus varying levels of rights protection.

The interest (economic and social) the Union has in encouraging freedom of movement is often seen as pushing for harmonised standards.[64] However, the freedom of movement which a citizen possesses within the Union does not *necessarily* mean that uniform standards should apply. Indeed, freedom of movement can be used to justify differential standards, on the basis that you are free to move somewhere else where the level of legal protection better corresponds to your own values. It is interesting here to compare the US Supreme Court case *Texas v Lawrence*,[65] concerning the constitutionality of Texan laws prohibiting homosexual intercourse, with the approach of the ECtHR in the *Dudgeon*[66] case. The result in both cases was the same: the laws were disapproved of. However, the Supreme Court of the federal United States took 22 years longer to reach the conclusion reached by an international court in Europe. It also drew an (in)famous dissenting opinion from Judge Scalia. I can simplify this dissent in the following way: 'political communities within the US should be free to determine basic moral standards and enforce these with the criminal law: if you do not agree with one community's standards, you are free to move to another' (or, more crudely, if you are a Texan who wants to engage in homosexual intercourse, move to New Hampshire). In the *Dudgeon* case on the other hand, the ECtHR considered that sexual preference was such a central part of most people's personalities that it was unacceptable to ask someone to deny it, in return for the privilege of living in the place he/she was born, in the applicant's case, Northern Ireland (which, unlike Texas, is not even sunny).

While highly relevant for fundamental boundaries, these cases are admittedly not about balancing rights as such, but restricting a right for reasons of morality. A more pertinent comparison between the two courts concerns their differing approaches to abortion, which arguably does involve balancing the right of a woman to decide over her own body (privacy) with the rights of the foetus/unborn child (though even the issue of whether it involves balancing two rights is disputed). The US Supreme Court in the famous case of *Roe v Wade*[67] ruled that States' laws must allow abortion at least in certain circumstances. This was a great legal victory in my view, but there seem to be few issues which have had a more

---

[64] eg Eeckhout posed the question whether the moving citizen triggers the application of the Charter, while noting that the concept of limited powers operates against this, P Eeckhout, 'The EU Charter of Fundamental Rights and the Federal Question' (2002) 39 *CML Rev* 945, 972.
[65] *Lawrence et al v Texas* 539 US 558 (2003).
[66] *Dudgeon v United Kingdom* (1981) Series A no 45 (ECtHR, 22 October 1981).
[67] *Roe v Wade* 410 US 113 (1973).

divisive effect in recent US politics, with the *Roe v Wade* judgment having been repeatedly challenged.

By contrast, the ECtHR long managed to avoid ruling about the issue of whether the ECHR requires states to decriminalise abortions. In *Tysiac v Poland*[68] it stated that a state must not make it impossible, in practice, to obtain an abortion in circumstances when the law itself provides for this possibility. But in *A, B and C v Ireland*, the ECtHR had to face this issue head-on. Even such a case where one would have thought that only a yes/no answer was possible, the majority of the ECtHR managed to find some form of compromise. The ECtHR found a violation of Article 8 ECHR in that the Irish legislature had – still – not clarified the relatively restricted situations in which the Irish Supreme Court had indicated that abortions could be legal under the Constitution. This meant a disturbing lack of legal certainty for many people, the women involved most of all, but also medical staff. However, on the central issue of whether the Convention requires states to allow certain abortions, the majority of the ECtHR invoked the freedom of movement Irish women have under EU law to seek abortions in other states (eg the UK) as a reason for *not* finding the Irish prohibition of abortion as being in violation of Article 8.[69]

Regardless of one's views about the merits of these particular judgments,[70] it is easy to hold in principle that the ECtHR as a half-international, half-constitutional court should accept relatively wide divergences between European states when it comes to balancing rights.[71] The ECtHR is not in the business of creating a union of states. It is more in the nature of a 'rationality check'. Where one underlying moral or political justification has been totally, or largely, ignored by the national government or legislature, then there can be value in a European arbiter saying: you should have factored in this justification too. But where the legislator has already weighed the two justifications, it is more difficult to see what the ECtHR can or should add.

As already noted, the ECtHR accepts in principle that it should defer to national balancing exercises, but only when these have been performed in accordance with principles laid down by the ECtHR. Thus, it always has the option of examining the balance struck and the process of striking it. The more its willingness to delve anew into the facts and circumstances of each case, the more likely that a situation of rights competition will arise.[72]

---

[68] *Tysiac v Poland* App no 5410/03 (ECtHR, 20 March 2007).

[69] The Court found, however, that the lack of specific legislation setting out when and under what circumstances abortion was lawful was a violation of Art 8.

[70] The old remark about 'an activist court is a court with which one disagrees' seems particularly pertinent here.

[71] See A Mowbray, 'A Study of the Principle of Fair Balance in the Jurisprudence of the European Court of Human Rights' (2010) 10 *Human Rights Law Review* 289, 313. 'Balancing the rights at stake, as well as the gains and losses of the different persons affected by the process of transforming the States' economy and legal system, is an exceptionally difficult exercise. In such circumstances, in the nature of things, a wide margin of appreciation should be accorded to the respondent State': *Broniowski v Poland* App no 31443/96 (ECHR, 22 June 2004) para 182.

[72] *cf* the dissenting opinion of Judge Lopez Guerra in *Axel Springer AG v Germany*, above n 35.

It is even less likely that the CJEU, the guardian of a proto-federal system, will be willing to accept a simple 'rationality check' function, and the sort of divergences an international court can and should accept. One can of course envisage varying degrees of federalism, depending not on whether the right in question can be seen as part of the 'core' of personal integrity but rather on how well-established EU norms are in the area in question. Eeckhout argues that the CJEU is likely to be more active in the well-established areas of the internal market (eg data protection) or where the EU goal is harmonisation of a core area (eg asylum) rather than areas which have traditionally been largely outside of EU competence (eg civil rights).[73] While the EU should certainly not have a 'race to the bottom' when it comes to social rights, it is instructive to remember Weiler's point that, as far as rights are concerned, it cannot uncritically have a 'race to the top' either. He gives the example of a hypothetical Irish right to clean air. The CJEU cannot state that it is the Irish standard which should apply throughout the EU, as this will make heavy industry, production of chemicals, etc, very much more expensive in other states.[74] Weiler's proposed solution is that, in the more controversial area of CJEU review, review which has the (indirect) effect of making Member States' legislation in violation of EU law inapplicable, the CJEU should only apply the minimum ECHR standard. I would suspect that CJEU judges see the Charter as giving the CJEU the legitimacy to go further than the ECHR.

My third point relates to the issue as to whether the Charter standard can ever fall *below* the minimum ECHR standard. The *Kadi* case[75] illustrates that the EU legislator can indeed legislate in violation of fundamental rights – even if the problem originated not in Brussels but New York. The CJEU has tried to solve the problem, although it is not solved yet, and it has taken 10 years of litigation (so far).

Personally, I think there is no guarantee that the majority of judges (7 in a 13-judge chamber) will stand on the side of human rights when these are seen as blocking EU legislation promoting more effective economic integration. Moreover, even if the CJEU always stands up for human rights, it may well have good reasons to keep its discussion vague, meaning that further clarification of a human rights issue from the ECtHR may be necessary.[76]

By interpreting a Charter right extensively, the CJEU will not fall foul of the equivalent minimum ECHR right *unless* the ECtHR considers that there is a *competing* ECHR right, and the ECtHR balances these two competing rights differently. There are no rights in the ECHR which are not also in the Charter, but internalisation of all values in the Charter will not solve the problem, as it is the

---

[73] Eeckhout, 'The EU Charter of Fundamental Rights and the Federal Question' above n 64, 976–77.
[74] Weiler, 'Fundamental Rights and Fundamental Boundaries', above n 22. One could say, cynically, that this is about all Ireland can afford during the present financial crisis. However, even in Ireland, foregoing the electricity generated by peat-fired power stations would be expensive (and unpopular).
[75] Cases C-402/05 P and 415/05 P *Yassin Abdullah Kadi and Al Barakaat International Foundation v European Council and European Commission* [2008] ECR I-6351.
[76] Below, text at n 83.

balance between competing rights which is the issue. This can be illustrated by the – naive – official Swedish approach (expressed at the time of incorporation of the ECHR) to the situation when both Swedish constitutional law and the ECHR provided for protection for a right.[77] If this situation occurred, then the 'higher' level of protection would apply. However, this only applies if there is no competing ECHR right. To go back to the already mentioned disagreement the ECtHR has had with the Austrian cases regarding integrity contra freedom of expression: which set of courts, the Austrian or the ECtHR, has applied the 'higher' level of protection?

Fourthly, in at least some EU states, the Charter has a greater potential to be used to challenge national law compared to the ECHR. This is because EU law has a stronger status in the national legal order compared to the ECHR. The point can be illustrated by the Swedish developments after the *Zolotukhin* case[78] concerning *ne bis in idem*. When the ECtHR explicitly reversed its earlier case law and found that two separate criminal proceedings for the same conduct were not permissible, it created a major problem for the Swedish system of administrative penalties in tax matters. The ECtHR had previously found that these were a 'criminal penalty' but that, as proving them did not require criminal intent (but only a negligent, and incorrect, tax return), they did not have the same 'essential elements' as tax offences which did require intent.[79] Thus a subsequent prosecution for tax crime was not blocked by the fact that the tax authorities had previously issued a tax penalty for the same conduct (or vice versa).

Zolotukhin fairly clearly changes this. However, there was other ECtHR case law, albeit very sketchy, that indicated that it might be permissible to make an exception to the principle of *ne bis in idem* and impose two penalties where this is foreseeable and there is a sufficiently strong link in time and subject matter between the two penalties imposed.[80] The issue came up before both the Swedish Supreme Administrative Court and the Supreme Court.[81] The Supreme Administrative Court found, in a summarily reasoned judgment, that the Swedish system was not in violation of the ECHR. The Supreme Court applied the already mentioned evidential threshold before engaging in constitutional review, and the majority of the Court (albeit with some misgivings) found that there was no 'clear support' on the basis of ECtHR case law that the Swedish system was in violation of the ECHR.

Subsequently, people who have been subjected both to a tax penalty and a criminal prosecution for tax crime have invoked Article 50 of the Charter. To do so, they must find a cross-border dimension. At least one lower Swedish court

---

[77] The Swedish legislator compounded this error by going on to state that the *lex specialis* principle could be used to solve any remaining problems. But *lex specialis* cannot be used to solve conflicts between two norm systems, of varying degrees of abstraction, created by *different* legislators. The conflict does not disappear.

[78] *Sergey Zolotukhin v Russia* App no 14939/03 (ECtHR (Grand Chamber), 10 February 2009).

[79] *Nils-Inge Rosenquist v Sweden* App no 60619/00 (ECtHR, 14 September 2004).

[80] *Christoffer Nilsson v Sweden* App no 73661/01 (ECtHR, 13 December 2005).

[81] RÅ 2009 ref 96, NJA 2010 s 168 I–II.

has, however, accepted that an argument can be made on this basis and requested a preliminary ruling on the matter. The case is still pending. The point I want to make here is that national courts cannot and will not, apply an evidential threshold to avoid an issue of conflict between national law and the Charter. On the contrary, national courts must intervene to protect EU law, including EU fundamental rights. This also indicates that the CJEU is likely to get some issues – probably those with considerable financial implications – before the ECtHR does. On the one hand, this gives the CJEU freer hands. On the other, it means that it must act with less guidance from the ECtHR, something which may make it more difficult to apply Weiler's proposed solution to the legitimacy problem in the situation, namely that the CJEU should not apply more than the minimum – ECHR – standard.

XI. Means of Avoiding Competition and Concluding Remarks

The most obvious reason why clashes can be mostly avoided between national supreme/constitutional courts within EU states, the ECtHR and the CJEU is that none of these courts is interested in conflict.

For example, the BVerfG has gone out of its way to stress the openness of the German constitutional rights catalogues to interpretation in an EU- and ECHR-conform way.[82] As already mentioned, the BVerfG has stressed that there is always a duty to take an ECtHR judgment into account and if at all possible to apply it. The CJEU takes ECtHR case law into account.

The ECtHR for its part, has granted the CJEU something larger than a margin of appreciation. From the perspective of the ECtHR, the defensiveness that some CJEU judges display vis-à-vis the ECtHR, and the reluctance that apparently exists amongst them to accept EU accession to the ECHR, look like fundamentalism ('there is only one true European law, and the CJEU is its interpreter'). The sensitivity of the CJEU, or at least certain judges on it, means that cases where the ECtHR interprets EU law and the EU charter, which it must do, to determine whether the protection offered matches the minimum level set by the ECHR, can be seen as actual or potential rights competition.

The prime means of avoiding or minimising the resultant problems, one advanced by a recent interesting contribution to the debate by Torres Pérez, is

---

[82] See eg the approach of the BVerfG to the ECtHR judgment in *von Hannover v Germany* App no 59320/00, above n 32, in the '*Caroline II*' case, BVerfG, 1 BvR 1602/07, judgment of 26 February 2008. English translation available at www.bundesverfassungsgericht.de/entscheidungen/rs20080226_1bvr160207en.html. See further A Voßkuhle, 'Multilevel cooperation of the European Constitutional Courts: Der Europäische Verfassungsgerichtsverbund' (2010) 6 *European Constitutional Law Review* 175.

'dialogue'.[83] Dialogue in good faith means that the CJEU judges must accept that dialogue is not, or not simply, the opportunity for the CJEU to warn off, or admonish, the ECtHR.

How will a good faith dialogue work in concrete terms? The ECtHR, as it was originally constructed, had an in-built informal dialogue mechanism, in that the judges were part-time. As far as multilateral dialogue is concerned, there are annual meetings with the national supreme and constitutional courts on the one hand and the CJEU on the other, where relevant (controversial, or potentially so) cases are chosen by the two sets of courts and discussed. Bilateral 'dialogue' within the ECtHR is provided by the presence of the national judge in any chamber or Grand Chamber judgment. After accession, the same will apply for the EU.

Bilateral and multilateral dialogue mechanisms are also provided by the ECHR. First, the ECtHR can either explicitly reconsider or 'clarify' a judgment in a later case on the basis of clarifications given subsequently by a national court.[84] Secondly there is procedural mechanism for ensuring a particular degree of respect for provisions of national law regarded as of special importance, namely the possibility of referral, or appeal, of a chamber judgment to the Grand Chamber. A topical example of this is the *Lautsi* case, concerning the obligatory crucifixes in Italian schools (a requirement of the Lateran Treaty of 1923, to 'compensate' the Vatican for their loss of influence over teaching). A unanimous chamber found a violation of Article 9 ECHR in that this did not respect non-Christians' freedom of conscience. Ten states (and several other intervenors, including the Holy See) filed amicus curiae briefs in the appeal and the Grand Chamber reversed the chamber judgment.[85]

Ultimately, a recalcitrant national supreme/constitutional court can engage in 'dialogue' with the ECtHR by noting that there are problems with applying an ECtHR judgment, or even explicitly stating that it will not do so.[86] It might seem strange to call this a dialogue. But the case will probably be from another state, and thus, the national court will have considerable discretion in 'translating' it to the national context. If the ECtHR left a margin of appreciation this will give even

---

[83] A Torres Pérez, *Conflicts of Rights in the European Union: A Theory of Supranational Adjudication* (Oxford, Oxford University Press, 2010).

[84] The part of the judgment in *Mulkiye and Ahmed Osman v UK* App no 23452/94 [1998] ECHR 101, which was troublesome for the UK, was reconsidered in *Z and others v UK* App no 29392/95 (ECtHR, 10 May 2001), 'The Court considers that its reasoning in the Osman judgment was based on an understanding of the law of negligence ... which has to be reviewed in the light of the clarifications subsequently made by the domestic courts and notably the House of Lords'. A recent example of clarification is *von Hannover (No 2) v Germany* App no 40660/08 and 60641/08 (ECtHR, 7 February 2012).

[85] *Soile Lautsi and others v Italy* App no 30814/06 (ECtHR, 18 March 2011).

[86] 'There will, however, be rare occasions where this court has concerns as to whether a decision of the Strasbourg Court sufficiently appreciates or accommodates particular aspects of our domestic process. In such circumstances it is open to this court to decline to follow the Strasbourg decision, giving reasons for adopting this course. This is likely to give the Strasbourg Court the opportunity to reconsider the particular aspect of the decision that is in issue, so that there takes place what may prove to be a valuable dialogue between this court and the Strasbourg Court', *R v Horncastle and others* [2009] UKSC 14, [2009] WLR (D) 358. Thanks to Mads Andenas and Eirik Bjorge for useful comments on this point.

more room for manoeuvre. It is only if the national court refuses to follow an earlier ECtHR judgment which concerns the same state and an identical fact situation that we can speak of a conflict between the two courts. And if we really accept the principle of 'multilevel protection' of rights in Europe, then any court in the system, not just the national court, could have 'got it wrong'.

In this respect, an essential part of the ECtHR's modus vivendi with national courts, including national constitutional courts, was the casuistic nature of its judgments, leaving considerable room for manoeuvre in similar but not identical cases. But for a variety of reasons, in particular the need to provide better guidance to national courts, the ECtHR practice is changing. It spells out more often the consequences of its judgments, either generally for all states, or specifically for the respondent state.

The CJEU, for its part, has also had a modus vivendi with national courts by producing a preliminary ruling which allows the national court considerable freedom of interpretation when the case returns for the decision. Formally, of course, a preliminary ruling does not determine the case (even though, in the past, the specificity of its ruling meant that it occasionally come very close to doing so). A Delphic preliminary ruling can also result from an inability to agree a consensus judgment. Either way, the CJEU avoids conflicts with national courts, and hopefully preserves its own legitimacy. The interesting question here is whether dynamics of the Charter, or more generally the post-Lisbon process of European integration, will act to make the CJEU less able to be vague when vagueness is a virtue.[87] One can ask, too, will the CJEU be willing to be vague, when this will leave more room (and need) for the ECtHR to enter into the field and clarify matters?

Here I can urge caution. The CJEU is also engaged in a form of abstract review. The biggest infringement of legislative competence tends to be an abstract review which results in the conclusion that a law is compatible with the Constitution *if* it is interpreted in a particular way. This is because it closes off political room for manoeuvre more than a simple 'cassation'.

Another method of avoiding conflicts is preventive checks. The Council of Europe states are supposed to build in a proper system of pre-legislative scrutiny against the ECHR, but it is only a minority of states which do this adequately.[88] Sweden, as already noted, primarily protects rights through the legislative process but the tax penalty problem shows that looking for guidance in the *travaux préparatoires* is useless when a supranational court, the ECtHR or the CJEU, has (re)interpreted a right *after* this process is concluded and this reinterpretation is then raised in litigation at the national level.

The implications for Sweden are that, if it wants to maintain the primacy of the legislative process as rights protection, then both the Charter and the ECHR must

---

[87] See A Ward, 'National and EC Remedies under the EU Treaty: Limits and Role of the ECHR' in C Barnard and O Odudu (eds), *The Outer Limits of European Union Law* (Oxford, Hart Publishing, 2009). Ward points out that there has been a lack of clear and coherent CJEU reasoning on access to national courts, remedies and sanctions.
[88] See generally the essays in Keller & Stone Sweet, *A Europe of rights*, above n 37.

be better integrated into the legislative process, and their requirements interpreted 'generously'. Otherwise, when a new judgment is given by the ECtHR or CJEU, colliding with existing law, it will definitely be indefensible for the Swedish courts to interpret this new judgment restrictively.

The EU has taken preventive measures to 'mainstream' human rights in the legislative process.[89] Here one can content oneself with noting that a certain tension has already been generated with the Council of Europe over the work of the EU Fundamental Rights Agency.[90]

I can conclude by saying that institutional and other factors will make some rights competition inevitable, and that this is likely to increase in the future. But this is not necessarily a negative thing. The ECtHR does have a role to play in encouraging the CJEU to respect the balance between the human rights set out in the Convention, and criticising it when it does not do so, just as it serves the same role for a national constitutional or supreme court. But respect for the values of European integration, as well as for democracy and institutional competence, means that the ECtHR should be better at developing principles of self-restraint, indicating in a coherent fashion when, and to what extent, it will be willing to intervene when, exceptionally, it draws that balance differently.

---

[89] Commission, 'Strategy for the effective implementation of the Charter of Fundamental Rights by the European Union' (Communication) COM(2010) 573 final. For an earlier discussion see O de Schutter, 'Mainstreaming Human Rights in the EU' in P Alston and O de Schutter (eds), *Monitoring Fundamental Rights in the EU: The Contribution of the Fundamental Rights Agency* (Oxford, Hart Publishing, 2005).

[90] See Parliamentary Assembly of the Council of Europe, 'Need to avoid duplication of the work of the Council of Europe by the European Union Agency for Fundamental Rights' (2010) Resolution 1756. assembly.coe.int/main.asp?Link=/documents/adoptedtext/ta10/eres1756.htm#1#1. The assembly noted that a risk of duplication exists 'and concerns remain as to the risk of confusion in interpreting human rights standards in the 27 Council of Europe member states belonging also to the EU ... fruitful co-operation in the future [between the FRA and the COE bodies] is dependent on the Council of Europe's *acquis* in the area of human rights protection at the European level being used as the main point of reference in the Agency's work' (paras 2 and 4).

Conference Report

The Protection of Fundamental Rights in the European Union after Lisbon

How Fundamental are the Changes Brought About by the Lisbon Treaty for the Protection of EU Citizens' Fundamental Rights?

EVA SUZANNE LACHNIT, LLM*

The conference 'The Protection of Fundamental Rights in the European Union after Lisbon', which took place on 11 March 2011, concerned the changing protection of European Union citizens' fundamental rights after the introduction of the Treaty of Lisbon. This report aims to give a concise impression of the presentations given that day, along with the subsequent discussions between the speakers and the audience.

Sacha Prechal[1] made the opening statement for the day. She provided a reflection on the current issues concerning the Charter of Fundamental Rights (Charter). Prechal addressed the initial hesitance of the Court of Justice to invoke the Charter and the important change in the Court's attitude after the entry into force of the Lisbon Treaty. She also briefly touched upon the relationship between the Charter and the European Convention of Human Rights (Convention) and pointed at the possibility of having a 'race to the top' in the area of fundamental rights protection in Europe.

The Charter's scope and justiciability were also addressed. In that sense, Prechal considered the newly-found distinction between rights and principles to be a step back from current practice. Though she warned against the frequent translation of problems into a fundamental rights application, Prechal predicted that the Charter would remain an important part of European law and practice.

---

* Eva Suzanne Lachnit is a PhD Candidate in Public Economic Law, Europa Institute, Utrecht University.
[1] Sacha Prechal is a Judge of the European Court of Justice.

Safeguarding Fundamental Rights in Europe's Internal Market

The first round of presentations (entitled 'Safeguarding Fundamental Rights in Europe's Internal Market') was chaired by Sacha Prechal and consisted of contributions by Stephen Weatherill, Catherine Barnard and Sybe de Vries.[2]

Stephen Weatherill's presentation 'From Economic Rights to Fundamental Rights' described the development from the internal market and its economic rights towards the Lisbon Treaty and its Charter of Fundamental Rights. Weatherill provided an extensive overview of the development of fundamental rights in the European Union by dealing with the most important case law in each stage of development. He discussed the various rights that were at stake in the specific cases and wondered whether the Charter would have greater force now it was declared binding by the Lisbon Treaty.

Pavlos Eleftheriadis[3] disagreed with this, because he felt that the Charter had actually led to a trivialisation of rights. He argued that there is a difference between what the Charter labels 'fundamental rights of the Union' and the 'absolute fundamental rights', such as integrity of the body or the right to have a lawyer present in criminal proceedings. Even though he agreed that the first category of rights is to a certain extent interpretable to serve economic purposes, Eleftheriadis felt that the latter category of rights should not be reconciled at all. He therefore believed that the Court of Justice's balancing test (used in numerous examples of case law) was irrelevant. Instead, Eleftheriadis argued that absolute fundamental rights (included in the Charter mainly prior to Article 16) call for the review by an impartial court that is able of disregarding the policy objectives that the Union pursues.

Weatherill agreed with the distinction between economic rights and absolute rights, but he on the other hand maintained that the Court of Justice is in fact capable of balancing economic rights with competing, non-absolute fundamental rights, because it had done so in a satisfactory manner before.

Also Catherine Barnard acknowledged the poor characterisation of rights in the Charter, because it had placed absolute fundamental rights, such as the prohibition of torture, alongside of more economic rights, such as the right to conduct a business.[4] She did argue, however, that because these economic rights are officially recognised within the European legal order, citizens must have the possibility to have them weighed against other European interests. In Barnard's opinion, the Charter had brought a more rounded perception of fundamental rights within the Union – whether absolute fundamental rights, economic rights or social rights

---

[2] Stephen Weatherill is Jacques Delors Professor of European Law, Sommerville College, University of Oxford. Catherine Barnard is Professor of European law, Trinity College, Cambridge. Sybe de Vries is an Associate Professor of European Law at the Europa Institute, Utrecht University.

[3] Dr Pavlos Eleftheriadis, is University Lecturer in the Faculty of Law and Fellow and Tutor in Law at Mansfield College, University of Oxford.

[4] Charter of Fundamental Rights of the European Union, [2000] OJ C364/01, Arts 3 and 16.

– which facilitated an actual reconciliation between the four freedoms and fundamental rights. Regarding these four freedoms, the Court of Justice had made clear in the case of *Viking* – in which the freedom of establishment was prioritised over the fundamental right to collective action[5] – that they would remain the starting point of any balancing test.

In a reaction to that, the audience proposed to avoid a balancing test altogether, which in case of *Viking* and *Laval*[6] could have been done by assuming that trade union action was not captured by the Treaty. However, Barnard noted that in these cases the Court of Justice had ordered the trade unions to take account of the Treaty, which – to some extent – put them in the same position as the state. She agreed that this might have been an unfair assumption, since the interests of a trade union are far more unilateral than those of a state. Sybe de Vries on the other hand, feared that excluding trade unions from the realm of the Treaty beforehand would have the effect of categorisation, which in his opinion leads to unjustifiable value judgments.

De Vries further elaborated this perspective during his presentation, in which he focused on the balance between fundamental rights and economic freedoms. He reviewed the landmark cases in which the Court engaged in a balancing exercise (*Schmidberger, Omega* and *Sayn-Wittgenstein*[7]) and he advanced two alternatives that the Court could use (or on occasion already has used) instead of the balancing of rights: categorisation and the procedural test.

These alternatives were not further dealt with, but on a more fundamental level, Jan Zglinski[8] doubted whether the above-mentioned cases even concerned a clash between two Union rights. He argued that in *Omega*, for example, the Court could also have ruled that there was a clash of national constitutional rights instead, by interpreting one of the rights that was at stake (human dignity) as an exception of public policy. The audience, however, was unconvinced by this argument and argued that human dignity is an actual fundamental right, acknowledged by the Union. This made the audience wonder whether the character of the fundamental rights is of importance in the Court's balancing exercises. The right at stake in *Sayn-Wittgenstein*, for example, was considered more of a curiosity of Austrian law.

De Vries disagreed and held that the character of the fundamental right is irrelevant. He indicated that the main issue in *Sayn-Wittgenstein* was not the right to hold a noble title, but the protection of the national constitution and the national identity, a field in which the Member States enjoyed a certain margin of appreciation.

---

[5] Case C-438/05 *International Transport Workers' Federation and Finnish Seamen's Union v Viking Line ABP and OÜ Viking Line Eesti* [2007] ECR I-10779.
[6] Case C-341/05 *Laval un Partneri Ltd v Svenska Byggnadsarbetareförbundet and others* [2007] ECR I-11767.
[7] Case C-112/00 *Eugen Schmidberger, Internationale Transporte und Planzüge v Republik Österreich* [2003] ECR I-5659, case C-36/02 *Omega Spielhallen- und Automatenaufstellungs-GmbH v Oberbürgermeisterin der Bundesstadt Bonn* [2004] ECR I-9609 and Case C-208/09 *Ilonka Sayn-Wittgenstein v Landeshauptmann von Wien* (ECJ, 22 December 2010).
[8] Jan Zglinski, Corpus Christi College, University of Oxford.

However, he admitted that the Court's approach in this case differed from its approach in the *Viking* and *Laval* cases, in which the conflicting legislation could also have been qualified as typically national and therefore part of the national identity, but in which the Court applied a strict proportionality test nevertheless.

The argument of de Vries was supported by Weatherill. He put forward that the main issue in all the above-mentioned cases was not the character of the rights, but the way these rights were weighed against Treaty provisions. Nevertheless, he found it striking that the Court had opted to conceptualise certain rights (*in casu* human dignity) into Union law, which indicated that the Court was not exclusively concerned with rights with an economic character.

Underlining this conclusion, Barnard then further analysed the social rights in her presentation, entitled 'The Protection of Social Rights in Europe after Lisbon'. She pointed out that the post-Lisbon changes on social policy had actually been a codification of existing practice. She found it unfortunate that the Lisbon Treaty had not yet resolved the three main conflicts in this field: conflicts of sources, conflicts of policies and conflicts of rights. Barnard proposed for these conflicts to be resolved by looking at the German constitutional principle of proportionality, though she recognised that the practical application of this principle still creates some uncertainty.

In the realm of that uncertainty, Xavier Groussot[9] wondered whether a discussion about proportionality would be justifiable when it comes to fundamental rights. Instead, courts should be more concerned with legal certainty and transparency, thus subsuming a procedural test in the proportionality test. De Vries argued that the Court of Justice had already taken this course of action, although he personally disagreed. In his opinion, a proportionality test should be a review that exceeds a mere scan of procedural requirements.

The Scope of Fundamental Rights in EU Law

The second round of presentations, chaired by Stephen Weatherill, was entitled 'The Scope of Fundamental Rights in EU Law'. Ulf Bernitz and Martin Mörk[10] jointly discussed the horizontal dimension of fundamental rights and its judicial protection. Xavier Groussot addressed the scope of EU fundamental rights after Lisbon.

Only two days after the Lisbon Treaty entered into force, the Swedish Labour Court gave a final judgment in the *Laval* case, relying on an EU principle of liability. Mörk discussed whether such a principle was indeed necessary to cover a supposed lacuna in effective judicial protection.

The main point of discussion after the presentation by Bernitz and Mörk was the compensation of damages. The *Laval* judgment had made clear that trade

---

[9] Xavier Groussot is Professor of European Law at Lund University.
[10] Ulf Bernitz is Professor of European Integration Law at the Universities of Stockholm and Oxford. Martin Mörk is a lawyer at Öberg and Associés in Stockholm.

unions should respect the obligations flowing from the fundamental freedoms, but had not addressed the question whether they could also be held accountable for breaches of these freedoms. The Court's earlier jurisprudence, however, seemed to imply that they could.[11] This premise was partly accepted by the audience, though they wondered to what extent the national legislator would be responsible for the creation of an effective remedy for such a breach.

Regarding the first argument, Mörk argued that no breach of European law by trade unions could exist without a concurrent breach of European law by the state. He explained that if a certain topic were insufficiently regulated by a Member State and the trade union action were committed in the scope of this lack of regulation, the Member State would be responsible in the end. In that light, those who also rejected trade union liability named *Frankovich* liability[12] as a possible remedy.

Bernitz acknowledged this possibility, but he stressed that even though European law facilitates individuals to protect their rights, such protection would not necessarily have to result in the payment of damages. Besides, Mörk added that once an effective remedy like *Frankovich* liability was available, the national legislator would be under no obligation to create other remedies. In the case of *Laval*, the liability could have been based on Article 28 of the Charter.

Member State liability was not the only topic of interest in the second round of presentations. In his presentation, Groussot signalled that horizontal application of fundamental rights was of increasing importance. He wondered what impact this horizontal effect might have on the application of the Charter. The Court of Justice could, for instance, interpret the Charter as a federal standard (a yardstick to evaluate national rules). Despite the advantages, Groussot noted that any federal effect of the Charter would be effectively tempered by the limits of Article 51. De Vries partly disagreed, because he felt that some members of the Court had already attempted to bypass Article 51 in the case of *Zambrano*.[13] In this case, the advocate-general had suggested that the competence of the Union alone would trigger the application of the Charter.

This observation caused a discussion on whether the Charter would be automatically triggered if a citizen of another member state was involved. Groussot's response was negatory; he considered such an abstract-level application of the Charter to be impossible. In his opinion, some kind of link to European law was indispensible. Nevertheless, Groussot agreed that, regarding the strength of that link, the Court had delivered far reaching judgments in the past. In this respect, he referred back to *Zambrano*, in which the Charter was invoked on grounds of European citizenship, even though the disputed citizen had not yet made use of any of his European citizens' rights as such.

---

[11] For example Joined Cases C-46/93 and C-48/93 *Brasserie du Pêcheur SA v Bundesrepublik Deutschland* and *The Queen v Secretary of State for Transport, ex parte Factortame Ltd and others* [1996] ECR I-1029.

[12] Joined cases C-6/90 and C-9/90 *Andrea Francovich and Danila Bonifaci and others v Italy* [1991] ECR I-5357.

[13] Case C-34/09 *Gerardo Ruiz Zambrano v Office national de l'emploi (ONEm)* (ECJ, 8 March 2011).

As noted before, Article 51 of the Charter itself prevents the Court of Justice to create a 'federal standard' against which all national rules may be evaluated. De Vries wondered how this limit relates to the reasoning of the advocate general in *Zambrano*, in which it was suggested that the competence of the Union alone would trigger the application of the Charter.

The Constitutional Dimension of Fundamental Rights

The third and last round of the conference, entitled 'The Constitutional Dimension of Fundamental Rights', consisted of presentations by Sionaidh Douglas-Scott, Iain Cameron and Katja Ziegler.[14]

Douglas-Scott discussed the relationship between the European Court of Justice and the European Court of Human Rights (ECtHR) after Lisbon, particularly in the light of the binding status of the Charter and the provision for European Union accession to the Convention. She wondered whether these changes would make the current system of human rights protection more effective, or just more complex.

Douglas-Scott's presentation triggered a debate on how the Court of Justice would react to new and binding judgments of the ECtHR. According to some members of the audience, the latter was growing more aware of its international status and promoted cooperation between its acceding states in order to give human rights substantial impact in their legal orders. Regardless of the hesitance of some national constitutional courts, the Court of Justice actually had adopted such a cooperative approach in the past.[15] Nevertheless, its recent pronunciation against EU accession to the Convention made the Court's approach to future judgments somewhat unpredictable.

Ziegler expected the reaction of the Court of Justice to depend on the required amount of cooperation. She and Douglas-Scott explained that the Court of Justice was not fundamentally opposed to accession to the Convention, but showed some initial apprehension because of the uncertainty about the division of competence. However, the Court of Justice now seemed to have realised that accession might solve its credibility problems with the level of human rights protection in the European Union, an issue which was repeatedly attested by national constitutional courts.

Even though Cameron agreed that the Court of Justice was moving towards becoming a constitutional court, he warned against the exaggeration of the role of ECtHR. In addition, Cameron gave an outline of a few of many approaches to human rights in his presentation 'Competing Rights and Competing Principles'.

---

[14] Sionaidh Douglas-Scott is Professor of European and Human Rights Law, Lady Margaret Hall, University of Oxford. Iain Cameron is Professor of Public International Law at Uppsala University. Katja Ziegler is Reader in European and Comparative Law, St Hilda's College, University of Oxford.

[15] As put forward by Cameron, using the *Roquette Frères* case as an example. Case C-94/00 *Roquette Frères SA v Directeur général de la concurrence, de la consommation et de la répression des fraudes, and European Commission* [2002] ECR I-9011.

This led Zglinski to inquire whether Cameron would agree that Robert Alexy's approach towards conceptualising rights[16] was a viable and fruitful one for EU law. Unfortunately, because of time limitations this question was not further discussed.[17]

The last speaker of the day, Ziegler, discussed constitutionalism in the European Union and the role of European fundamental rights. With this presentation the final speaker of the conference outlined the constitutional dimension of the European fundamental rights debate.

This brought the audience to discuss the constitutional implications of the recent developments. Some of the members of the audience put forward that the courts should stop balancing rights, because this could endanger the constitutional equilibrium as pursued by the legislator. Furthermore, the idea of the Court of Justice functioning as a self-standing constitutional court was rejected. Instead, they advocated a dualist system in which the Court of Justice would work alongside national constitutional courts and in which a European judgment could not overrule a national constitutional decision. In response, Ziegler pointed out that at that stage, the Court of Justice already had a dualist function. It was not a self-standing human rights court, but it incorporated human rights in the scope of European law. Ziegler did recognise, however, that the gaining of prominence of human rights in litigation has made this distinction harder to maintain.

Cameron partly disagreed and maintained that it is a court's fundamental task to adjust a general system, because it is impossible for the legislator to create impervious law. In his opinion, individuals should not become victims of legislative mistakes or forgetfulness. He held that, on a European level, these adjustments had to be made by the Court of Justice, whose course of action in some cases had definitely been influenced by the European Court of Human Rights.

Douglas-Scott concluded this discussion by stating that even though the Court of Justice might not perfectly fit the role of a human rights court, its more favourable turnaround time might increase the number of applications in the field of human rights.

Conclusion

The protection of human rights in the post-Lisbon European Union remains an infinite ground for discussion. The general attitude towards a more extensive and binding human rights catalogue is predominantly positive, though the constitutional and jurisdictional problems with such a binding document cannot be overlooked. Time will tell the effect of the changes brought about by the Lisbon Treaty and how the Court of Justice, the European Court of Human Rights and the national constitutional courts will deal with them.

---

[16] Robert Alexy and Julian Rivers, *A Theory of Constitutional Rights* (Oxford, Oxford University Press, 2002).

[17] In this respect, Cameron referred to his paper: 'Competing Rights' (ch 8 of this volume).

Index

actions against state *see under* horizontal liability
age discrimination 46–7
Alexy, R 76–7, 182–3
association, freedom of *see* collective action
autonomy, EU legal order 168–71

balancing theory
   categorisation 77–8
   exclusionary reasons 78–9
   law of balancing 76–7, 182–3
   margin of appreciation *see under* margin of appreciation
   procedural test 79
   see also internal market, balancing; rights competition
Bernitz, U 121
Bosphorus case 155–6, 174

Cassis de Dijon case 14–15, 19–20, 30
categorisation 77–8
Charter of Fundamental Rights (CFR) 2, 59, 71
   additional value 74–5
   binding nature 30, 63, 153, 178–9
   content 71–6
   court dialogue 161–4
   and EU law 72–4
   limitations/proportionality 76
   mixed approach 71
   rights/freedoms, conflict 75–6
   rights/principles, distinction 71–2, 86–7
collective action 69–70
   economic rights 26–8, 34
   Laval case, judicial rights 119, 142–4
   social rights *see under* social rights
collective agreements 55–6
competing rights *see* rights competition
competition, undistorted, commitment 32–5
consensus doctrine/test
   European Convention on Human Rights (ECHR), EU accession 175–7
   and margin of appreciation 77
Council of Europe 159, 166, 175, 178
Court of Justice of the EU, relationship with ECtHR 153
   court dialogue 157–61, 161–4
   jurisdictional issues 154–6
   see also European Convention on Human Rights (ECHR), EU accession

damages
   horizontal liability 120–1, 126–31, 133–8

Laval case *see under Laval* case, judicial rights
De Vries, S 128
discretion 68–9
   margin of discretion 20
Dynamic Medien case 68–9, 74, 75, 89, 90

ECHR *see* European Convention on Human Rights (ECHR)
ECJ *see* Court of Justice of the EU, relationship with ECtHR
economic rights 208
   broader justifications 18–22
   collective action 26–8, 34
   family rights' protection 28–9
   free movement 5
      collective action 26–8, 34
      family rights' protection 28–9
      freedom of expression 23–6
      and fundamental rights 22–9
      of goods 11–12
      laws 17–18
   freedom of expression 23–6
   internal market
      broader justifications 18–22
      marketising effect 13–16
      national product standards 14–16
   limited competences 16–19, 21, 35
   Lisbon Treaty
      constitutional identity 31–2
      horizontal clauses 30
      softening effect 29–30, 33, 36
      undistorted competition, commitment 32–5
   margin of discretion 20
   and national law 13–14
   public interest test 19–20
   reasonableness 19
   sport 18, 21–2
   undistorted competition, commitment 32–5
ECtHR *see* Court of Justice of the EU (ECJ), relationship with ECtHR
Elefthariadis, P 208
equality, social rights 46
ERT principle 101–3, 113, 116–17
EU citizenship rights
   and fundamental rights 62–3
   member state action 103–5
EU legal order autonomy 168–71
European Convention on Human Rights (ECHR), EU accession
   basic position 6, 153, 165–6, 175, 212–13

European Convention on Human Rights
    (ECHR), EU accession (*cont.*):
  co-respondent mechanism 171–4
  Committee of Ministers 175
  concerns 175–9
  consensus doctrine/test 175–7
  Council of Europe 159, 166, 175, 178–9
  EU legal order autonomy 168–71
  issues 168–75
  judges' role 175
  pre-EU accession 154–64
    basic position 154, 175
    Bosphorus case 155–6, 174
    court dialogue 157–61, 161–4
    direct actions v EU 154
    jurisdictional issues 154–6
    member state, discretion/liability 154–6
  procedure 166–8
  scope 174–5
  state autonomy 177–8
  see also Court of Justice of the EU (ECJ), relationship with ECtHR
European Court of Human Rights (ECtHR) *see* Court of Justice of the EU, relationship with ECtHR
Eurozone crisis, social rights 54–6
exclusionary reasons *see under* balancing theory
expression, freedom of 23–6

family rights' protection 28–9
Francovich case 120, 124, 126–8, 130, 145
free movement
  economic rights *see under* economic rights
  social rights *see under* social rights
free movement of goods 63–5
freedom of association *see* collective action
freedom of expression 23–6
fundamental rights
  autonomous application 62–3
  case law development 5, 60–3, 209
  conference report 207–13
  current issues 3–4, 209, 210
  and EU law 7
  institutional (EU) infringement 61
  internal market *see under* internal market
  member state infringements 61–2
  origins 1–3

Gitlow v New York (US) case 101
Greer, S 49–50
Gutiérrez-Fons, JA 136

horizontal liability
  actions against state 126–31
    effectiveness 126, 127–31
    underlying responsibility 126–7
  conclusion/summary 137–8
  damages 120–1, 126–31, 133–8
  economic rights *see* economic rights, Lisbon Treaty, horizontal clauses
  effective rights protection 123–31
    basic issues 123–4
    equivalence 131
    margin of appreciation *see under* margin of appreciation
    predictability requirement 131–2
  private rights protection
    background 6, 139–40
    case law development 140–1
    categories 140–2
    Charter rights 141–2
    nationality discrimination 140–1
  proportionality issues 135–7
  retroactivity issues 132–5
  Unibet liability 124–6
  see also Laval case, judicial rights
human dignity, respect for 65–6

industrial relations 50–1
institutional (EU) infringement 61
internal market
  background 59–60
  balancing
    fundamental rights/economic freedoms 87–90
    horizontal/flanking policy interests 79–82
    proportionality principle/test, in case law 90–3
    see also balancing theory
  case law 63–70
  collective action 69–70
  conclusion/summary 93–4
  discretion 68–9
  Dynamic Medien case 68–9, 74, 75, 89, 90
  economic freedoms, as fundamental rights 83–6
  economic rights *see under* economic rights
  free movement of goods 63–5
  fundamental rights 86–7
    economic freedoms
      a priori hierarchy 87
      balancing 87–90
      conflict 83–7
      protection as exception 87–90
  horizontal/flanking policy interests, balancing 79–82
    see also balancing theory
  human dignity, respect for 65–6
  Laval case 69–70, 89–93*passim*, 117
  Lisbon Treaty 70–1
  Omega case 65–6, 68, 93
  proportionality principle/test
    balancing in case law 90–3
    see also balancing theory
    procedural requirements 82
    public interest, impact 81

regulatory instrument, impact 81
   three elements 79–81
public policy 66–8
rule of reason 79
Sayn-Wittgenstein case 66–8, 90, 91, 92, 93
Schmidberger case 63–5
social market economy 85–6
supranational legitimisation 85
Viking case 69–70, 89, 90–3 *passim*, 117
Internationale Handelsgesellschaft case 2–3

judicial rights protection *see Laval* case, judicial rights

Kommers, D 48
Kücükdeveci case 106–7, 110–11

Laeken Declaration 35
Laporta, F 135*n*
Laval case, judicial rights 209, 210–11
   collective action 119, 142–4
   conclusion/summary 137–8
   damages 120–1, 126–31, 133–8
   horizontal liability
      basic issues 6, 122–3
      in ECJ 122–3
      Francovich case 120, 124, 126–8, 130, 145
      in national court 121
      ruling 119–22
      and *Viking* case 122
   internal market 69–70, 89–93 *passim*, 117
   member state action 89–93 *passim*, 117
   private rights protection
      background 139–40
      basic principles 145
      damages 142, 144–7
         critique of decision 147–50
      in ECJ 142–4
      tort liability 146–7
   see also horizontal liability; *Viking* case
Lenaerts, K 35, 136
Lisbon Treaty 59
   basic commitment 1
   constitutional identity 31–2
   economic rights *see under* economic rights
   internal market 70–1
   post-Lisbon developments 1–2
   pre-Lisbon cases 2–3

Maastricht Treaty 59
Mangold case 107–10, 111
margin of appreciation
   balancing theory 77
   and consensus doctrine/test 77
   horizontal liability 129–30
margin of discretion 20
marketising effect *see under* economic rights, internal market

member state action
   background 97
   basic issues 98
   complementary rights 105–6
   direct effect doctrine 109–10
   ERT principle 101–3, 113, 116–17
   EU citizenship rights 103–5
   federalising effect 6, 98, 99–106
   fundamental rights, reliance 114–16
   general principles 111–12
   horizontal effect 106–12, 116–17, 118
   implementation/derogation categories 98
   infringements 61–2
   Kücükdeveci case 106–7, 110–11
   Mangold case 107–10, 111
   new classification 113–17
   private parties 107, 118
   scope of EU law 99–102
   social rights, conflicts 41–3
   summary/conclusion 117–18
   Wachauf case 113, 114, 116–17
   Zambrano case 103–5
Mörk, M 147–50

national product standards *see under* economic rights, internal market
national state action *see* member state action
Nice Treaty 59

Omega case 65–6, 68, 93
Ordo-liberal school 84

Pérez, T 203–4
Plato, *The Republic* 60
practical concordance 48–50
Prechel, S 128
private rights protection *see under* horizontal liability; *Laval* case, judicial rights
procedural test (balancing) 79
proportionality
   horizontal liability 135–7
   principle/test *see under* internal market
   social rights 47–51
public interest test/impact
   economic rights 19–20
   internal market 81
public policy 66–8
public procurement, social rights criteria 51–4

reasonableness 19
Reich, N 121
retroactivity issues 132–5
rights competition
   avoidance 203–6
   background 6–7, 181
   balance issues 201–2
   basic issues 181–2, 212–13
   Court of Justice, and Charter 187–8, 195–7

rights competition (*cont.*):
  dialogue 204–5
  ECHR
    and Charter 195–7
    ECtHR 186–7
    national protection 191–3
  ECtHR
    and ECHR 186–7
    national protection 189–91
  factors 197–203
  fundamental boundaries 198
  meaning 182–3
  minimum standards 198–201
  national protection
    and Charter 202–3
    constitutional rights 193–5
    ECtHR 191–3
    human rights 191–3
  preventive checks 205–6
  social rights *see* social rights, rights' conflicts
  summary/conclusion 206
  Swedish approach 183–6
    basic position 183
    courts' role 185–6
    Instrument of Government rights 184–5
    legislative process 183–4
  see also balancing theory
rule of reason 79

Sayn-Wittgenstein case 66–8, 90, 91, 92, 93
Schmidberger case 63–5
social market economy 85–6
social rights
  background 5, 37, 208–9, 210
  basic issues/conclusions 37–8, 57
  policies' conflicts 38, 51–6
    collective agreements 55–6
    concerns/solutions 56
    Eurozone crisis 54–6
    public procurement, criteria 51–4
    wage/productivity levels 54–5
  practical concordance 48–50
  proportionality 47–51
  rights' conflicts 37–8
    age discrimination 46–7
    basic issues 45–6
    equality 46
    free movement/collective action, conflict 45–6

  industrial relations 50–1
  practical concordance 48–50
sources' conflicts 37, 38–45
  basic issues 38–9
  concerns/solutions 44–5
  EU
    international bodies, conflict 43–4
    member states, conflict 41–3
  EU collective agreements, national/subnational, conflict 42–3
  EU legal order, autonomy 44
  EU legislation
    national law, conflict 41–2
    self-conflict 40–1
  horizontal conflicts 39–41
  openness/accommodation 43–4
  treaty provision v legislation 39
  vertical conflicts 41–5
Socrates 60
sources' conflicts *see under* social rights
sport 18, 21–2
SPUC v Grogan 13
state actions *see* horizontal liability, actions against state
Stauder case 2–3
supranational legitimisation 85
Sweden *see* rights competition, Swedish approach

trade unions *see* collective action
triptych of cases 2–3

undistorted competition, commitment 32–5
Unibet liability 124–6
US Supreme Court 100–1, 105–6

Van Gend en Loos case 11
Viking case 69–70, 89, 90–3 *passim*, 93, 117, 209, 210
  and *Laval* case 122, 136–7
Volker and Schecke case 2–3

Wachauf case 113, 114, 116–17
Weiler, JHH 198
Wyatt, D 136

Zambrano case 103–5
Zglinski, J 209